1796.
Saunderton
Red Lane
Bottom Farm
Radnage
Rennet End
Stoken Church
Paufleys
Radnage Common
Small Dean
Slough
Upper North Dean
Lower North Dean
Bradenham
Noble Farm
Lee Castle
Napple Common
Coomb Farm
Harrow House
Naphill
Green End
Lamburn
Chaulkey
Downley
Hitchingdon
West Wycombe
Flint Hall
Obelisk
Flomer hill
Little Worth
Bottom Farm
Tarriers
Brick Kiln
Ham Farm
Towerage
Chips
Huckington
Mill End
Francis Mill
Friars Mill
Ball's Mill
Lane's Mill
Kings Wood Lane
Totteridge
North End
Poston House
Wheeler End
Rackleys
Bottom Farm
Desborough
HIGH WYCOMBE
Mickle Fields
Penn
Groves End
Cadmor End
Bolter End
Park Lane
Lane End
Park Hill
Oakridge
Pest House
Turville Heath
Turfield
Fingest
Stockwell
Limmers
Booker Green
Mundys Farm
Dawes Hill
Wycombe Marsh
TURVILE PARK
Turfield Court
Pinkets
Little Frieth
Ackhamsted
Chapel
Bowmers
Clay Lane
Crefsicks
Homers Farm
Handy Cross
Hardy Barn
Harty Foine
Whinch Bottom
Nat Mill
Loudwater
Stonor
South End
Frieth
Moor End
PART OF OXON
Pumoor
Chisbeach
Chisbeach Cross
Beechen Barn
Monktye
Heath End
Horsepur
Kimble
Cocksleys
Hambleton Wood
End
Hill House
Widmer Cross
Pheasants
Colsthorp
Bockwell
Cold Harbour
Whitmers
Harper's Heath
Dean House
Shipridge
Wood Barn
Wye Mills
Clary Mill
Wooburn Moor
Hill Farm
Heath
Northern Scrub
Wooburn Green
Bosmer
Fawley
Fawley Bottom
Pheasants Hill
Hawkins
Holywick
Huttons
Seymours
Blunt Farm
Marlow Bottom
Work House
Little Marlow
Marlow Fern
Well End
Lilly Field
Hambleton
Botten Row
Bockmer End
Borough
Marlow Common
Bovingdon Green
St Westhrop
Spade Oak Wharf
Abby
Coars End
Wooburn
WOOBURN HEATH
GREAT MARLOW
Hebbern Lee
Bourn End
Hedsor
Horse Ferry
Dropmer Hill
THAMES
RIVER
Fawley Court Farm
Fawley Court
Mill End
Remenham
Medmenham Abby
Danesfield
Harleyford
Low Grounds
Bisham
Temple Mills &
Cookham
Clifden House
HUNDRED
BURNHAM HUNDRED

CW01650638

CHILTERN *Images*

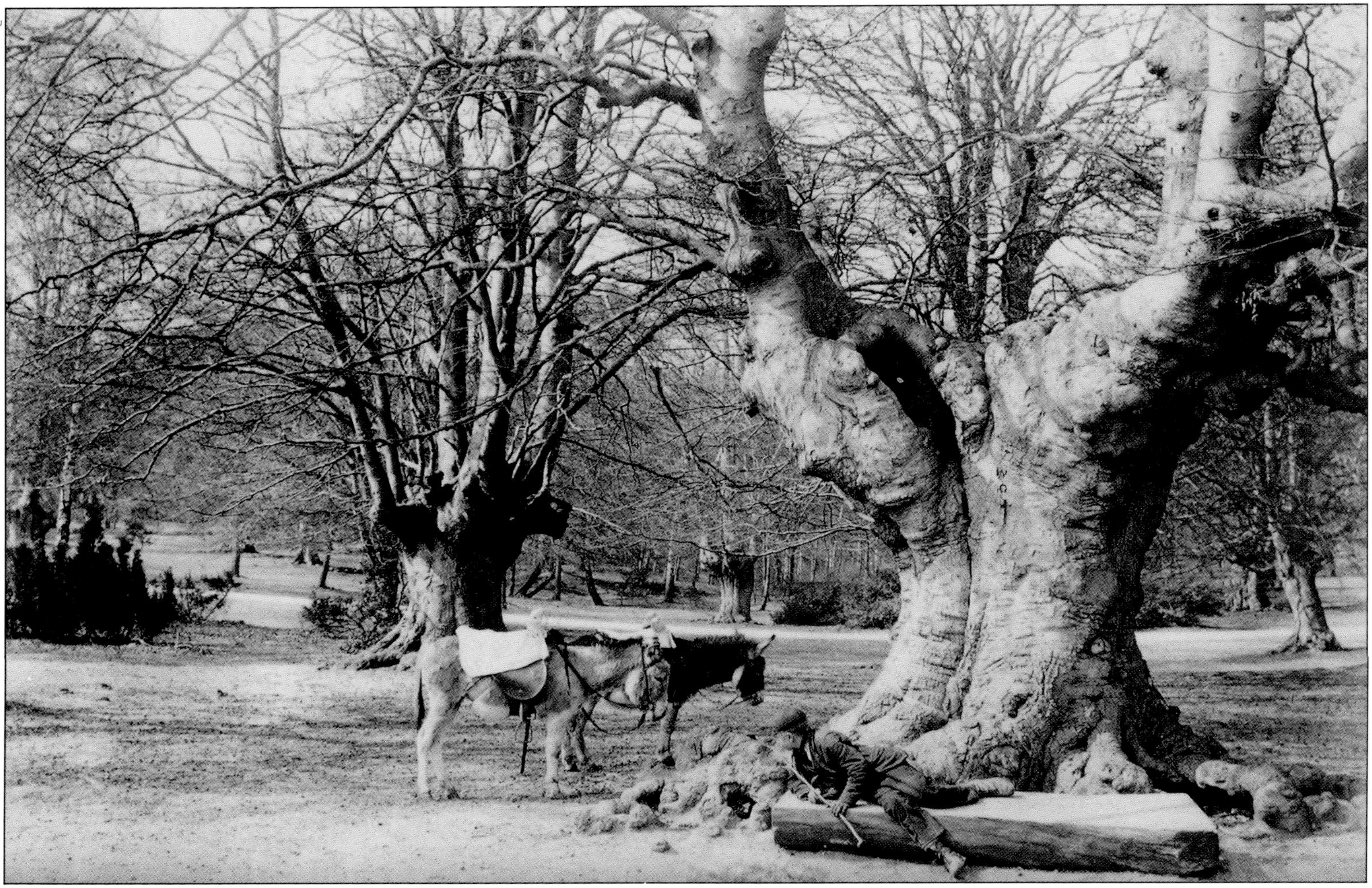

Donkey boy in Burnham Beeches

CHILTERN *Images*

SUSAN READ and DAVID EMPRINGHAM

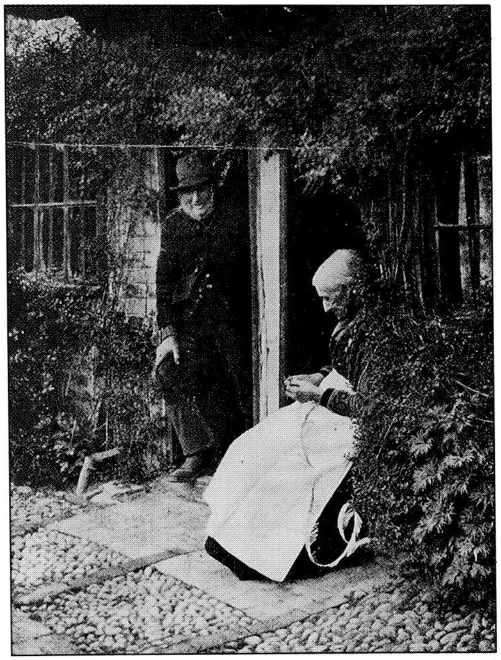

ALAN SUTTON

First published in the United Kingdom in 1992
Alan Sutton Publishing Ltd · Phoenix Mill · Far Thrupp · Stroud · Gloucestershire

---

First published in the United States of America in 1992
Alan Sutton Publishing Inc. · Wolfeboro Falls · NH 03896–0848

Copyright © Susan Read and David Empringham 1992

All rights reserved. No part of this publication may be reproduced, stored in a retrieval system, or transmitted, in any form, or by any means, electronic, mechanical, photocopying, recording or otherwise, without the prior permission of the publishers and copyright holders.

British Library Cataloguing in Publication Data

Read, Susan
Chiltern Images
I. Title II. Empringham, David
942.5

ISBN 0–7509–0007–5

Library of Congress Cataloging in Publication Data applied for

Endpapers: county maps from front to back: R. Plot, *The Natural History of Oxfordshire,* 1676; Revd T. Langley, *History of the Hundred of Desborough and the Deanery of Wycombe*, 1797; W.H. Smyth, *Aedes Hartwellianae*, 1851; Sir H. Chauncey, *The Historical Antiquities of Hertfordshire*, 1700.

Typeset in 11/13 Bembo.
Typesetting and origination by
Alan Sutton Publishing Limited.
Colour and duotones by Yeo Valley Graphics.
Printed in Great Britain by
Bath Press Colourbooks Ltd, Glasgow.

Introduction

Approaching London from the Vale of Aylesbury, the dominant feature of the landscape is a long band of hill, rising up for all the world like the barrier to a forgotten kingdom, and indeed for centuries this densely forested part of ancient Britain called the Chilterns was just that. Alongside these chalk hills, edges nervously one of the oldest roads in the country; the Icknield Way runs contiguously with the Ridgeway and forms a link between the Wash and the vast plateau of Salisbury Plain. Stonehenge, shrouded in mystery, is actually less perplexing than Grim's Ditch which snakes unpredictably over the Chilterns. Robert Gibbs, writing in his BUCKINGHAMSHIRE MISCELLANY offers our imaginations a vivid picture of these past times:

Here, too, you may trace for some miles the course of Grim's Dyke, which, your rustic guide will tell you, was all made in one terrible, tempestuous night by grizzly Gryme, the wicked wizard; and perhaps the learned antiquary would not be able to give you a more truthful account of its origin, so completely hidden is it in remote antiquity. On these hills may be traced vestiges of British and Roman settlements, and the chronicled sites of Saxon and Danish battles.

Many have carefully avoided speculating upon the geographical boundaries of the Chiltern Hills. However, generally these are acknowledged to be part of a chain of heights rising in Cambridgeshire as the Gog-Magog hills, running through Hertfordshire and Bedfordshire, and entering Buckinghamshire by Ivinghoe and passing in a south-west direction to exit from this county at Chinnor. Through Oxfordshire the Chilterns pursue their course in the same direction until they reach the Thames. For the purpose of our book, however, the limits are from the Dunstable area to the Thames Valley. This includes places within a line drawn roughly from Stoke Poges to Hemel Hempstead, taking in Ashridge Park. The omnipresence of the Chilterns is such in the Vale of Aylesbury that they can both with some justification be considered in the same breath. Viewed from many points along the escarpment the Vale gives a feeling of unique pastoral stillness and confirms the mutual benefit each bestows on the other. It is in this spirit rather than in due deference to geographical niceties that we include the area from Aylesbury to Wallingford.

It is worth our while to take a short excursion back in time to find out how the Chilterns were created; geologically they are the remnant of an old sea bed now lifted out of its original position and worn away at the margins. If one were to drill deeply enough in Piccadilly Circus, one would certainly feel the long arm of the law, but given the chance would eventually reach the same seam of chalk that crops out at such eminences as Coombe Hill, one of the highest points in the Chilterns at 257 metres (843 ft) above sea-level. The porous nature of the chalk means that only a few valleys support running water and then often intermittently. This shortage of water dictated the siting of early settlements and later the construction of dew ponds

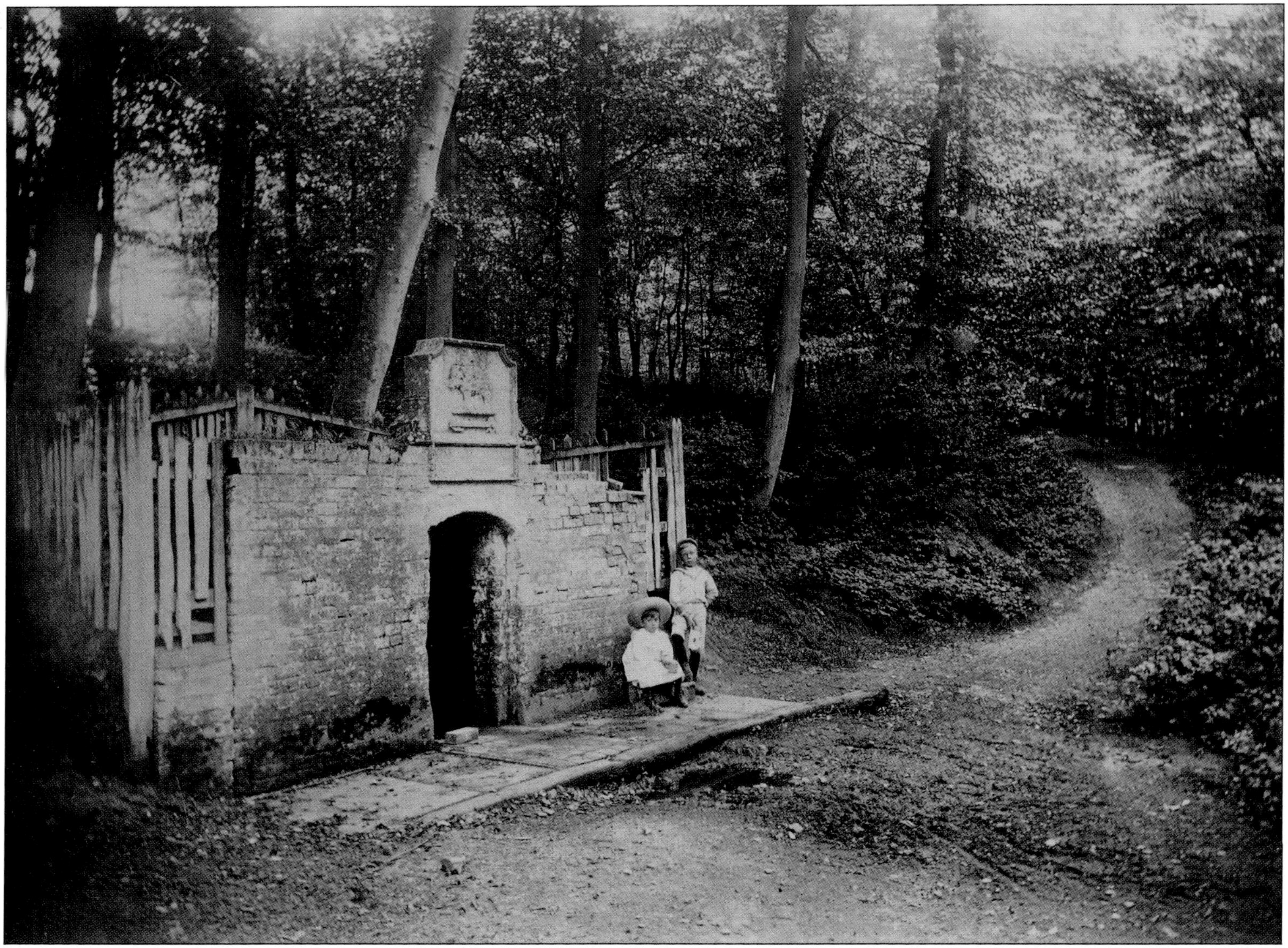

Spring head at Peppard

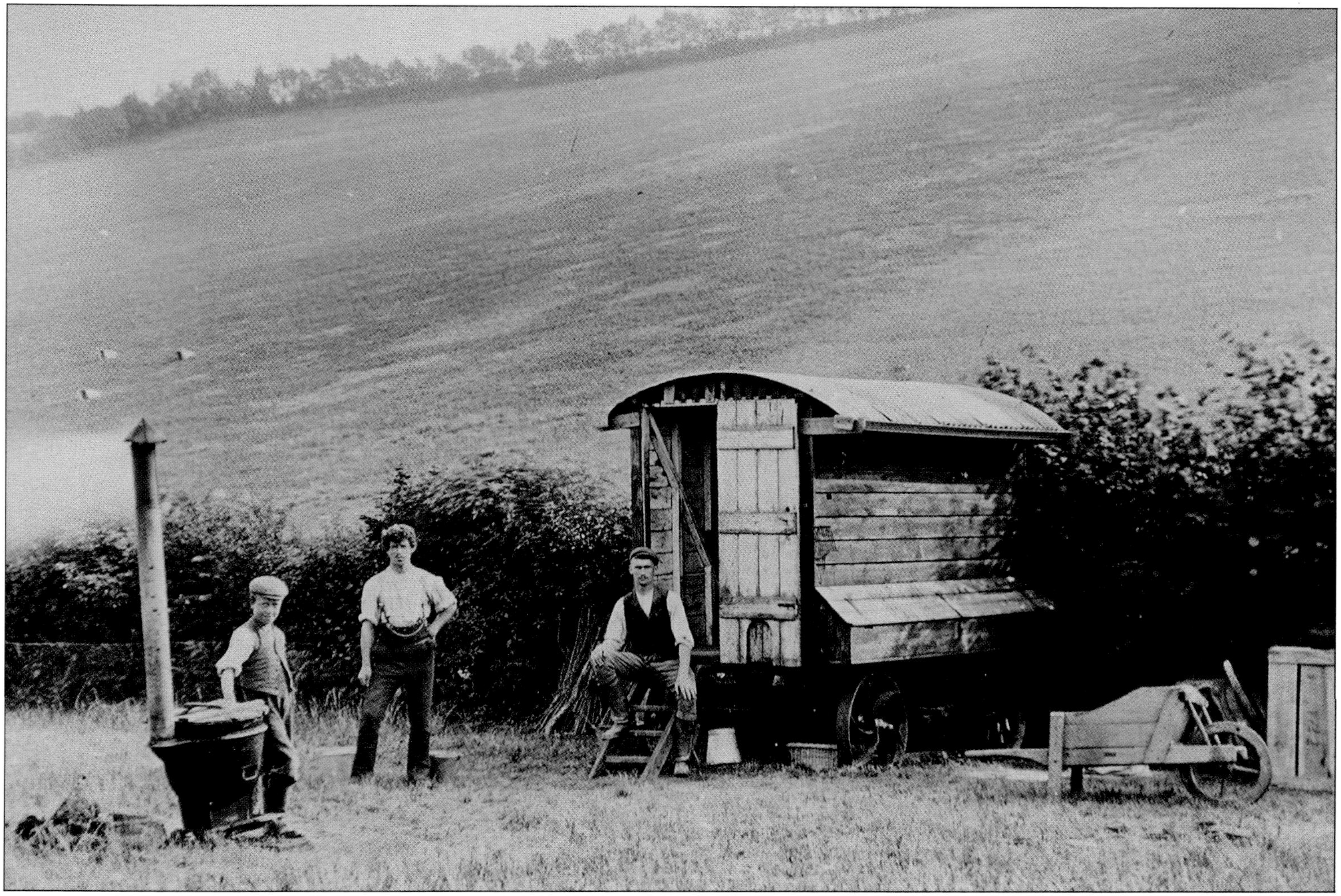

The Hampdens

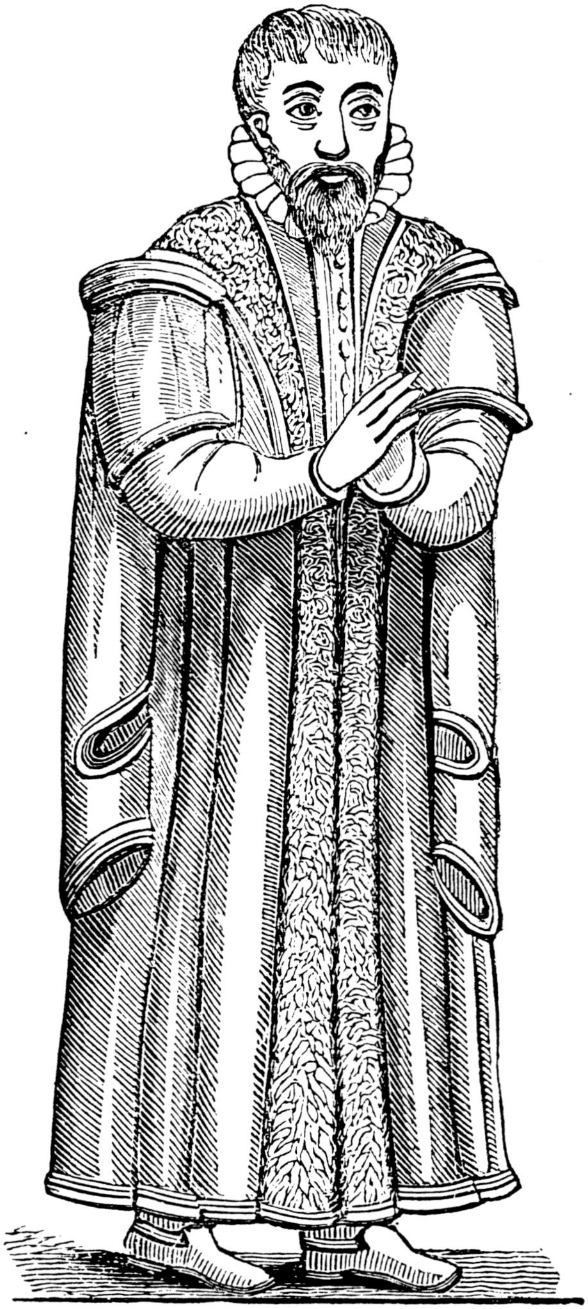

and in some places the digging of very deep wells. The most notable valley is still 'permanently wet' and was formed during the last Ice Age when the melt water, trapped between the ice and the chalk, burst through at Goring and thus formed the Thames, once a wide inundating stretch of water, now a sedate river of incomparable charm.

This same geological event, with its southern limit at the Thames, was responsible for depositing a layer of boulder clay on the chalk hills to which the indigenous beech tree tenaciously clings. The underlying flints, found here in great numbers, were of course used in earlier times for lighting fires and to make cutting tools, but later became one of the main building materials of the region. Their use, together with locally produced brick, is responsible for the pervading character of the region, displayed to advantage in churches as well as public houses and cottages, and always creating a wonderfully mellow and satisfying group.

Who better to describe the result of all this chemistry than the Revd Bryant Burgess, an eminent writer on the Chilterns in the nineteenth century:

Viewed in profile, the hills present a series of lofty slopes and bold brows or headlands, some of very sharp descent, and turfed, others covered with hanging woods, in which are found the box and juniper, as well as the ash, oak, and beech. . . . It may be observed further, that this platform of high land, showing invariably its steepest face on the north west limit, is penetrated by vallies running into it at intervals from the plain which carries off its waters. It is at the opening of the vallies or among the declivities of the hills, that there are found those hanging woods and wild glades, which have gained for such spots as Velvet Lawn or Bledlow, their well deserved name for picturesque beauty. Within the high rampart of the hills slopes gently down, for many a mile to the south eastwards, what may be termed the Chiltern country. It forms a high but undulating tract of hill,

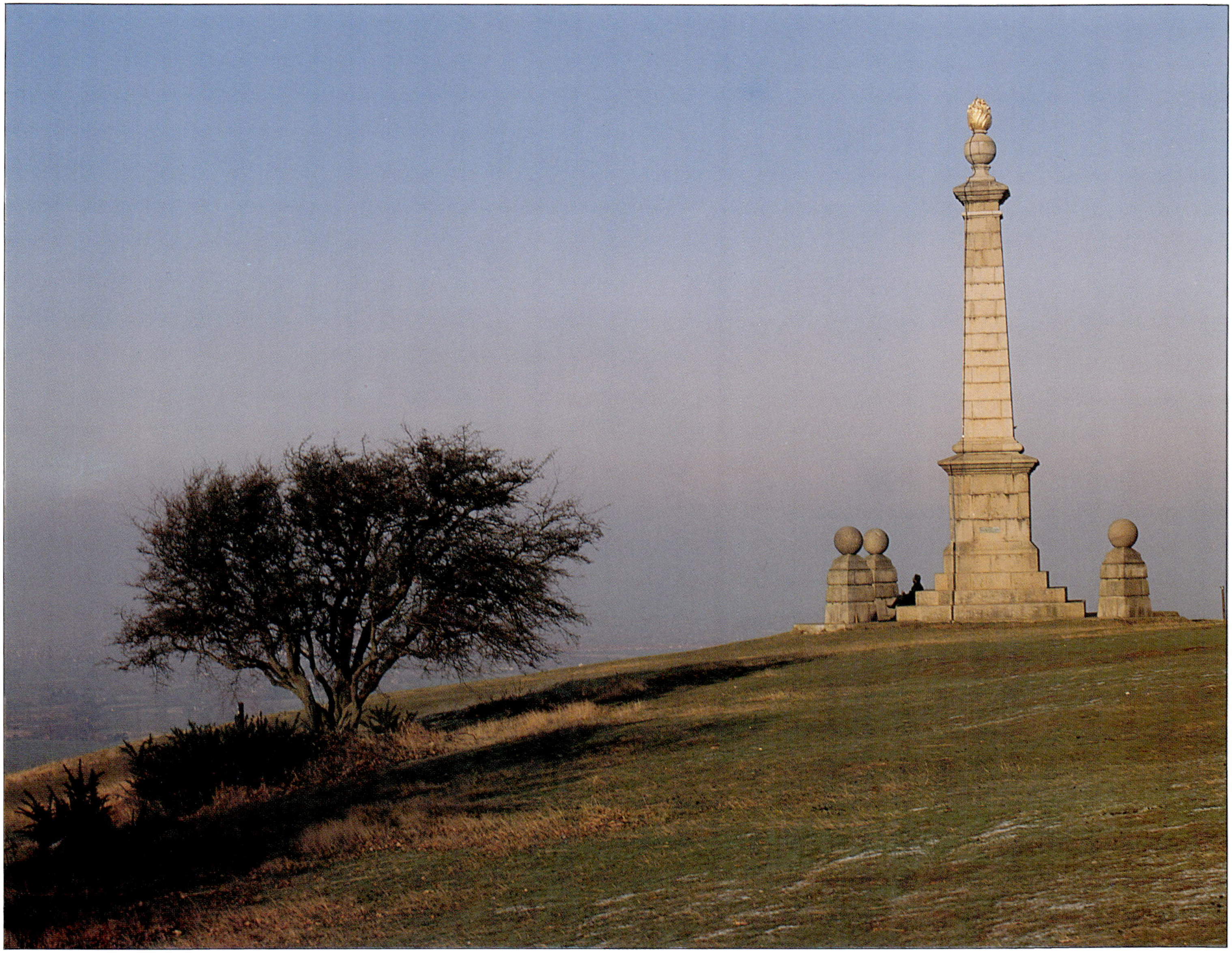

Coombe Hill

vale, and wood, in which the upland Hamlets, with 'secure delight', have invited and might still invite the visits of a Milton and in which quiet and picturesque farms, country towns and villages, seated generally by the brook in the vale, a few pleasant with some noble mansions, may claim for the district a character for cheerful rural beauty. Assuredly, from an acquaintance of some years with this country, the writer can promise the lovers of good exercise, fine air, and pleasant scenery, many an agreeable walk or ride over the open commons, or through the shady lanes and fertile fields of this variegated hill country. Let the scenery of Marlow, Missenden, Penn, and Wycombe attest that this is no undue partiality.

It would not be totally unfair to say that in certain areas one could no longer be swayed by undue partiality. The M40 has stamped its authority on the landscape, but little more in retrospect than the great railway undertakings of a hundred or so years before. Travelling in to this region in days gone by was a fairly hazardous business; particularly before Macadam revolutionized road construction, and the risk of being molested by robbers was ever present. Main roads and railways were inevitably driven through this previously forbidding area and London drew ever nearer.

People came to leafy Bucks, and some stayed; not just the politicians, poets and priests whose voices have helped to shape our thinking, but also those who made it their business to write about the countryside and the folk who lived in it. Disraeli made his home in Hughenden near High Wycombe and became part of Chiltern history; Grey immortalized Stoke Poges; men who were actually involved in the Civil War wrote about their experiences, and earlier travellers such as Leland and Defoe drew a picture of the Chilterns in their time. It is from such sources that our extracts are drawn, beginning with the sixteenth century and ending in the early part of the twentieth; a tapestry of words and pictures woven together to make *Chiltern Images*.

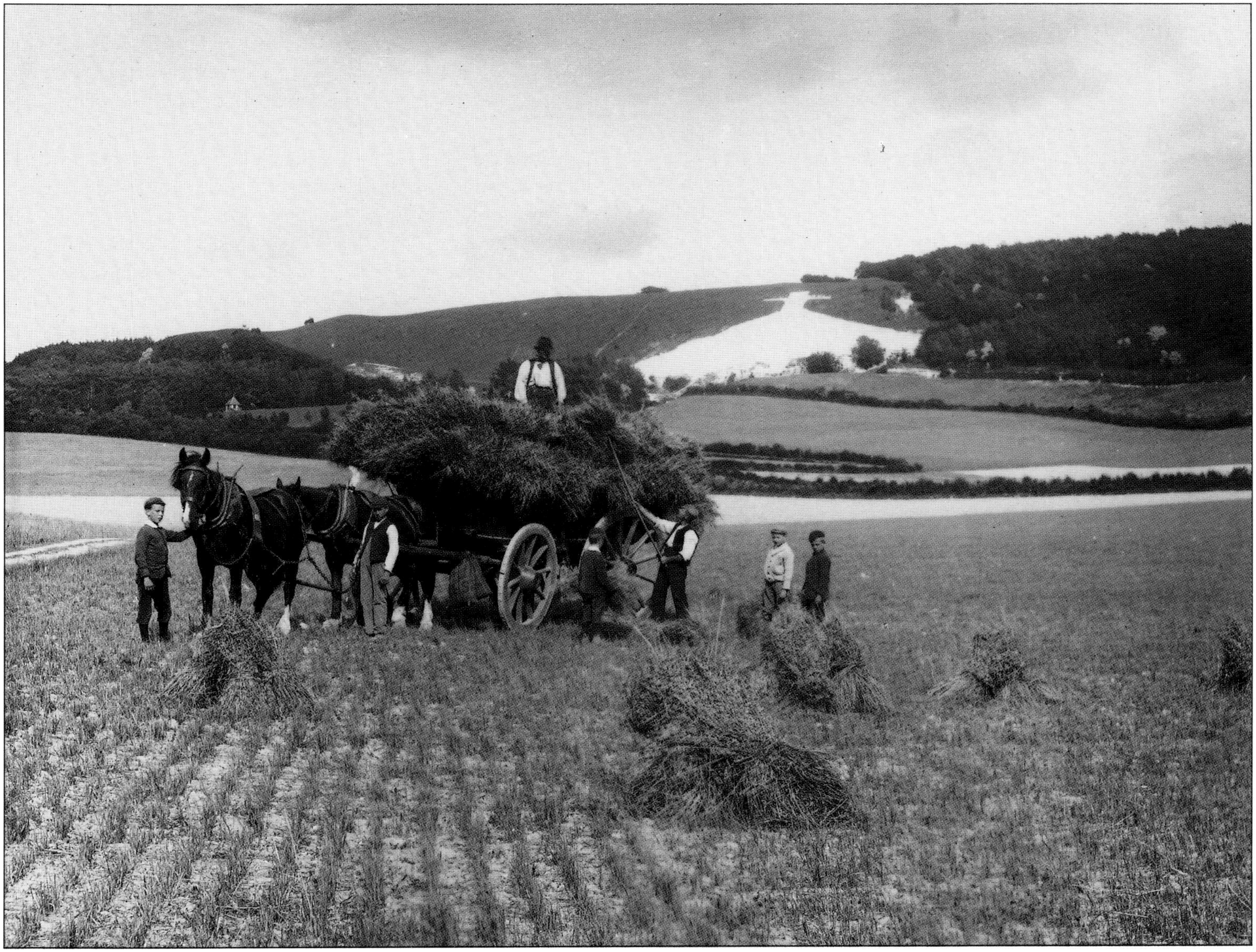

Whiteleaf Cross

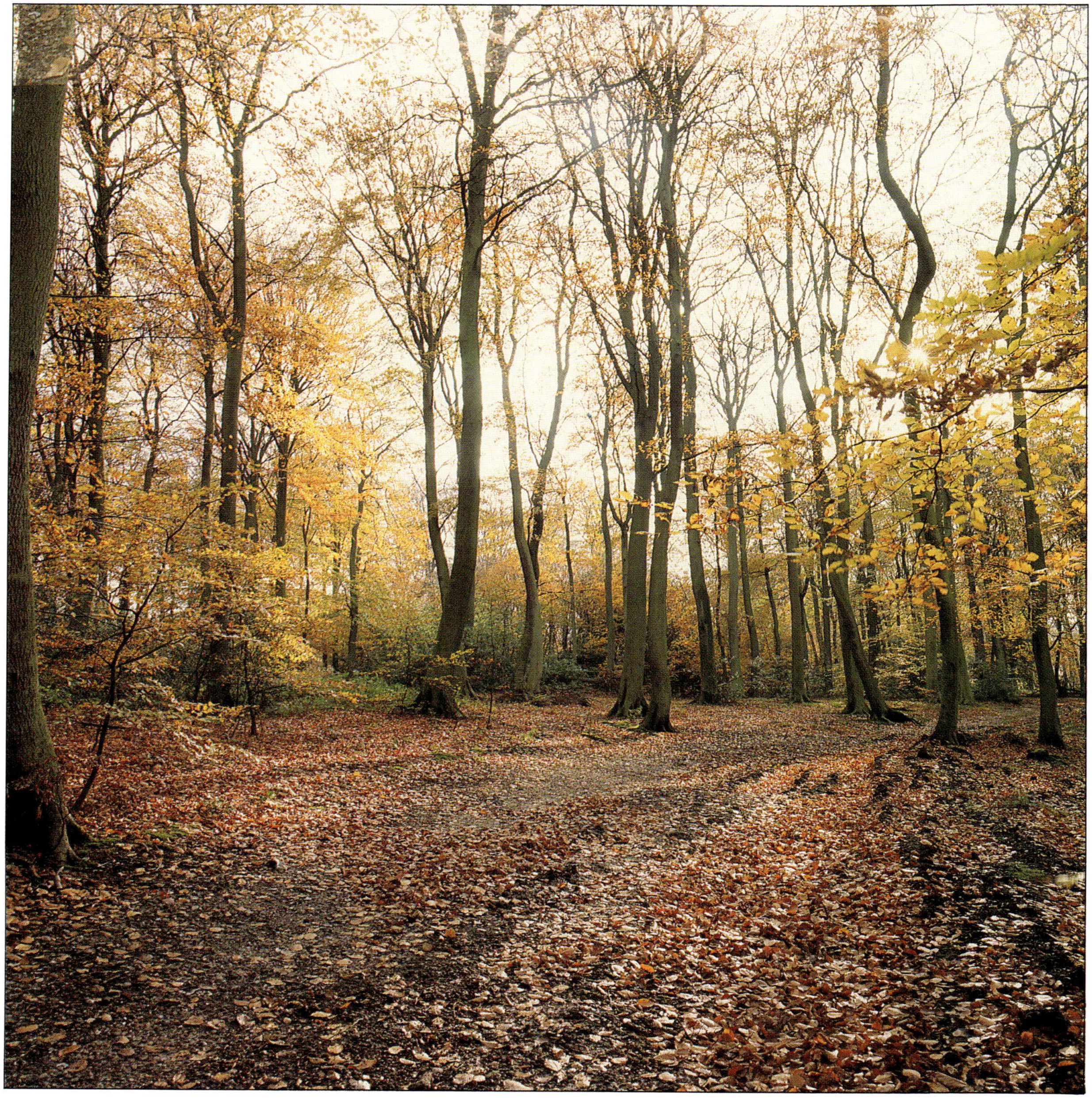

Bradenham

CHILTERN *Images*

John Leland, the antiquary and topographer, passed through the Chilterns on his famous ITINERARY through England, which he committed to paper between 1535 and 1543. He used the term 'Chiltern-hilles' frequently, which gives us a clear indication that these were already a significantly and clearly defined range of hills.

We are made aware that gone are the days of the defensive castle, as at Berkhamsted, and that we are left by this time with little more than a romantic ruin. Such relics are being replaced by the substantial country houses of the nobility and country gentlemen, each with its own 'fair parke'.

Our journey with Leland begins at Maidenhead Bridge and passes through the Thames valley to Caversham.

A 2. or 3. miles beyond the passage over Burne I cam to Maidenhead bridge of tymbre apon the Tamise.

There is a great warfeage of timbre and fier wood on the west ende of the bridge, and this wood cummith out of Berkshir, and the great woddis of the forest of Windelesore, and the great Frithe.

The toun of Maidenhed stondith a praty distance from the Tamise side, and is meately welle buildid.

The south side of the toune is yn the paroch of Bray.

The north side is in the paroche of Cookham.

From Maidenhedde toun a 2. miles by narow wooddy way to the Frithe. And so through the Frithe 3. miles and more.

Then to Twiford a praty tounelet a 2. miles.

At the west ende of this tounlet rennith Loden a praty ryver, and so brekith out in armes that therby I passid over 4. bridges.

Thens a mile and a half to Sunning, an uplandish toune, but set on a fair and commodius grounde. The Tamise rennith under it in a plesant vale.

I markid no very great antiquite in the chirch; it is impropriate onto the decanerie of Saresbyri.

Ther is an old chapelle at the est end of the chirch of S.Sarik, wither of late tyme resortid in pilgrimage many folkes for the desease of madnes.

The Bisshop of Saresbyri hath had at Sunning afore the Conquest an auncient maner place, and hath be lordes there. And yet remainith a fair olde house there of stone, even by the Tamise ripe, longging to the Bisshop of Saresbyri: and therby is a fair parke.

From Reading to Causeiham, shorty caullid Causham, about half a mile, wher is a gret mayne bridge of tymbre over Tamise, wher I markid that it restid most apon fundation of tymbre, and yn sum places of stone.

Towards the north end of this bridge stondith a fair old chapelle of stone on the right hond, pilid in the fundation for the rage of the streame of the Tamise.

Ther is no bridge on the Tamise upward betwixt this and Walingford, distant about 10.miles of. And byneth this Causham bridge to Henley five miles, and a half lower is first Sunning bridge of tymbre, and Grat-Marlaw-bridge.

Bisham Priorie in Barkshir on the Tamise a 3.miles above Maidenhed.

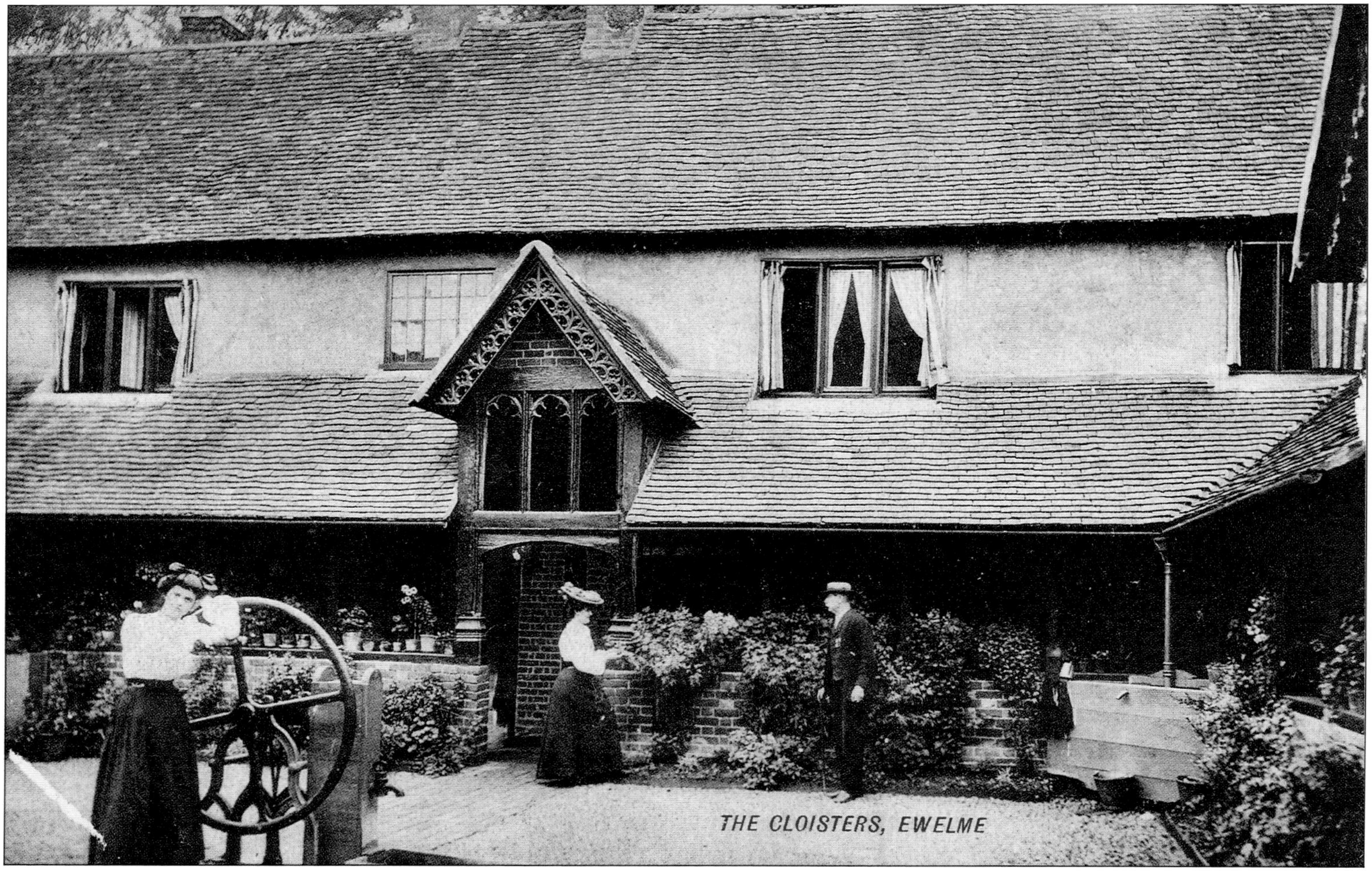

Ewelme

Hurley apon the Tamise, a celle to Westminster, a mile above Bisham.

Litle-Marlaw, wher the priorie of nunnes was, a 2.miles above Maidenhed, stondin in Bukinghamshir.

Great-Merlaw, wher the bridge of timbre is over the Tamise, a mile above it.

Menmenham, a celle to Woburn in Bedfordshir, a mile above Bissham as the Tamise goith in Bukinghamshir.

Beyond Causham bridge is Causham villag in Oxfordshir.

Then I rode a v.miles or more al by great wooddes.

And thens by chaumpaine hilly ground a 4.miles to Ewelm, an uplandish village.

Ewelme was the inheritance of the Chaucers.

Thomas Chaucer the last heire male owner of it is buried yn an high marble tumbe in a fair chapelle in the paroch chirch of Ewelm. . . .

Alice, doughter and heire to Thomas Chaucer and Matilde, tooke to husband William de la Pole Duke of Southfolk: the which for love of her and the commodite of her landes fell much to dwelle yn Oxfordshir and Barkshir wher his wifes landes lay.

This William translatid and encreasid the manor place of Ewelme.

I think that Ewelme tooke name of a great poole afore the manor place and elmes grouing about it.

Ewelme paroche chirch a cumly and new peace of work stonding on an hille was lately made by William Duke of Southfolk and Alice his wife.

William was slayn, and Alice supervivid, and after was byried yn the paroche chirch of Ewelme on the south side of the high altare in a riche tumbe of alabastre, with an image of woves crounid lying over it.

The pratie hospitale of poore men is hard joynid to the west ende of Ewelm paroche chirch: and much after the building of the vicars houses at Windesore yn a circle.

In the midle of the area of the hospitale is a very fair welle.

The master or provost of the almose house hath ther a praty lodging. Every poore man hath 14d. a week.

The maner place of Ewelme is in the valley of the village; the base court of it is fair, and is buildid of brike and tymbre. The inner part of the house is sette with a fair mote, and is buildid richely of brike and stone. The haul of it is fair and hath great barres of iren overthuart it instede of crosse beames. The parler by is exceding fair and lightsum: and so be all the lodginges there.

There is a right fair parke by the manor place.

Remaining in the Thames valley we move from Wallingford to Henley and it's vicinity:

Tame and Ise metith aboute half a mile beneth Dorchestre bridg in the medowis.

From Dorchester to the fery over the Tamise about a mile.

Here the hither ripe by north is low and medow ground. The south ys high al alonge like the long bak of an hille.

From the fery to Walingford a mile by marvelus fair champain and fruteful ground of corne.

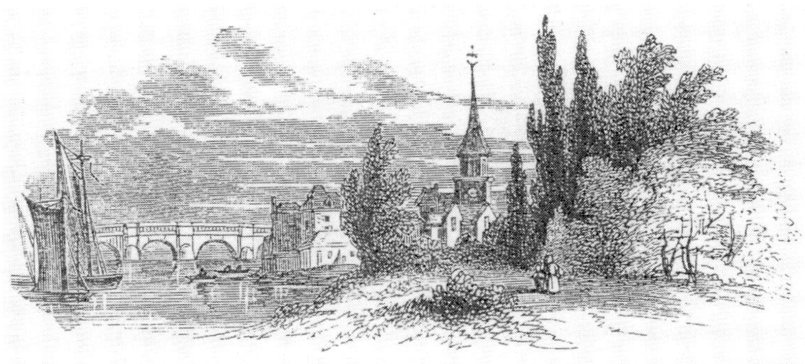

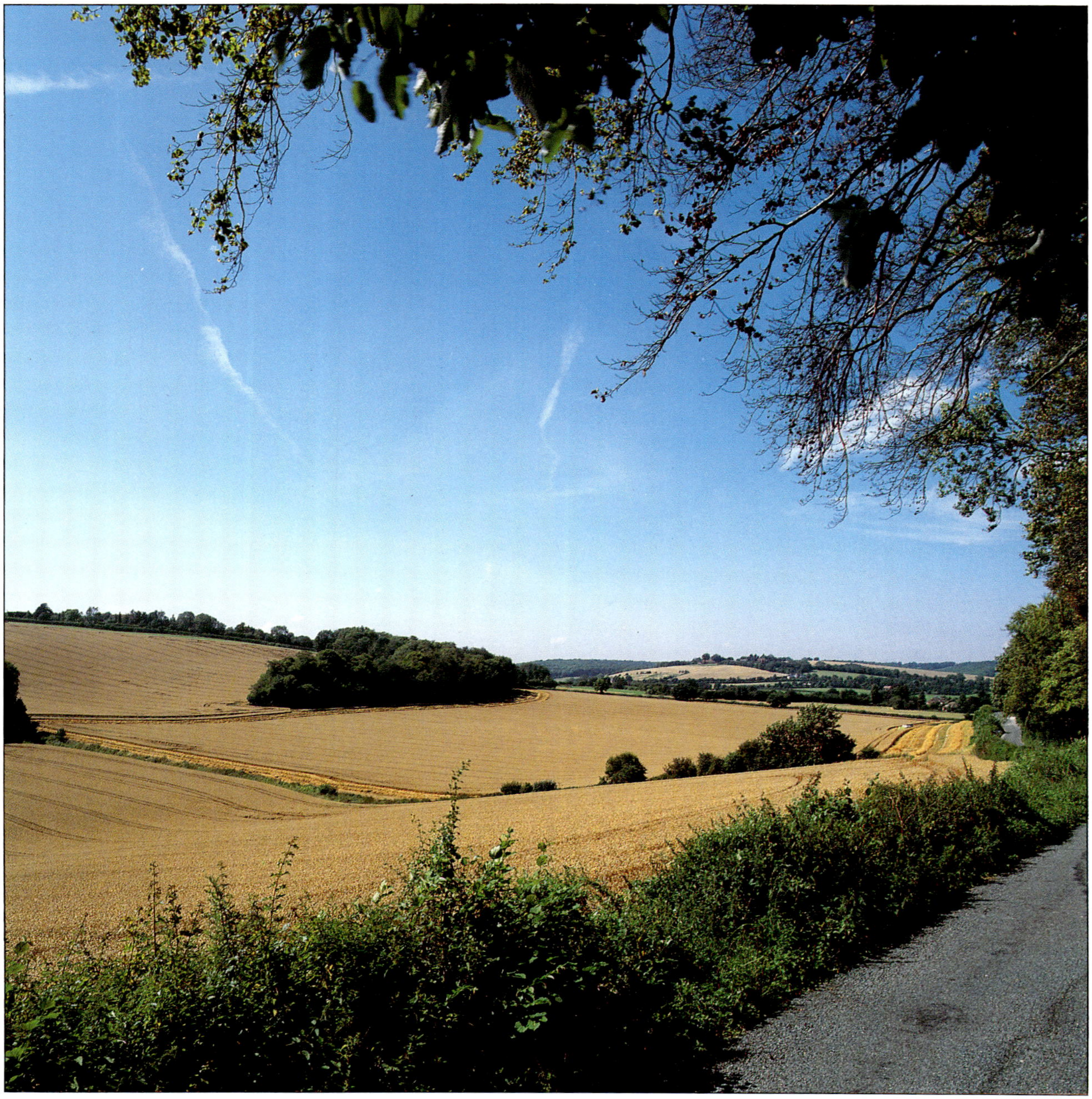

Radnage

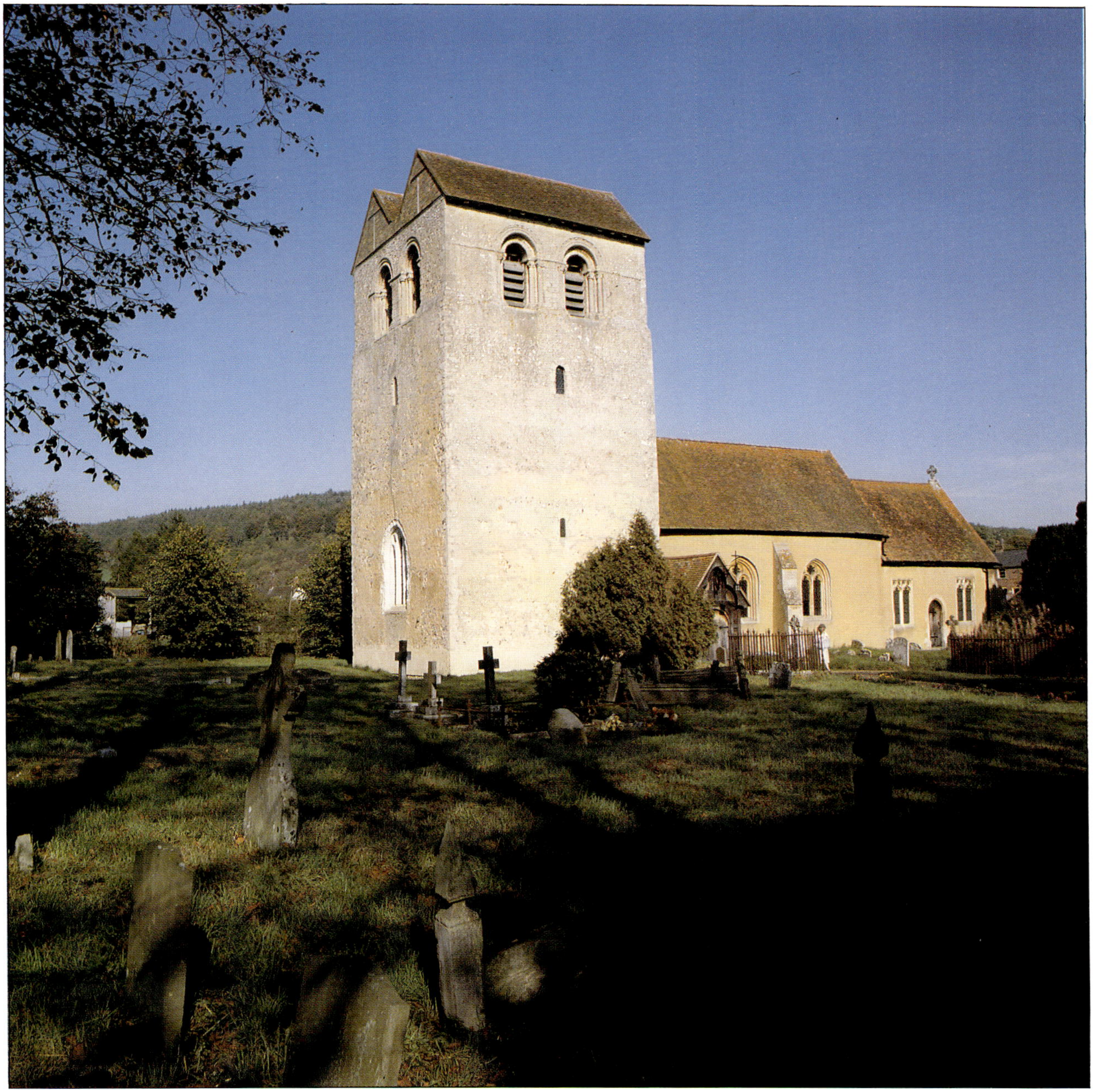

Fingest

The toun of Walingeforde hath beene a very notable thing and welle waullid.

The diche of the toun and the crest wheron the waulles stoode be yet manifestely perceyvid, and begin from the castelle going in cumpace a good mile and more, and so cummith to Walingford bridg a large thing of stone over the Tamise.

Cummyne to Henley I saw in the valley the priorie of Hurley, a celle to Westminster, standinge on the right ripe of the Thames.

The bridge at Henley is all of tymbre, as moste parte of the bridgs be ther about.

It was of stone, as the foundation shewithe at a low water . . .

Plenty of wood and corne about Henley. The soyle chalky and hillinge.

Rotherfeld about a mile from Henley. There is a parke. It is of moste men caulled Rotherfelde Gray, by cawse that one of the Gray of Ruthyne came to be owner of it . . . There appere enteringe into the maner place on the righte hand 3. or 4. very olde towers of stone, a manifest token that it was sume tyme a castle. Ther is a very large courte buildyd about with tymbar and spacyd withe brike; but this is a latter worke. Men of Henley may yet remembar that it was the Lord Lovel's pocession. Sens by attainture it cam by gifte to Knolls.

Stoner is a 3. miles out of Henley. There is a fayre parke, and a waren of connes, and fayre woods. The mansion place standithe clyminge on an hille, and hathe 2. courtes buyldyd withe tymbar, brike and flynte. Syr Waltar Stonar now pocessor of it hathe augmentyd and strengthed the howse . . .

In a totally different landscape we are guided through Aylesbury and it's vale and eventually back to the Chiltern Hills beginning at Wendover:

From Birdsteine to Aillesbiri a faire markett toune, al by champayne, [a 3. miles. Of this towne all the champaine] thereabout is called the vale of Alesburye.

This vale goithe one waye to the forest beyond Tame market. It goithe otharwyes to Bukinghame, to Stony Stratford, to Newporte Panell, and along from Ailesbery by the rootes of Chilterne Hills almoste to Dunstaple.

Or evar I pasyd into Aillesbyri I rode over a little bridge of stone caullid Woman's Bridge, undar the whiche passithe a brooke downe on the right hand as I rode; and from this bridge to the towne is a causey of stone. [This is, as farre as I can gather, Tame water.]

The towne selfe of Aillisbyry standithe on an hill in respecte of all the ground thereabout, a 3. miles flate northe from Chilterne Hills. The towne is metly well buyldyd with tymbar, and in it is a celebrated market. It standithe in the highe waye from Banbyry to London, and in the highe way from Bukingham to London. There is a domus civica in the midle of the markett place, a late reedified by [John] Baldwine cheife Justice [of the Common-Pleas]; but the kynge gave the tymbar unto it. The common gaolie or prison for Bukyngham-shire is in this towne.

There is but one paroche church in the towne standinge west northe west in it; but that is one of the most auncientist in all thos quartras . . .

There was an howse of the Gray-Friers in the towne toward the sowthe, foundyd about the tyme of Richard 2. There rennithe a praty brooke undar a wooden bridge almoste at the very end of Aillesbyri towne, by southe. This watar cummithe downe from este and rennithe by weste into Tame, by the lefte ripe of it about a mile bynethe Aillesbyri, some what lower then Stone-bridge on Tame. I take the hedde of this broke to be toward Wyndover thrwgh-fayre 3. miles of the southe.

Tame rivar selfe, as I there lerned, rysethe in the ester parts of all the Chiltern Hills towards Dunestaple, and the

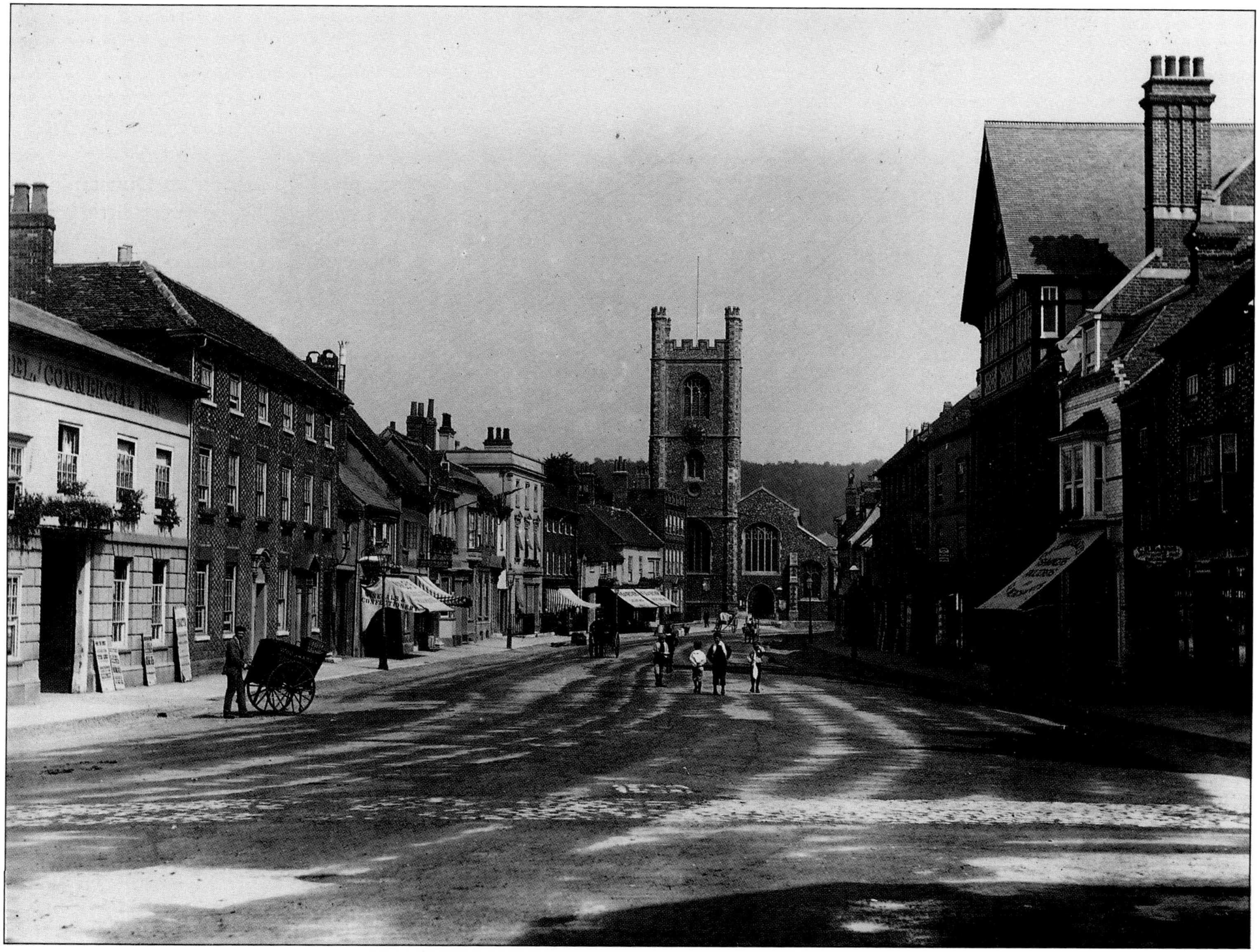

Henley

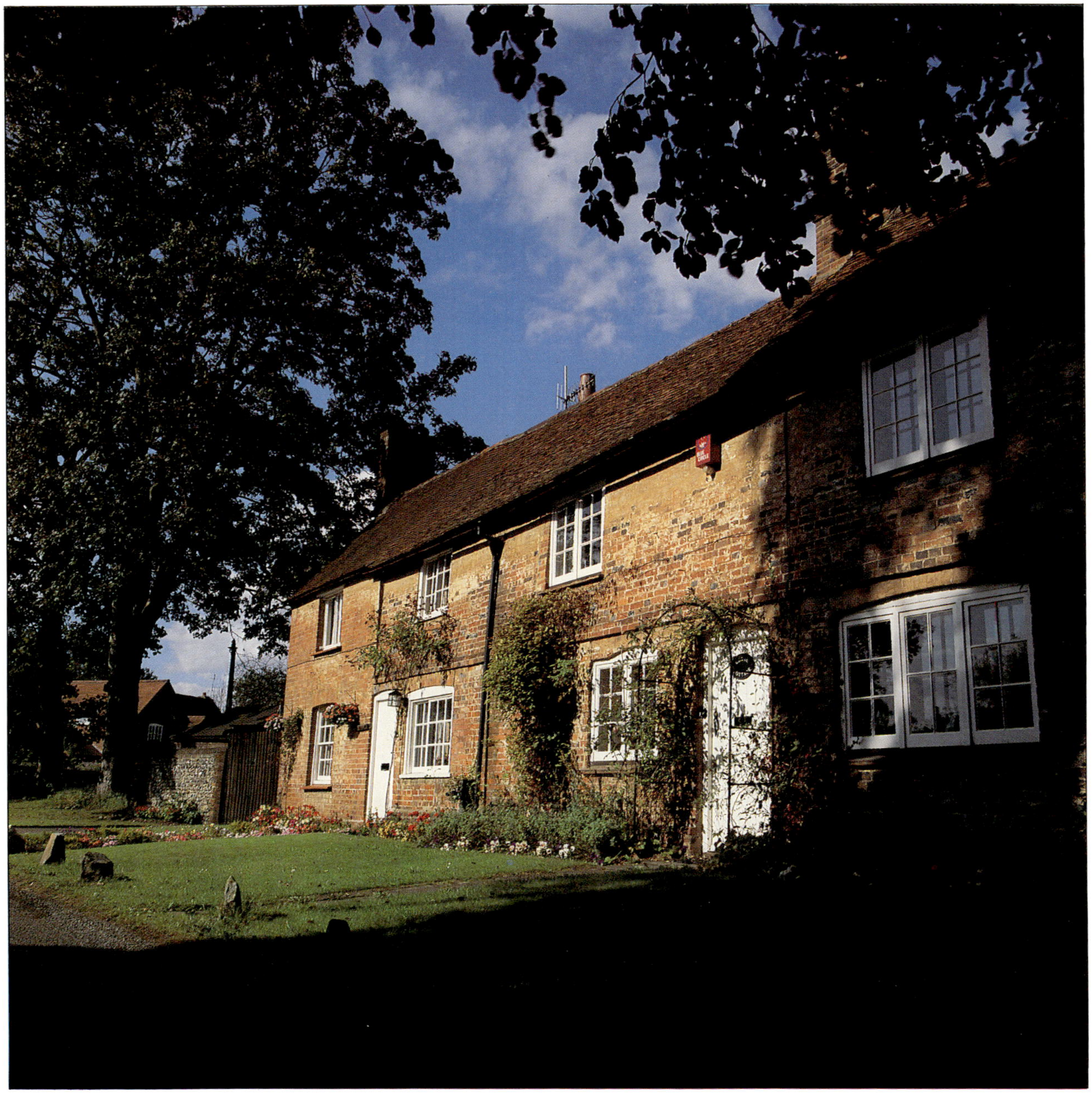

Great Missenden

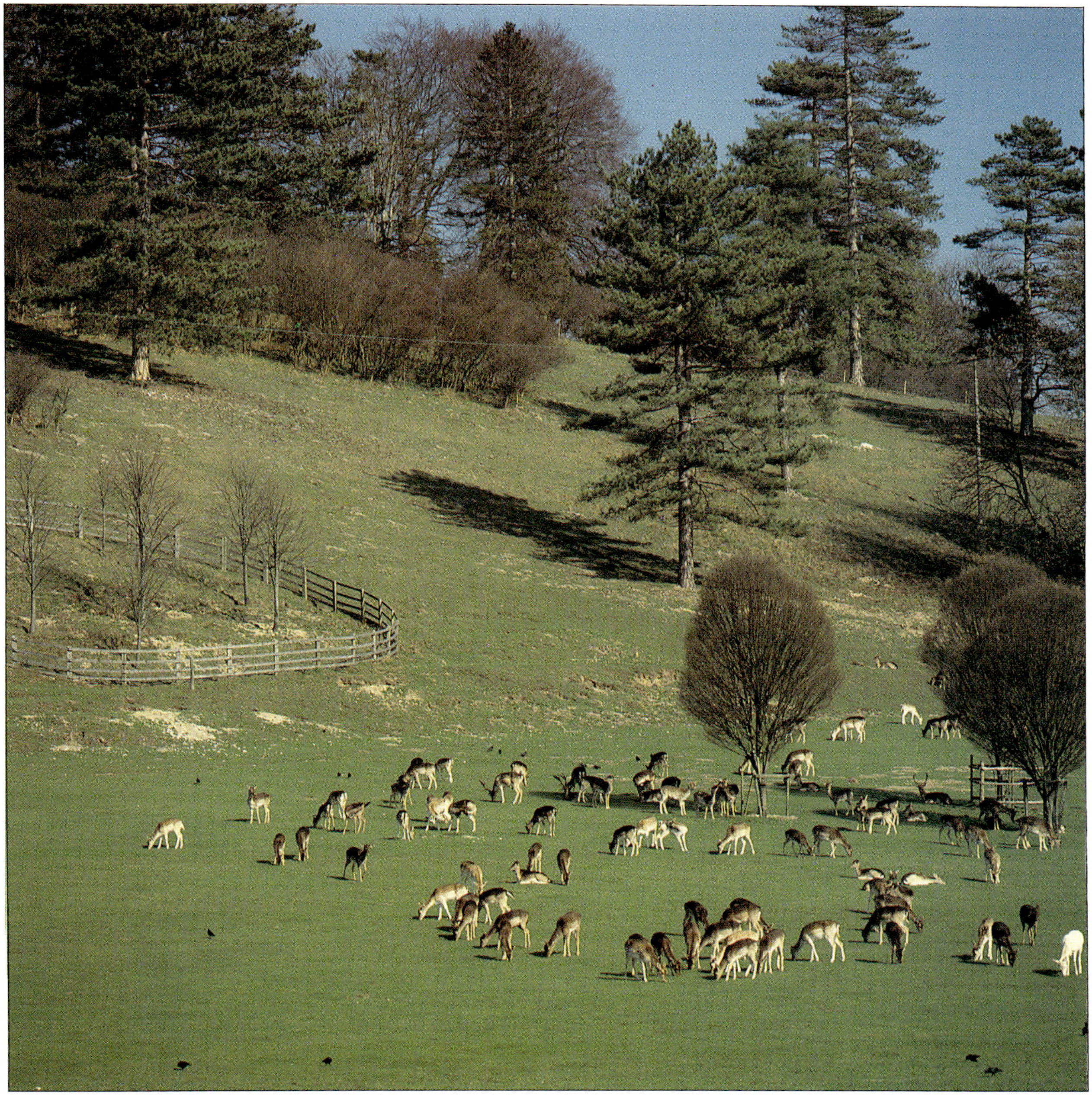

Stonor Park

hede of it by estimation is 7. miles from Stonebridge on Tame betwixt Querendune and Aillesbyri. . . .

Wyndover a praty thrwghe fayre, havynge 2 stretes well buildyd with tymber, a 3. miles of. There is a causey made almoste thrwghly to passe betwixt Aillesbery and it, els the way in wet tyme as in a lowe stiffe claye grownde were very tedius and ille to passe by.

The tounelet selfe of Wyndover stondythe partely apon one of the north-est cliffs of Chilterne Hills. The residew and north-est parte of the towne stanythe in the rootes of the hills. Looke as the conterye of the vale of Aillesbyre for the most parte is clene baren of woodde, and is champaine; so is all the Chilterne well woodyd, and full of enclosures.

From Windover to Great Missenden in Chiltern a 3. miles. It is a praty thrwghe fayre, but no market towne. There is a praty chapell of brike in the southe part of it, and a little by southe without the towne was Missendene, a priorie of black channons. It standithe in the very botom of an hill, and hathe goodly ground about and dyvers praty hills well woodyd toward the est and southe.

A mile and a halfe furthar toward London is a strete caullyd Litle Missendene. Hagmondesham, alias Hamersham, a right praty market[towne] on Friday, of on strete well buildyd with tymbar, standynge in Bukinghamshire and Chiltern, 2. miles and halfe from Litle Messenden. The Duke of Bukyngham was chefe lorde of it, syns the kynge, now the Lord Russell by gyft, that dwellithe at Cheynes 3. miles[of] by east . . . There comithe a brooke almoste from Missenden, and passeth hard by Hagmondesham levinge it almoste by full southe on the right ripe, and aftar rennithe downe by the valeys of Chiltern Hills toward Colne streme . . .

. . . I passid half a mile by hilly ground as in the beginning of Chilterne, and there I saw in a praty wood side S. Leonardes on the lifte hand, scant half a mile of toward north weste. Where of late tyme was a priorie of nunnes . . .

Finally our itinerary with Leland takes us into the Hertfordshire Chilterns:

So forthe by Chiltern-hilles and woddes a 4. miles and a half to [Gaddesden] wher the Lord of Darby hath a praty maner place of tymbre.

And or I came to this village I rode over a little brooke that cummith not very far out of Chiltern-hilles and resortyth to Langley where the friars are dwelling. Thens by Chiltern-hilles and baren, wooddy, and ferne ground for the moste parte, the soile waxing chalky and flinty, as al Chiltern ys, a 3. miles to Barkhamstede. Wher is an old large castelle in a roote of an hille stonding sum what low, and environid with a mote, to the which as I could perceyve, part of the water of the ryver there hard by doth resorte.

I markid dyverse towers in the middle warde of the castelle, and the dungeon hille. But to my sighte it is much in ruine. The house of Bonehomes, caullid Asscheruge, of

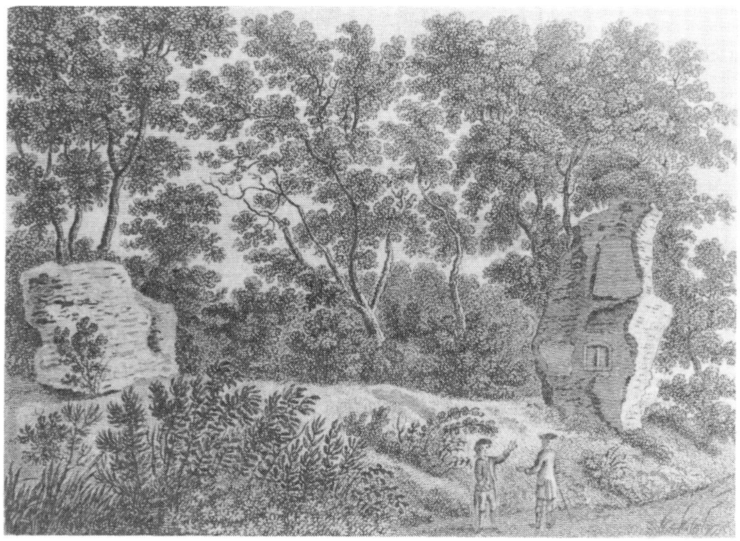

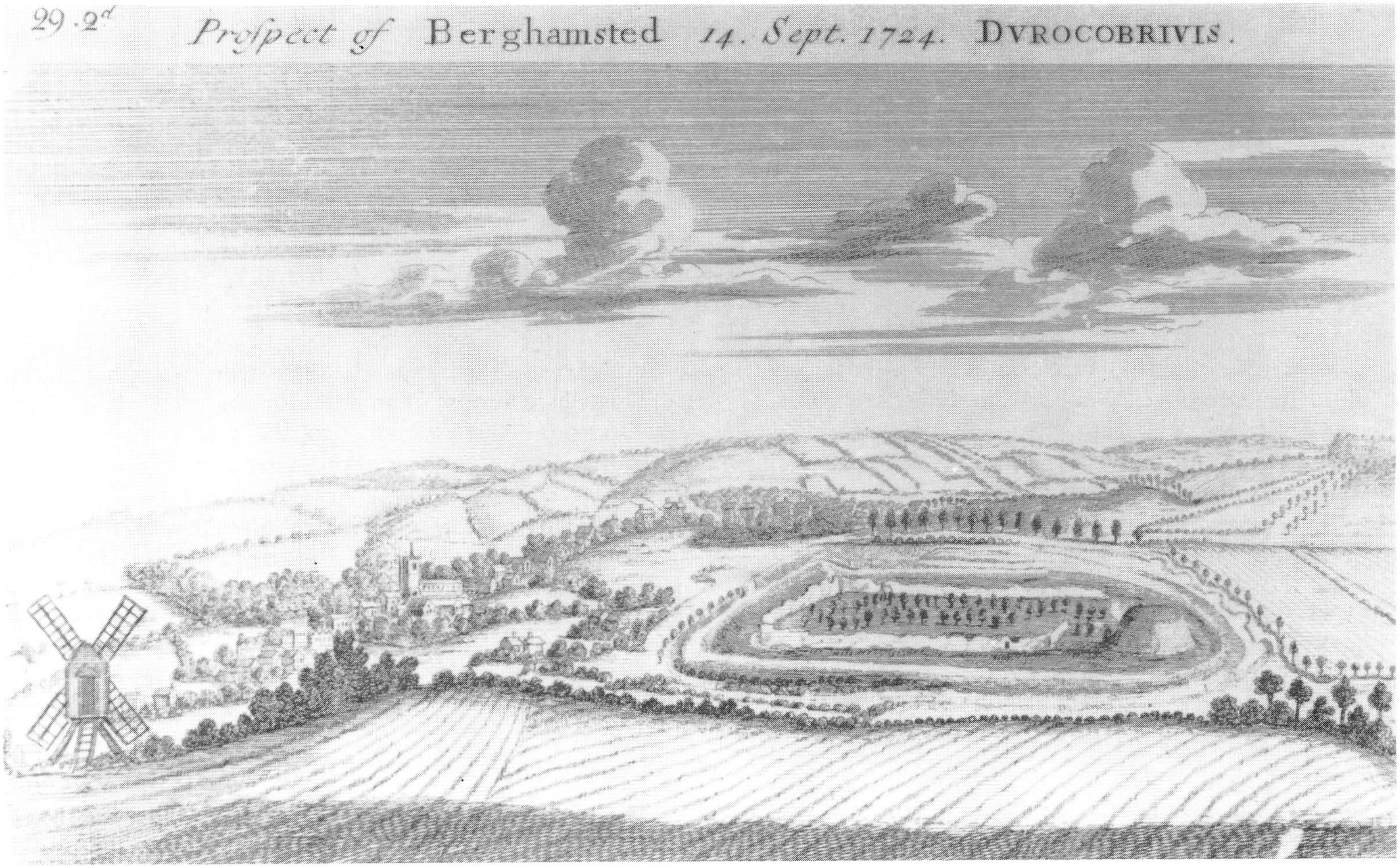

the fundation of Edmunde, Erle of Cornewale, and owner of Berckhamstede-Castel, is about a mile of, and there the king lodgid. After that I had veuyd the castel, I passid over the ryver wher as is a Bridge of wood. This ryver cummith by northe-west from Penley, a place yn Chiltern a 3. miles of, and so renning by the est ende of Barkhamstede towne goith doun a xij. miles southwarde to the more water about the quarters of Richemannesworthe.

Berkhamstede is one of the best markette townes in Hertfordeshire, and hath a longe streate metely welle builded from the north to the south: and another, but sumwhat lesser, from the west to the est, where the ryver rennith.

The chirch is in the midle of the town.

In the botom of the ryver of eche side be very faire medowes.

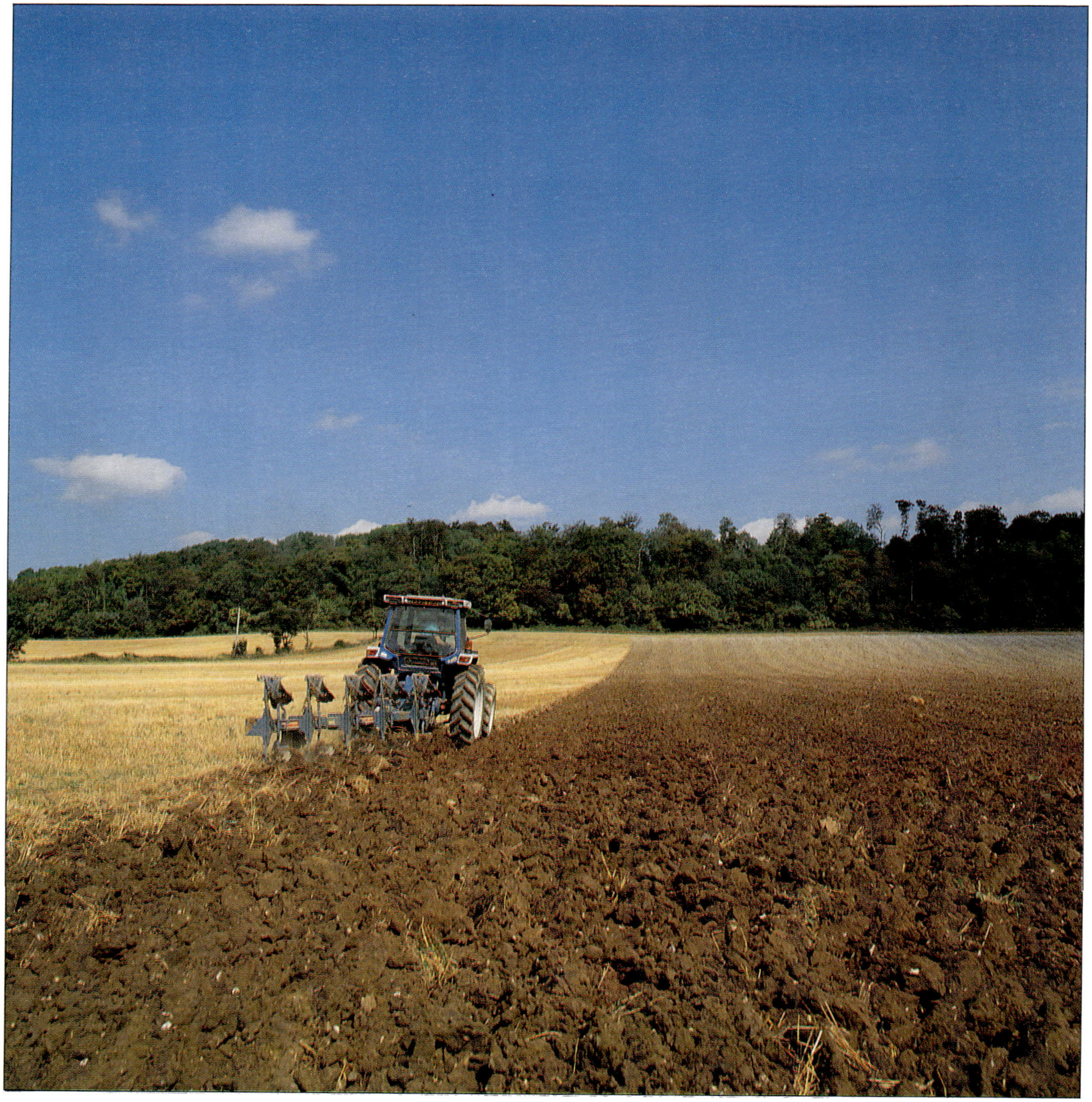

Saunderton

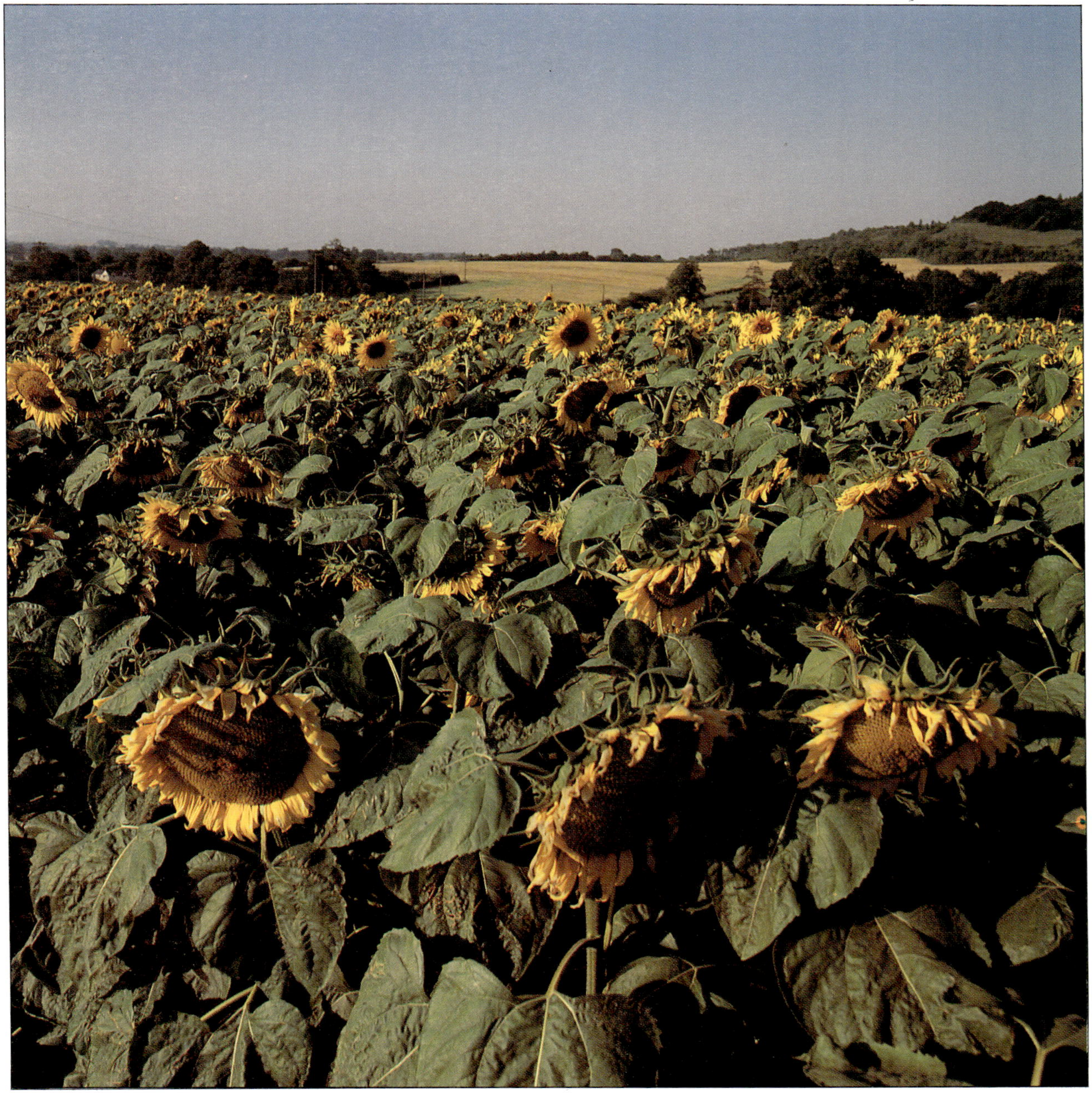

Watlington

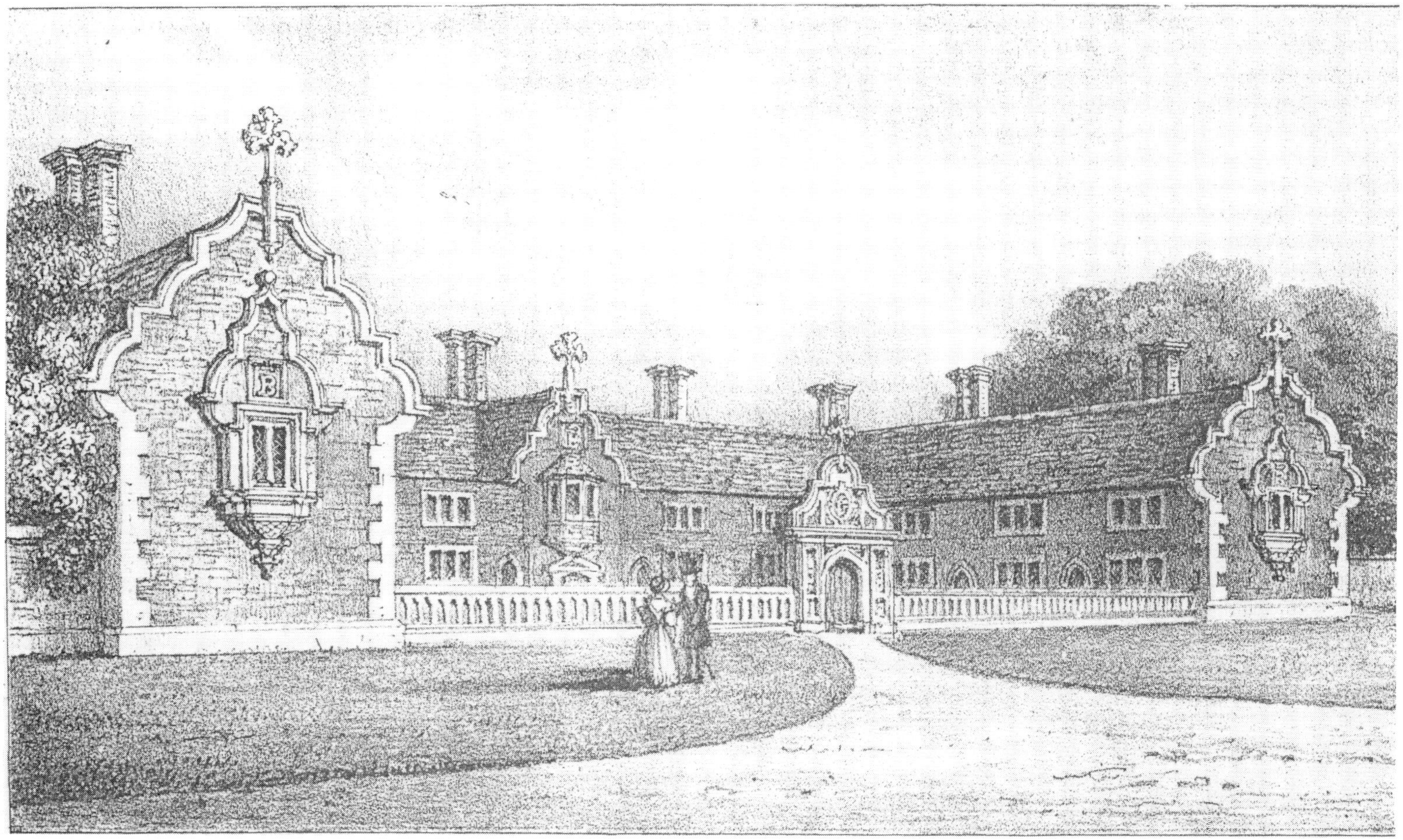

Thens I passid by hilly, woddy, and much baren ground to Cheynes v. miles of.

And or I cam very nere Cheynes I passid over a little brooke, and even in the valley by Cheineys over another, and they resorte aboute Richemansworth to the moore water.

The olde house of the Cheyneis is so translatid by my Lorde Russel, that hath that house on the right of his wife, that litle or nothing of it yn a maner remayneth ontranslatid; and a great deale of the house is even newly set up made of brike and timber: and fair logginges be new erectid in the gardein.

The house is within diverse places richely painted with antique workes of white and blak.

And there about the house 2. parkes, as I remembre.

The maner place stondeth at the west ende of the paroche chirche.

In the paroche on the north side of it, as in the chapelle,

be 2. tumbes of the Chaynes lordes of the manor ther, and the smaul village bering their name.

From Leland's writing we learn that many of the small villages scattered through the Chiltern countryside and along the Thames were often based on religious establishments. His period was to see the dramatic change wrought by Henry VIII. All were gradually swept away, yet the villages remain to this day inheritors of their distinguished past.

The following letter is a personal and touching appeal made by Margaret Vernon, the last prioress of Little Marlow Nunnery, to Thomas Cromwell. It was his task to see that all such religious institutions were subjected to the iron will of Henry VIII. Unlike the nearby Abbey of Reading, where the abbot was committed to death for his refusal to accept the supremacy of the monarchy and the abbey itself dissolved, the prioress here made her surrender to the hand of fate, and the nunnery received more gentle treatment, being annexed to Bisham Abbey in 1534.

To the Ryght onurabyll and hyr most specyall good mayster, mayster secretary vnto the Kynges most nobyll grace. – After all dew commendacyons had vnto yowre good maystershyp with my most vmble thankes for the greate cost mayd on me and my pore madyn at my last beynge with yowre maystershyp, fathermore plesyth yt yow to vnderstonde that yowre vysytors hath bene here of late who hath discharged iij of my systers, the one is dame Katheryn the other ij is the yonge women that were last professyd whyche yt not a lyttyll to my discomforte, nevertheless I must be content with the Kynges pleasure, but now as towchynge my nowne parte I most vmbly beseeche yow to be so specyall good mayster vnto me yowre poore bedewoman as to geve me yowre beste advertysment and counseyle what waye shalbe best for me to take seynge there shalbe none left here but myselfe and thys pore madyn, and yf yt wyll plese yowre goodness to take thys pore howse Into yowre owne hondes other for yowre selfe or for my nowne m[ayster] yowre sonne, I woyld be glad with all my hart to geve yt Into yowre maystershypes hondes with that ye wyll commaunde me to do therin: Trustynge and nothyinge dowptynge In yowre goodness that ye wyll so provyd for vs that we shall have syche onest lyvynge that we shall not be dreven be necessyte nether to begge nor to fall to no other vnconvenyence, and thus I offer my selfe and all myne vnto yowre most hygh and prudent wysdom, as unto him that ys my onely Refuge and comfort In thys world, besechynge god of hys goodnes to put In yow hys holy sprete that ye maye do all thynges to his lawde and glory, –
By yowre owne assured bedewoman, **Margaret Vernon**.

Religious persecution was not a new phenomenon, particularly in this part of the country. Dr Fuller, who we will meet in the next century, makes the following potent comment in his CHURCH HISTORY: 'It is no small praise to Buckinghamshire that though it is one of the lesser counties of England, it had before the time of Luther more martyrs and confessors than all England besides.'

John Foxe in his ACTES AND MONUMENTS, published in 1563, records the ruthless persecution at the beginning of this century of those who were considered heretics. The Lollards were particularly active in the Chilterns:

In 1500, also, we meet with William Tylsworth, who was burned at Amersham, or Agmondesham, in Bucks; when the cruel savages compelled his only daughter, as a penance for Lollardy, to set fire to her father's burning; and her husband, and at least sixty more, many of which are given by name, were obliged to bear a faggot, and afterwards to wear badges, and to be exhibited in several market towns. William Page and some others were also burned on the cheek; and Robert Bartlet, a rich man, was sentenced to lose his farm and goods, imprisoned in the monastery of Ashrigg seven years, with a badge upon his

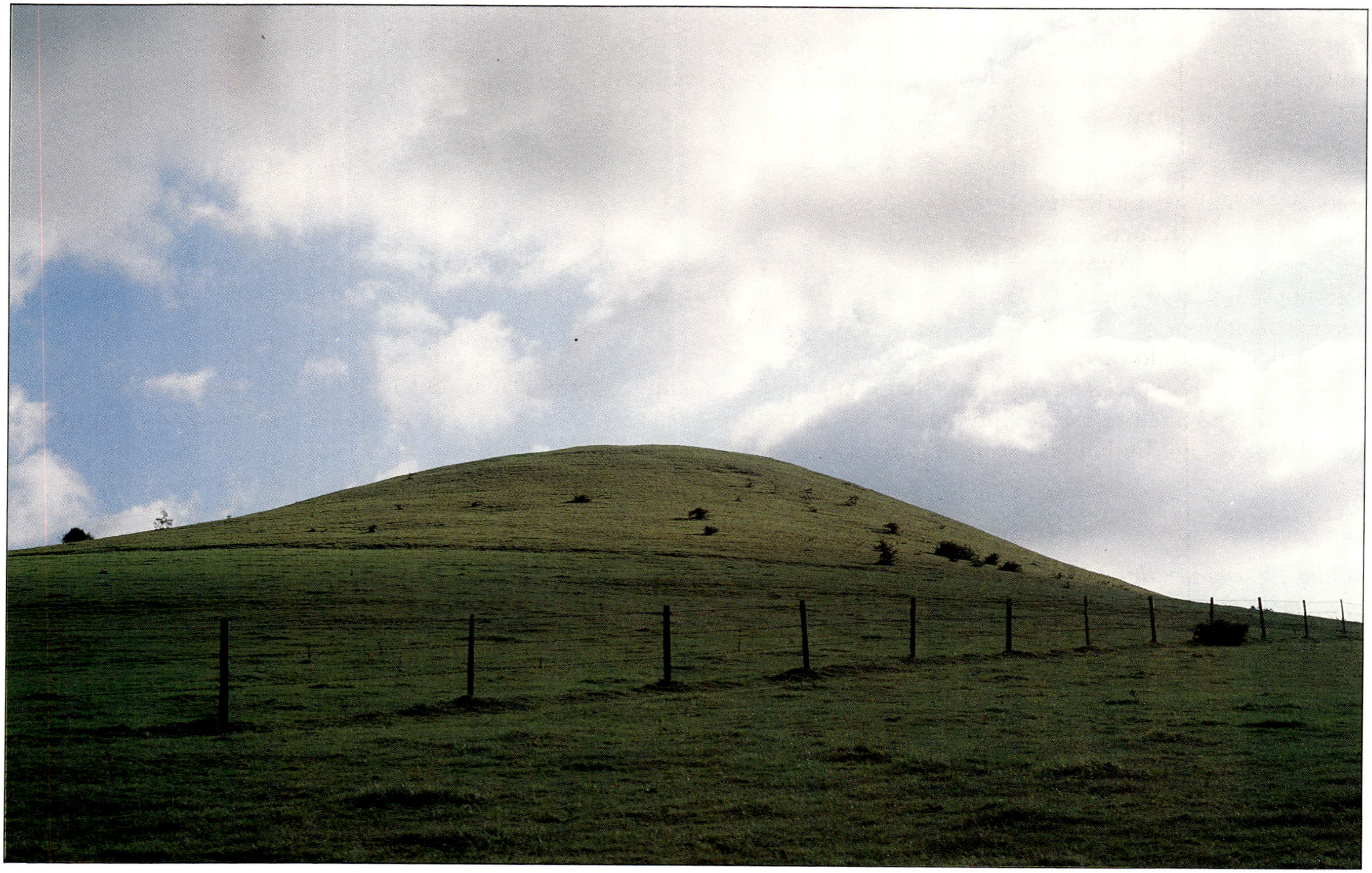

Cymbeline's Mount

right sleeve. Robin Cosin was also burned at Buckingham, on the same day as Tylsworth, or the day following being a miller of Missenden; when about twenty persons were compelled to bear faggots, and submit to other penance. About the year 1503, also, Thomas Bernard, a husbandman, and James Morden, a labourer, were burned at Amersham. William Littlepage was there burned on the cheek, and Father Rogers; as was also Father Reive, who afterwards suffered martyrdom. Father Rogers had been in the bishops prison fourteen weeks, oppressed with cold, hunger, and irons; and, when discharged was so lame in the back that he could never afterwards stand upright. In the year 1506 Thomas Chase of Amersham was apprehended and conducted to the bishop of Lincoln, at Wooburn, in Bucks, and by him was committed to his prison there called Little Ease; where he was strangled and pressed to death.

William Camden writing his famous BRITANNIA (1586) covers some of the same ground as his predecessor Leland, and yet reading the two they compliment one another, Camden frequently expanding on the descriptions of certain towns and villages. In turn his own work was augmented in later editions, including an explanation of the connection between King Cunobeline and the hill called Cymbeline's Mount; the battle purported to have taken place here is described by Shakespeare in his play CYMBELINE KING OF BRITAIN.

Camden takes us county by county through the length and breadth of England. We start in the old county of Berkshire at Wallingford, and from here pass down the Thames to Maidenhead.

In old times it was compassed about with walls, which, as men may see by their tract, tooke up a mile in circuit. It has a Castle situated upon the river, verie large (I assure you) and stately: so fortified in times past, that the hop in it, (as imprenable, and invincible) made divers over-bold and stowt. For, when England burned (as a man may say) in a generall flame of warres, we read, that it was by King Stephen belaied once or twice with sieges, but all in vaine. The greatnesse and magnificence thereof I much wondered at when young, and removed thither from Oxford (for a place it is now for the Students there of Christchurch, to retire unto) as having a double range of walles about it, and being compassed round likewise with a duple rampire and ditch: and in the mids of it, there standeth a tower or keepe, raised upon a mightie high mount: in the steep ascent whereof by steps, we saw a well of exceeding depth. The Inhabitants are verily perswaded, that it was built by the Danes; but I should rather judge, that something was heere erected by the Romans, and afterwards rased by the Saxons and Danes, what time Sueno the Dane, ranging and roving this way spoiled, and harried the countrey. That it was at length reedified under King William the first, we know assuredly by Domesday book, seeing that it yeeldeth record (as even now I noted) of eight Hages or Houses destroyed for the Castle.

And verily about the time when the most mortal Plague which followed the conjunction of Saturne and Mars in Capricorne, reigned hotly through Europe in the year of our Lord 1348. This town was so dispeopled by reason of continual mortalitie here, that whereas before time it was passing well Inhabited, and had twelve Churches in it, it can shew now no more than one or two. But the cause of this desolation of the Inhabitants lay rather upon the bridges of Abbindon and Dorchester, whereby London portway was turned from thence.

Scarce halfe a mile from Reading, betwixt most greene and flowing medowes, the Kennet is coupled with the Tamis, who now runneth with a broad streame by a small village called Sunning, which a man would mervaile to have beene the Sea of eight Bishops who had this Shire and Wiltshire for their Diocese (yet our Histories report as much) the same afterwards by Herman was translated to

Shirburne, and in the end to Salisburie, unto which Bishopricke this place still belongeth.

From Sunning the Tamis passes by Bisteham, now called short, Bisham, at first a Lordship of the Knights Templars, then of the Montacutes and amongst them, William the first Earle of Saisburie of his familie founded a Priory, wherin some say he was buried. . . . Now it is the possession of Sir Edward Hoby Knight, of me especially to be observed, who singular kindnesse towards me the often consideration thereof shall keepe so fresh, that it shall never vanish out of my remembrance.

Tamis having now left Bisham behind it, fetcheth it selfe with a compasse about to a little towne named in the former ages, Southaelington, afterward Maiden-hith and at this day Maidenhead . . . Neither is this towne of any antiquity; for no longer agoe then in our great grandfathers daies, there was a Ferry in a place some-what higher at Brabhams end. But after they had built heere a bridge of timber piles, it beganne to flourish with Innes and goe beyond her mother Bray hard by, which notwithstanding is farre more ancient, as having given name to the whole Hundred.

Moving into the Buckinghamshire Chilterns our course is set through Marlow to High Wycombe and eventually to Aylesbury:

The Chiltern hath its name from the nature of the soil, Cylt or Chilt, in Saxon, signifying chalk; for it riseth, for the most part, into chalky hills, covered with woods and groves of beeches. For, theretofore, it was so thick with trees that they rendered it impassable, till they were, in a good measure, cleared by Leofstan abbot of St. Alban's, as a common receptacle and harbour of thieves. In this part, where the Thames winds itself round the bottom of the hills, is seated Marlow, a pretty considerable town, which has its name from a sort of chalky clay which we call marle; this, being spread upon the fields, so fattens and enriches the soil, when it is worn out, that, after one year's lying fallow, they are always fit for tillage; and what they receive of the husbandman they repay with wonderful increase.

Near this town, a little river cuts its way through low grounds into the Thames; on the turning of which is seated High Wickham, or rather Wicomb; and, perhaps, it may have received its name from thence: for the German-Saxons call the winding of a sea or river Wick, and in England there are abundance of places of like denomination. This town, for largeness and beauty, compares with the best in the country, and, as it is governed by a mayor, is justly prefered to most of the rest. North of Wicomb is the highest eminence of these parts, where it still keeps the British name Pen [for they call the head or top of anything Pen; whence the Pennine Alps, and the Apennine, and several mountains among us, seem to be derived]. Near Pen lies Bradenham, of a commodious and healthy situation, the chief residence of the barons of Windsor.

More inward are two places which we must by no means pass over; Stoke-Pogeis, called so from the Pogeis, formerly lords of it, from whom it devolved, by the right of inheritance, to the Hastings. The other place is Fernham, the same (as I take it) which is called Fernham Royal; this the barons Furnival heretofore held by service, 'that, on the coronation-day, they should be obliged to find a glove for the king's right hand, and to support his left arm, that day, while he held the royal sceptre'. The Coln, being joined higher by another rivulet from the west, carries it along: and, upon this, the first place observable is Missenden, where a monastery was founded by the D'oily's, and augmented by the noble family sirnamed de Missenden. Next, in the vale, stands Amersham which could heretofore neither boast of buildings nor populousness, but is now both populous and well-built, and may by justly proud of its lord Francis Russel earl of Bedford, who lived an exact pattern of virtue and true honour, entirely beloved by all good men. The chief seat of the earls of Bedford is Cheyneis, more to the east; where John, the first earl of this family, and his son, the before-mentioned Francis, and their successors, lie intombed together. To Cheyneis adjoineth Latimers, called heretofore Isel-Hampstead; but it has the present name fro the lords of it, the ancient barons Latimer.

Passing hence, scarce three miles northward, we come to the ridge of the Chiltern hills, which divides the whole shire, from south-west to north-east, along many little villages; of which the most considerable is Hampden, whence an ancient and numerous family in this county took their name. [Not far from hence is Princes-Risborough, near which, on the top of a hill, is a camp; and the way which goes by it is called by the vulgar Acknel-way. At the foot of the hill, was found a coin of the emperor Vespasian; and from the top of it, is said to be a prospect of thirteen counties. Near this is Monks-Risborough, which Aescwin, bishop of Dorchester, gave to the church of Canturbury and to Aelfric, the archbishop, about the year 995; it was afterwards assigned for a portion to the monks of Canturbury, whence it received the present name. In these parts, are two places which seem to be of great antiquity; the first is Ellesborough, near the church whereof, on a round hill, is an ancient fortification called Belinus's Castle, where the inhabitants tell you, by tradition, that king Belinus resided; above which is also an high hill, that still retains the name of Belinesbury-hill: the second is Kymbel (great and little) which are supposed to take the name from Cunobeline king of the Britons; the places being also, in ancient records, written Cunebel. And this (together with several trenches and fortifications in these parts) confirms the notion, that the county was the seat of the action wherein the two sons of Cunobeline were slain; and from hence they might probably retire, to give battle to Aulus Plautius.]

On the eastern angle of the hills, upon a descent stands Ashridge, formerly a house of pleasure of the kings, where Edmund earl of Cornwall, son of Richard king of the Romans, founded a monastery for an order of religious, then lately instituted and by him first brought into England, called Bon-hommes; they wore a sort of sky-coloured habit, after the manner of the hermits. From the top of these hills, we have a clear and full prospect of the large vale, which I said was the other part of the county; it is almost all champain; the soil is chalky, stiff and fruitful; the rich meadows feed an incredible number of sheep, whose soft and fine fleeces are sought after, even from Asia itself.

Not far from the said river (Thame), which watereth the fourth part of the vale, stands on a rising ground a very fair market-town, large, and pretty populous, surrounded with a great number of pleasant meadows and pastures, and now called Ailesbury; whence the whole vale is named 'the Vale of Ailesbury'. In the time of the Conqueror, this was a manor Royal, and several yard-lands were here given by the king, on condition 'that the holders of them should find litter (i.e. straw) for the king's bed (I hope the nice part of the world will observe this) whenever he should come thither'. It owes much to the munificence of Baldwin chief justice, who not only adorned it with public edifices, but raised an excellent causey about three miles in length, where the road is deep and troublesome. All about, vast numbers of well-fleeced sheep are plentifully fed, to the great profit and advantage of their owners.

Entering Oxfordshire, we make our way to Thame, and then drop down to the more southerly part of the county:

As soon as Isis and Cherwell have joyn'd their streams below Oxford, the Isis with a swift and deeper current passes on to the south, to find out the Tame which it seems long to have sought for. Nor does it run many miles before the said Tame, rising in the County of Bucks,

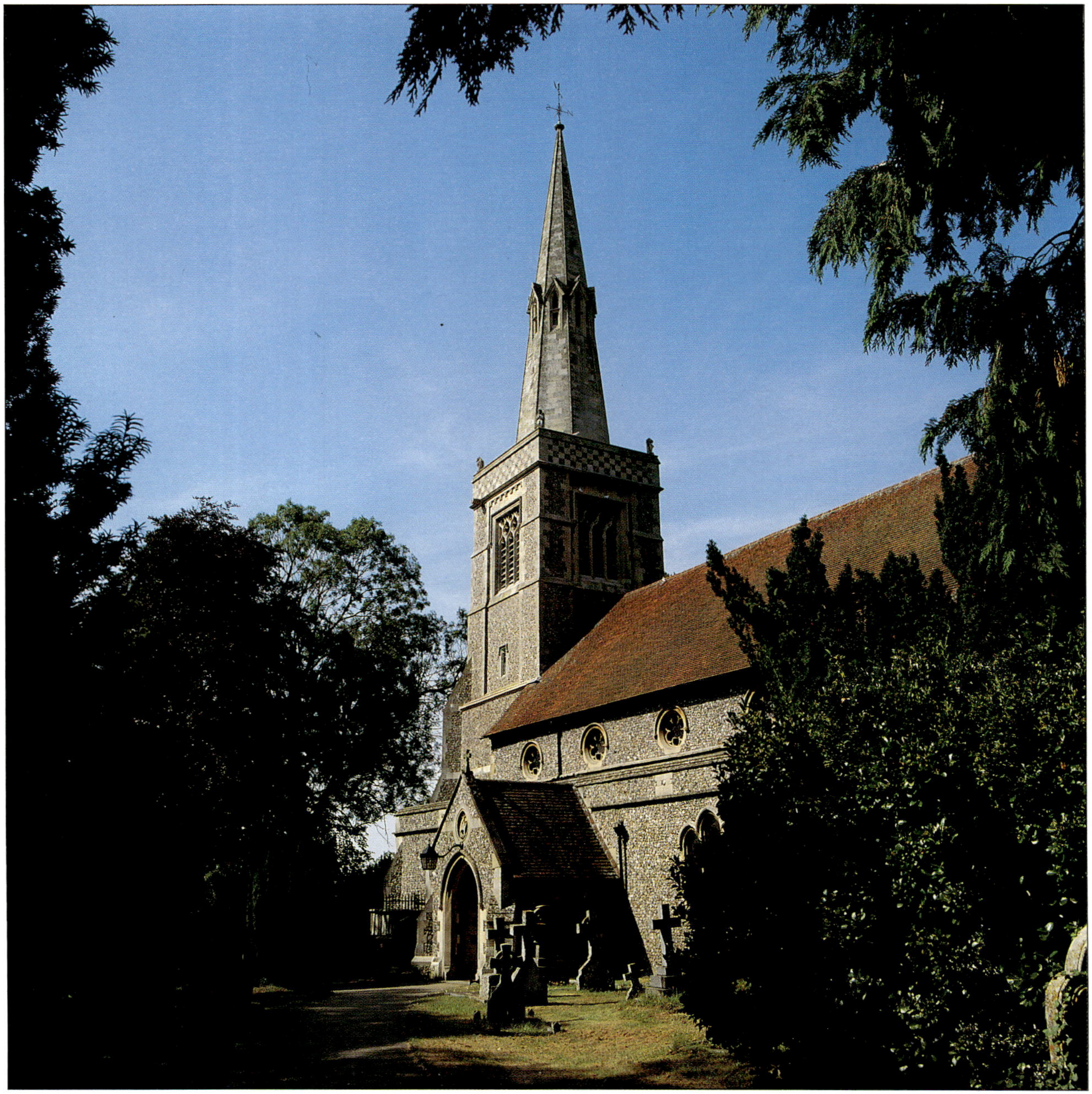

Princes Risborough

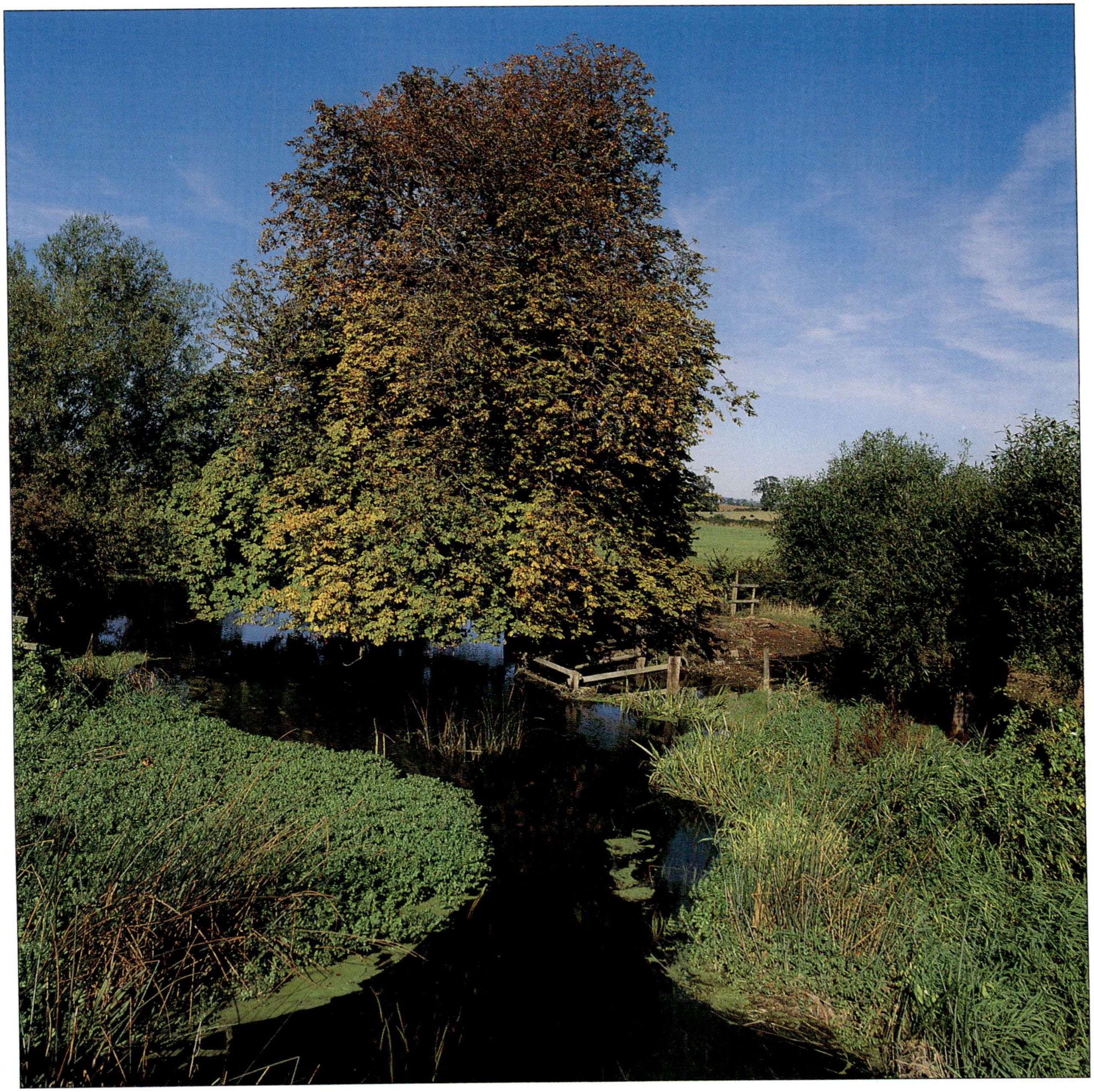

Thame

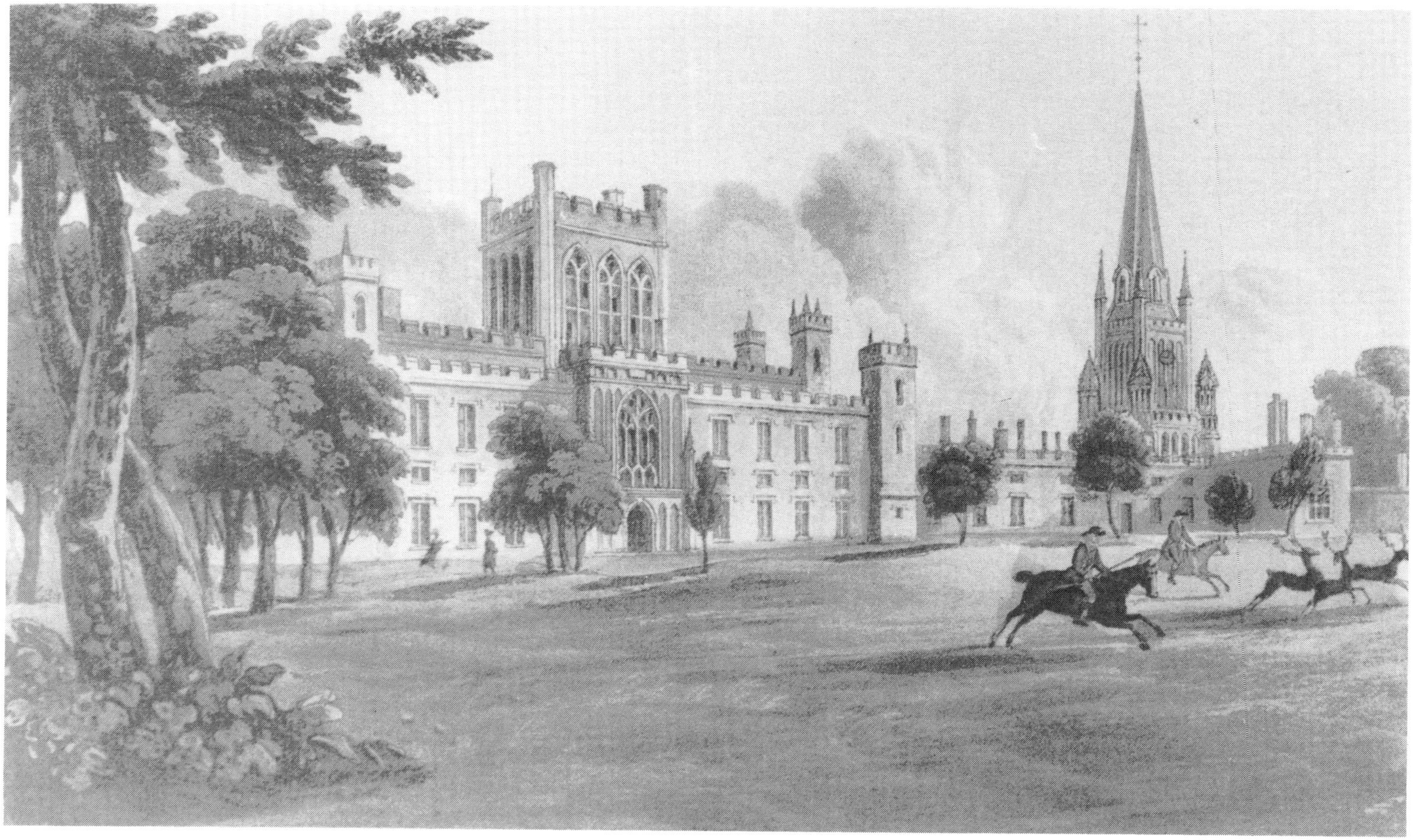

comes and joyns it; which river, at the entrance into this County, gives its own name to a Market-town of pleasant situation among rivers: for the river Tame washes the north part of the town, and the two little brooks shut it in on the east and west sides. This place has been in a flourishing condition, ever since Henry Bishop of Lincoln, in the reign of Henry the third, brought the great road, which lay below the town, through the middle of it. Alexander, that munificent Bishop of Lincoln, Lord of this Manour, to alleviate the general odium he had contracted by his extravagant expences in building Castles, refounded here a small Monastery.

And many years after, the Quartermans, a Family in former times of great repute in these parts, built here an Hospital for the maintenance of poor people. But neither of these foundations are at present to be seen; however instead of them, Sir John Williams Kt. founded here a beautiful School, and a small Alms-house.

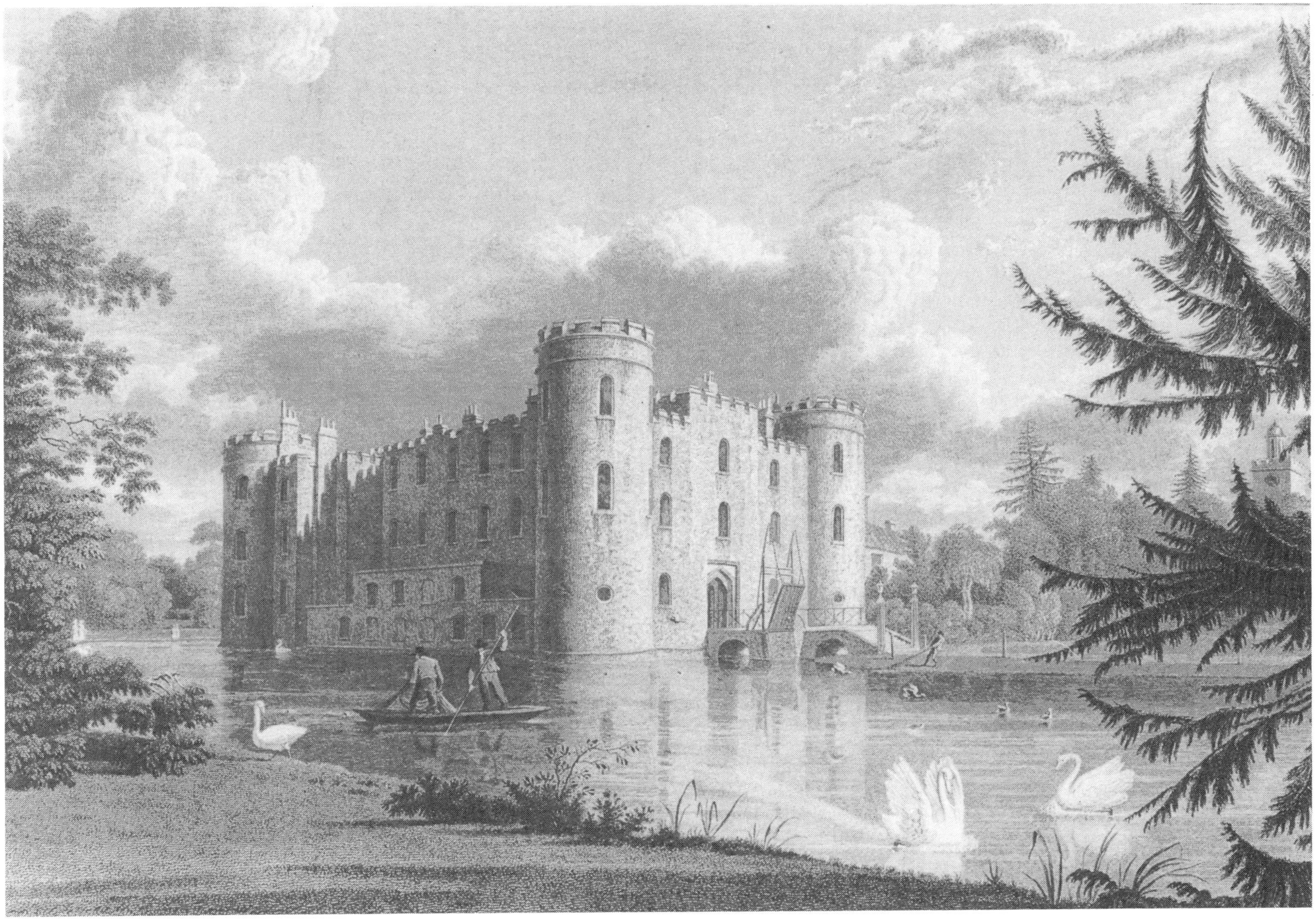

From thence, the Thames fetches a large and winding compass, round the Hundred of Henley, which is hilly and woody . . . From Henley, the Chiltern-hills run in a continued ridge to the north, and separate this county of Oxon from that of Bucks: at the foot whereof are seated many little towns, of which the most remarkable are Watington, a small market-town, belonging formerly to Robert D'oily. Then at the foot of the same hills, is Shirburne heretofore a small Castle of the Quartermans.

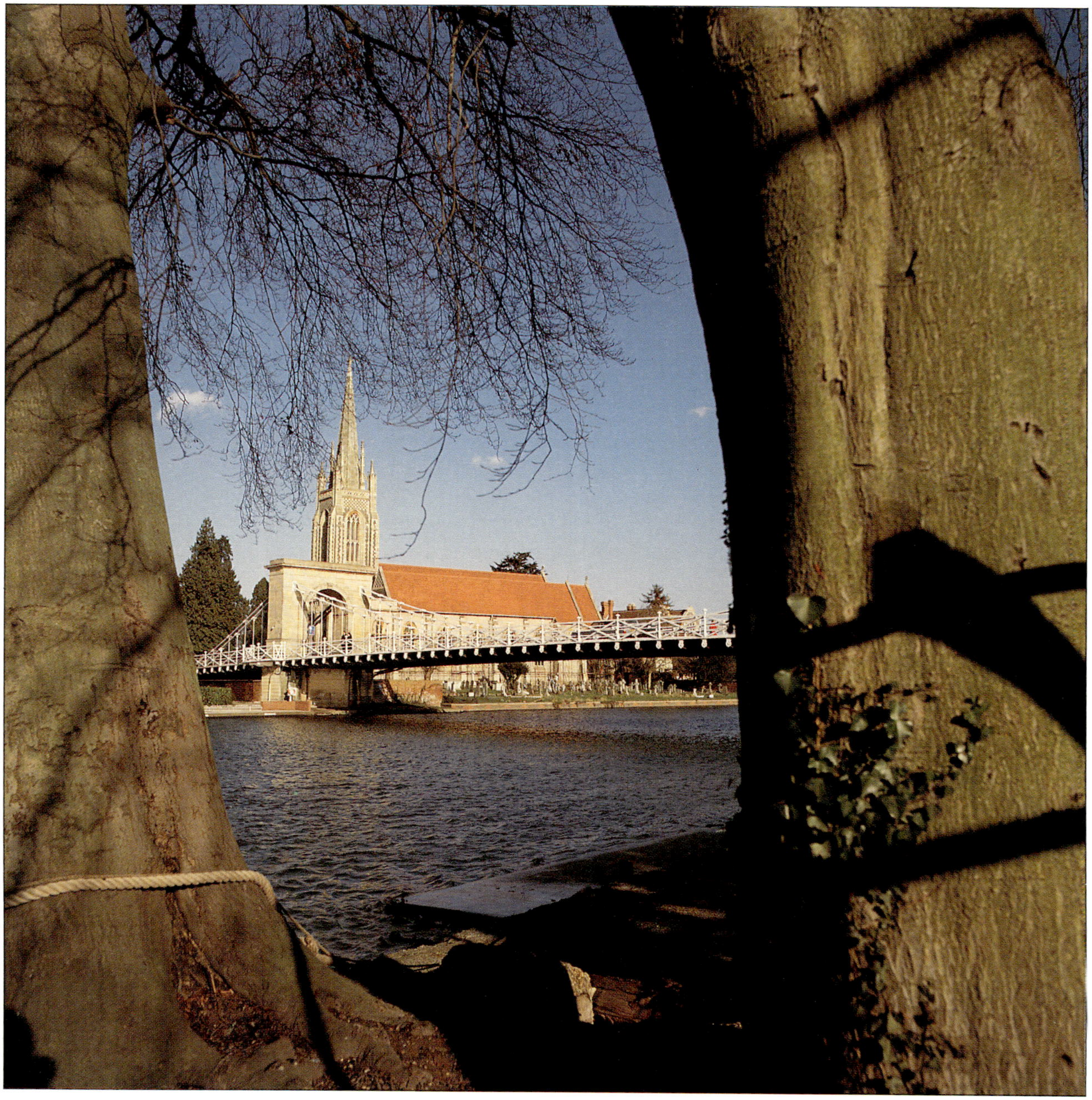

Marlow

Finally we pass into the Hertfordshire region of the Chilterns:

Hence I passed southward to Hemsted, a small Market-town call'd Hehan-hamsted, when King Offa made a grant of it to the monastery of St. Albans. It is seated among hills by the side of a small river, which, a little lower, runs into another that goes through Berkhamsted. In this place, the Nobles of England had a meeting, when, by the perswasion of Fretheric Abbot of St. Albans, they were conspiring to throw off the new Norman Government.

Thither came William the Conqueror in person (as we read in the life of this Fretheric) much concern'd, for fear he should, to his great disgrace, lose that Kingdom which he had gain'd with so much blood. And after many debates in the presence of Lanfranc the Archbishop, the King, to settle a firm peace, took an Oath upon all the Reliques of the Church of St. Alban, and upon the holy Evangelists, which the Abbot Fretheric administer'd, that he would inviolably observe all the good, approv'd, and ancient laws of the Kingdom which the holy and pious Kings of England his predecessors, and especially King Edward, had established. . . . But most of these Noblemens estates were soon after seized and confiscated by him, and he bestow'd this town upon Robert Earl of Moriton and Cornwall, who, according to common tradition, built here a Castle with a double ditch and rampart. . . . The Castle is now nothing but ruin'd walls, and one rude heap of stones; above which, upon a small hill, Sir Edward Cary Knight, Master of the Jewel-House to the King, built a noble and exceeding pleasant seat.

Michael Drayton, a prolific writer of topographical, historical and religious verse, published his POLYOLBION during the early years of the seventeenth century. He seems to have followed Spencer in his personification of natural objects such as hills, woods and rivers. In the following extract he unites the bride – Isis – with the bridegroom – Tame – at Dorchester. The venerable parents of the happy couple are represented by the Cotswolds, the Vale of Aylesbury and 'old Chiltern':

That Isis, Cotswold heir, long woo'd, was lastly won,
And instantly should wed with Tame, old Chilterns son.
And now that woodmans wife, the mother of the flood,
The rich and goodly vale of Alsbury, that stood
So much upon her Tame, was busied in her bowers,
Preparing for her son as many sutes of flowres
As Cotswold for the bride, his Isis lately made;
Who for the lovely Tame, her bridegroom, onely
  staid . . .
But whilst things are in hand, old Chiltern (for his life)
From prodigal expense can no way keepe his wife;
Who feedes her Tame with marle, in cordiall wise prepar'd
And thinks all idly spent, that now she only spar'd
In setting forth her sonne: nor can shee thinke it well,
Unless her lavish charge doe Cotswold's farre excel.

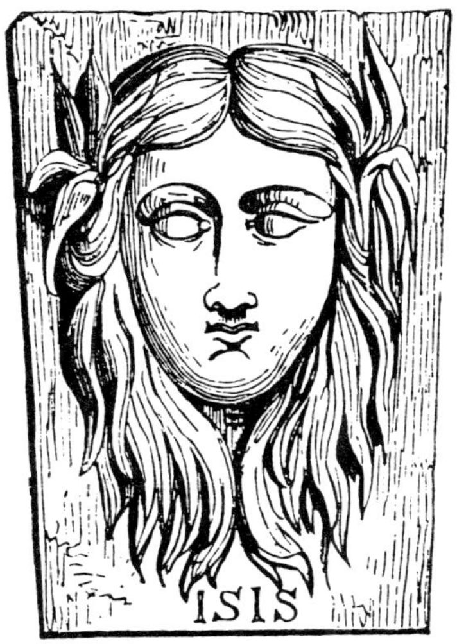

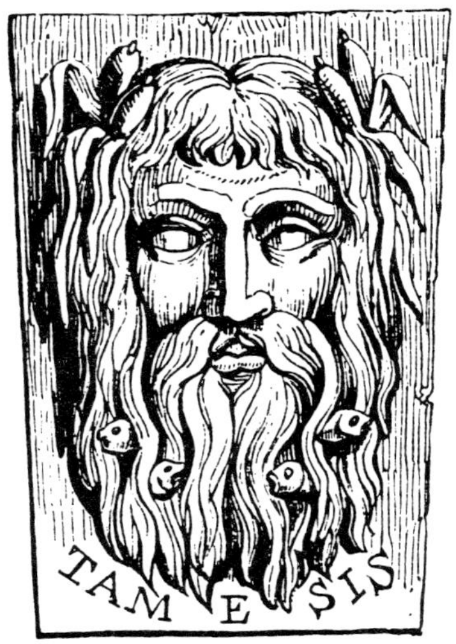

For, Alsbury's a vale that walloweth in her wealth,
And (by her wholesome ayre continually in health)
Is lustie, frim and fat, and holds her youthfull strength.
Besides her fruitfull earth, her mightie breadth and length,
Doth Chiltern fitly match: which mountainously hie,
And beeing very long, so likewise she doth lie;
From the Bedfordian fields, where first she doth begin,
To fashion like a vale, to th' place where Tame doth win
His Isis' wished bed, her foil throughout so sure
For goodness of her gleabe, and for her pasture pure,
That as her graine and grasse, so shee her sheepe doth breed,
For burthen and for boane all other that exceed:
And she, which thus in wealth abundantly doth flowe
Now cares not on her child what cost shee doe bestow:
Which when wise Chiltern saw (the world who long has try'd
And now at last had layd all garish pompe aside;
Whose hoar and chalky head descry'd him to be old,
His beechen woods bereft, that kept him from the cold)
Would fain perswade the vale to hold a steddy rate;
And with his curious wife, thus wisely doth debate: . . .
And Tames, got, borne and bred, immediately doth flowe
To Windsor-ward amain (that with a wond'ring eye,
The forrest might behold his awful emperie)
And soon becoming great, with waters wext so rank,
Till happily attayn'd his grandsire Chilterns grounds,
Who with his beechen wreaths this King of rivers crownes.
Amongst his holts and hills, as on his way he makes,
At Reading once arriv'd, clear Kennet overtakes:
Her lord the stately Tames, which that great flood againe,
With many signes of joy doth kindly entertaine.
Then Loddon comes next in, contributing her store;
As still we see, the much runnes ever to the more.
Set out with all this pompe, when this emperiall streame,
Himselfe establisht sees, amidst his watery realme,
His much love'd Henly leaves, and proudly doth pursue
His wood nymph Windsor's seate, her lovely site to view. . . .

Into this Arcadian wedding feast unwelcome guests were very soon to burst, changing forever the role of monarchy in the land.

'Who with great spirit and consummate Ability, began a noble Opposition to an arbitrary Court, in Defence of the Liberties of his Country, supported them in Parliament, and died for them in the Field.' Thus reads the inscription to John Hampden in the Temple of Worthies at Stowe in north Buckinghamshire. To pay for the Royal Navy the so called ship-money was levied by King Charles, first in 1634 on ports and later on inland towns as well. It was Hampden's refusal to pay this unconstitutional tax which led to his arrest along with four other Members of Parliament, and the subsequent trial in which the Court of the Exchequer found for the king; a finding which not only incensed supporters of Hampden but also those who had paid the money as a favour and now found the levy being exacted as a legal right. As Burke said, 'Would 20/- have ruined Mr Hampden's future? no, but the payment of half 20/- on the principle it was demanded would have made him a slave.' This whole bitter episode ultimately fanned the sparks of confrontation into the devouring flames of civil war which raged from 1642 until 1646. Soon after the battle of Edge Hill King Charles made his headquarters or 'second capital city' complete with its own mint at Oxford. Parliament had the advantage of controlling London along with most of the ports and the more densely populated areas. Between these two centres of power lay the Chilterns and the Vale of Aylesbury through which ran several vital lines of communication including the River Thames. It was in these regions, because of their strategic importance, that many skirmishes took place with various garrisons changing hands several times.

When the king raised his standard at Nottingham he was joined by his nephew, the colourful, not to say infamous Palatine, Prince Rupert. His reputation for reckless courage, gained in the war against the oppression of Protestantism in Austria, first under Gustavus Adolphus and then the Prince of Orange, was soon to spread among his adversaries on English fields. It has been said that had his gallantry been subordinated to a capable commander he would have made an ideal cavalry leader.

The battle of Edge Hill on 23 October 1642 was to prove this point, where, although he swiftly cut through opposing forces, he neglected the main battle and the king was left dangerously exposed.

Shortly after this indecisive engagement the prince fell on Aylesbury and the following report was published immediately afterwards:

YE BATTELL OF ALISBURY 1642

Good and Joyful Nevves ovt of Buckinghamshire, being an exact and true Relation of a Battell, stricken between Prince Robert and Sir William Balfore, Lieutenant Generall to his Excellency the Earl of Essex, near Alisbury in that County, on Tuesday last, the first November, wherein the said Sir William obtained a happy and glorious Victory.

London, Printed for Francis Wright, 1642

. . . on Tuesday last, All Saints Day, destined for holier uses, Prince Robert with his well beaten troops . . . sought to refresh themselves in the pleasant and plenteous County of Buckingham, in which all things exuberate that might please their appetites, or satisfy their wants, they left no expressions of their hostility and rapine unperformed; Souldiers (especially wanting ones) wishing no better place for plunder than a rich and fertile Province, till they arrived at Ailesbury, a towne one of the most signall and wealthy of the Shire, where Prince Robert with some ten thousand horse and foote, on Tuesday morning, about six of the Clock, entered to the great amazement and feare of the honest inhabitants, who little expecting such a sudden greeting from the Enemy, were unprovided for defense. The faithful Militia of that good towne, being unable to make resistance against such a multitude of desparate men, made a vertue of necessity, and gave them a free entertainment. . . . Sir William Balfore . . . who investigating the enemies passages had certaine intelligence that Prince Robert, with some of the profligated troopers, were returned into Buckinghamshire, and had fixed their rendezvous at Alisbury, whither with all speed the sais Sir William made, knowing that delaies in affaires military as in all other actions beget dangers, with his fifteen hundred men, being six horse troops, and the foot part of Colonel Hampdens, and part of Colonel Grantham's regiments, which were the army of six thousand foot and Horse . . . but he (Prince Robert) having drawn forth his companies into one entire body, without the towne, he espied within a quarter of a mile the Parliament's Forces, which were as ready to charge him as the Prince was them; but their wise and prudent chiefe, Sir William Balfore, knowing that hasty attempts beget dangerous and uncertain successes, kept them in, facing the Prince with a narrow body of horsemen, his troopes being drawn out like a pyramid, sharpe at the top, and broad by degrees in the grosse. Prince Robert with his owne troope, the flower of the Cavalry, charging through Sir William Balfore his front, and thinking to make us find an easie passage through the rest, was bid to a bloody dinner in the heart of his squadrons. The horsemen being there at least ten broad in Rank, thundering death from those engines of destruction, their Carbines and patronels, into the bosome of the Princes Souldiers; who neither knew well to advance nor to retreat. Another Troope, if I mistake not young Master Pym's, charging them hotly in their right flanks, till Sir Lewis Dives, fell in pell mell to the princes rescue; having behind each of his horsemen a musketeer, who, being at competent distance, alighted and diffus'd their dreadfull

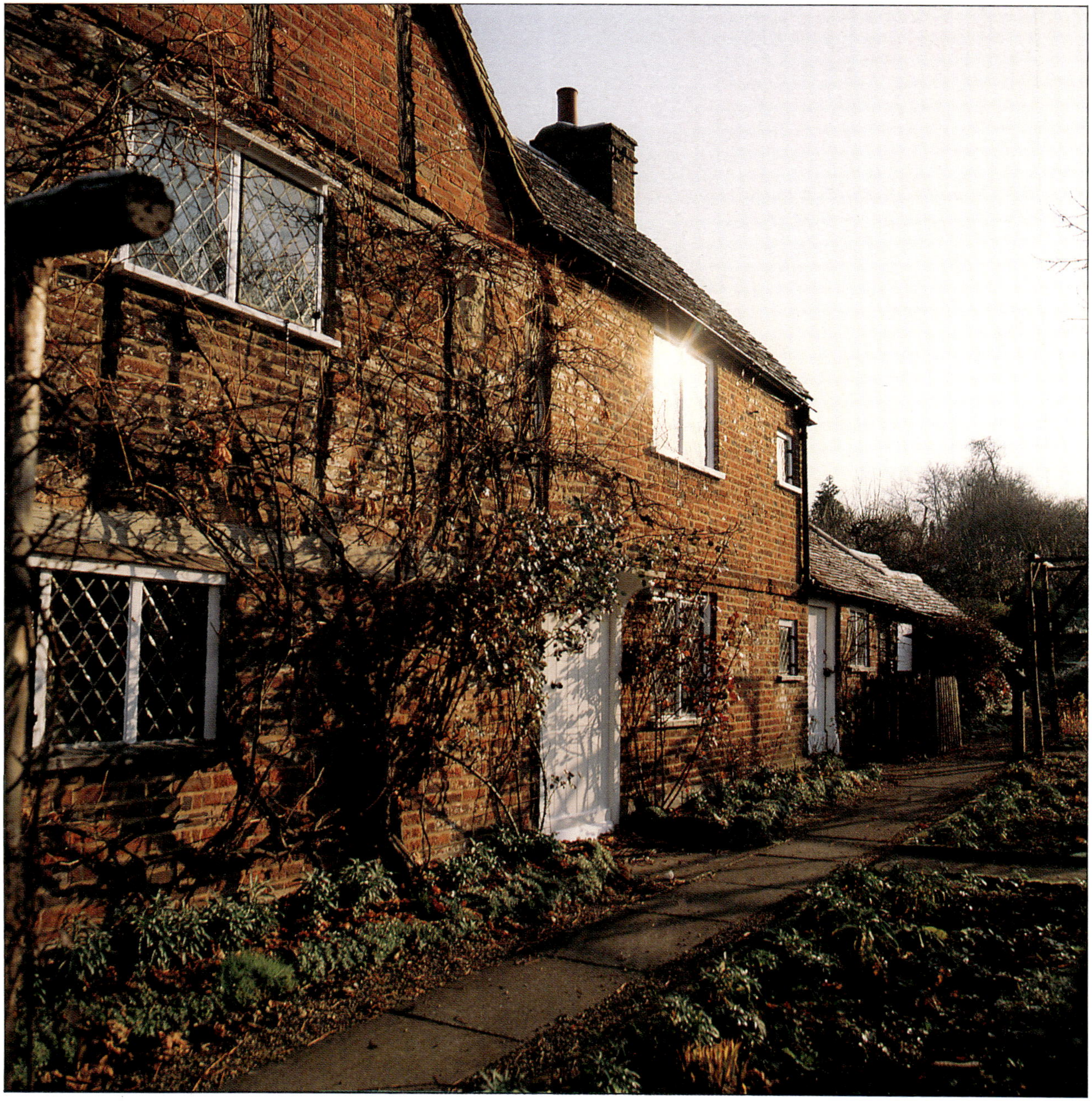

Milton's cottage at Chalfont St Giles

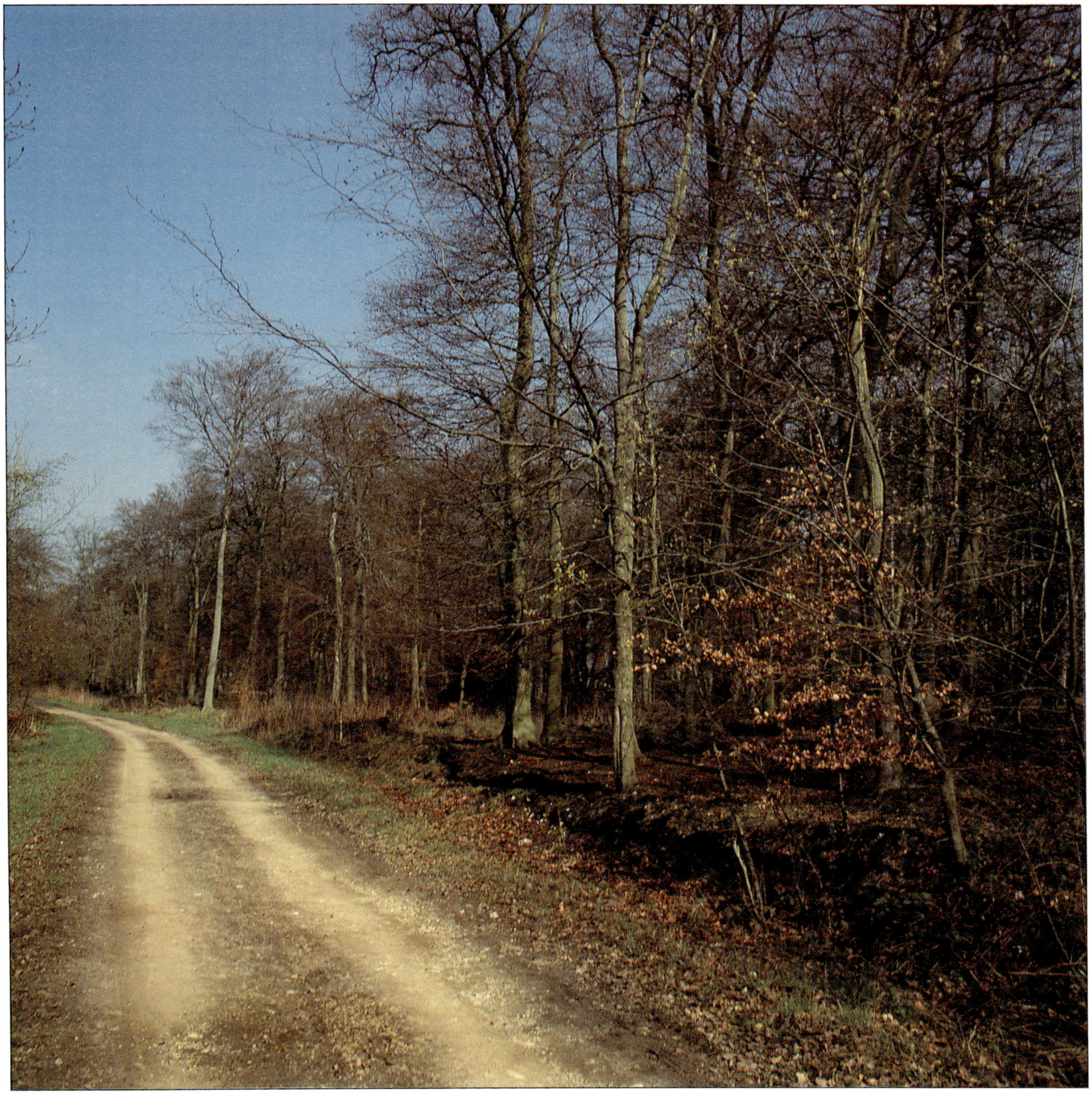

Poynatts Wood, near Skirmett

and death-bearing bullets through our squadrons, which then began to totter from their order, Some ten or fourteene falling in that furious charge; till Captain Herbert Blanchard Captain of the Earl of Peterborrowe's Troope came in with much courage to the aid of Sir William Balfore's Troope, and the foot forces on our side having gained both wind and Sun, sent cheerful volleys of fire and smoak and bullets, on the left flanke of the Prince's Squadrons, the Horses gald with the shot over-throwing their riders . . . Commissary Willmott who all this while had stood as a reserve to the Prince's Forces, then falling into this game of blood and slaughter, reduced the conflict to an equal scale, killing some three score of our men, when Sir William Balfore who leaving his own Troops to the charge of his Lieutenant, had retired into the rear of his horse and brought them up to the face of the Enemie, our foot in the interim wheeling about, came in upon theirs with a full charge, beating them from their stations, and disordering their ranks. They sent at least 200 of their men to salute the earth, never more to rise thence. The Prince all this while made good the fight against Sir William with his horse till Commissary Willmott receiving a shot into the shoulder, They began to shock each together and as it were to retreat; when the flight of their foot, who began to use the vertue of their legs: drive them, spite of Prince Robert's fury, to bear them company and outstrip them at their own exercise of running away: that troope and those two foot companies advancing forth of the town to the reliefe of their companions were undertaken by Captain Ascough's Troope and some foot forces till the Townes men near being rid of their unwelcome guests, to the number of two hundred well arm'd, charged them upon the backs, then they fell into an apparent rout, following their flying fellowes; our horsemen having them in the chase, they did execution on their foot for the space of a miles riding: killing in the chase and the fight to the number of six hundred, most of which were the infantery, their Cavalry escaping by the benefit of their horses, found the Proverb verified 'one paire of legs is worth two paire of hands' . . . Sir William Balfore after his victory, marching to Alisbury, spent the rest of that day in prayers and thanksgivings for his good successe, to that Great God of battels, in whose dispose is Conquest, and by whose almighty and outstretched arme, this victory arriv'd to his servants; Prince Robert with his flying Troopes as it were, in revenge of that overthrow, burning the poore country villages in his retreat towards Oxford. . . .

High Wycombe had the misfortune of being a strategic garrison town and a good source of supplies as we shall see in the extracts from Samuel Luke's journal. Although protected by other garrisons in the surrounding area it was attacked several times and the following contemporary account indicates that much blood was shed. In this skirmish and the attack made by Sir John Urry on 24 June 1643 statistics seem to be unreliable. No doubt facts were suppressed or exaggerated for propaganda purposes, or as Gibbs says in his HISTORY OF AYLESBURY: *'After the Restoration all documents in the hands of individuals relative to the Parliamentary cause would be concealed; and among the inhabitants of a town, such as Aylesbury, which had taken part in the contest against a triumphant antagonist, probably no pains would be taken to preserve a memorial.'*

On 6 December Royalist forces under the command of Thomas Lord Wentworth entered the town from the direction of Wycombe Marsh and approached the defences thrown up in the area now known as Queen Victoria Road by forces under the command of Captain Hayes:

Lord Wentworth arrived neere the said forces . . . where he sounded his trumpets and made a glorious shew upon the tops of two great hills thinkeing the day to be his owne, for he had information that the forces which lay there about, did not amount to above foure or five thousand of them and had set then in two vayllyes one the left side of Wickham, carrying their colours low, and every man traylling his Pike because the enemy should not descry them, and gave them strict charge that everyman should be silent. When they see the enemy advance towards Wickham they should fall on so soone as they heard the ordnance fire, which command they very diligently observed. No sooner had the ordnance discharged but they fell on fighting with extraordinary courage and much policy which when the enemy seeing were amazed to see such a company behind them and another before them. The ordnances played very fast, and the Commander of the volunteers shewd very discretion, so that for the space of foure houres they fought very valiantly, till at last the enemy retreated leaving behind them at least nine hundred of their confederates slaine and maymed in the filed, the young Lord Wentworth being dangerously wounded all this done with loose of three hunden men (Parliamentary forces).

There can be fewer places in the Chilterns that witnessed as much of the cut and thrust of the civil war as Henley. Not only did it have a wharf on the Thames and a critical crossroads, but it was also adjacent to Phylis Court, Fawley Court, and Greenlands House; all deemed important by the military. At the end of 1642 Prince Rupert established his headquarters at The Red Lion and sent a regiment of horse to occupy Fawley House. Sir Bulstrode Whitlock, Member of Parliament for Great Marlow, had the misery of seeing his house ruined about his ears, and then, having moved to Phylis Court, found his house being turned into a fort by the Parliamentary General. In May 1644, the Earl of Essex lay siege to Greenlands House held for the king by Sir John Doyley. This Royalist stronghold capitulated in July, by which time the building had been devastated. In 1651 the house was sold to Sir Bulstrode who thus became the owner of three riverside ruins!

Charles I stayed at The Red Lion on his way to Oxford in 1632 and again in 1642 when things seemed to be going his way. However, it was a totally different Charles who, escaping from Oxford in 1646, fled along the footpath by Deer Park in order to reach Hambledon Manor. His downfall was the result of a more effective 'model army' and the sort of unflinching opposition portrayed in the following incident:

LETTER OF CAPTAIN SAMUEL TURNER TO HIS BROTHER IN LONDON 26 JAN 1643

Loving Brother,

. . . About nine of the clock at night we come to this Towne, where before we could get in, by reason the bridge was not quite laid down, we were enforced to stay an houre and an halfe at the least. So soon as we were come in, and our men gone to their quarters, some of us, amongst which myself was one, rid round to view the Towne how it lay which when we had done, we appointed 4 Companies to watch that night, one towards Redding, and the other at the Bridge, a third at the upper end of the Town, and myselfe having the main guard, it being mine for that night as I was the eldest captain of all that watched: I divided my Company, and sent my Lieutenant, with about 40 men to guard some works which the Towne had made on the way to Oxford, I having the rest on the maine guard, which was kept in a little house close to the Towne Hall, where the 4 wayes divide themselves; having thus ordered our men, and having placed our Ordnance, which were but three in all, one of our biggest pieces towards Redding rd, and the other, which was our best, towards Oxford, and the third, which was but a Drake, wee planted towards the upper end of Towne, by that time this was done, it grew neere eleven of the Clocke. . . . about two of the clock in the morning, being in a house with the Major, and most of our Gunners, discoursing together, news was brought that the enemy had come, and had fired

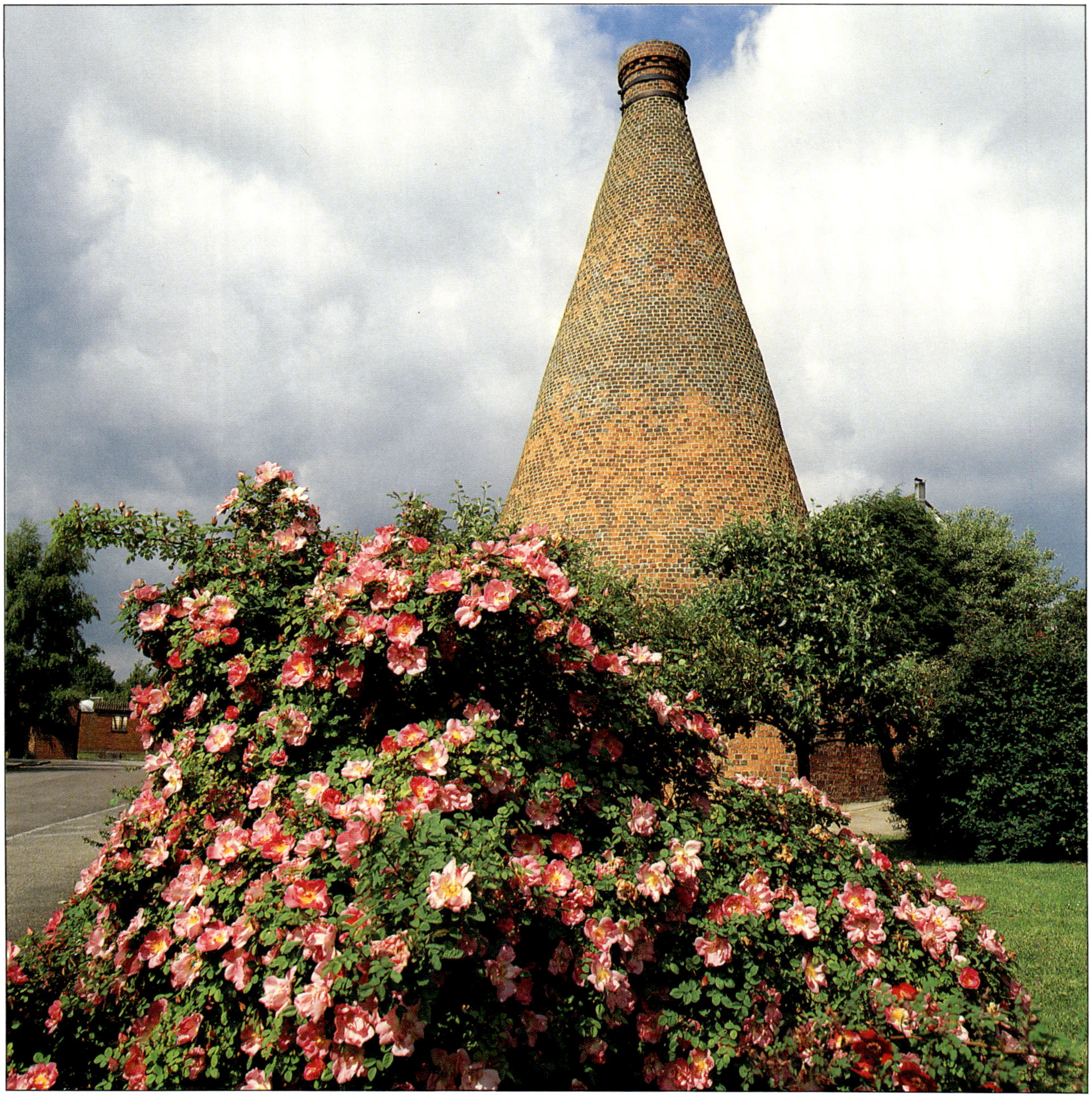

Nettlebed

upon our Centinels, which caused an Alarme through the Towne . . . at last they broke their way through, and came along the Lane towarde the Towne, the way they came being but narrow . . . our Parliament dog lay ready to fire upon them, which being laden with one great shot, and two cases of shot, containing 120 Musket bullets, at length the way being cleare of our owne men, but full of theirs, we let flie my self being within a yard or two at most when it gave fire, and saw the execution it did: Some of their horse came so desparately on, that they were even ready to enter upon the mouth of the Canon . . . we found 3 men, and 4 horse lie dead within less then a quoites throw off the mouth of the piece, and an Ensign which was found halfe dead, and half alive, having his leg shot short off and some three shots more in his body besides. . . . and we are informed by some who came from a place called Caw-some, that there are divers lie wounded there, besides our men saw them lift up on their horses which they carried away, some dead, others wounded, so that we conceive they lost thirty men at least, the whole Skirmish, from the time they entered, to the time they ran away, was not a full quarter of an hour. We lost of our men but three in all one of which was mine . . . I had almost forgot to tell you that the two troopes of horse which were appointed with us, left us at the Townes end, and went away to their quarters, so that we were left naked; only God fought on our sides: if the enemy had got into the Towne, I believe few of us had been alive at this present, thus fearing to be over tedious to you, I rest,

Your ever loving Brother,

SAMUEL TURNER.

Throughout the Civil War the ability of the officers to move their men freely was governed partly by their ability to control the various river crossings in the region, hence the conflicts at Henley and Caversham.

On 15 April 1643 Essex laid siege to Reading; the Royalist attempt to relieve the town from Oxford was repulsed at Caversham and the garrison surrendered on the following day.

By 3 October the Royalists had re-established themselves at Reading and much of the ground won by Essex during the year was lost again.

CAVERSHAM FIGHT 25 APRIL 1643

An account by Richard Atkyns

We were then commanded to march towards Oxon, to the relief of Reading, besieged by the Earl of Essex, with the Kings whole army that quartered thereabout: where I had the honour to command the forlorn-hope again; 8 or 10 days after, the general rendezvous was by Wallingford; and the forlorn-hope consisting of about 160 horse, we sent out between eight and nine of the clock in the morning; we marched to Nettlebed, and so to Cawsam-house; through as bad way for horse to march as ever I saw: for the way was so thick of woods and furzes, that in

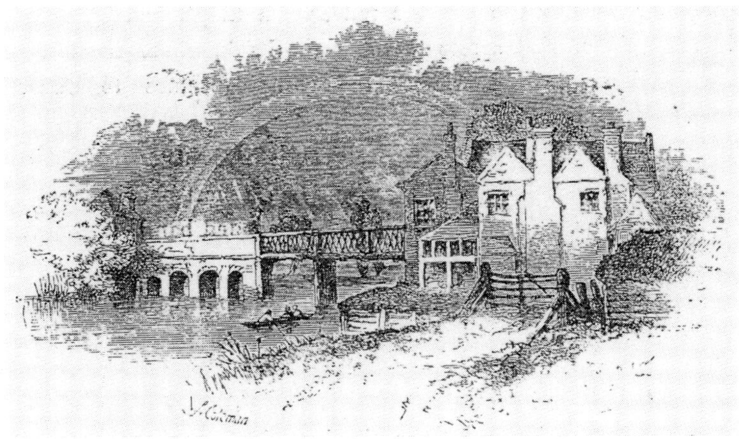

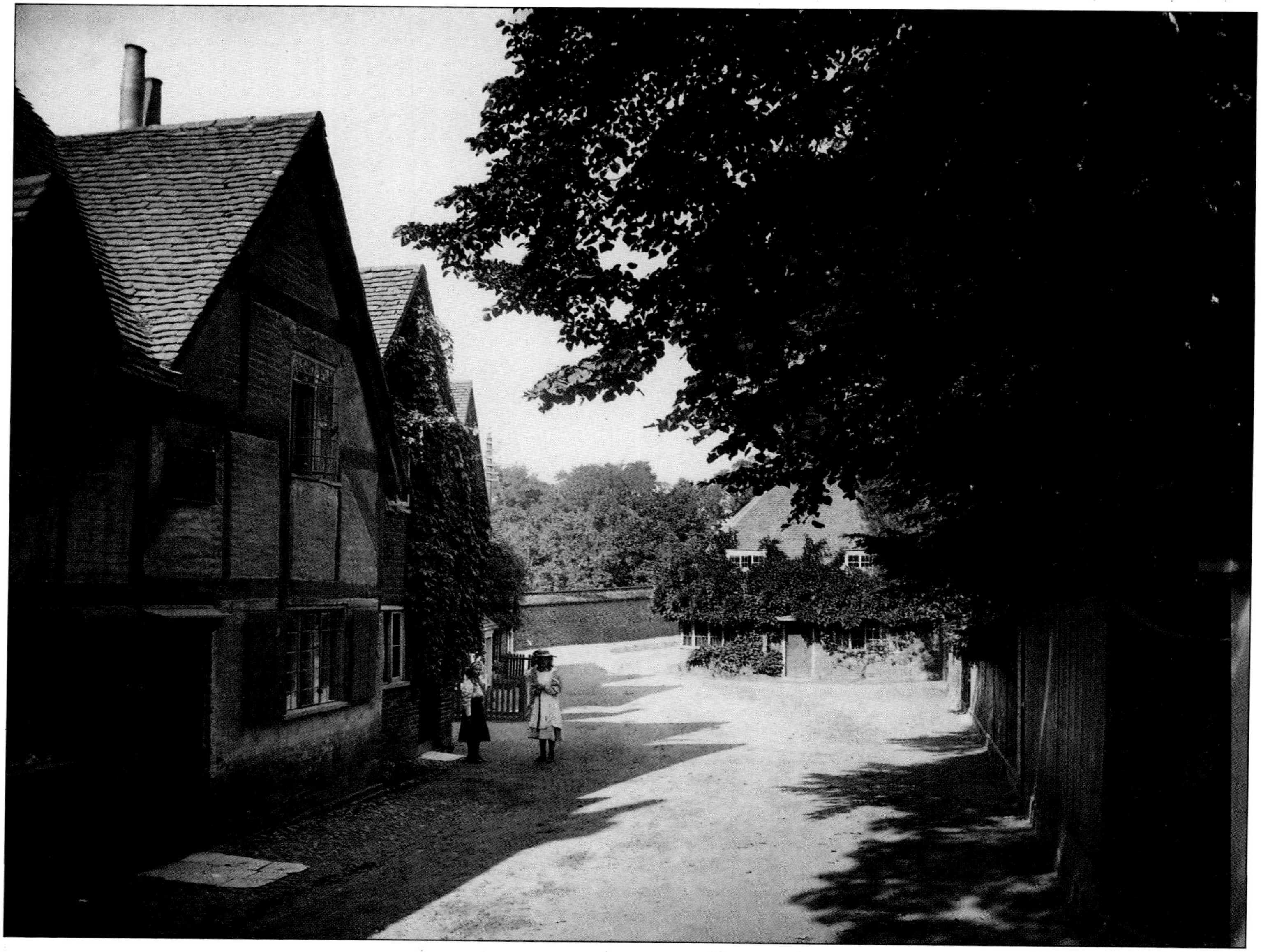

Sonning

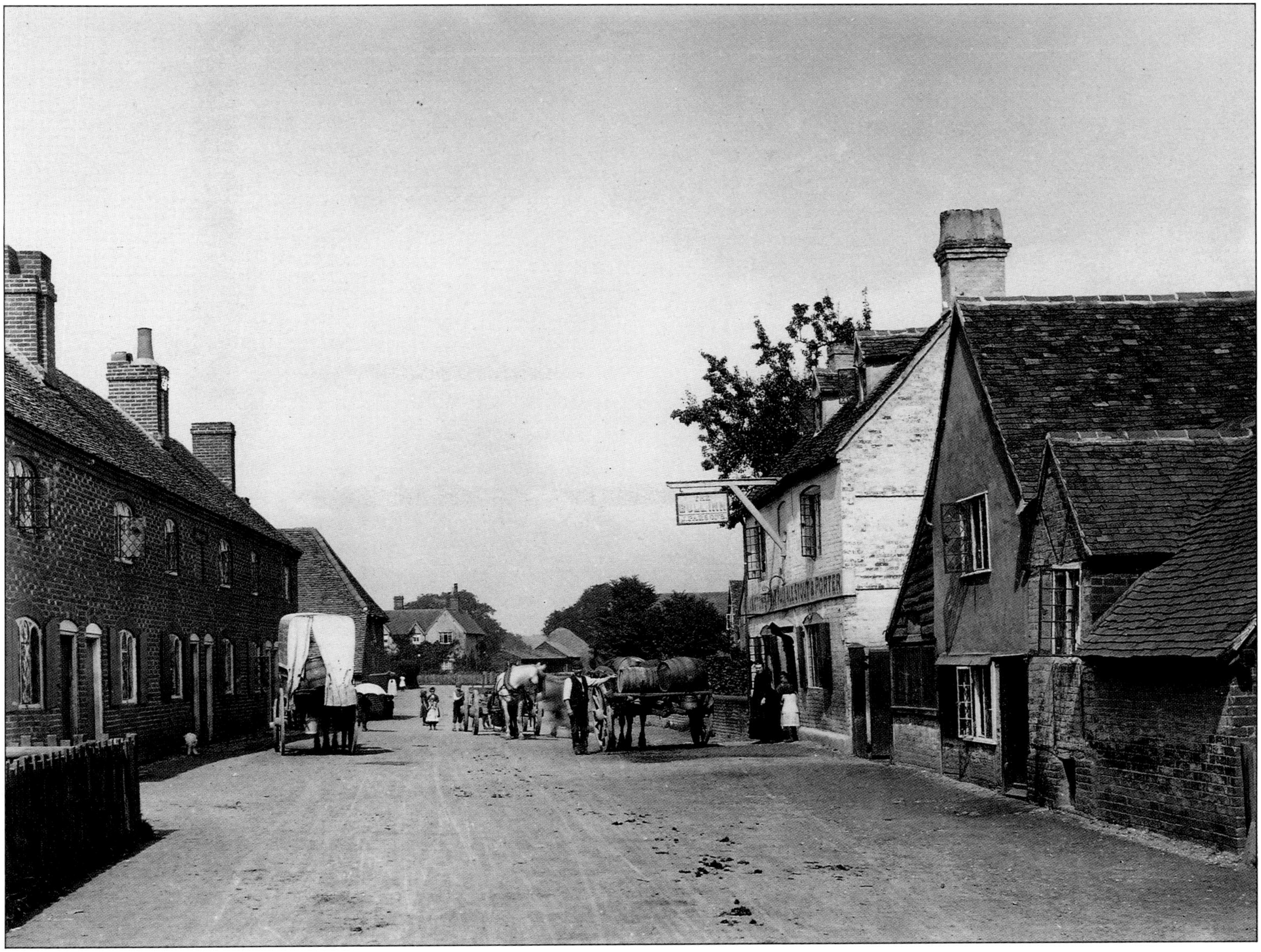

Bisham

two miles we could not draw up 8 in front, so as a small party of horse might easily have retarded our march, and killed several of us. Our security might be the illness of the way; for none that knew not of our march before, would ever expect horse to march in that place: we saw not one scout, or armed man, till we approached Cawsam Bridge, and there we found their army prepared to entertain the King's. My station was (not directly but obliquely) between the river (Thames) and a large barn (Harrisons Barn), within musket shot of both . . . 'Twould grieve one's heart, to see men drop like ripe fruit in a strong wind, and never see their enemy; for they had made loopholes through the walls, that they had the full bodies of the assailants for their mark, as they came down a plain field: but the assailants saw nothing to shoot at but mud walls, and must hit them in the eye, or loose their shot. Upon this disadvantage I need not tell you what men we lost; about three of the clock, my party was relieved for half an hour, and then the party that relieved us were drawn off again.

After this futile attempt to break the defence of Caversham bridge the men under Atkyns became somewhat mutinous until at dusk Prince Rupert sent orders to retreat.

Sir Samuel Luke, a relative of Cromwell's was a man of action as well as letters. On 30 July 1642 he was made captain of a troop of horse and fought at the battle of Edge Hill. As the records show he was involved in other actions as well, and in January he was commissioned as Scout Master General attached to the headquarters of the Earl of Essex. According to a tribute in MERCURIUS BRITTANICUS: 'This noble commander watches the enemy so industriously that they eat, sleep, drink not, whisper not, but he can give us an account of their darkest proceedings'. In truth, much of the credit must go to his scouts who daily risked their lives penetrating enemy lines to bring back their intelligence; indeed there is one report, apparently false, that one of his men was caught and hung.

Our first entries are centred on the town of Wallingford which, as at the time of the conquest, was a strategic river crossing.

Satturday the 29th Aprill 1643

Ralph Norton returned this day and saith . . . there are warrants come forth from his Majestye or some of his chiefe comanders to search all the howses in the contry thereabouts for all manner of armes, pikes, halberds, musketts, birding peeces and to bring them into Wallingford Castle, that all the ovens thereabouts are imployed in baking of biskett, and that they intend to pull downe all the workes about the towne and many as possible can to betake themselves to the Castle and the rest to march to Oxford, where it is reported his Majestye intends to have a pitcht feild.

Monday 8th May 1643

Robert Goddard saith that hee was at Tame . . . and that one Thomas Fletcher a hemp dresser whoe useth to carry hempe to the Kings army to make match withall and if any speake of the Parlyments side hee brings warrants from them along with him and makes him fly the towne. That the Cavallyers have planted 8 peeces of ordnance on both sides of the way to Crowmarsh and Wallingford, and hidd them in the banks to cutt of our men as they passe alonge.

Satturday 20 May 1643

Samuell Brayne returned this day and saith . . . That in Wallingford there are but small forces not above 400 men both in the towne and castle, and 4 peeces of ordnance, but very strong workes, and they are making a new drawbridge and a gatehouse at the entrance into the castle.

Tuesday 23 May

John Webb and Ralphe Norton returned this day and saith

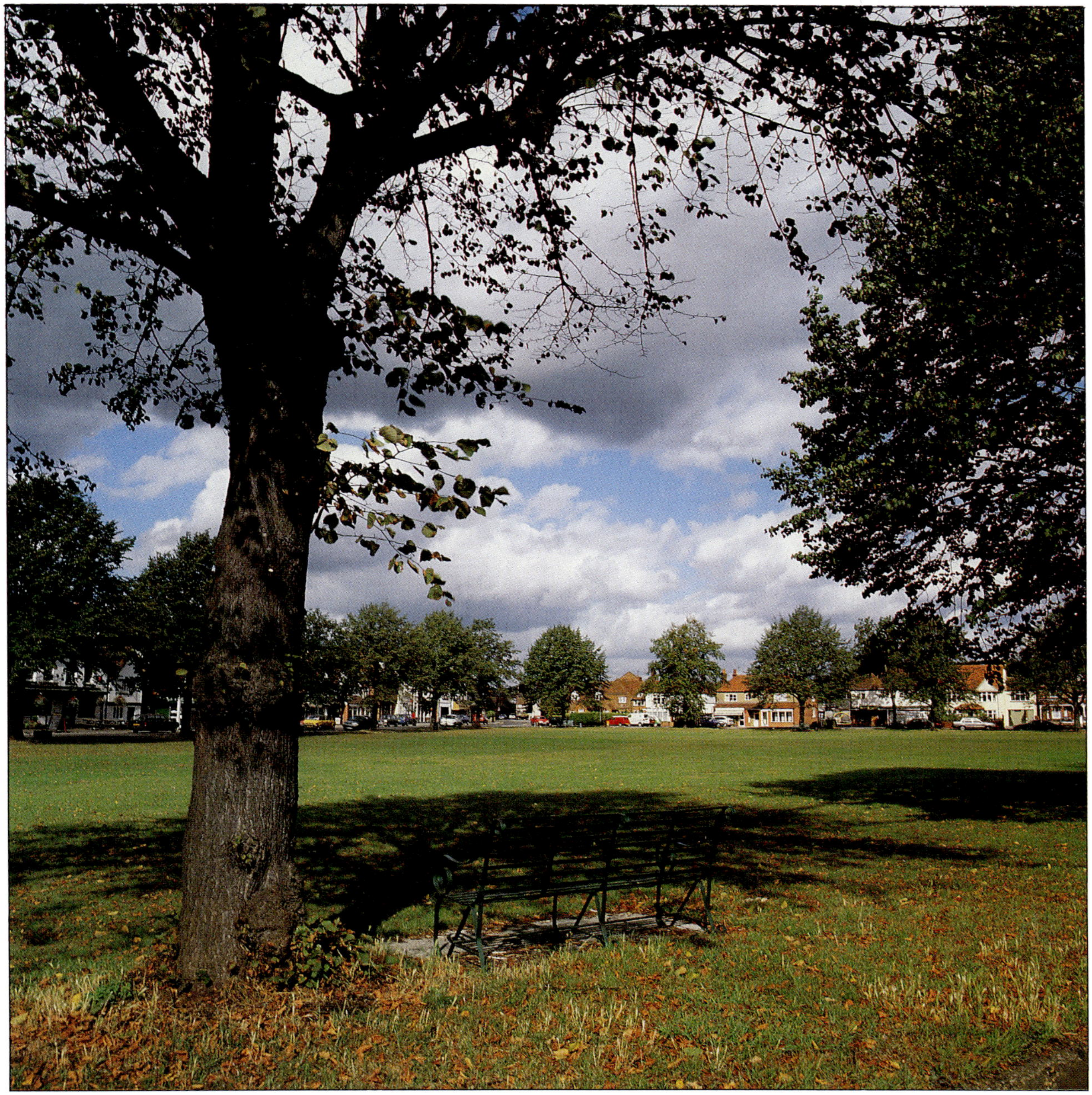

Wooburn Green

. . . That there was yesterday a loade of powder, match and bullett carryed from Abbington to Wallingford guarded with about 30 men, and many of the papists and rich men in the contry are gone into Wallingford castle and carryed their goods mony and plate along with them.

Thursday 25th May

Ralph Norton returned this day and saith that . . . Att Wallingford the water nowe runnes round the towne, and they have made the gates soe that noe cart can come in but att one place but a little wickett dores for a horse to goe in att. Alsoe the brooke which runnes round about the towne which is verie deepe fills the moates about the castle full of water, and there is a place a mile beyond the towne called the locke that the sluce may be pulled up and they cannott have any water but what they have from the Thames and by that meanes the river may be made drye.

29th. May. Monday

John Webb returned this day and saith . . . That the Lord Digby with 7 troopes of horse sallyed out and come towards Nettlebed and tooke 9 of our troopers, kild 2, and one ran into the wood, and that upon their bringing in, the Cauallyers abused them, and tooke away their clothes. That in Wallingford there is come into the towne a regiment of foote.

Tuesday 30th of May

Edward Sherwyn returned this day and saith that all the contry within 7 miles of Wallingford are in great feare of the Cauallyers comming to plunder them whoe having already taken away their goods, and imprisoned their persons, and that they greatly desire that our forces would advance that way to secure them. That on Sonday last a party of the Kings forces came to Nettlebedd and tooke 11 of our men and killd 2 of them. That none of the Kings forces sallyed out of Wallingford or any other place yesterday at 6 of the clocke at night towards Nettlebed or any lyeing in the woods or high wayes.

Fryday 2 February

Raph Norton came this day from Twyford, and saith he heares . . . That the King sent this weeke to Wallingford for 200 soldiers to march with the Irish forces to Gloucester or some place thereabouts. Whereupon the governer went to his Majestye and told him that there were soe few in the towne that hee could not spare any, being most of them run away for want of their pay, where at the King was very angry and strucke him twice over the head with his caine.

The Earl of Essex had been chosen to lead the Parliamentary Army partly because of his noble birth and also because of his experience in the continental wars. Even when suffering reverses his devotees still clung to the belief that he would ultimately bring them the sweeping victory they yearned for. However, by the end of 1644 their patience had been tried too far and he was voted a pension of £10,000 per year but died less than two years after his resignation.

At the time of the Chalgrove battle his headquarters were at Thame, but following the defeat at this battle and other incursions by Rupert, he withdrew to Aylesbury and then by the beginning of July 1643 to Great Brickhill.

Ever prepared to take caution as the better part of valour, as at Edge Hill and Newbury, and preferring to keep all his pieces on the board rather than try to press home any advantage, it is not surprising that in the following report by him, he is fairly dismissive of Hampden. Hampden it has been said, risked his life unnecessarily in this action, but this was his nature and one reason possibly why there had been talk of his replacing Essex as a commander. He believed that while Essex continued his Fabian tactics the war would be fatal to puritan hopes.

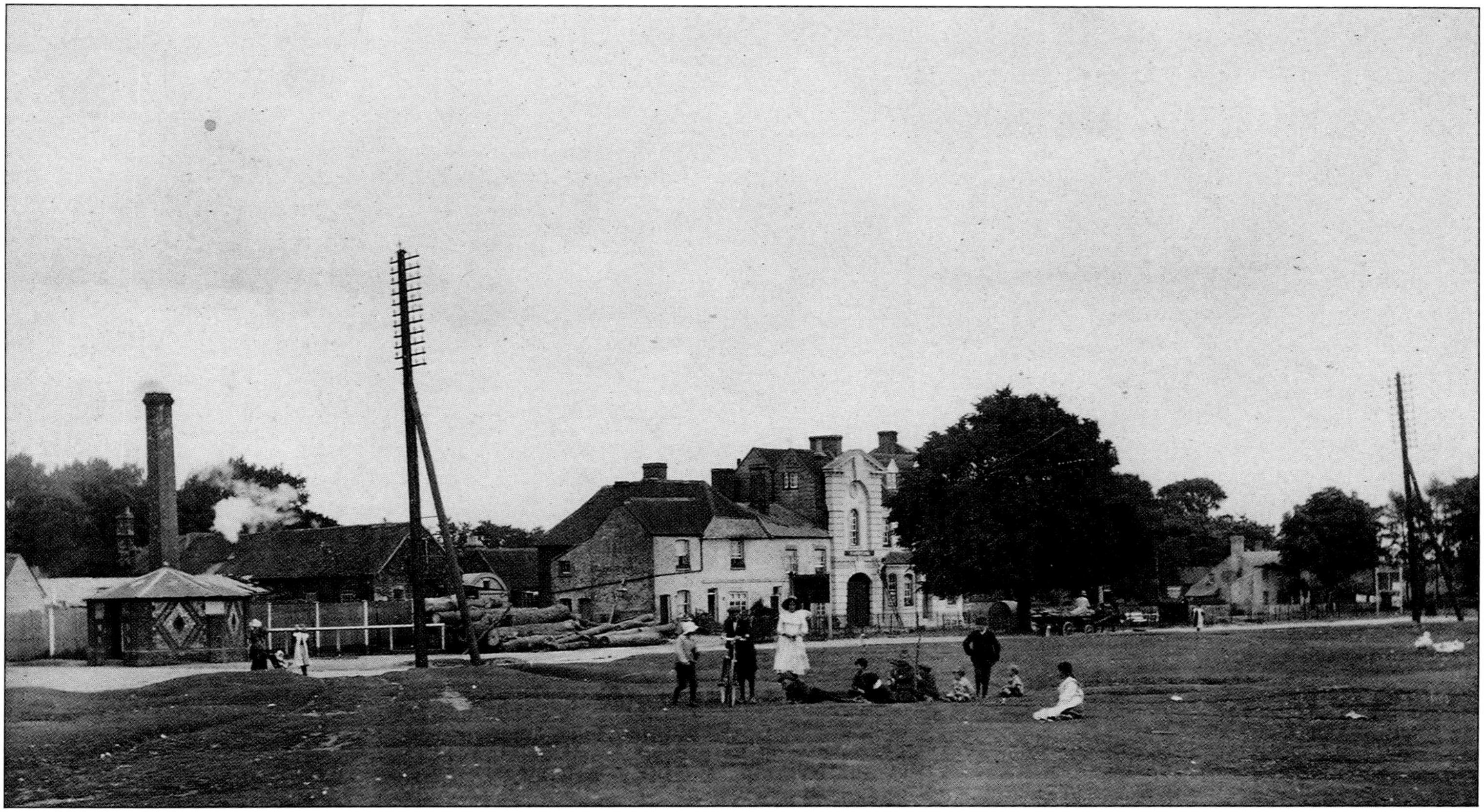

Stokenchurch

A LETTER FROM HIS EXCELLENCY
ROBERT EARL OF ESSEX,
DIRECTED TO THE SPEAKER
OF THE HOUSE OF COMMONS

Sir,

There being some of my Horse that had an Encounter with the Enemy yesterday being Sunday, I thought fit to give the House an Accompt of the particulars of it, knowing how apt many are to mis report things to our disadvantage.

About two of the clock on Sunday morning the enemy with about 1200 Horse and a great body of Dragoons fell into the Town called Porcham [Postcombe], where one Troop of Horse (being Colonell Morleyes) was quartered, of which they took the greatest part, and from thence went not farre to another village called Chinner, where they beat up some of the new Bedfordshire Dragoons and took some of them Prisoners, and three of their Colours; and some of the Officers behaving themselves very well, and defending the houses wherein they were; they set fire on the Town; these being out Quarters, the Alarum came where Major Gunter lay with three Troops (viz) his own, Captain Sheffields, and Captain Crosses, whom he presently drew out and marched towards the Enemy; Colonell Hampden being abroad with Sir Samuel Luke and onely one man, and seeing Major Gunters Forces, they did go along with them, Colonel Dulbeir the Quarter-master Generall did likewise come to them: with these they drew neare the Enemy, and finding them marching away, kept still upon the Reare for almost five miles. In this time there joined with them Captaine Sanders Troop and Captain Buller, with fifty commanded men, which were sent to Chinner by Sir Philip Stapleton, who had the watch here that night at Thame: when he discovered the fire there, to know the occasion of it he likewise sent one troop of Dragoons under the command of Captain Dundasse who came up to them. There were likewise some few of Colonell Melves Dragoons that came to them: at length our men pressed so neare, that being in a large pasture Ground they drew up, and not withstanding the inequality of the numbers, we having not above 300 Horse, our men charged them very gallantly, and slew divers of them; but while they were in fight, the Enemy being so very strong, kept a body of horse for his reserve, and with that Body wheel'd about and charg'd our men in the Reare, so that being encompassed and overborne with the multitude, they broke and fled, and though it was not very farre; For when I heard that our men Marched in the Rear of the Enemy, I sent to Sir Philip Stapleton, who presently Marched toward them with his Regiment; and though he came somewhat short of the Skirmish, yet seeing our Men Retreat in that disorder, he stopt them, caused them to draw into a Bodie with him, where they stood about an hour: Whereupon the enemy marched away. In this Skirmish there were slain fortie and five on both sides, whereof the greater part were theirs They carried of the Bodies of divers persons of qualitie. On our side Major Gunter was killed, but some say he is prisoner and so hurt; a man of much courage and fidelitie, his bravery engaging him and his small Partie too farre: Colonell Hampden put himself in Captain Crosse his Troop, where he charged with much courage, and was unfortunately shott thorow the Shoulder. Sir Samuel Luke thrice taken prisoner, and furtunately rescued: Captain Crosse had his Horse killed under him in the Middest of the Enemy, and was mounted by one of his own men, who quitted his own Horse to safe his Captain. Captain Buller was shot in the Neck, who shewed very much resolution in this fight, taking one prisoner after he was shot. Monseir Dulbeir with Captain Bosa and Captain Ennis did likewise carry themselves very well. We like-wise lost two Colours viz. Major Gunters, and Captain

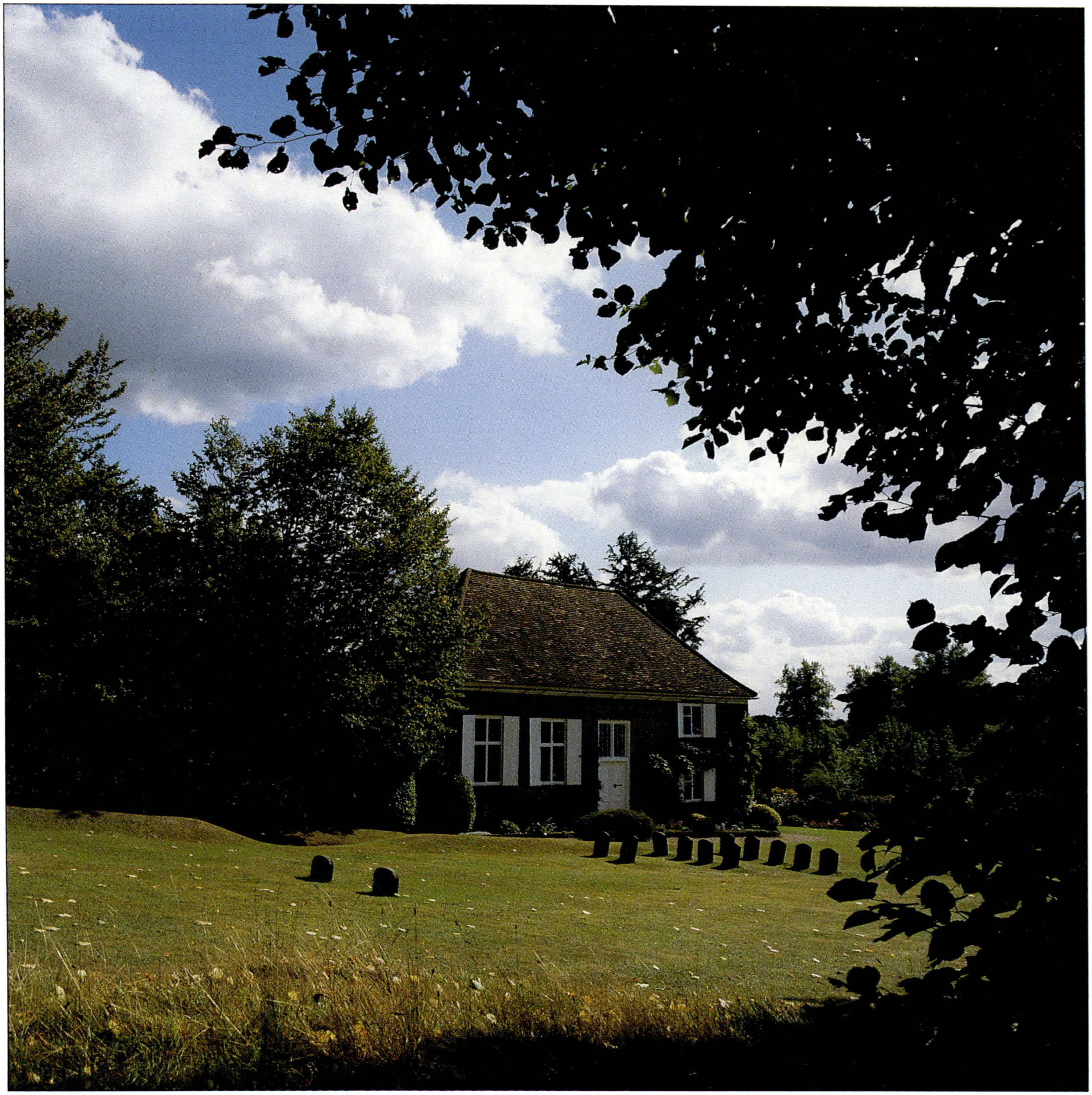

Jordans

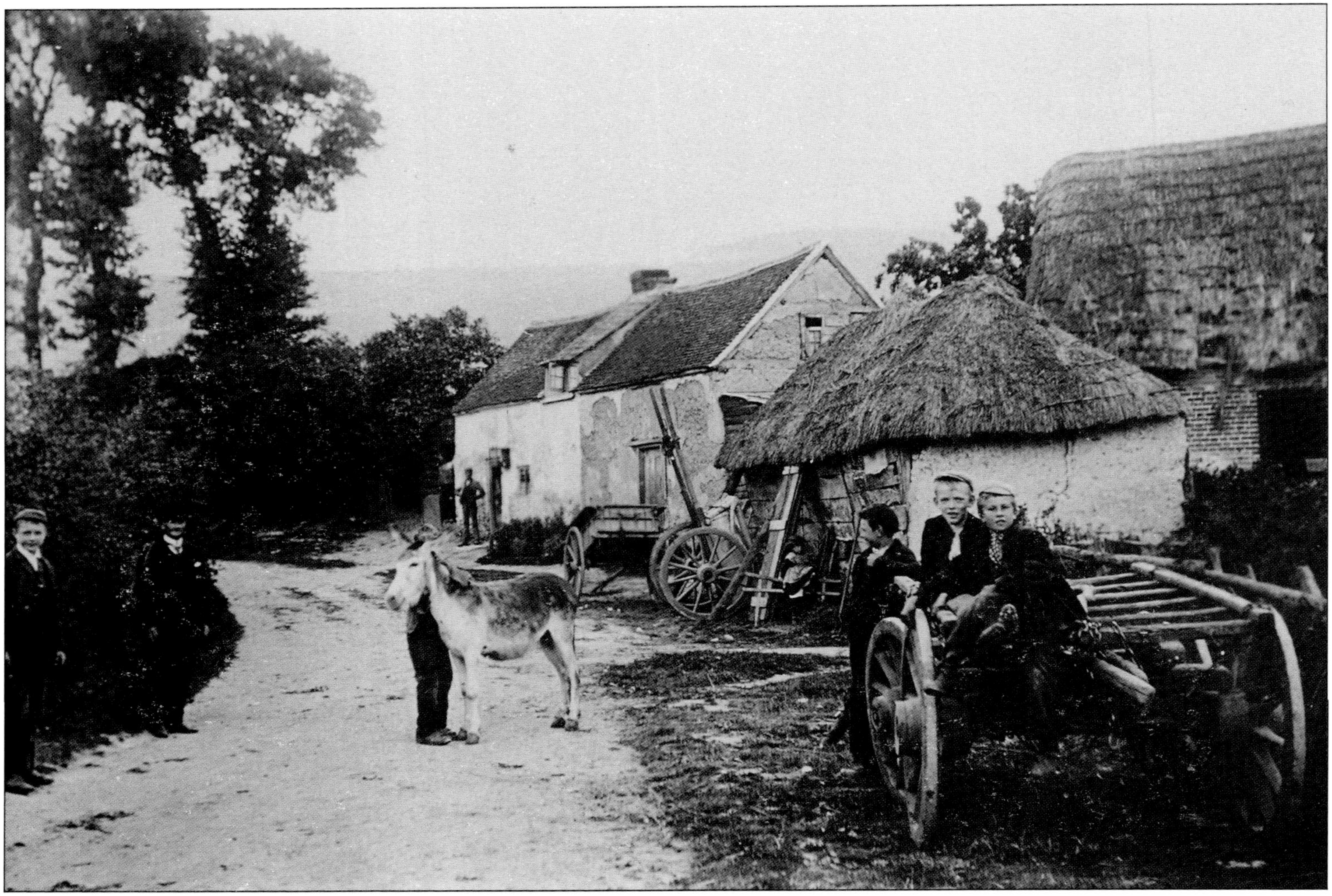

Chinnor

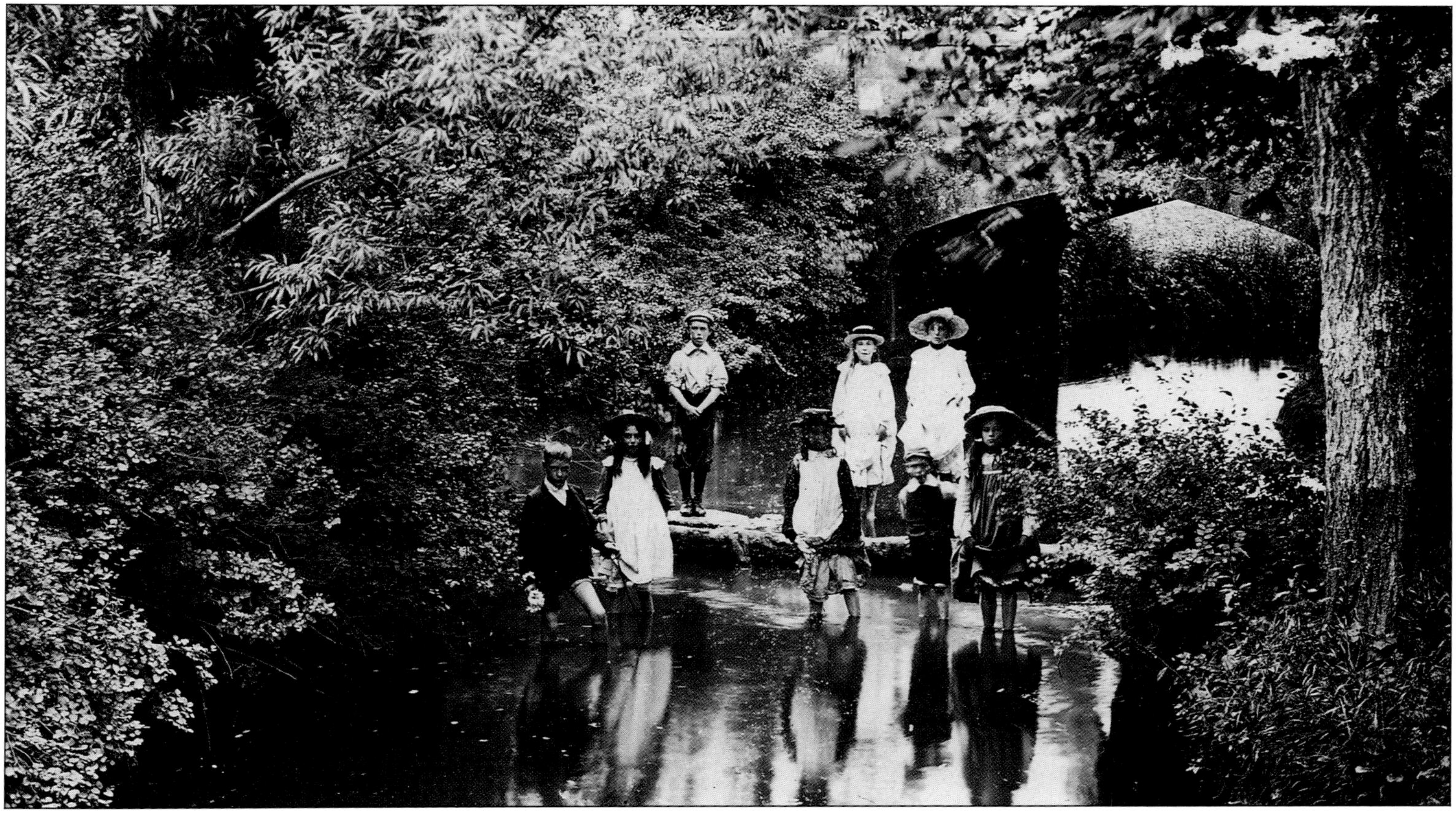

The Ford, Hardwick

Sheffields; no Prisoners of qualitie were taken by the Enemy, but Captain Sheffields Brother. Prince Rupert was there in person, and the Runagado Hurry. We took prisoner one of the Earl of Berks sons, Captain Gardener, the late Recorders sonne of London, and Captaine Smith, with some others of qualitie, and divers prisoners.

Sir, this is the true Relation of what passed in this business. I rest,

Thame Your assured Friend

19 June, 1643 Essex

FINIS

It would be almost heresy not to refer to Clarendon whose HISTORY OF THE REBELLION was first printed from a transcript under the supervision of his son in 1702–4. It is uneven in accuracy but nevertheless remains a classic reference work and still savours strongly of the events when 'the passion, rage and fury of this time shall be forgotten'.

Thus he writes of John Hampden:

He was a gentleman of a good family in Buckinghamshire, and born to a fair fortune, and of a most civil and affable deportment. In his entrance into the world, he indulged to himself all the licence in sports and exercises, and company, which were used by men of the most jolly conversation . . . He was rather of reputation in his own country, then of public discourse, or fame in the kingdom, before the business of Ship-money: but then he grew the argument of all tongues, every man inquiring who and what he was, that durst, at his own charge, support the liberty and property of the kingdom, and rescue his country, as he thought, from being made a prey to the Court . . . After he was among those members accused by the King of high treason, he was much altered; his nature and carriage seeming much fiercer than it was before. And without question, when he first drew his sword, he threw away the scabbard . . . Many men observed (as upon signal turns of great affairs, as this was, such observations are frequently made) that the field in which the skirmish was, and upon which Mr Hambden received his death's wound, Chalgrove field, was the same place in which he had first executed the ordinance of the militia, and engaged that county, in which his reputation was very great, in this rebellion . . .

Following the battle at Chalgrove in which Hampden was fatally wounded:

. . . But that which could have been looked upon as a considerable recompense for a defeat, could not but be thought a great addition to the victory, which was the death of Mr Hambden; who, being shot in the shoulder with a brace of bullets, which brake the bone, within three weeks after died with extraordinary pain; (he was buried according to the parish register on 25th and therefore as most historians state, died in six days) to as great a consternation of all that party, as if their whole army had been defeated, or cut off.

After receiving his wound on the battlefield, Hampden made for his father-in-law's house at Pyrton but found his way barred by Royalist troops. He then made his way in great pain to Thame where he later succumbed to his injuries. Amid scenes of great sorrow his body was taken to his home at Great Hampden where he was laid to rest with his forbears. The following touching letter, written by his close friend Arthur Goodwin, was addressed to his daughter the Lady Wharton, of Upper Winchenden:

THE LAST HOURS OF JOHN HAMPDEN

Deere Jenny, – I an now heere at Hampden in doinge the last duty for the deceased owner of it, of whome every

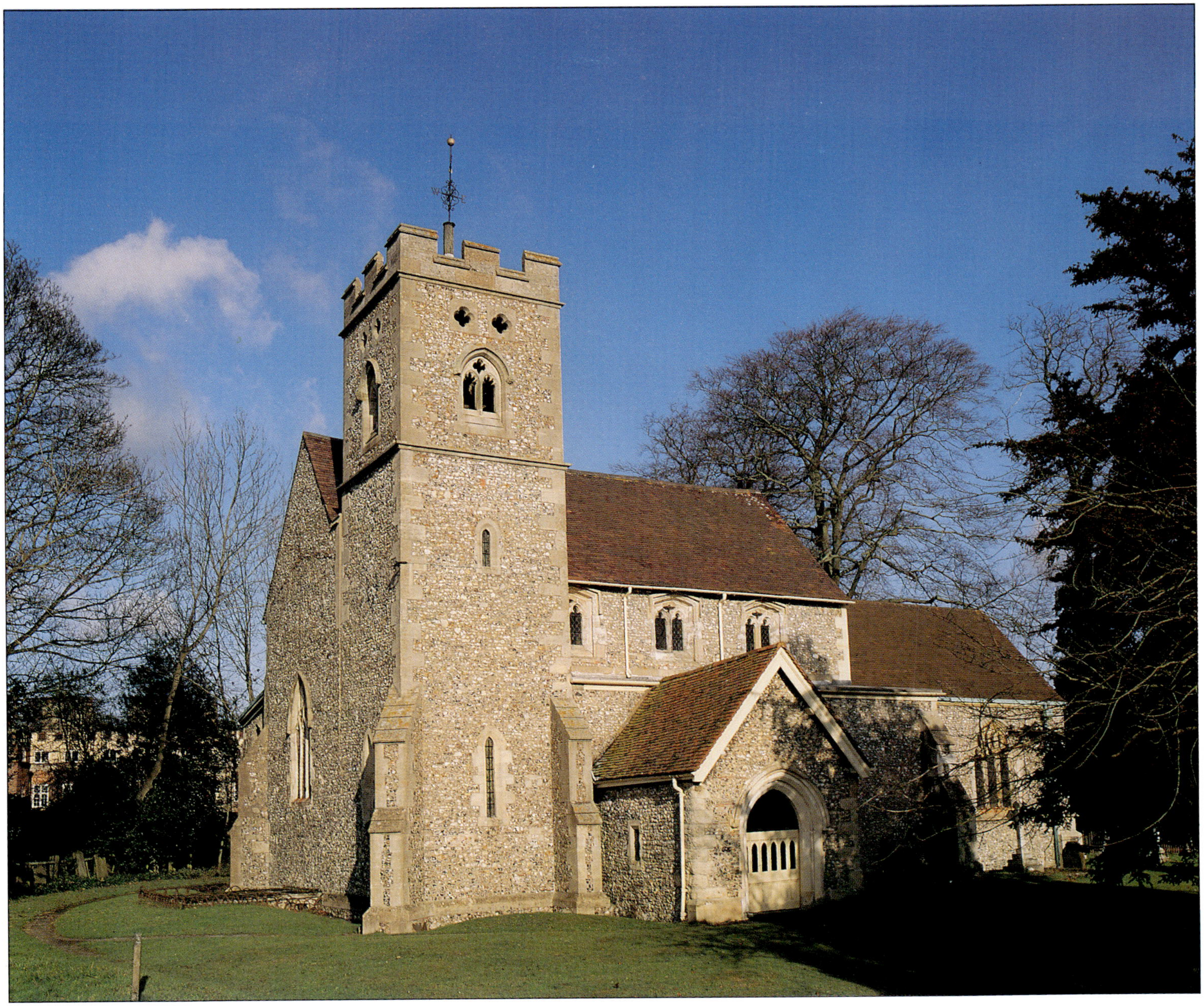

Great Hampden

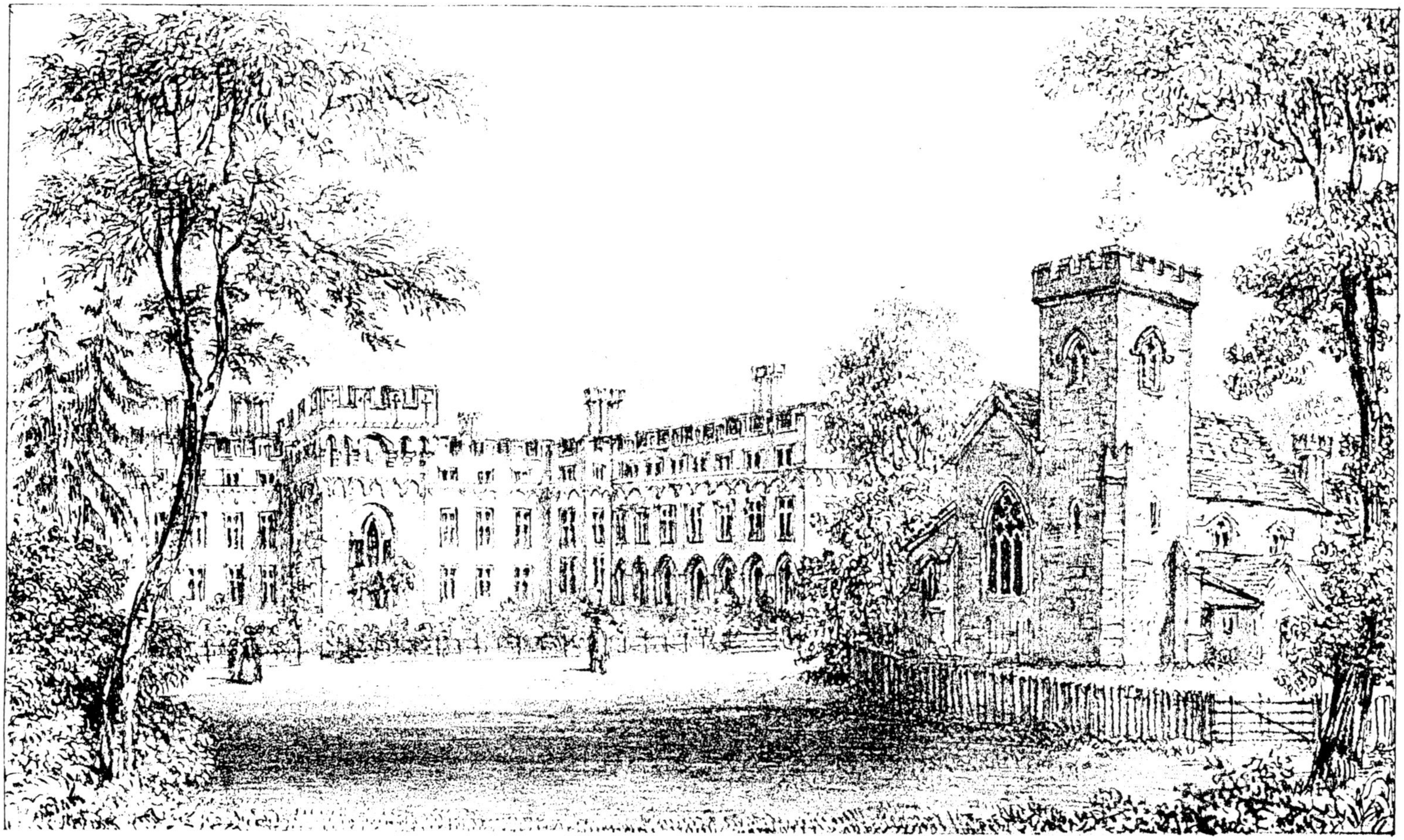

honest man hath a share in the losse, and therefore will likewise in the sorrowe. In the loss of such a friend, to my own particular, I have no cause of discontent, butt rather to bless God that he hath nott, accordinge to my deserts, bereft me of you, and all the comforts deerest to me. All his thoughts and endeavours of his life were zealously in for this cause of God's, wch he continued in all his sickness even to his death; for all I can heere the last words he spake was to me, though he lived six or 7 hours after I came away, as in sleepe; truly Jenny (and I know you may easily be persuaded to it) he was a gallant man, an honest man, an able man; and take all, I know nott to any man livinge second. God now in mercy hath rewarded him . . . I have writt to London for a black suite. I pray lett me begg of you a broad blacke Ribbon to hange about my standard; my faithful service to my Lady, my Lord Sir Rowland, Sir Thomas, my wife, and the young ladyes. I would we could all lay it to hart, that God takes away the best

amongst us. I pray the Lord to bless you. Yr ever, deere Jenny, most affectionate father, Ar. GOODWIN. Hampden, June 26, 1643
Col. Goodwin to Lady Wharton.

Returning to the journal of Samuel Luke we find that Thame, having been abandoned by Essex, is suffering at the hands of the Cavaliers, and that they still have designs on Aylesbury. A letter to Hampden and Goodwin, read in Parliament on 18 May 1643, complains bitterly about the condition of 'this country' and how the Royalists 'sweep clean divers of our pastures, leaving no cattell behind them'.

Monday 22 January

Roger Cunington retorned this day from Tame, and saith that there was in the towne and thereabouts 3000 horse and foote and the commaund of Prince Rupert and Collonell Hurrey. Collonell Hurrys regiment lyes at Tame and intend to goe against Alesbury. William Blewit retorned yesterday from Alesbury, and saith that the Lord Digby promised Leiftenant Collonell Mosley of Alesbury 2,000£ if hee would betray the towne to them.

(Col. Aldrich, governer of Aylesbury was written to by Sir John Byron 16 Oct suggesting the betrayal of Aylesbury, but Aldrich informed Parliament for which he was duly rewarded, and the subsequent attack by Rupert was aborted.)

Thursday 25 January

Raph Norton returned from Tettesworth, and saith . . . That Prince Robert was soe private when hee went out upon his late desigen from Aylesbury, that hee caused all the bridges to bee pulled upp and noe man suffered to goe out of the citty for feare they should give notice to the Parliament. But the contry reports that when hee came backe hee was ashamed and putt his head in a blacke bagg as he ridd.

William Blewett returned this day from Redding, and saith that there are about 2000 horse and foote and 8 peeces of ordnance in the towne, and 2 troopes of horse are quarterd at Sunning under the command of Sir Charles Blunt, and they keepe very strong guards about the towne. That there is a troope of horse alsoe in Henly, and about 100 foote in Greenland howse, and have fortified it, but they have not above 30 musketts amongst them all. That the Cavallyers threaten to plunder and burne the town of Wickham if they bring not in 40£ tomorrow, which they have assessed them to pay. That a troop of horse marcht this day through Missonden and intended to quarter at Chessam, but the townesmen arose and beate them out, whereupon they returned to their old quarters. And that companies of dragoones under the command of Captaine Aldridge and Captaine Fleetwood were in pursuite of them.

Monday 29th January

John Carpenter retorned yesterday from Bledlow, and saith . . . Hee heard at Barkhamsted that a party of the Kings horse came this morneing from Henly to Amersam, where they plundered a captaines house of this side, and divers other houses in the towne and set fire one wone end of the towne, and an other party of the Kings horse at the same instant were plundering Missenden.

Wednesday 9 August 1643

James Carey returned this day and saith that there were about 30 of the Kings forces yesterday at Tame and tooke away all the horses they could find, and pillaged onely one mans howse because when some of the prisoners which were taken on the Kings side at Chinner were brought thither hee wisht them all hangd and Prince Robert alsoe. That there were 9 or 10 more neere Stoken Church where they robbd one man and one of their scouts was shott with a brace of bulletts by one of ours in the towne.

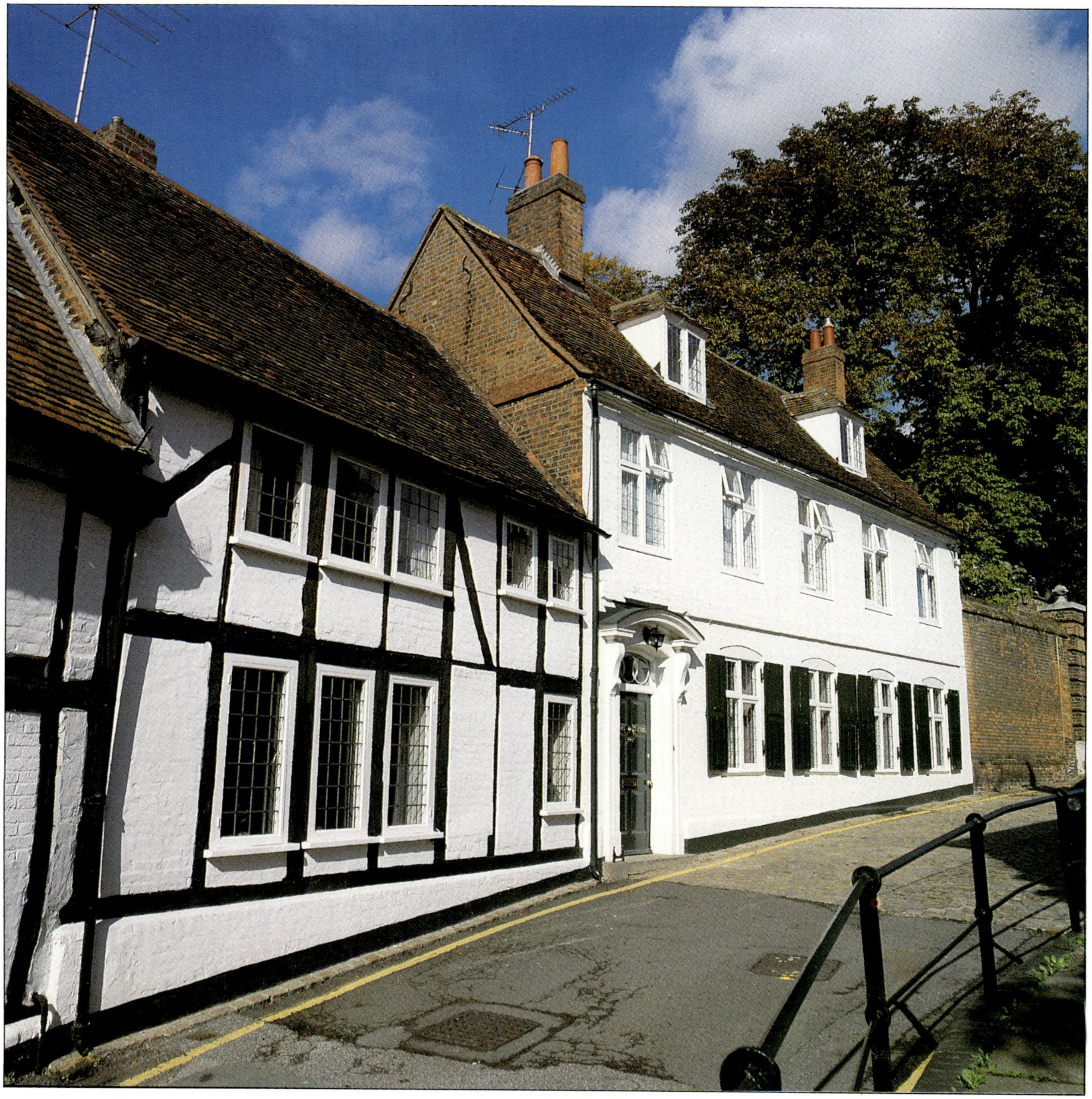

Aylesbury

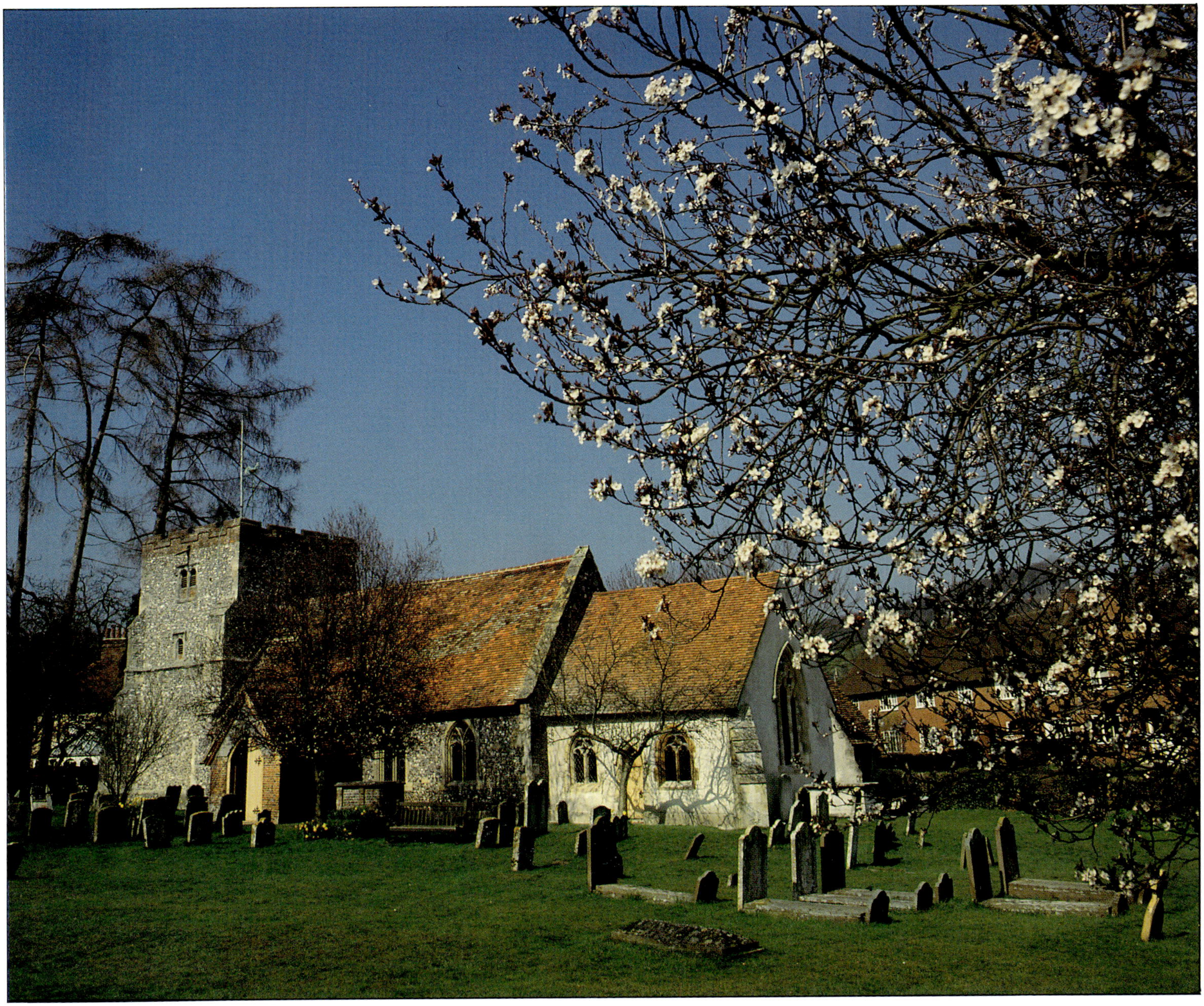

Turville church

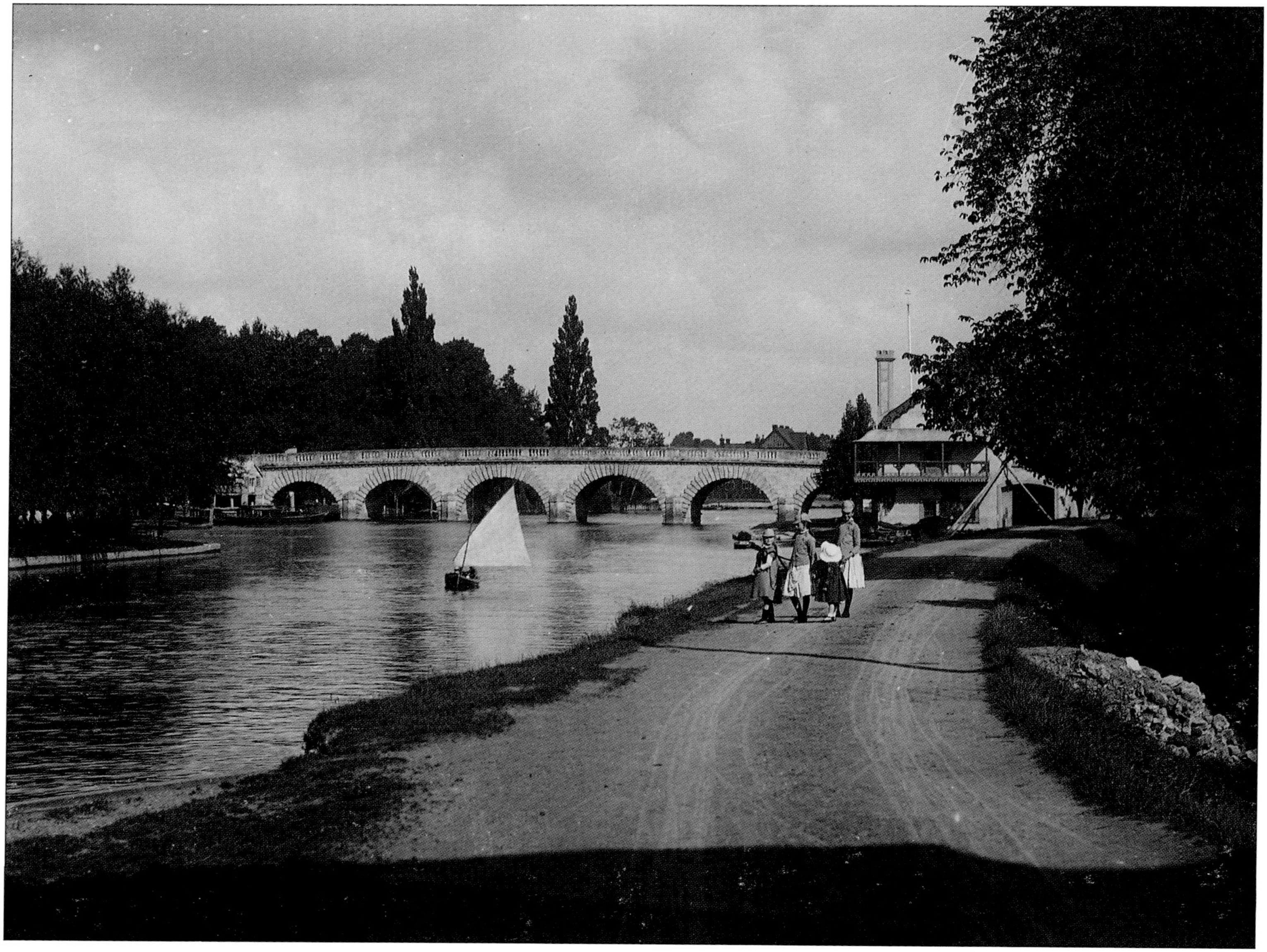

Maidenhead

Thursday 10the August

Thomas Gardner returned this day and saith that on Thursday last the Cavallyers came to Henley and apprehended one Mr Freeman a shopkeeper in the towne at whose howse Collonell Holborne lay, and took him upp behind one of the their troopes and threatened to carry him away, but for 10 li. they released him at the townes end.

Satturday the 12th of August

Thomas Shilborne sith . . . That there are some [forces] at Bister some at Lamton (Launton) and divers other places betwixt Buckingham and Oxford, and it is feard that they intend to fall upon Alesbury where they are sicke, weake and in great want both of men and money.

Next we see the whole mixture of frenzied activities used by the Cavaliers to advance their own cause or to deny their enemy any advantage; corruption of traders, harassment of civilians, extortion, and destruction of property – Sandford bridge was also pulled down and the miller charged 'upon paine of death to suffer none to passe that way to Okeingham' (Wokingham).

As with much of Luke's journal, scattered pieces of information begin to form a more recognizable picture. The repeated reference to the strengthening of defences at Greenlands House is clearly a prelude to the siege which took place through the following spring and summer.

Thursday 5 October

Ralph Norton returned and saith that . . . they have pulld upp Twyford Bridge and burnt the mills at Twyford and Sanford [Berks.] and will not suffer any man to passe that way to London and presse all men they can lay their hands on, and that hee sawe some of their dragoones this afternoone in Maydenhead Thickett, and sent 2 of their company into Maydenhead privatly to see if any of the Parliament soldiers were there. . . .

Satturday 4 November

Henry Connington saith that goeing to Oxford hee was apprehended yesterday morning by the Cavallyers at the Swann at Beconsfeild and tooke away his bootes, horse and mony, and carryed him tallmost to Henley. That there

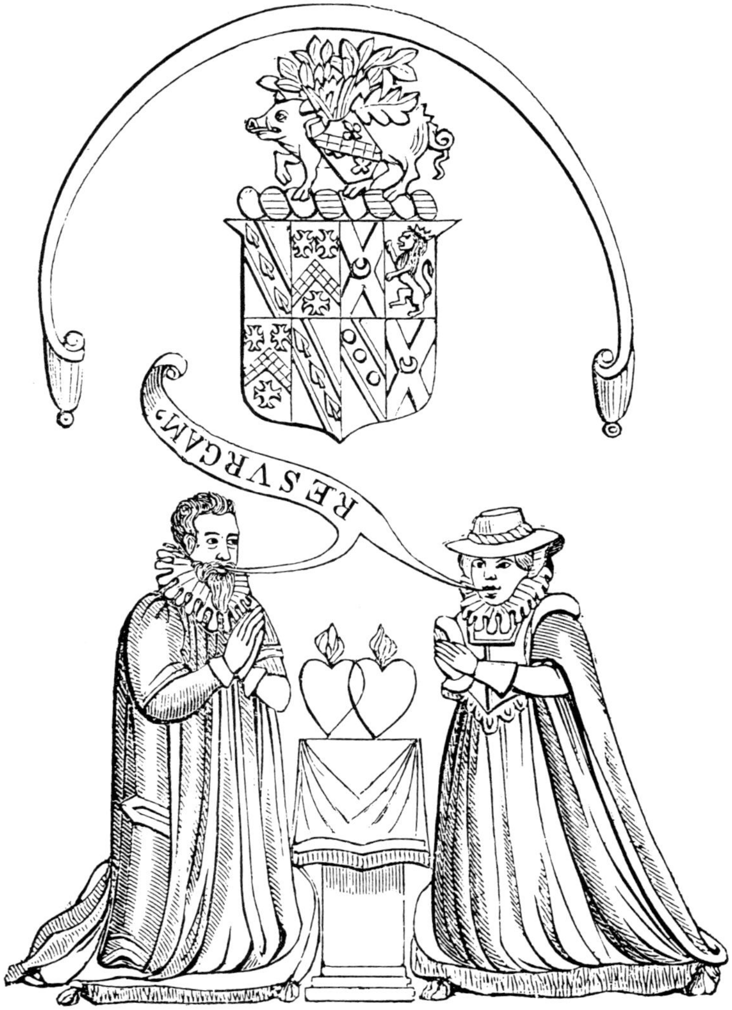

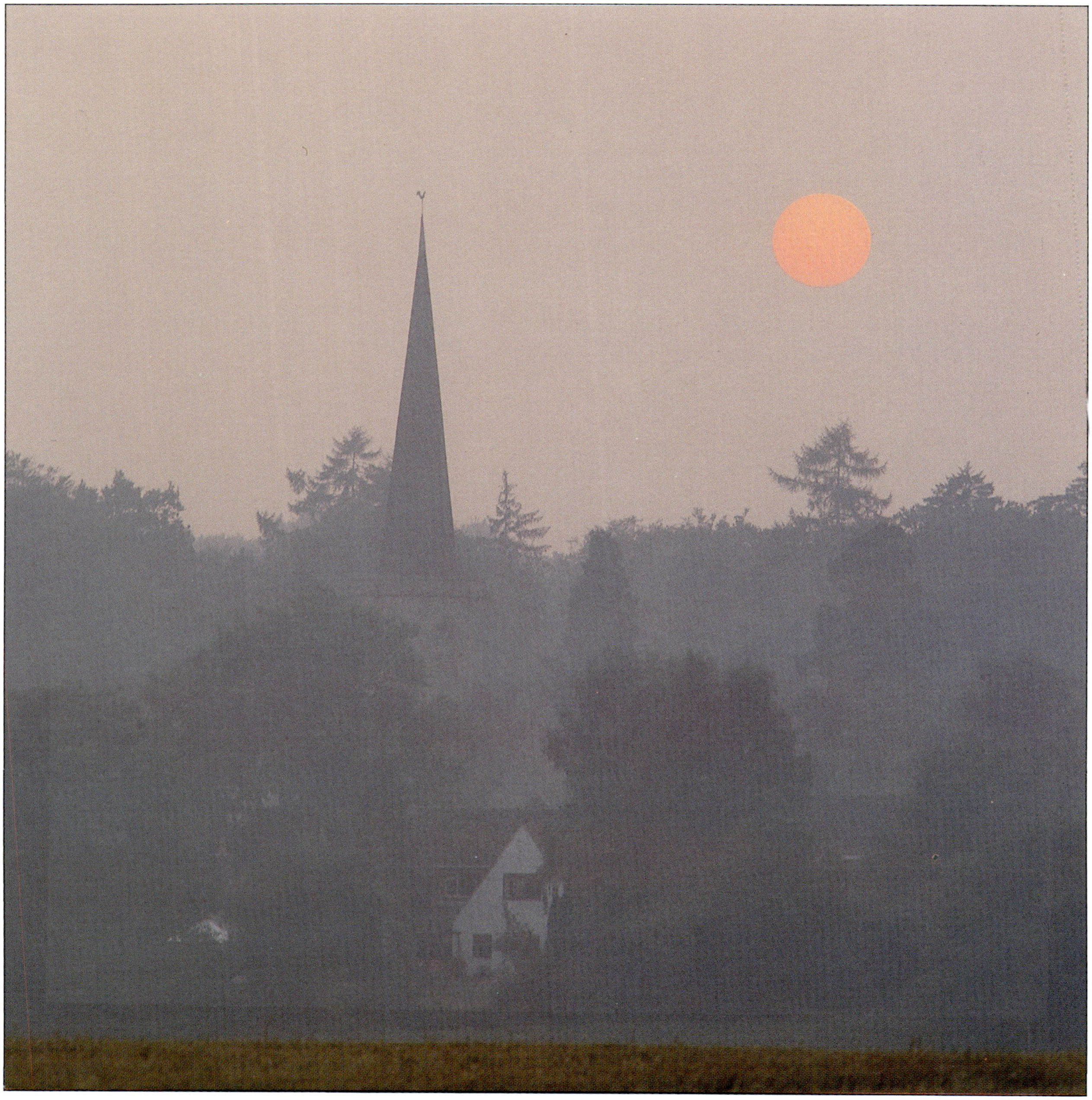

Penn Street

were about 14000 of them whoe were come from plundring Uxbridge, that they kept their randevous halfe a mile beyond Beconsfeild where hearing of the comming of our forces to the towne they prepared themselves to encounter them, but seeing none approach them they went to Henley and soe from thence to Redding.

9th Nov

John Appleby . . . came this day through Chessam where he found the whole towne in armes under one Captain Fleetwood who had 200 musketeeres besides others with prongs and bills. The reason of it was some Cavaleers appearing in a body on Wickham Heath last night, and it was reported, with intent to plunder theire towne. But they resolved rather to dye every man than be plundered by such rascalls.

December 2nd 1643

Thomas Hunt retorned this day from Oxford and saith . . . Upon Tuesday last there were 80 of the Queenes regiment at Tame. They drove away a greate store of bease from Wickham butchers to Oxford.

December 6th 1643

William Harris returned this day from Oxford and saith . . . that all commodityes which the Cavileers want are sent from London to Wickham under Wickham mens names, and soe sent in the night to Oxford by waggon loads at a tyme.

December 10th 1643

Thomas Hunt returned this day from Reading and saith . . . Upon Friday last there went 500 horse and foote from Reading to Grinland on this side of Henly to Mr Dawley's house, [Sir John Doyley] there they seysed upon all his goods, some of his goods they sent to Reading and the rest they keepe for their owne uses for there is 300 foote quarter there this winter and 200 horse at Hambledon. They send for the countrymen to come to helpe to intrench Grinland. Yesterday there came 5 waggons loaden with ammunicon from Reading to Grinland. Upon Wednesday last a party of Reading forces pilledged Sir John Burlacy's [Sir John Borlase] house at Bockmore and tooke away all that they layd their hands on.

December 13th Wednesday

James Carey came from Marlow and saith that there were about 1000 of the Kings horse yesterday, about 40 or 50 of them came yesterday to Wickham and plundred some howses in the towne and carryed some of the inhabitants prisoner along with them, and they intend to make a garrison towne of Marlowe and stopp all the passage upon the Thames. They are making of bulwarkes at Greeneland howse a mile on this side of Henley, and have warned in the contry thereabouts to come and assist them and have planted 3 peeces of ordnance upon them.

William Harryes came this day from Wickham and saith that there came about 30 of the Cavalyers thither yesterday, and plundred some howses in the towne and carryed away 4 of the townesmen. That the Maiors wife of Wickham followeing them for her goods, they detayne her as a prisoner and will not release her unlesse they have 45 li paid eyther by her or some other for her. That they are fortifieing of Greenland howse neere Henley, and the reason is, as it is reported, because they intend to stop the barges, and prevent them from carrying of billetts and faggotts and all manner of tymber to London. That Wickham is assessed at 5 li. a weeke to bee paid every Fryday, and they are to send every day 20 men for 4 dayes to helpe to make upp the workes at Greenland howse.

Saturday 16th December

Ralph Norton went towards Lord Hopton, and informed . . . that there are noe soldiers Henley, but the townesmen

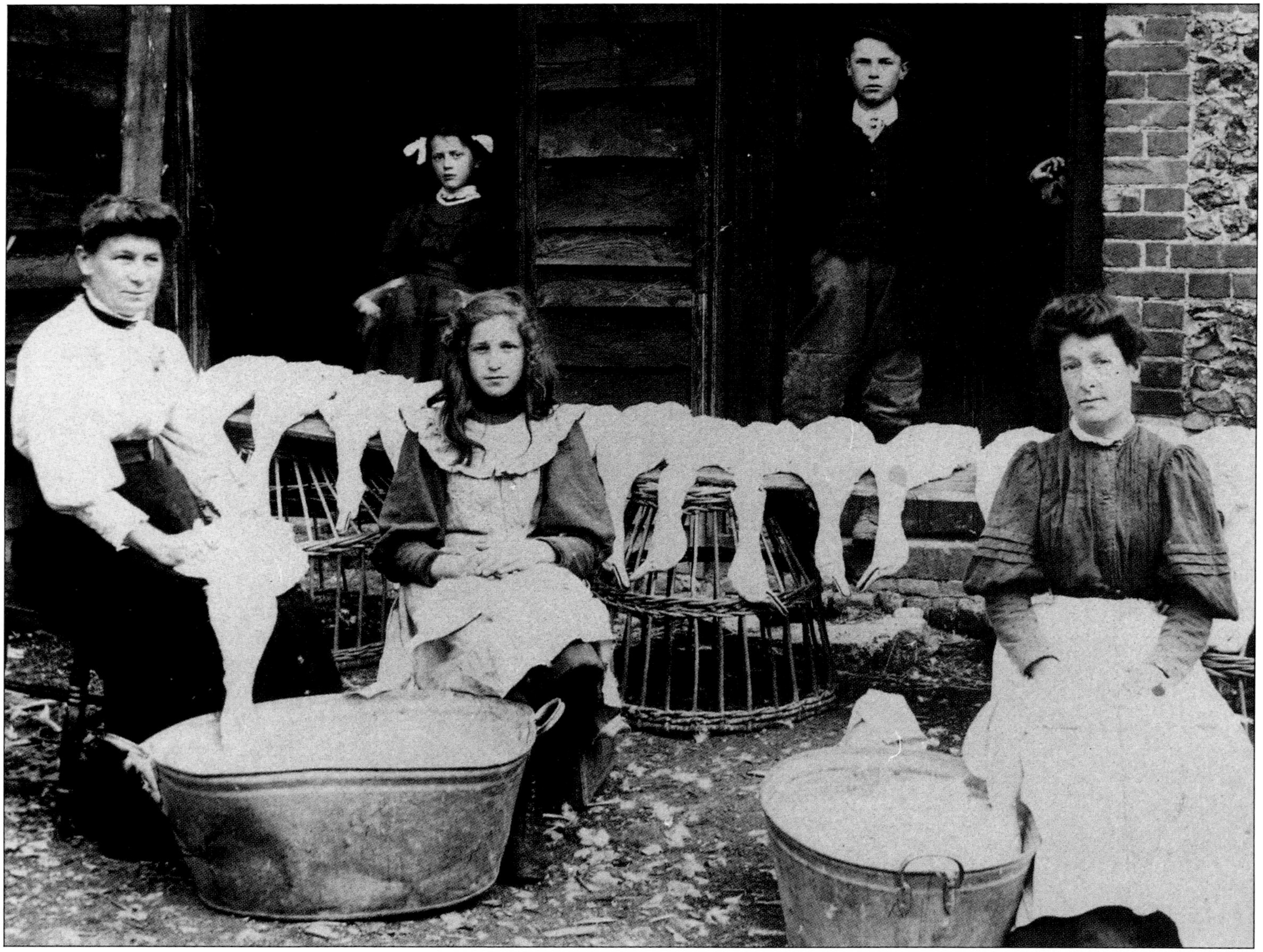

Plucking ducks at Chinnor

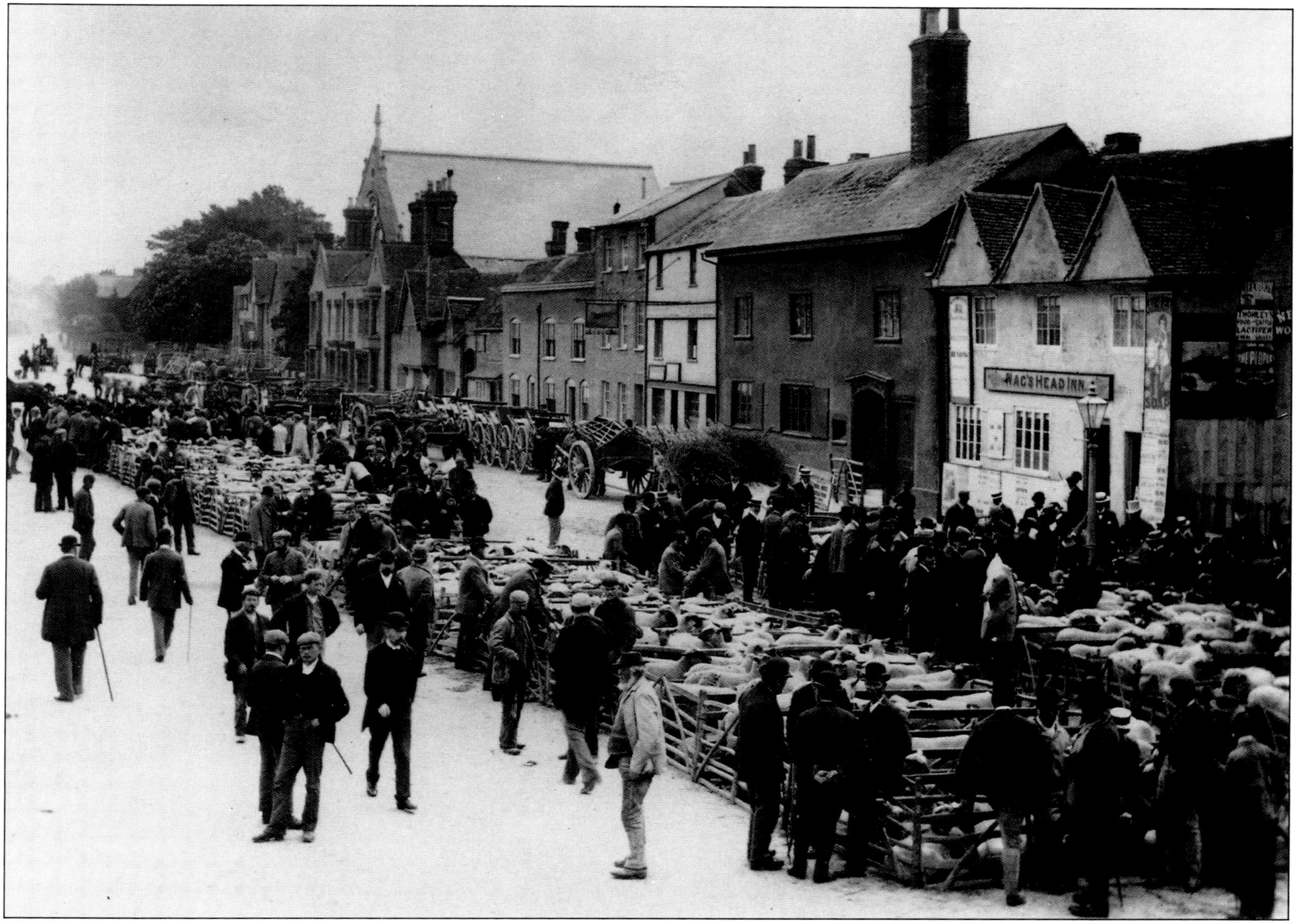

Thame

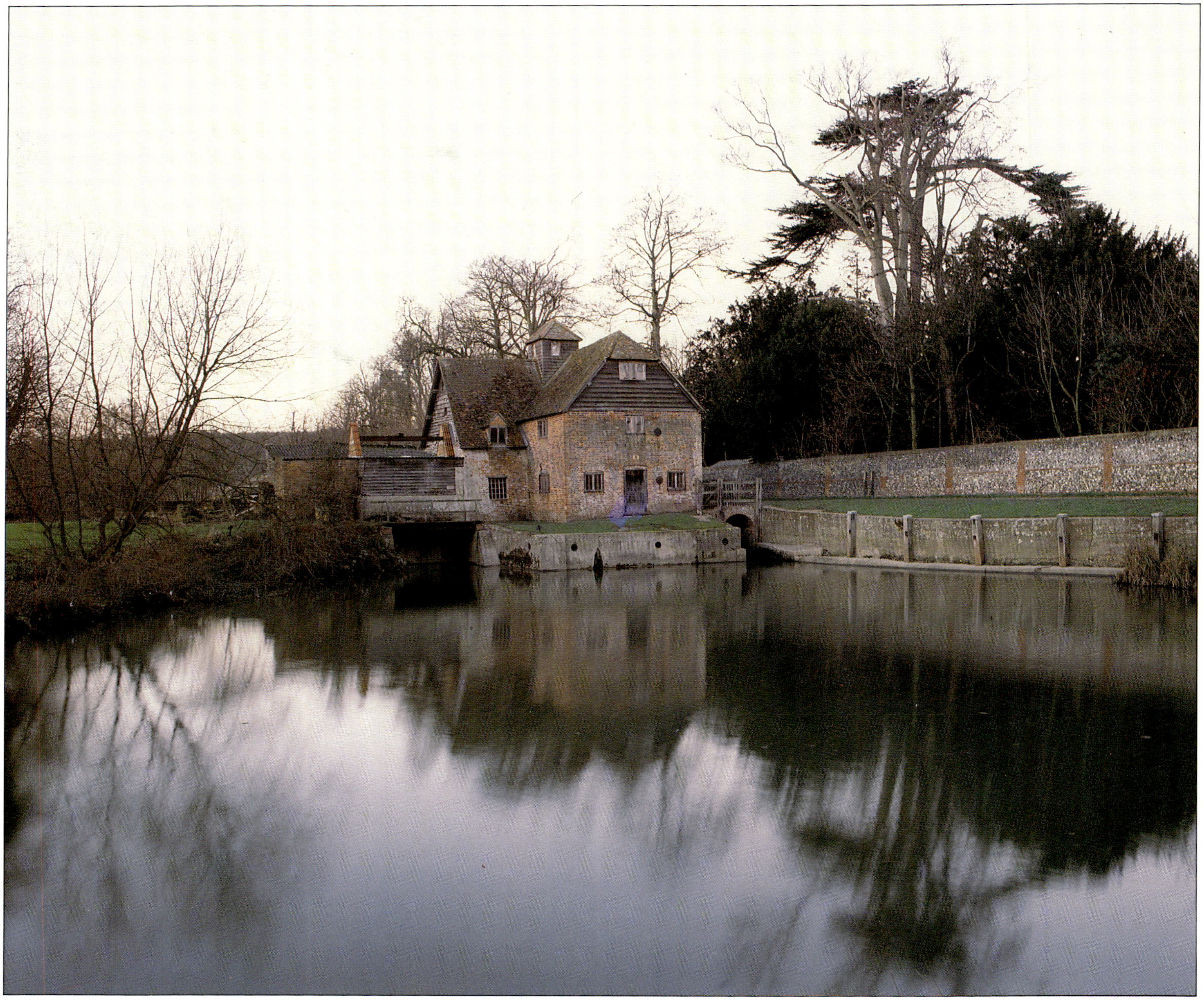

Mapledurham Mill

and all thereabouts are making of bulwarkes at Greyes and Greenland howse, where there are about 200 men, which cause the contry to bring in money, and provision . . . that since they have fortified Greenland howse, they stopp all passage by water, and will not suffer any fewell to bee conveyed that way to London.

Sonday 14 January 1644

Ralph Norton came yesterday from Mapledurham, and saith . . . That he came by Henley – there are neither horse nor foote in the towne but there are about 200 foote in Greeneland howse, where they are still fortifieing, and Sir Charles Blunt (hee heares) is made governer there.

The fortunes of the main participants in the war were mixed indeed. Prince Rupert, after his surrender at Bristol, was banished. Cromwell's body, only shortly after his death, was exhumed and his remains desecrated. Essex died at fifty-five, dubbed a failure, and King Charles paid for his Draconian policies with his head.

We return again to Clarendon for a glimpse of his pathetic last hours spent with his children:

That the king much desired to have the sight and company of his children, and that if they might not be allowed to be longer with him, that at least they might dine with him; and he sent them word that, on such a day, the King, who attended the motion of the army, and was quartered only where they pleased, would dine at Maidenhead. There his children met him, to his infinite content and joy; and he being to quarter and to stay some time at Caversham, a house of the Lord Cravens, near Reading [Caversham Park], his children were likewise suffered to go thither, and remained with him two days; which was the greatest satisfaction the King could receive; and the receiving whereof he imputed to the civility of the General. . . .

To end we return to where we began – Aylesbury. This 'postscript' taken from J.J. Sheahan's HISTORY AND TOPOGRAPHY OF BUCKINGHAMSHIRE could really form a postscipt to all wars and civil wars in particular, where the real losers are the civilians and their property:

The battle of Aylesbury is supposed to have been fought near Holman's Bridge, on the Aylesbury and Buckingham road 'Contiguous to the turnpike road to Winslow, about six furlongs N.N.W. of Aylesbury', where in 1818, some labourers digging gravel near the brook 'Discovered many human bodies, buried promiscuously, in pits from two to four feet deep.' Lord Nugent caused the bones to be carried together, and buried in the neighbouring churchyard of Hardwick; and the following inscription to be engraved on a marble slab:

'Within are deposited the bones of two hundred and forty seven persons which were discovered A.D. 1818, buried in a field adjoining Holman's Bridge. From the history and appearance of the place where they were found, they are concluded to be the remains of those officers and men who perished in an engagement fought A.D. 1642 between the troops of Charles the First, under the command of Prince Rupert, and the garrison who held Aylesbury for the Parliament. Enemies, from their attachment to opposite standards in the sanguinary conflicts of that civil war, they were, together victims of its fury, united in one common slaughter. They were buried in one common grave, close to the spot where they had lately stood in arms against each other. May the memory of the brave be respected, and may our country never again be called to take part in contests such as these which this tablet records.
Erected by Lord Nugent.'

From his style of writing we immediately gain the impression that Dr Thomas Fuller, our next guide to the Chilterns, was a

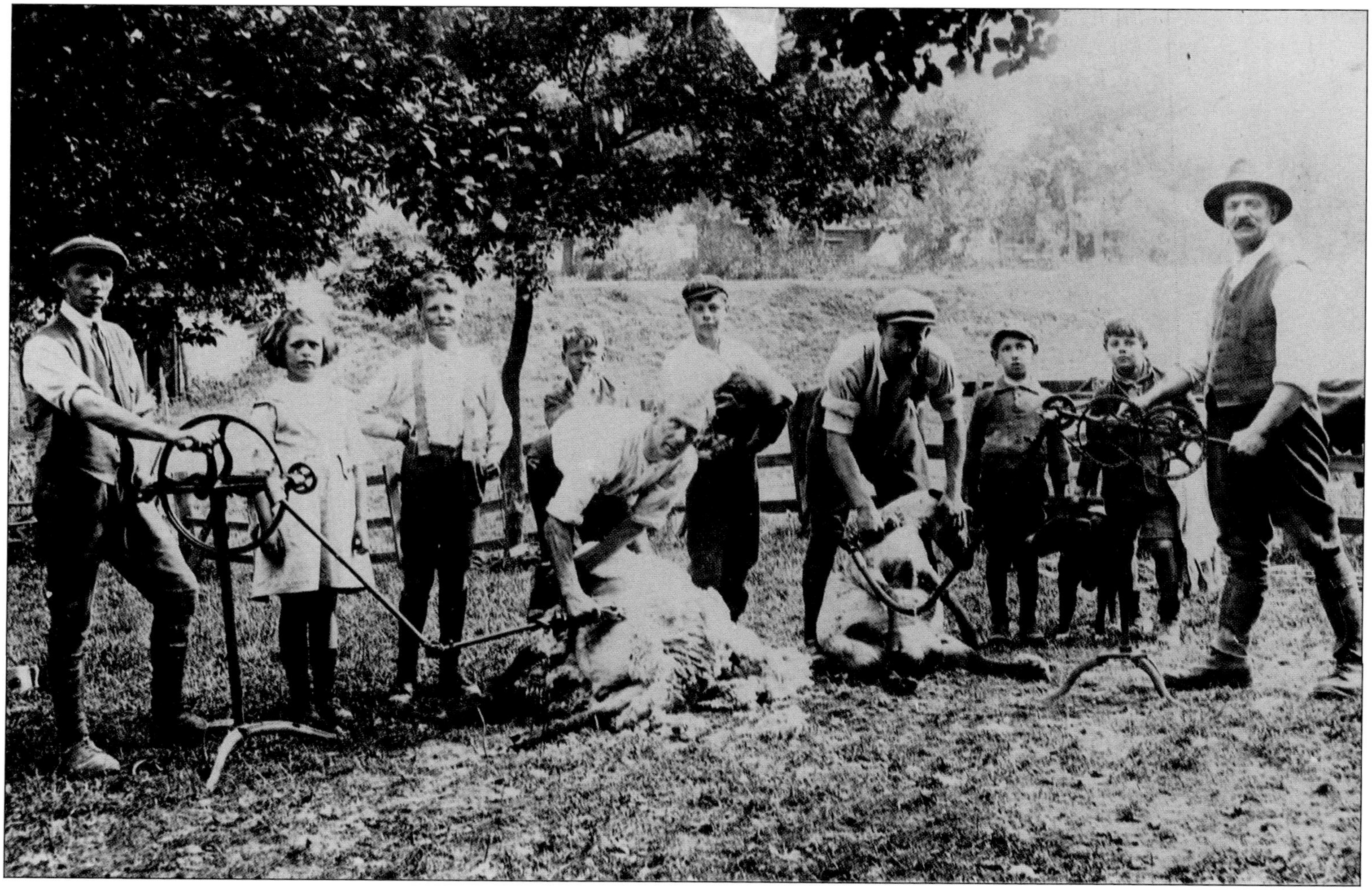

Sheep shearing

man of humour and eccentricity. A man of the cloth, he supported the Royalist cause and was chaplain to the notable soldier Sir Ralph Hopton. While travelling round England during the Civil War, he developed the idea of writing his substantial work, THE HISTORY OF THE WORTHIES OF ENGLAND, which was published in 1662 shortly after his death. County by county this covers much ground relating to people and places, their history and current situation, and an engaging collection of proverbs. As he himself describes his research: 'My pains have been scattered all over the land, by riding, writing, going, sending, chiding, begging, praying, and sometimes paying too, to procure manuscript material.'

Berkshire Proverbs

First we will despatch that sole proverb of this county 'The Vicar of Bray will be the Vicar of Bray still.'

Bray, a village well known in this county, so called from the Bibroces a kind of ancient Britain inhabiting thereabouts. The vivacious Vicar hereof living under the King Henry the Eighth, King Edward the Sixth, Queen Mary, and Queen Elizabeth, was just a Papist, then a Protestant, then a Papist, then a Protestant again. He had seen some Martyrs burnt (two miles off) at Windsor and found this fire too hot for his tender temper. This Vicar being taxed by one for being a Turn-coat, and an unconstant changeling, 'Not so,' said he 'for I alwaies kept my principle, which is this to live and die the Vicar of Bray.' Such many now adayes, who though they cannot turn the wind, will turn their mills, and set them so, that wheresoever it bloweth, their grist shall certainly be grinded.

Hartfordshire Proverbs

Hartford-shire Clubs and Clouted Shoon
Some will wonder how this shire lying so near London, the Staple of English Civilitie, should be guiltie of so much *rusticalness*. But the finest Cloth must have a List, and the pure *Pesants* are of *coarse* a *thread* in this County as in any other place. Yet, though some may smile at their *Clownishness* let none laugh at their *Industry*; rather because the *high Shoon* of the *Tenant* pays for the *Spanish-leather Boots* of the landlord.

Hartfordshire Hedge-Hogs

Plenty of Hedge-Hogs are found in this *High-Woodland-County*, where too often they suck the Kine, though the Dayre-maid conne them small thanks for sparing their pains in milking them. A creature alwayes in his posture of defence, carrying a *stand of pikes* on his back, so that, if as well *victualled* as *armed* he may *hold out a siege* against any equal opposition.

If this proverb containeth any further reflections on the people of this County, as therein taxed for *covertousness*, and their constant *nudling on the Earth* I will not so understand it, as hoping and believing this to be a false application.

Buckinghamshire Proverbs

Here if you beat a Bush, it's odds you'ld Start a Thief.
No doubt there was just occasion for this proverb at the original thereof, which then contained *satyrical* truth, proportioned to the place before it was reformed; whereof thus our great Antiquary:
'It was altogether unpassible in times past by reason of Trees, until that Leofstane Abbot of St. Albans did cut them down, because they yielded a place of refuge for thieves' (Camden's *Britannia Buckinghamshire*).

But this proverb is now antiquated as to the truth thereof, *Buckingham-Shire* affording as many *Maiden Assizes* as any County of equal populousness. Yea, hear how she pleadeth, for her self, that such High-way-men were never her Natives, but fled thither for their shelter out of neighbouring counties.

Buckingham Bread and Beef

The former is as fine, the latter as fat in this as any other county. If therefore the inhabitants thereof came with *hearty-grace* and *hungrey appetites*, no doubt both *strength* and *health* will follow on their repast.

Clearly the Vale of Aylesbury was as famous for its sheep as it was for its beef, as Fuller explains:

The best and biggest-bodied in England are the Vale of Ailsbury in this County, where it is nothing to give ten pounds or more for a Breed-ram. So that should a Forrainer hear of the price thereof, he would guess that Ram rather to be some Roman Engine of battery, than the creature commonly called so. Forrainers much admire at our English sheep, because they doe not (as those beyond the seas) follow their Shephards like to a pack of dogs but wander wide abroad; and the Popish Priests tell their simple flocks, that this disobedience of our sheep happeneth unto us because we have left the great Shephard the Pope, whereas they did so long before our separation from Rome, freed from the fear of wolves (infesting them in forraine parts), they feed safely in the fields, needing neither guide to direct, nor guard to defend them.

Here the worthy doctor introduces us to a lady, born in Latimer, who is remembered for her particularly extensive family, such that Fuller himself felt the urge to offer his own design for a monument charting her descendants!

Dame Hester Temple, daughter of Miles Sands Esquire, was born at Latmos in this County; and was married to Sir Thomas Temple of Stow, Baronet. She had four sons and nine daughters, which lived to be married, and so exceedingly multiplied, that this lady saw seven hundred extracted from her body. Reader I speak within compass, and having lost myself a reserve, having bought the truth thereof by a wager I lost. Besides there was a new generation of marriagable females just at her death; so that this aged vine may be said to wither, even when it had many young boughs ready to knit.

Had I been one of her relations, and as well enabled as most of them, I would have erected a Monument for her, thus designed. A fair tree should have been erected, the said Lady and her Husband lying at the bottom or root thereof; the Heir of the family should have ascended both the middle and the top bough thereof. On the right-hand hereof her younger sons, and left her daughters should as so many boughs be spread forth. Her grandchildren should have their names inscribed on the branches of these boughs; the great grandchildren on the twigs of these branches; the great-great grandchildren on the leaves of those twiggs. Such as survive her death be done in a lively green, the rest (as blasted) in a pale and yellow fading colour.

A more tangible tree, the beech has dominated the Chiltern landscape from very early times and, not surprisingly, most writers about the Chilterns make due reference to this splendid woodland tree – Thomas Fuller is no exception:

This was esteemed sacred amongst the Romans . . . It is also medicinall: though we would wish none sore lips and eyes, to try the truth of Pliny's report, where Beech-leaves cure the one, or the ashes of Beech-mast heal the other. Our ordinary use thereof (besides making of many utensils) is for building of Houses. One asked, when Beech would make the best Timber, meaning what season of the year was best to cut it down for that purpose. It was answered 'that Beech would make the best Timber, when no Oake was to be had,' a time, I assure you, which daily approacheth in our Land. [The following comment was added by John Nichols who produced a new edition of

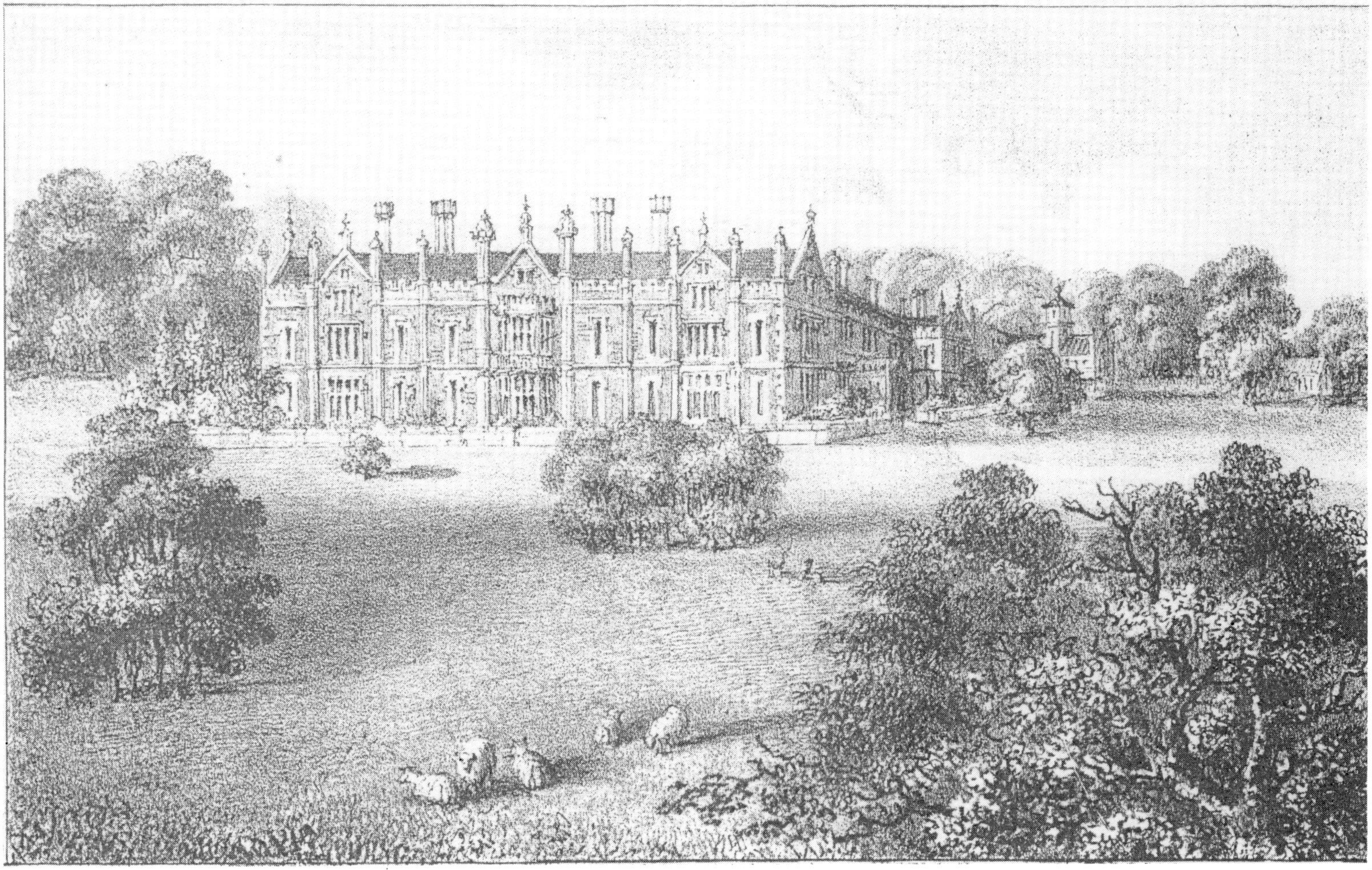

Fuller with explanatory notes in 1811: 'the prospect of Oak Timber becoming scarce, therefore, is not a modern chimera'.]

Hence it was, that such care was taken in the Reign of King Henry the Eighth (when Woods were in a better condition than now adays) for the preserving of standells of Beech. As also it was provided in the first of Queen Elizabeth, that no Timber-trees of Oak, Beech, and Ash (where Beech deservedly is made second) being one foot square at the stub, and growing within fourteen miles of the sea, or any Navigable river, should be converted to coal or fewell, as the debasing of that which, if Nature did not just intend Necessity must employ for better service.

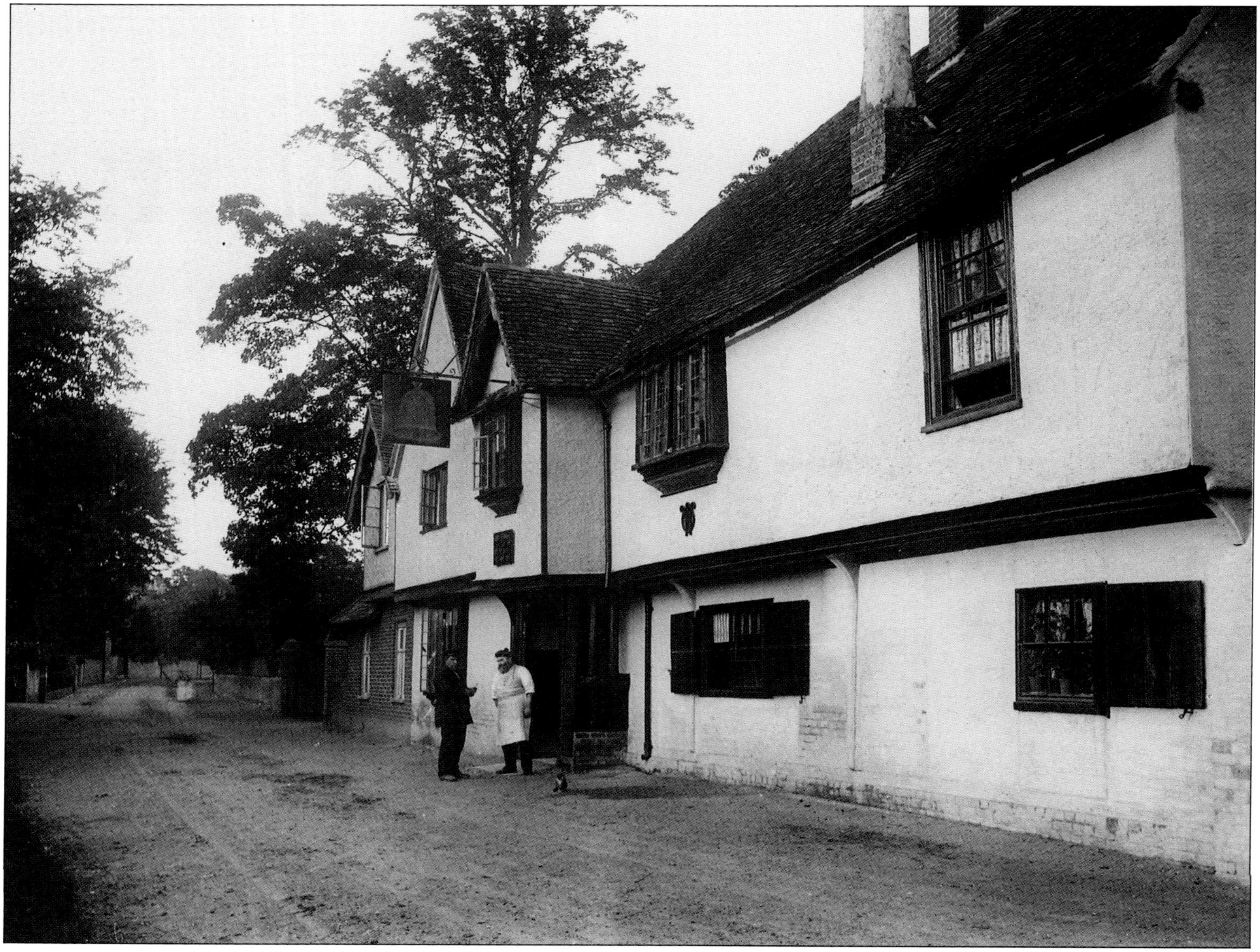

Hurley

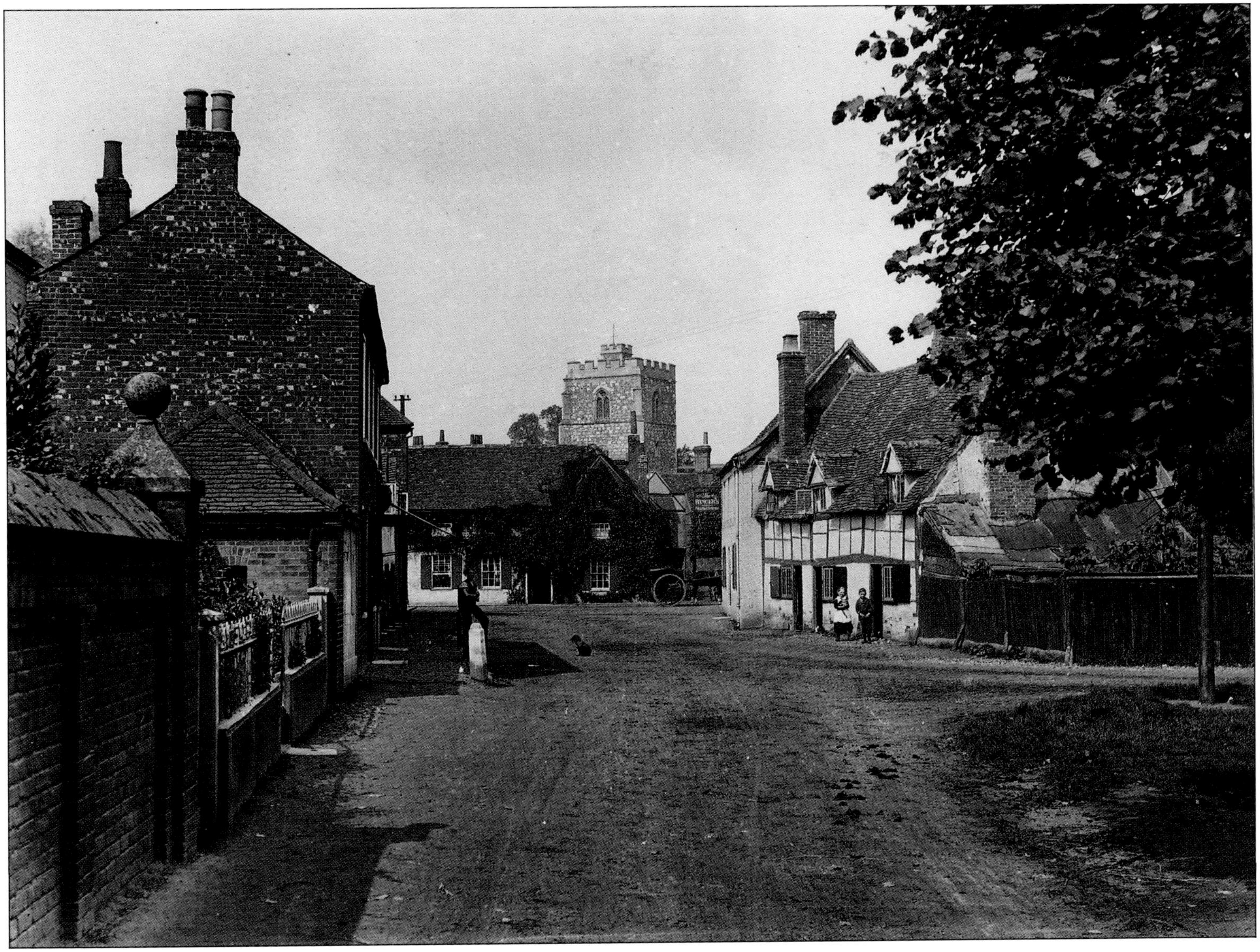

Bray

The 'ingenious Dr. Plot' in THE NATURAL HISTORY OF OXFORDSHIRE (1676), provides us with two natural curiosities, one relating to beech, the other to oak:

There was two Beeches in the way from Oxford to Reading, near a place called Cain End, more strangely joyned together a great height from the ground: for the Bodies of these Trees came from different Roots, and ascend parallel to the Top, but are joyned together a little before they come to bough, by a transverse piece of Timber entring at each End into the Bodies of the Trees, and growing jointly with them, for which reason tis commonly called the Gallow Tree, though the piece that intercedes them lies somewhat obliquely.

And at Ricote in the park of the Right Honourable the Lord Norreys, there was a Oak which extends its Branches from the Trunk of the Tree about 18 yds, so that the Diameter of its circumference being 36 yds, it takes within its area 972 sq yds; under the Umbrage of which Tree, upon the afore mentioned Proportions, no less than 324 horses, or 4374 Men may sufficently be sheltered.

The young Miss Deborah Milton, daughter of John Milton, to our great good fortune, kept a diary for the period May to September 1665 when the poet and his family were forced to take refuge in the country to escape the plague in London. Here we have a vivid picture of the cottage in Chalfont found for Milton by Thomas Ellwood, and with it the daily life of the family. The last passage is an insight into the problems faced by the poor, who were considered a burden on the parish at the best of times, but when disease was rampant these visitors were definitely unwelcome. Milton's kindly attitude is in sharp contrast to that of the village constable:

However, we really are preparing for Country Quarters, for young Ellwood hath this morning brought us Note of a rustick Abode near his Friends, the Penningtons, at Chalfont, in Bucks, the Charges of which suit my Fathers limited Means; and we hope to enter on it by the end of the week . . .

Half way to Amersham found Hob Carters Wagon, with Fathers Organ in't, sticking in the Hedge, without Man or Horse; and, by and by, came upon Hob himself, with a Party carousing. Ned gave it to him well, and sent him back at double quick Time. 'Twas too bad. He had left Town overnight, and promised to be at Chalfont by Noon. I should have be fain to keep him in Advance of us; howbeit, we were forct to leave him in the Rear; and, about two Miles beyond Amersham, we turned of the high Road into a country Lane, which soon brought us to a small retired Hamlet shaded with Trees, and surrounded with pleasent Meadows and Orchards, which was no other than Chalfont . . .

Dear Father, how is't with you? Are you comfortable here? 'Anything but that,' replies he, very shortlie. 'I am not in any Way at my Ease in this Place. I can get no

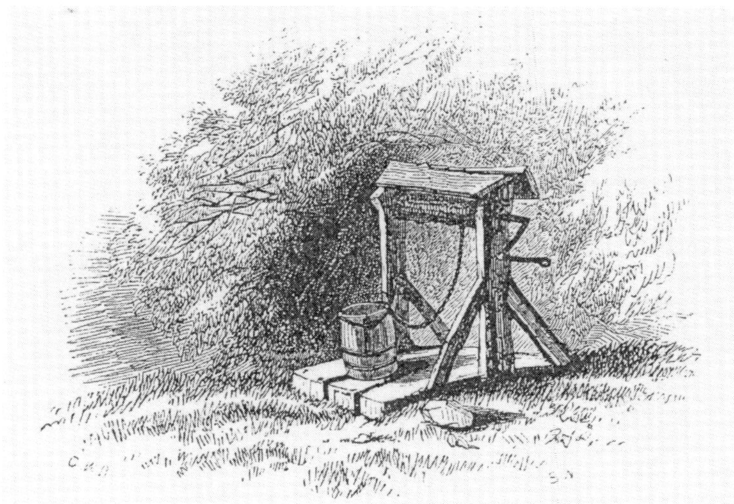

definite Notion of what 'tis like, and what notion I have is unfavourable. To finish all, they have stuck me up here, like a Bottle in the Smoke.' 'Look about, Child, and tell me, with Precision, what the Place is like.'

Soe I told him 'twas an irregular two storied Tenement, parcel Wood, parcel brick, with a deep Roof of old tiles that had lost their Colour, and were curiouslie variegated with green and yellow Moss, and that the Eaves were dentilled, with Birds Nests built in 'em, and a big Honeysuckle growing to the upper Floor; and there was a great and little Gable, and a heavy Chimney stack; a Casement of four Compartments next the Door, and another of two over it; four Lattice windows at the other End. In Front, a steep Meadow, enamelled with King-cups and Bluebells; alongside the gable end, a Village Road, with deep Cart ruts, and Hawthorn Hedges. Onlie one small Dwelling at hand, little better than a crazy Haystack; Sheep in the Field, Bees in the Honeysuckle, and a little rippling Rivulet flowing on continually.

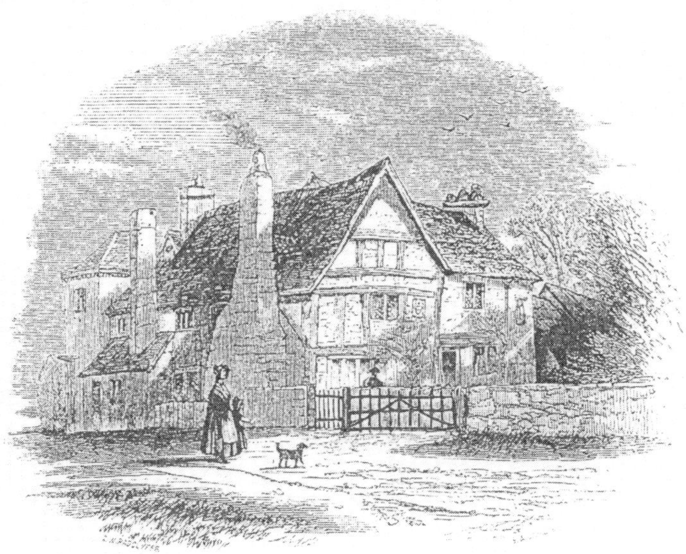

'Why, now you have sett me quite at Ease!' cries he, turning his bright Eyes thankfully towards the Sky.

Our life here is most pleasent. Father and I pass almost the whole of our time in the open Air – he dictating, and I writing; while Mother and Mary find 'emselves I know not whether more of Toyl or Pastime, within Doors, – washing, brewing, baking, pickling and preserving; to say Nought of the Dairy, which supplies us with endless Variety of Country Messes such as Father's Soul loveth. 'Tis well we have this Resource, or our Bill of Fare would be somewhat meagre; for the Butcher brings nothing but Mutton, except at Christmas. Then we make our own Bread, for now we keep strict Quarantine, the Plague having now so much spread, that there have e'en been one or two Cases in Chalfont.

Today, as we were sitting under the Hedge, we heard a rough Voice shouting, 'Hoy! hoy! what are you about there?' To which another Man's Voice, just over against us, deprecatingly replied, 'No Harm, I promise you, Master . . . We have clean Bills of Health; and my Wife and I, Foot sore and hungry, do but Purpose to set up our little Cabin against the Bank, till the Sabbath is overspent. 'But you must set it up Somewhere else,' cries the other, who was the Chalfont Constable; 'For we Chalfont Folks are very particular, and cant have Strangers come harbouring here in our Highways and Hedges, – dying and making themselves disagreeable.' 'But we dont mean to die or be disagreeable.' says the other. 'We are on our Way to my Wifes Parish; and, sure, you cannot stop us on the Kings Highway.' 'Oh but we can though.' says the Constable. 'And besides, this is not the Kings Highway, but only a Bye-way, which is next to private Property; and the Gentleman at present in Occupation of that private Property will be highly and justly offended of you go to give him the Plague.' 'Thats me,' says Father. 'Do tell him, Deb, not to be so hard on the poor People, but to let them abide where they are till the Sabbath is over. . . .

The friendship between Thomas Ellwood and Milton had been struck when the former went as a reader to the already blind poet, to improve his own learning. It is intriguing to think that a chance remark made at Chalfont should have induced the poet to write the companion volume to his famous Paradise Lost.

Some little time before I went to Aylesbury Prison, I was desired by my quondam master, Milton, to take an house for him in the neighbourhood where I dwelt, that he might go out of the City for the safety of himself and his family, the pestience in 1665 then growing hot in London. I took a pretty box for him in Giles's Chalfont, a mile from me, of which I gave him notice. Being now released and returned home, I soon made a visit to him, to welcome him into the country. After some common discourses had passed between us, he called for a manuscript of his, which, being brought, he delivered to me, bidding me take it home with me, and read it at my leisure, and, when I had so done, return it to him, with my judgement thereupon. When I came home, and had set mysely to read it, I found it was that excellent poem which he entitled 'Paradise Lost.' After I had with the best attention read it through, I made him another visit, and returned him his book, with due acknowledgement of the favour he had done me. He asked me how I liked, and what I thought of it, which I modestly, but freely told him; and after some further discourse about it, I pleasantly said to him, 'Thou hast said much here of Paradise Lost; but what hast thou to say to Paradise Found?' He made no answer to me, but sat some time in a muse; then brake off that discourse, and fell upon another subject. After the sickness was over, and the City well cleansed, and become safely habitable again, he returned thither; and when afterwards I went to wait on him there, he showed his second poem, called 'Paradise Regained,' and in a pleasant tone said to me, 'This is owing to you; for you put it into my head, by the question you put to me at Chalfont, which before I had no thought of.'

Views of paradise must have been far from Ellwood's mind when he subsequently found himself in Aylesbury prison along with other Quakers, all of whom were condemned for their beliefs. Quakerism played an important part in the story of the Chilterns with particular strongholds in such places as High Wycombe.

William Penn, a member of the Chiltern Penn family, joined the Quakers against his father's wishes and was persecuted for his beliefs. His founding of the Quaker state of Pennyslvania is renowned for being the only settlement of Europeans in America which was made without force of arms, and with due deference to the rights of the natives.

Once the colony was established he returned to England. Here he spent the rest of his life, and was interred in the meeting-house burial ground at Jordans. The following passage written 140 years after Penn's death by J. Leadbetter in A PILGRIMAGE TO THE SHRINES OF BUCKINGHAMSHIRE (1860), has a moving quality about it:

. . . after a few minutes' walk, we arrive at the little meeting-house of Jordans . . . surrounded by its verdant grave-yard, and half-ruined gateway and palisade, upon which time has wrought with its obliterating hand. . . . An old woman, her hair tinged with the frost of many winters, advanced towards us and said, 'Do you wish to see the meeting house, and the grave of William Penn, Sir?' We gladly assented, and, opening the little gate, she conducted us to the doorway of the chapel . . . We entered, and found ourselves in an oblong building panelled with oak, and bearing about it few marks of architectural embellishment . . . all was simple and plain as the quiet, yet earnest faith that in that lonely spot, had raised a temple to the Deity.

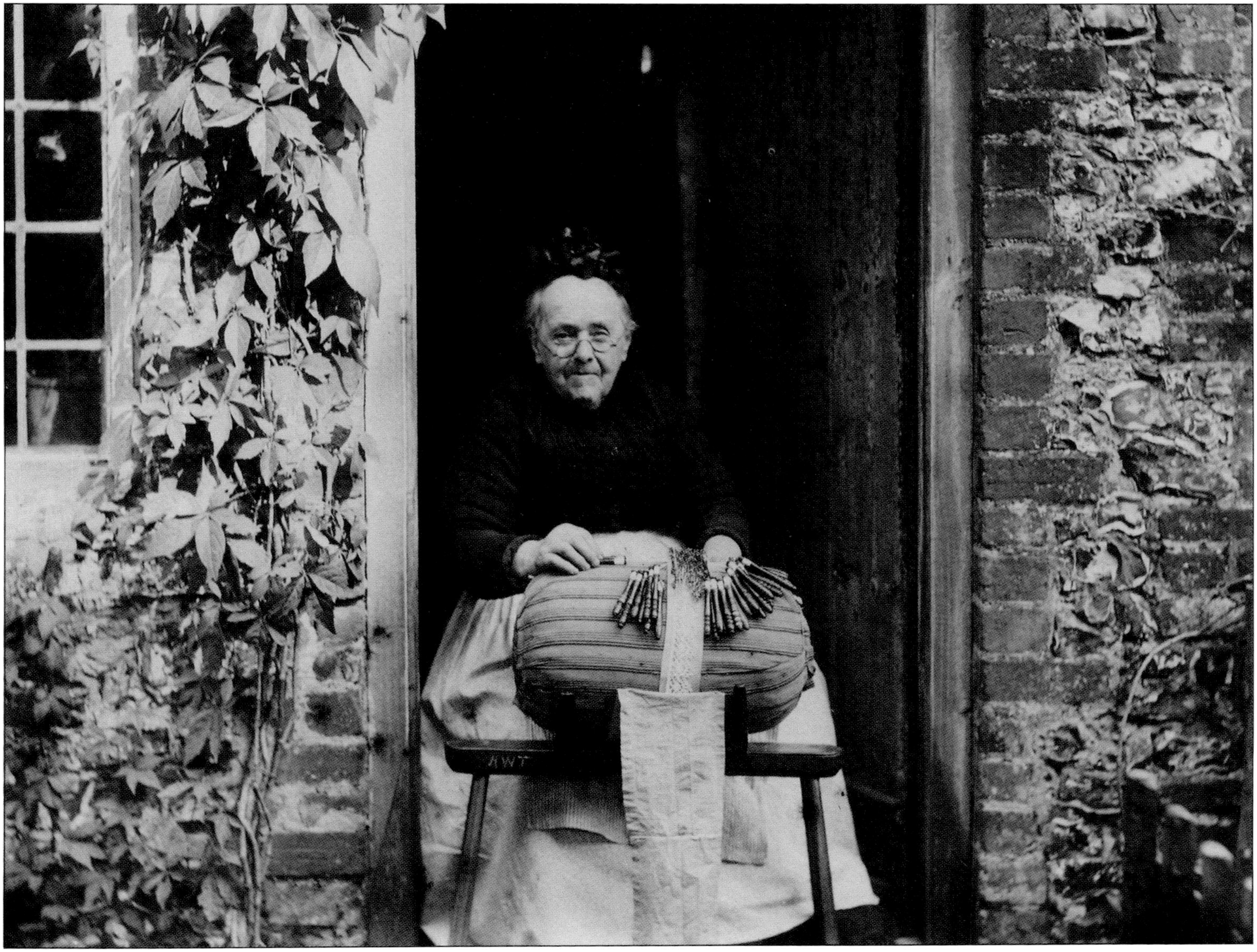

Monks Risborough

. . . we left the chapel, and entering the grave-yard, found a spot where a number of small mounds mark the resting places of Penn and his family. Here no monumental marble, or even a simple headstone marks the spot, where the founder of Pennsylvania found at last that rest and freedom from persecution, he had not experienced in his lifetime.

Every age and every part of the country produced its true eccentrics, and in the Chilterns of the seventeenth century we have two particular individuals. Taking the first of these, we have a certain Roger Crab who gained the nickname 'the Mad Hatter'. Margaret Verney has made a jocular suggestion that he was 'the undoubted ancester of the fourth guest who took tea in Wonderland with Alice, the Dormouse, and the March Hare.' It seems a strong possibility that Lewis Carroll in nearby Oxford may well have heard of this amusing and individual charcter. The DICTIONARY OF NATIONAL BIOGRAPHY *provides us with the following description of Crab, some of which is in the hatter of Chesham's own words:*

Roger Crab, hermit, a native of Buckinghamshire, was probably born about 1621. He says his mother had 20£. a year, or his father would not have married her. About 1641 he began to restrict himself to a vegetarian diet, avoiding even butter and cheese. From roots he got to a regimen of broth thickened with bran, and pudding made of bran and turnip leaves chopped together, and finally resorted to dock-leaves and grass. He drink nothing but water, and could live on three farthings a week. For seven years (probably 1642–9) he served in the parliamentary army. He states that while fighting for the parliament his skull was cloven to the brain, an injury which may account for some of his later eccentricities. The grounds of his abstention from animal food seems to have been the supposed moral effects of a flesh diet. 'Butchers,' he observed, 'are excluded from injuries; but the receiver is worse than the thief; so the buyer is worse than the butcher. His asceticism was connected with a rude kind of mystical revolt against established notions in religion. His notions often got him into trouble. Parliament, he says, imprisoned him for two years; and he 'got sentenced to death in the field from the lord Protector.' Leaving the army he became 'a haberdasher of hats' at Chesham; but he shut up his shop in 1651, and 'sold a considerable estate to give to the poor.' Settling on 'a small roode of ground' at Ickenham, near Uxbridge, he dwelt as a hermit in 'a mean cottage of his own building,' where he practised his austere regimen, wearing 'a sackcloth frock, and no band on his neck.' He dabbled in astronomy and physic, having from a hundred to a hundred and twenty patients at a time. Godbold, the minister of Uxbridge, told the people of Chesham he was a witch. . . . Ultimately he transfered his hermitage to Bethnal Green.

Our second eccentric is introduced by Robert Gibbs in his WORTHIES OF BUCKINGHAMSHIRE (1888), *who obviously felt that this character should not be omitted from his illustrious record:*

John Bigg – was known as the Dinton Hermit. It is said that in the earlier part of his life he was clerk to Simon Mayne, the regicide, who acted as a justice of the peace for Bucks for many years before his death. Bigg lived in a cave under ground; his method of mending his clothes, which he never exchanged, was by sewing fresh pieces of cloth or leather over the decayed parts. A shoe had been thus mended till the leather became more than tenfold its original thickness. . . . Some years ago the cave in which he lived was dug out with the hope of finding something relative to his history, but without success. He died in 1696.

Daniel Defoe in his work A TOUR THROUGH THE WHOLE OF GREAT BRITAIN 1724–26 *concentrates on*

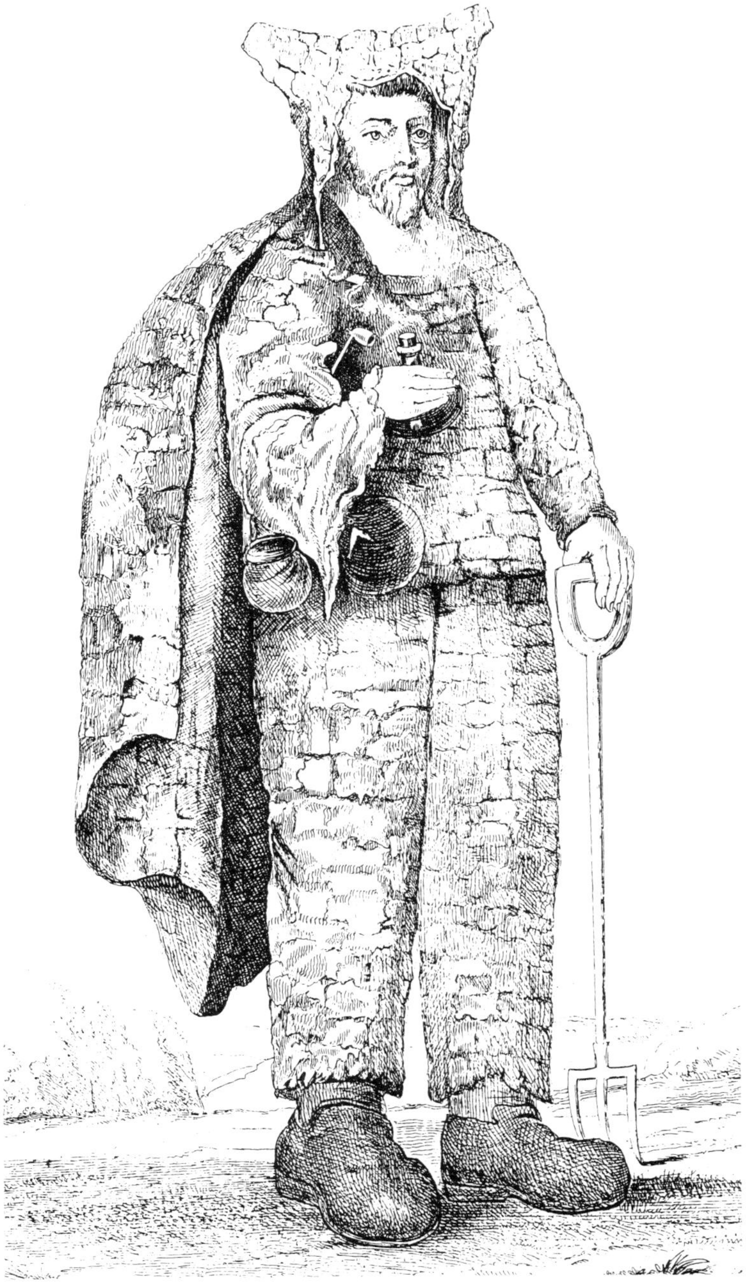

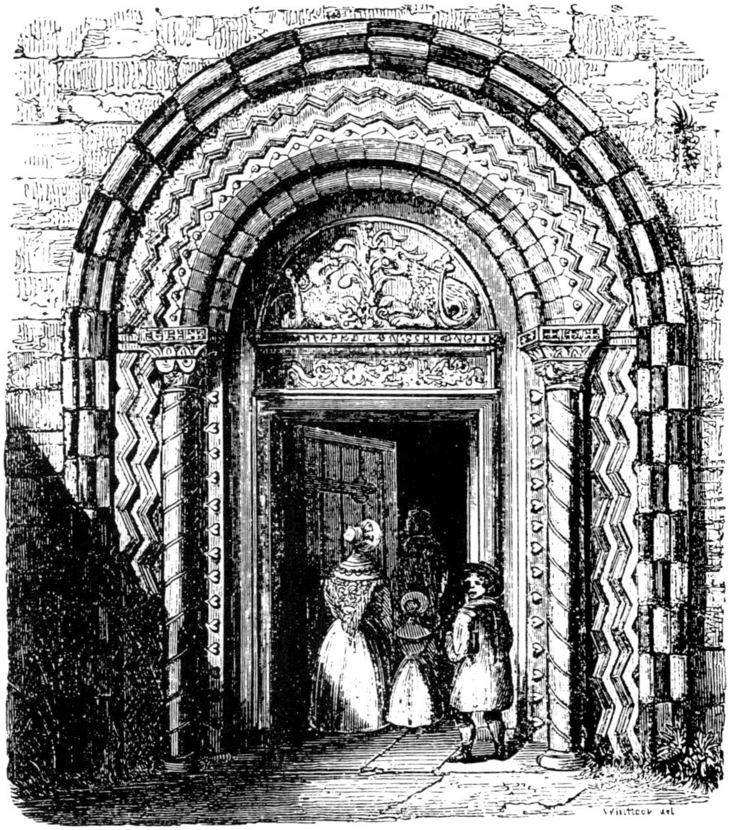

the fortunes of the merchant class with whom he clearly identifies. Though containing some inaccuracies (he refers to the River Loddon and means, in fact, the Wye), his work does reflect the economic and social conditions of England before the industrial revolution. The map of England in his time showed a very great concentration of wealth in the south of the country, particularly around the ports and the connecting rivers where transport was easiest.

The following extract describes a journey down the Thames valley which illustrates this aspect very clearly:

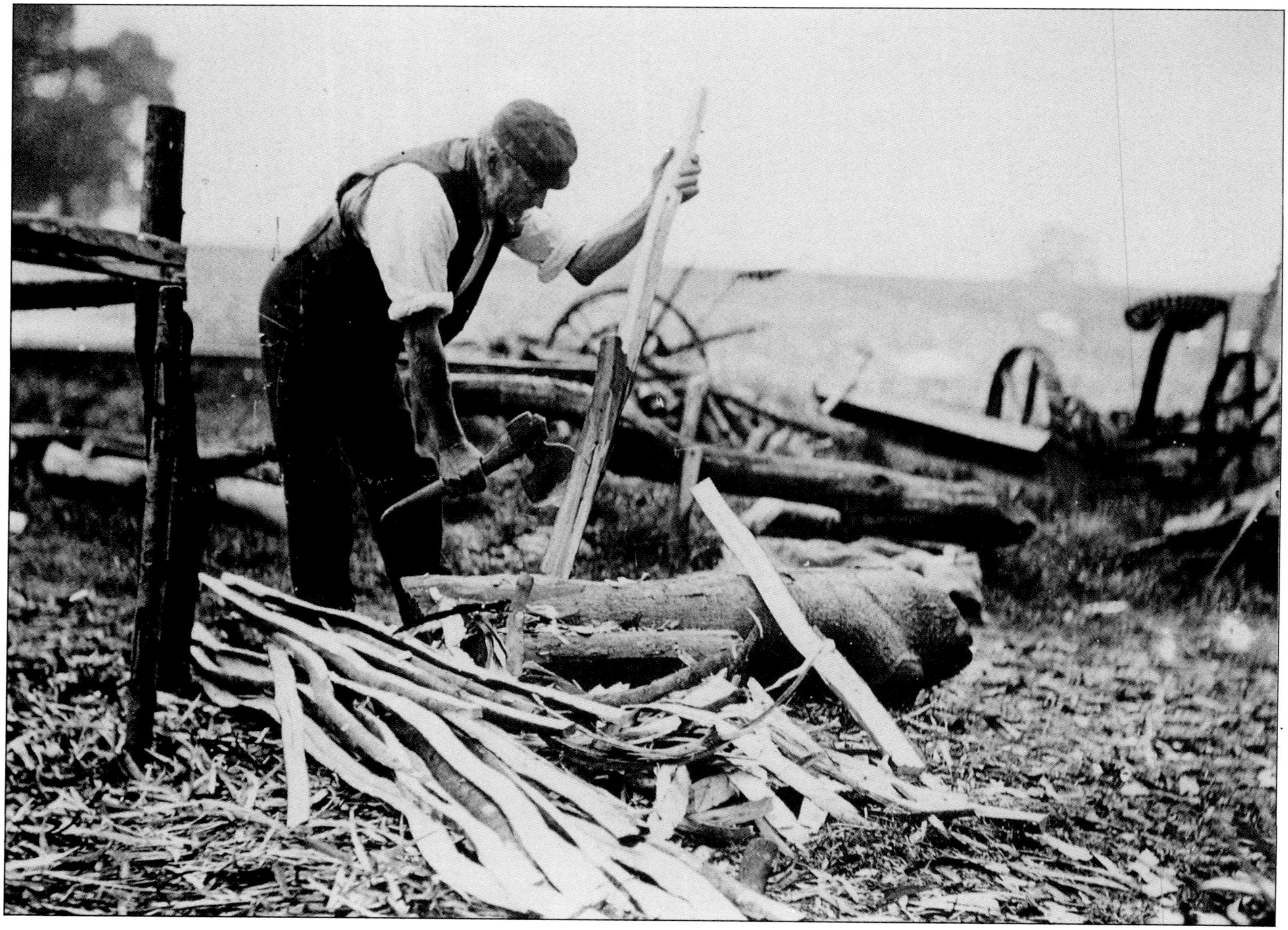

Hurdlemaker at Little Gaddesden

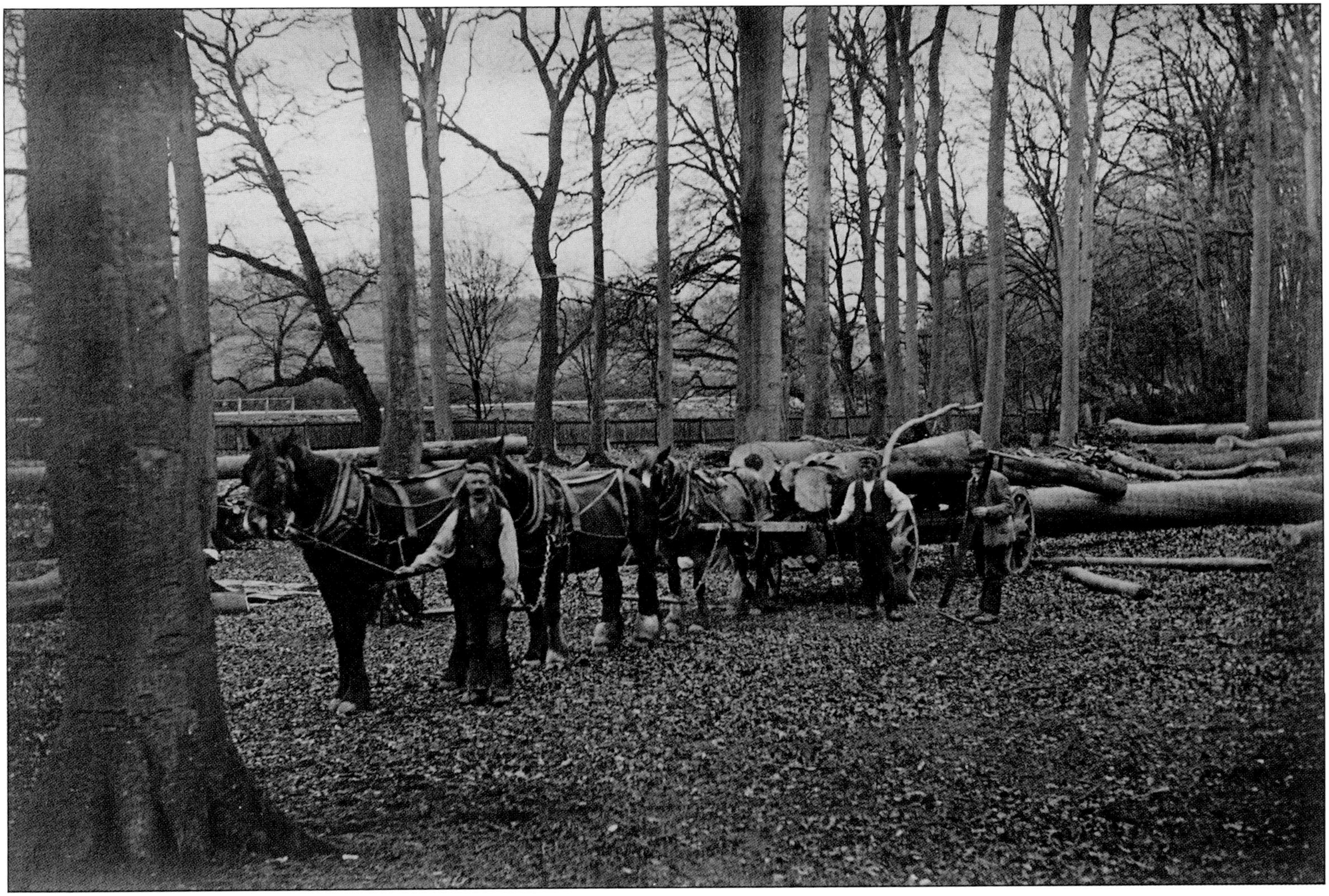

Timber hauling

My next stage from Reading, was to Great Marlow in Buckinghamshire, which, though not in the direct road, yet lying on the banks of the river of Thames, is, in my course, proper enough to be spoken of, and is particularly worth notice for several things.

1. It is a town of very great embarkation on the Thames, not so much for goods wrought here, (for the trade of the town is chiefly in bone lace) but for goods from the neighbouring towns, and particularly, a very great quantity of malt, and meal, is brought hither from High-Wickham, a large market town, about — miles off, which is one of the greatest corn markets on this side of England, and lies on the road from London to Oxford.

2. Between High Wickham and Marlow, is a little river called the Loddon, on which are a great many mills, and particularly corn mills; the first of these, grind and dress the wheat, and then the meal is sent to Marlow, and loaded on board the barges for London: and the second makes great quantities of printing paper, and that, very good of its kind, and cheap, such as generally is made use of in printing our news papers, journals, &c. and smaller pamphlets; but not much fine, or large, for bound books, or writing.

3. On the river of Thames, just by the side of this town, though on the other bank, are three very remarkable mills, which are called the Temple-Mills, and are called also the Brass-Mills, and are for making Bisham Abbey Battery Work, as they call it, viz. brass kettles, and pans, &c. of all sorts. They have first a foundary, where, by the help of lapis caliminaris, they convert copper into brass, and then, having cast the brass in large broad plates, they beat them out by force of great hammers, wrought by the water mills, into what shape they think fit for sale. Those mills went on by the strength of a good stock of money in a company or a partnership, and with very good success, 'till at last, they turned it into what they call a Bubble, brought it to Exchange-Alley, set it a stock-jobbing in the days of our South Sea madness, and brought it up to be sold at one hundred pounds per share, whose intrinsick worth was perhaps ten pounds, 'till, with the fall of all those things together, it fell to nothing again. Their treasurer, a tradesman in London, failed, having misapply'd about thirty thousand pounds of their money, and then, as is usual where want of success goes before, quarelling amongst themselves followed after, and so the whole affair sunk into a piece of mere confusion and loss, which otherwise was certainly a very beneficial undertaking.

4. Next to these are two mills, both extraordinary in themselves, one for making of thimbles, a work excellently well finished, and which performs to admiration, and another for pressing of oyl from rape-seed, and flax-seed, both which, as I was told, turn to very good account to the proprietors.

Here is also brought down a very great quantity of beech wood, which grows in the woods of Buckinghamshire more plentifully than in any other part of England. This is the most useful wood, for some uses, that grows, and without which, the city of London would be put to more difficulty, than for anything of its kind in the nation.

1. For fellies for the great carrs, as they are called, which ply in London streets for carrying of merchandizes, and for cole-carts, dust-carts, and such like sorts of voiture, which are not, by the city laws, allowed to draw with shod wheels or wheels tyr'd with iron.

2. For billet wood for the king's palaces, and for the plate and flint glass houses, and other such nice purposes.

3. Beech quarters for divers uses, particularly chairmakers, and turnery wares. The quantity of this, brought from hence, is almost incredible, and yet so is the country overgrown with beech in those parts, that it is bought very reasonable, nor is there like to be any scarcity of it for time to come . . .

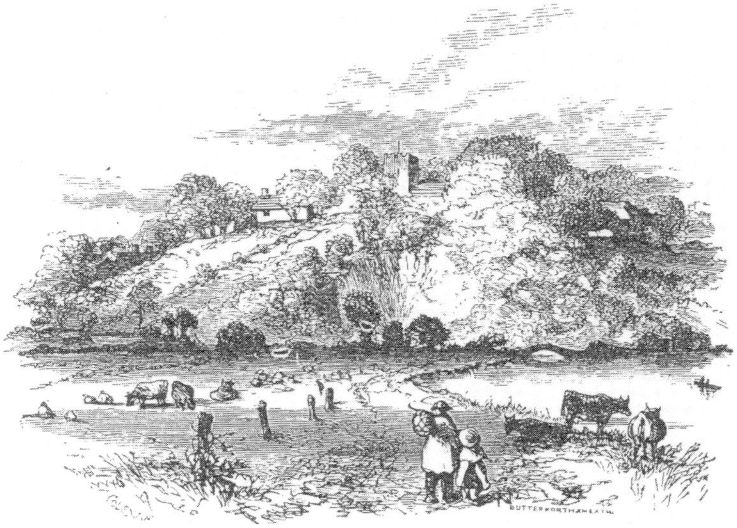

There are two other towns on the Thames, which I have already mentioned, viz. Henly and Maidenhead, which have little or nothing remarkable in them; but that they have great business also, by the trade for malt and meal and timber for London, which they ship, or load, on their great barges for London, as the other towns do.

With Defoe we move to Tring where his theme is enclosure of common land, a feature that eventually changed the landscape irrevocably until, by a twist of irony, the more recent and equally dramatic changes wrought by the so called 'prairie' farm.

At Tring . . . is a most delicious house, built a la moderne, as the French call it, by the late Mr Guy, who was for many years Secretary of the Treasury, and continued it till near his death . . . There was an eminent contest here between Mr. Guy, and the poor of the parish, about his enclosing part of the common to make him a park; Mr. Guy presuming upon his power, set up his pales, and took in a large parcel of open land, call'd Wiggington Common; the cottagers and farmers oppos'd it, by their complaints a great while; but finding he went on with his work, and resolv'd to do it, they rose upon him, pull'd down his banks, and forced up his pales, and carried away the wood, or set it on a heap and burnt it; and this they did several times, till he was oblig'd to desist; after some time he began again, offering to treat with the people, and to give them any equivalent for it: But that not being satisfactory, they mobb'd him again. How they accommodated it at last, I know not; but I see that Mr. Gore [*Mr Guy's house was bought by Sir William Gore and left by him to his eldest son.*] has a park, and a very good one but not large: I mention this as an instance of the popular claim in England; which we call right of commonage, which the poor take to be as much their property, as a rich man's land is his own.

As we leave Defoe in Tring, we meet William Ellis living in Little Gaddesden, and author of various books relating to farming, including the PRACTICAL FARMER *or* HERTFORDSHIRE HUSBANDMAN. *Apart from his more specific writing on farming methods, he provides us with some social comment relating to the area.*

In short, it is our Notion in Hertfordshire that Gentlemen, Yeoman, or Farmer manages best, who victuals his Harvest-men with Pyes, Pasties, Cheese, Milk, Beef, Bacon, or Pickled Pork, Beans and Pease, with other culinary preparations, and with well-brewed strong and small beer, for such a one stands the best chance of Hiring the best Hands, that will go on briskly with their work, and do a good Deal of it in a Day.

In Wheat Harvest Time, which commonly lasts about a Fortnight, our Men set out for the Field by four of the clock in the Morning, and return Home about eight at Night.

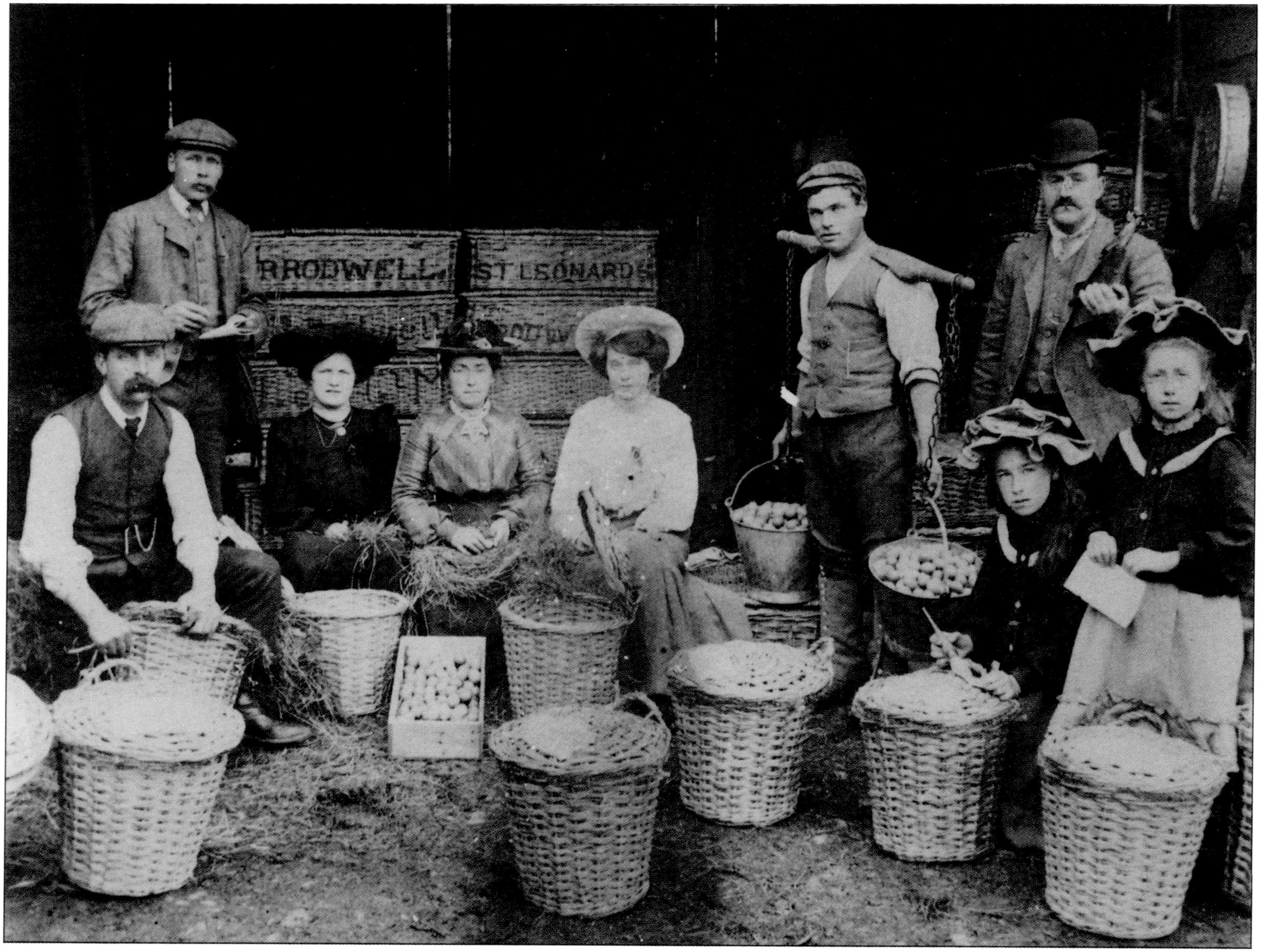

Packing pheasant eggs at Cholesbury/St Leonards

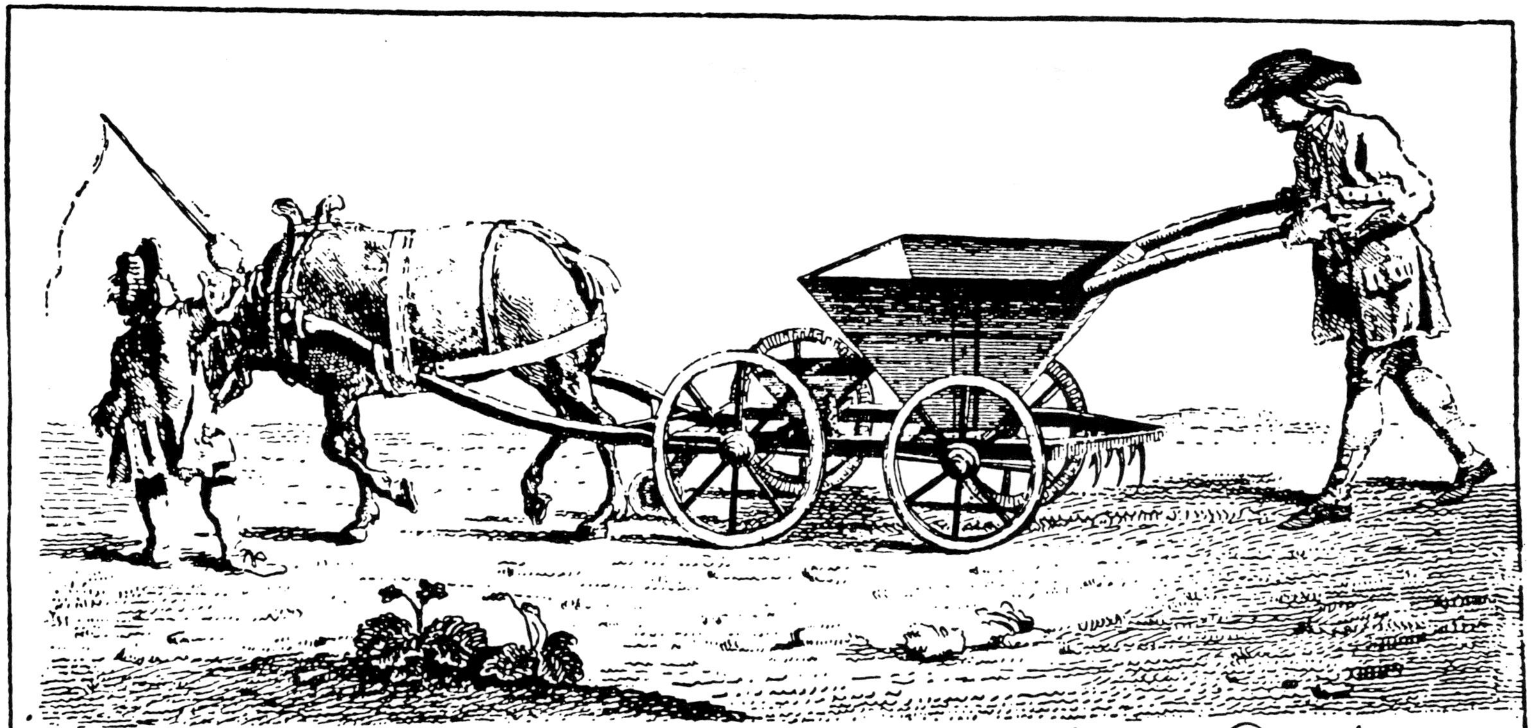

This four Wheel Drill Plow, with a Seed and a Manure Hopper was first Invented in the Year 1745 and is now in Use with Wm. Ellis at Little Gaddesden near Hempstead in Hertfordshire. where any person may View the same. It is so light that a Man may Draw it. but Generally drawn by a pony or little Horse.

The Men usually Eat five times a Day . . . At Dinner Time, which should always be at One o'clock, the victuals should be in the Field; for it was the Saying of a Notable Housewife, that as the Men expected it at that hour, if it was not Brought accordingly, they would Lag in their work, and lose Time expecting it. Broad Beans and Bacon or Pork one day, and Beef with carrots or Turnips or Cabbages or Cucumbers or Potatoes, is with Plumb Pudding, good Dinner Victuals.

The Hertfordshire Way of making Plumb-pudding in Harvest Time

Pudding is so natural to our Harvest-men, that without it they think they cannot make an agreeable Dinner . . . Now to make a Plumb-pudding of the better sort for six Harvest-mens Dinners, our Housewife makes use of a Pottle of Flower, a Quart of skim or new Milk, three eggs, half or three quarters of a Pound of Raisons, and half a

Pound of chopt Suet. This being stirred and well mixed together, with a little Salt, is to be tied up in a Linen Cloth or Bag; but not too tight, that it may have Room to swell. Boil it three or (better) four Hours; and if they cannot dine on this with good boiled Beef, or with Pork, or with Bacon and Roots, or Herbs, they deserve to want a Dinner.

We are told that Ellis, who had an obvious regard for the 1st Duke of Bridgewater, interrupted his own writing to compose the following personal obituary:

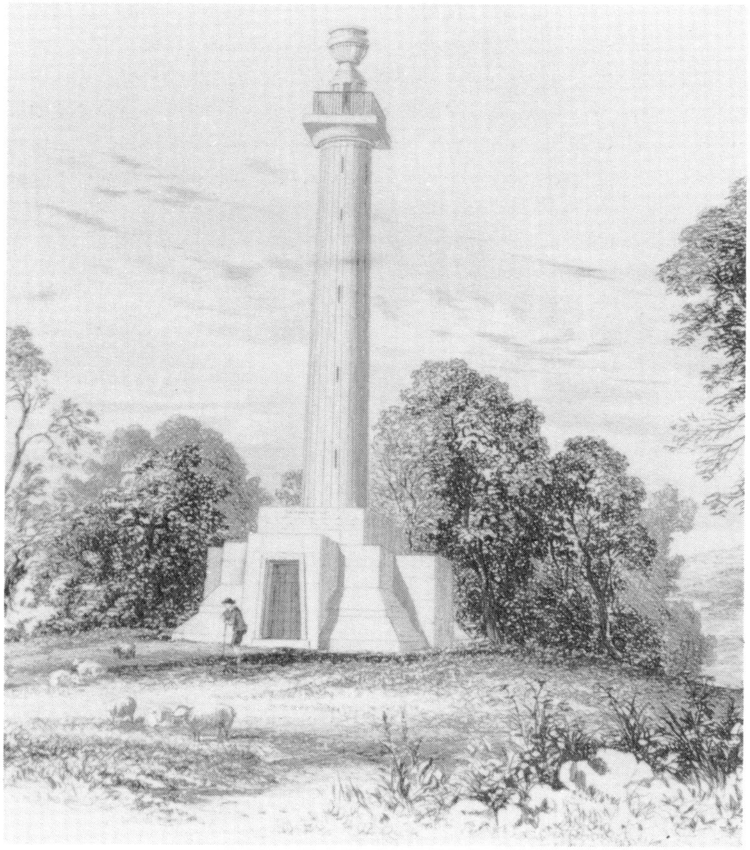

The Character of that great Economist Scroop Egerton, Late Duke of Bridgewater

This Nobleman was certainly possessed of many fine Qualities, particularly that of Temperance in eating and drinking and in many Branches of living. He was (I believe) never known to be intoxicated with Liquor, for he and his Duchess seldom or ever, exceeded a Pint or a Quart Bottle of Wine at Dinner.

His Breakfast was a Mess of Water Gruel, and he always rose betimes, while in the Country; when he had eaten it he would ride or walk out till ten, and then come home to a Tea breakfast, with his Duchess and Daughters.

His Supper was Tarts, Hasty Pudding, Pancake or other light Food, in refusal of Flesh; but he generally eat as hearty a Dinner as any Man, having extraordinary Plenty of all Manner of Dainty Provisions, and two Men Cooks to dress them.

His Exercise was walking amongst his many Workmen, with whom he was so delighted, that he seemed never better pleased, than when he was giving them Orders and seeing them work in the best planted Park in England, in his many inclosed Fields, Woods and Gardens.

And so extremely fond was this Gentleman of a Country Life, that he would even now and then take a Trip, even in Winter, down to his seat at Ashridge from London; and not withstanding the Fatigue of his Journey, I have seen him, the same Day, walk through a great Shower of Rain, to a considerable Distance in his Great Coat, to view a new-made Pond or other Novelty. His Number of Cart, Race, and other Horses was one hundred and fifty at least; his red and fallow Deer, above one thousand; his menial servants of all sorts, about sixty; and his Day Labourers, thirty.

And although he kept a large Pack of the finest fleetest Hounds in the Country, yet he would latterly seldom go with them; But on the Contrary has been heard to say, he wished in his Youth he had minded them less, and the Improvement of his Estate more. However he pretty well redeemed his lost Time, for he planted much, and seldom felled a Tree unless at a very great Age indeed. His Household and other Parts of his Economy were attended with a very close Inspection, particularly that of his Servants Accompts; his Housekeeping was exercised in Plenty, yet with Frugality; and there was always enough of every Thing that was good; his Corn-fields furnished his House with Bread, Malt, Oatmeal etc; and he sold much Grain besides at Hempstead Market; his Cows supplied Milk, cream and Butter, but his Cheese he bought . . . his Oxen, Sheep, Lambs and Calves he generally fatted in his own Grounds, and commonly killed an Ox every Week or Fortnight, besides smaller Meat, giving large Quantities of it ever Week to the Adjacent poor People, to the Making of their Families Hearts glad.

Peter Kalm, a Swedish traveller, en route to North America in 1748 broke his journey in England.

25th March 1748

In the morning I undertook at the cost and at the request of Herr Vice-President Baron Bjelke, a journey to see Mr. Ellis, who lived at Little Gaddesden in Hertfordshire. Mr. Ellis was a man who had a great reputation for his Practique in Rural Economy.

Kalm conveys in his writing the objectivity of an outsider, making pointed observations and comparisons with Sweden at the same period.

Here he is noticeably surprised to find that though winters in England are milder than in Sweden, far more fuel is used during this season:

But, I will name the reason. The fire-places are here built . . . so that there is nothing to retain the warmth. . . . No, here all the warmth goes freely up the chimney; windows, doors, roof, floor, etc., are not stopped or made tight, but the wind and cold get freely to play through them. There is no moss on the inner side or in the middle of the roof. Therefore it is not wonderful, if in the winter time it is as cold in as it is out.

In this country in the farm cottages, the fire-hearth is so low that it is on a plane with the floor itself. The chimney-places in these are also so large that three or four stools can be accommodated within the chimney-place, on which they sit to warm themselves.

As soon as the wind begins to be somewhat fresh, as it commonly is from and in a great part of October, till and in a great part of April, wood is for the most part burnt on the hearth from morning till evening. Round it the folk sit and warm themselves; and when the cold is somewhat more severe, the women are seen sitting near the fire, without doing the least things more than prate.

Again we recognize Kalm's incredulity regarding the work-load of English women compared with their Swedish counter-parts. However he is not without praise for English womanhood:

One hardly ever sees a woman here trouble herself in the least about outdoor duties, such as tending (beasts) in the arable and meadows etc. The duty of the women in the district scarcely consists in anything else but preparing food, which they commonly do very well, though roast beef and Pudding forms nearly all an Englishman's eatables.

Besides that, they wash and scour dishes and floors etc., for about cleanliness they are very careful, and especially in these things, to wash clothes, and to hem one thing and another minutely.

They never take the trouble to bake, because there is a baker in every parish or village, from which they always have new bread. Nearly the same can be said about

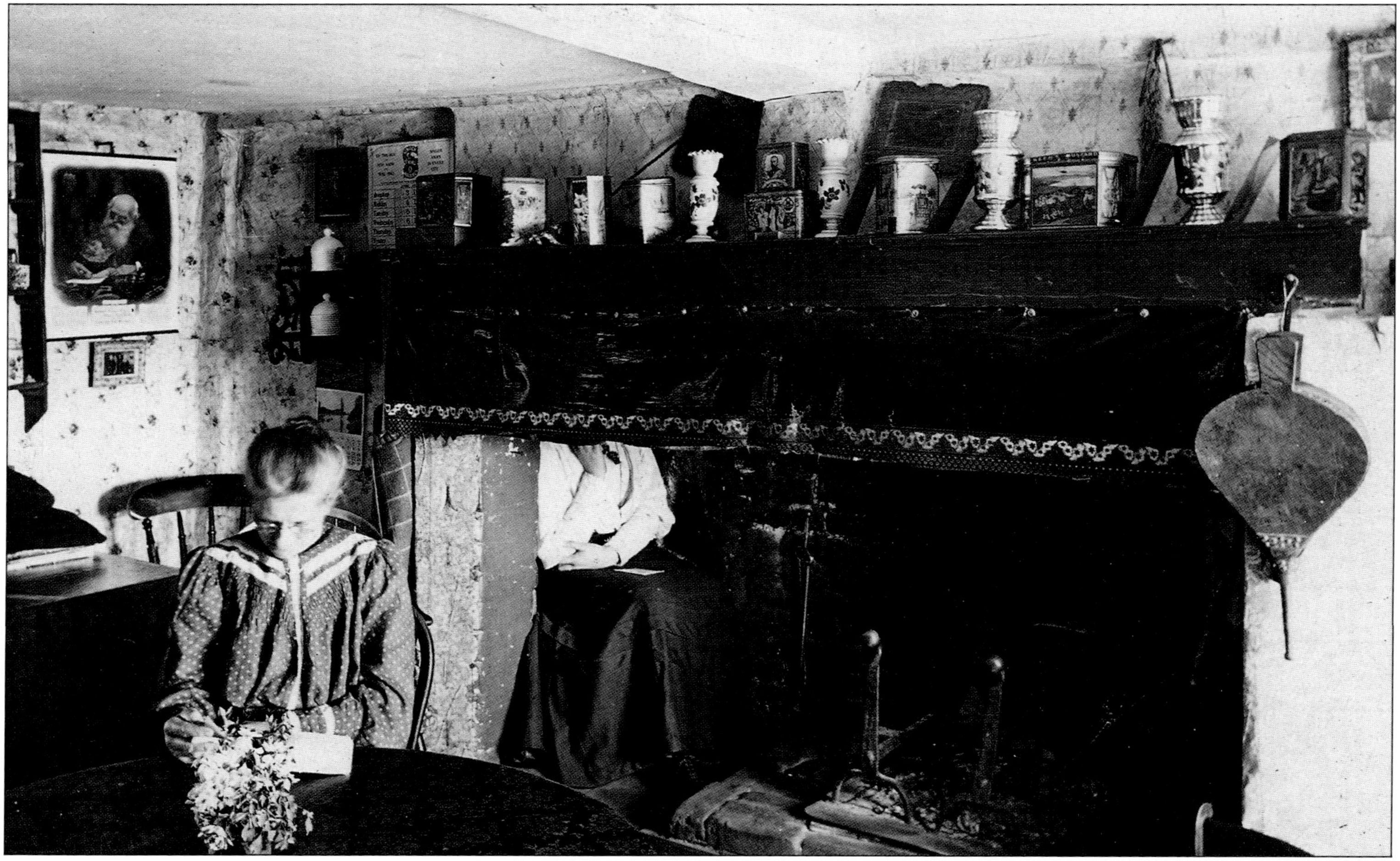

Chimney corner in Bucks

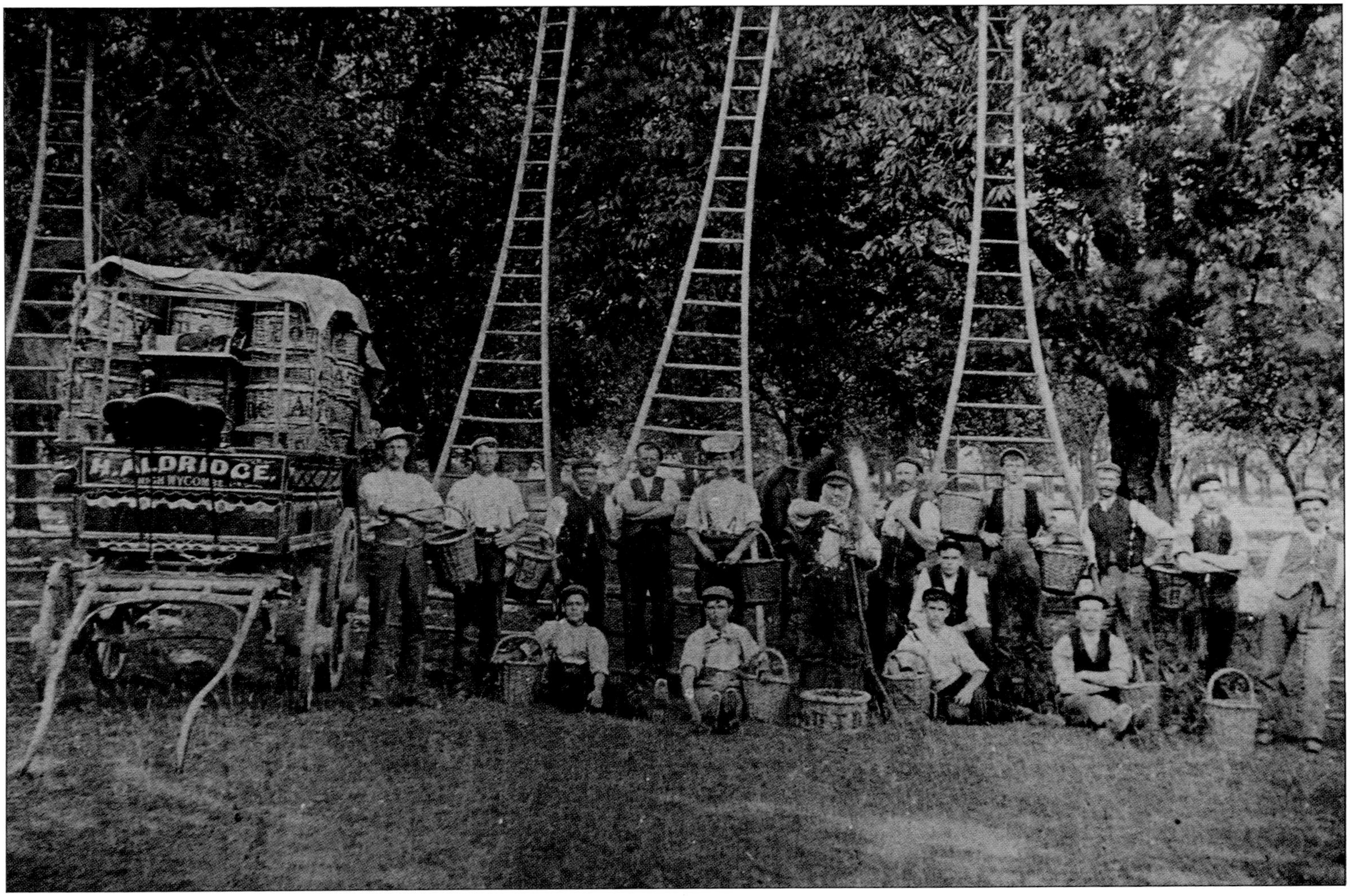

Cherry pickers

brewing. Weaving and spinning is also in most houses a more than rare thing, because their many manufacturers save them from the necessity of such. For the rest it belongs to the men to tend the cattle, milk the cows, and to perform all the work in the arable fields and meadows, and in the lodge and lathe etc. I confess that I first rubbed my eyes several times to make them Clear, because I could not believe I saw aright when I first came here, out in the country, and saw the farmers houses full of young women, while the men on the contrary, went out both morning and evening to where the cattle were, milk-pail in hand, sat down to milk, and afterwards carried the milk home.

In short, when one enters a house and has seen the women cooking, washing floors, plates and dishes, darning a stocking or sewing a chemise, washing and starching linen clothes, he has, in fact, seen all their household economy and all that they do the whole of God's long day, year in and year out. . . .

But they can never be deprived of the credit of being very handsome and lively in society. In pleasant conversation, agreeable repartie, polite sallies, in a word, in all that the public calls politesse and savoir vivre, they are never wanting.

They are lucky in having turned the greater part of the burden of responsible management on to the men, so that it is very true that England is a paradise for ladies and women.

Returning to William Ellis we make the acquaintance of another tree synonymous with the Chilterns. The famed cherry orchards, now largely displaced by housing, were once a common sight, as were human bird scarers or starvers, and the distinctively-shaped ladders of exceptional length.

The following passage comes from Ellis' CHILTERN AND VALE FARMING *of 1733*:

Several good properties of this tree have slipped the Knowledge and Notice of Authors both Ancient and Modern, I shall be the more singular in the illustration thereof; and because this county of Hertford does certainly more abound in plantations of the Common Black Cherry, than any other in England, and particularly in the western part where I now live, is as famous for the Black as Kent is for the Red or Flemish Cherry.

Reasons humbly offered on behalf of the counties of Hertford, Bucks, Kent etc for encouraging the growth of the Black and other Cherry Trees.

Whereas this Fruit is of itself of that healthful and cordian nature, that it is a collector of several sorts of liquors particularly in molosses and malt brandies: also in Beer Their excellancy is found, as well as in the wholesome wines, syrups and distilled waters that are made of them, whose medicinal qualities are best known to the Physician, Apothocary etc.

The Black, wild Cherry for many years has been a sort of Harvest both to the Owner and the Poor; to the first, in that it is a fruit that most opportunely preceeds the Corn Harvest, and thereby is of such Consequence to the Farmers Interest, that it often returns Money enough to defray the Charge of Inning his General Harvest; the latter are employed in gathering them as they sufficiently ripen, and so become a subsistence for some time to their poor Family. The higgler also that buys them, shares their Advantage by turning the Penny at the London Market, where they are generally twice retailed, and where the Distiller used to furnish himself for making a spirit from this Fruit, and collecting his Brandies by their salubrious infusions.

The Black Cherry Tree in particular is endowed with several beneficial Qualities: for it is a wood that is next serviceable to the Oak for the inside Buildings of Houses, Barns etc. And because of its long Duration, and Strength, is of Service to the Commonwealth in general; and for its fine red colour, which is increased by letting it lie two or three years on the Ground after it is cut down: and then it

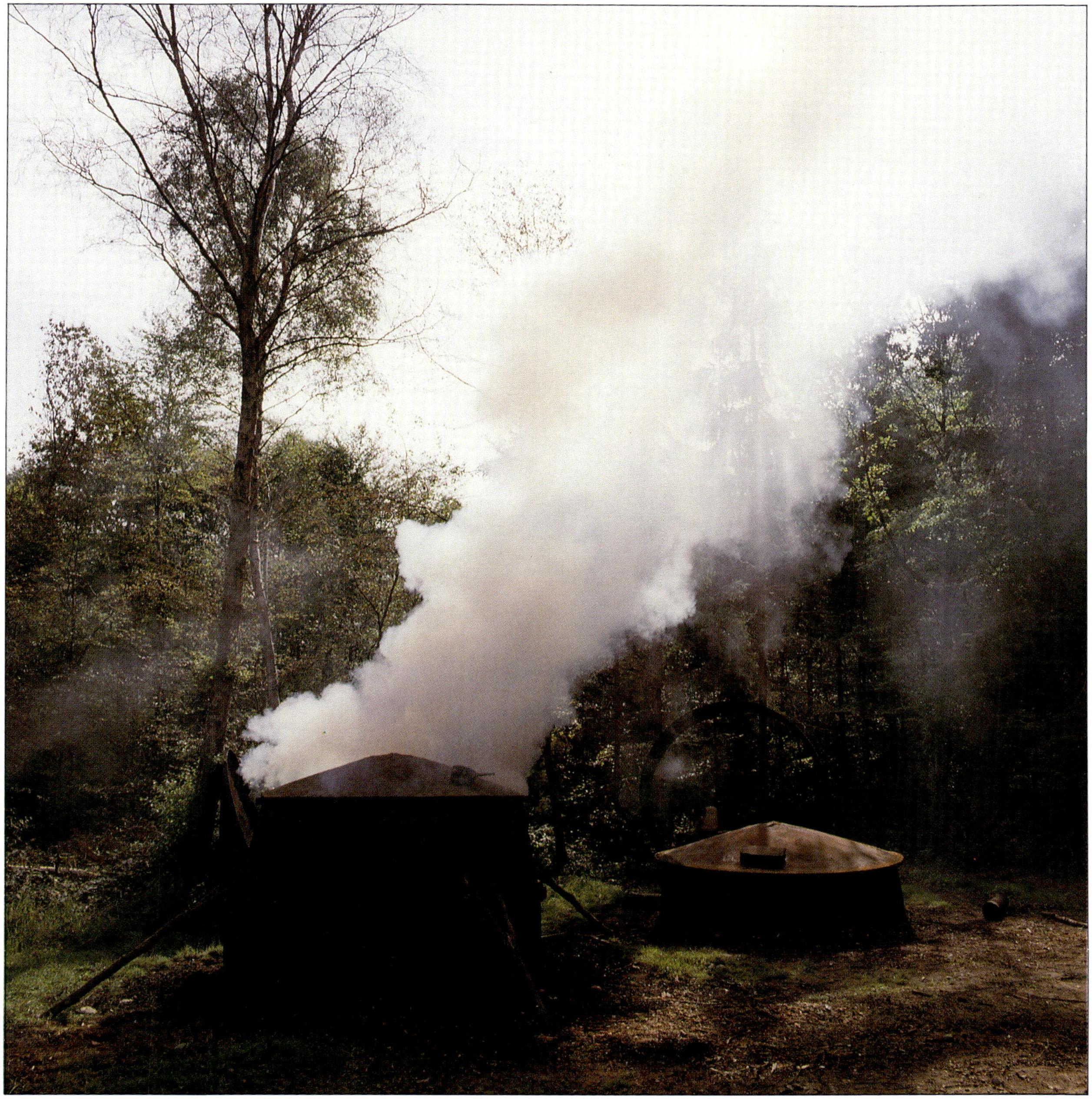

Charcoal burning near Tring

so neatly counterfeits Mohogony wood, as hardly to be discerned in the difference, both in its Grain and Colour, by the help of a certain Liquor that the Joyner stains it with.

Just crossing the boundary into the nineteenth century, the Revd St John Priest in his GENERAL VIEW OF THE AGRICULTURE OF BUCKINGHAMSHIRE (1810), provides us with a further comment on the cherry industry and also one on human conceit!

Many cherries are grown, and sent to Aylesbury and London market. It would puzzle a moralist to conjecture how a cherry ground should be made the cause of local pride; but so it is at Flackwell-heath. With shallow vain persons, let anything be done, either by a accident or natural means, which produces effects of public notoriety, and even though they themselves had no concern in producing them, but merely live in the neighbourhood, yet they are so infatuated as to feel an unaccountable pride in any advantage attending it, and depression of spirits at its disadvantages. Flackwell-heath abounds with cherries. Should the season be propitious to the growth of this fruit, this neighbourhood vaunts itself, and is as much puffed up, as if they were the cause of the abundance; so that if upon the road you meet at the cherry season a person belonging to the place, and necessity obliges, or curiosity induces you to ask him from whence he comes, he replies immediately, 'From Flackwell-heath. Where do you think?' On the contrary, should some perverse cause have prevented the growth of cherries, or adverse winds and frost have cut them off, and you should have occasion to put the same question, he replies (But mark his depression), 'From Flackwell-heath – God help us!'

A custom relating to a village in the heart of the Chilterns, Drayton Beauchamp, is recorded by a writer under the intriguing pseudonym of KAPPA in the RECORDS OF BUCKS for 1858. Though the custom appears to span many decades, he is referring to a specific occasion in the late eighteenth century or early nineteenth century. These customs could become a burden to those who had to provide – be it squire or vicar – but the moral of this story must be that it is unwise to take remedial action into one's own hands!

An ancient custom existed in the parish of Drayton Beauchamp, called Stephening, a brief notice of which may not only be amusing, but may elicit some evidence as to its origin, which at present is totally unknown in the neighbourhood. On St. Stephen's Day all the inhabitants used to pay a visit to the Rectory, and there assert their right to partake of as much bread and cheese and ale as they chose at the Rector's expence. On one of these occasions, as tradition states, the then Rector, being a penurious old batchelor, determined to put a stop, if possible, to this rather expensive visit from his parishioners. Accordingly, when St Stephen's Day arrived, he ordered his housekeeper not to open the window-shutters or unlock the doors of his house, and to be perfectly silent and motionless whenever any person was heard approaching. At the usual time, the parishioners began to cluster about the house. They knocked first at one door, then at the other, then tried to open them, and on finding them fastened, called aloud for admittance. No voice replied; no movement was heard within. 'Surely the Rector and his housekeeper must both be dead!' exclaimed several voices at one, and a general awe pervaded the whole group. Eyes were then applied to the key-holes, and to every crevice in the window-shutters, when the Rector was seen beckoning to his old terrified housekeeper to be still and silent. A simultaneous shout convinced him that his design was understood. Still he consoled himself with the hope that his larder and cellar were secure, as the house could not be entered. But his hope was speedily dissipated. Ladders

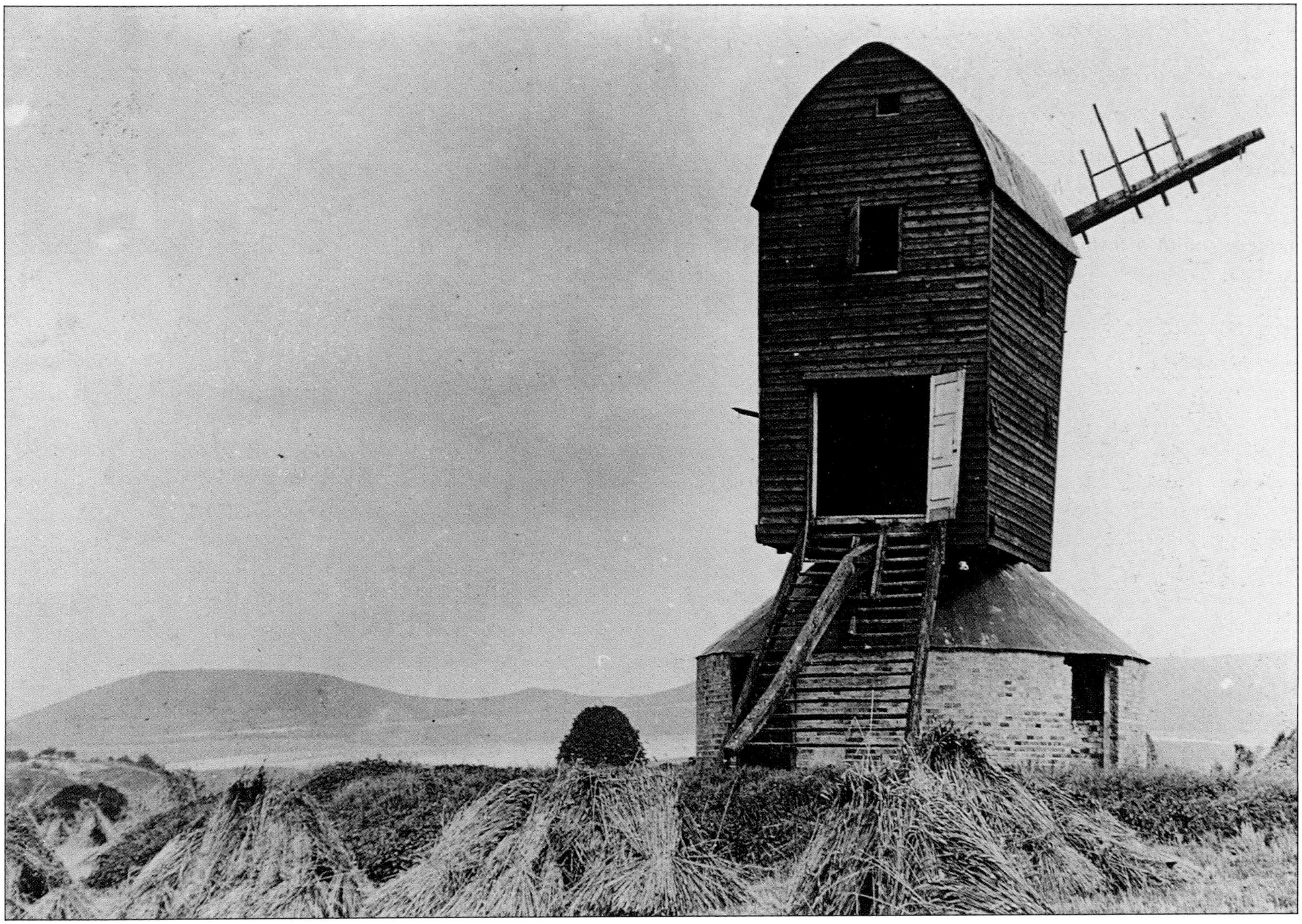

Pitstone

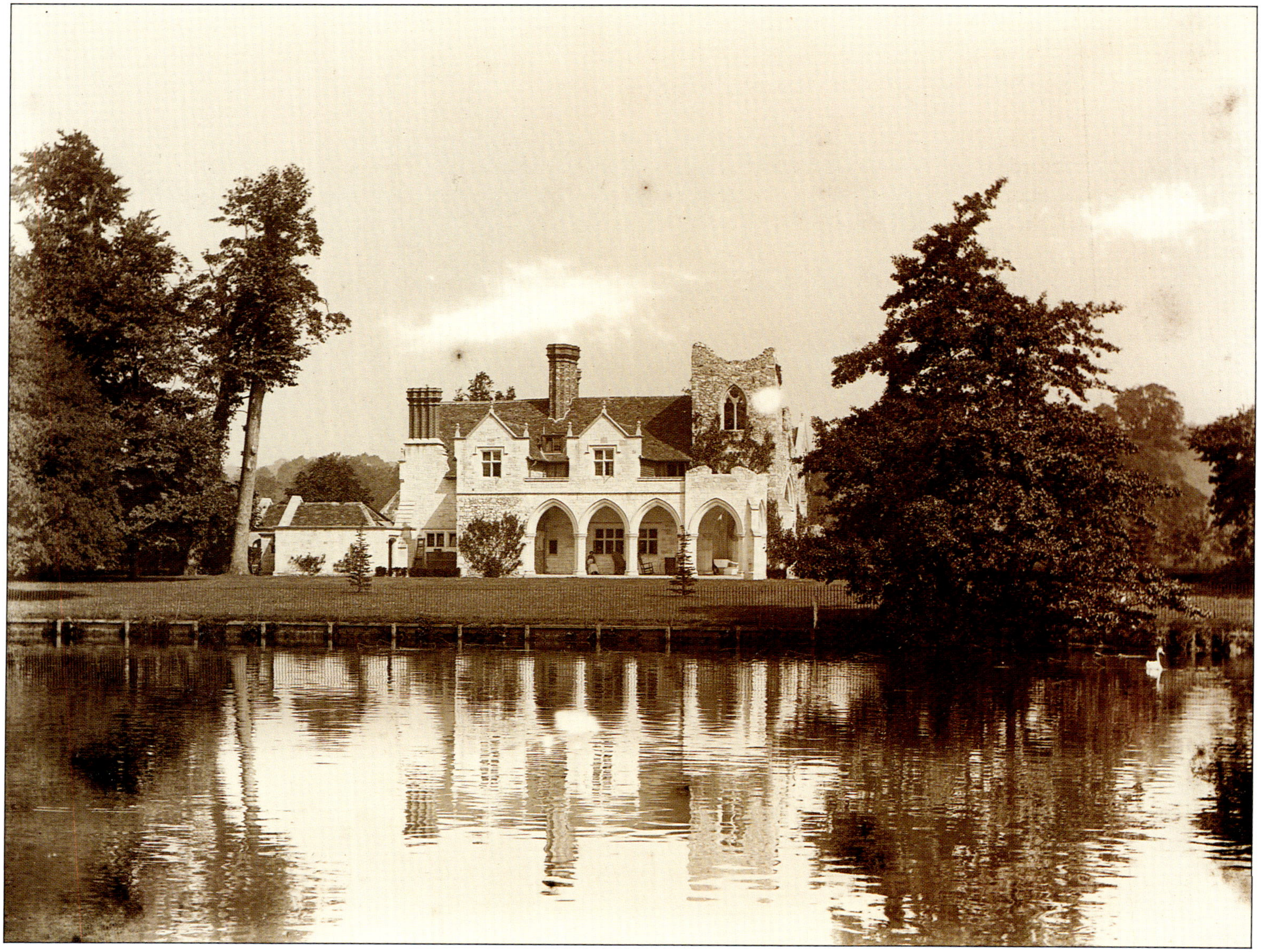

Medmenham Abbey

were reared against the roof, tiles hastily thrown off, half a dozen sturdy young men entered, rushed down the stairs, and threw open both the outer doors. In a trice a hundred or two unwelcome visitors rushed into the house, and began unceremoniously to help themselves to such fare as the larder and cellar afforded; for no special stores having been provided for the occasion, there was not, of course, half enough bread and cheese for such a multitude. To the Rector and his housekeeper the festival was converted into the most rigid Fast-day they had ever observed.

The Hell Fire Club, usually associated with the caves at West Wycombe, had its true home at Medmenham Abbey on the banks of the River Thames.

At the time of the dissolution the Commissioners returned the following details:

Of the Order of St. Bernard; the clear value £20 6s.2d.; monks there 2, and both desyren to go to houses of religion; servants, none; bells worth £2 6s.8d.; the house wholly in ruin; the value of the movable goods, £1 3s.8d.; woods, none; debts, none.

In stark contrast the quasi-religious order founded in 1745 is given a pungent description, laced with Victorian morals, by the Honourable G. Berkeley:

The Hell Fire Club, of which Sir Francis Dashwood was a member, as well as several others . . . was established, as it seemed, simply to outrage all the refined usages of society, as well as to manifest contempt for religion, and the attributes of Divine worship. It was this desire to defile all things that are usually held sacred that lead the club to select the ruins of Medmenham Abbey as a place for their coarse and detestable debaucheries.

Gibbs, in his WORTHIES OF BUCKINGHAMSHIRE, suitably respectful of Sir Francis Dashwood in general, could not allow his dubious activities to pass unmentioned:

Lax as were the morals of the age in which he lived, it may be questioned whether he was surpassed by any of his contemporaries in profaneness, obscenity, and vice. His wild and irreverant frolics were the constant talk of his time.

The demise of the club followed the supposed actual events which were later vividly portrayed by Charles Johnstone in his satirical novel CHRYSAL, OR THE ADVENTURES OF A GUINEA (1760–5):

. . . for which injustice he resolved to revenge himelf in the most signal manner. For this purpose, he had contrived the night before to bring into his cell a great baboon, which he had provided for the occasion. When the brotherhood retired to their cells after dinner . . . to prepare for the ceremony, he availed himself of the office of keeper of the chapel, which he had then filled, to convey this creature, dressed up in the fantastic garb, in which childish imagination clothes devils, into the chapel; where he shut him up in a large chest . . . To the spring of the lock of this chest he fastened a cord, which he drew under the carpet that was on the floor to his own seat . . . and, by giving it a pull, open the chest, and let the baboon loose whenever he pleased, without being perceived by any of the rest of the company. Accordingly, when they were all in the height of their mirth, on my master's kneeling down, and with hands and eyes raised towards heaven, repeating an invocation, in the perverted phrase of Holy Writ, to the being whom they served, to come down among them, and receive their adorations in person, he pulled the cord, and let the animal loose, who, glad to be delivered from his confinement, gave a sudden spring upon the middle of the table.

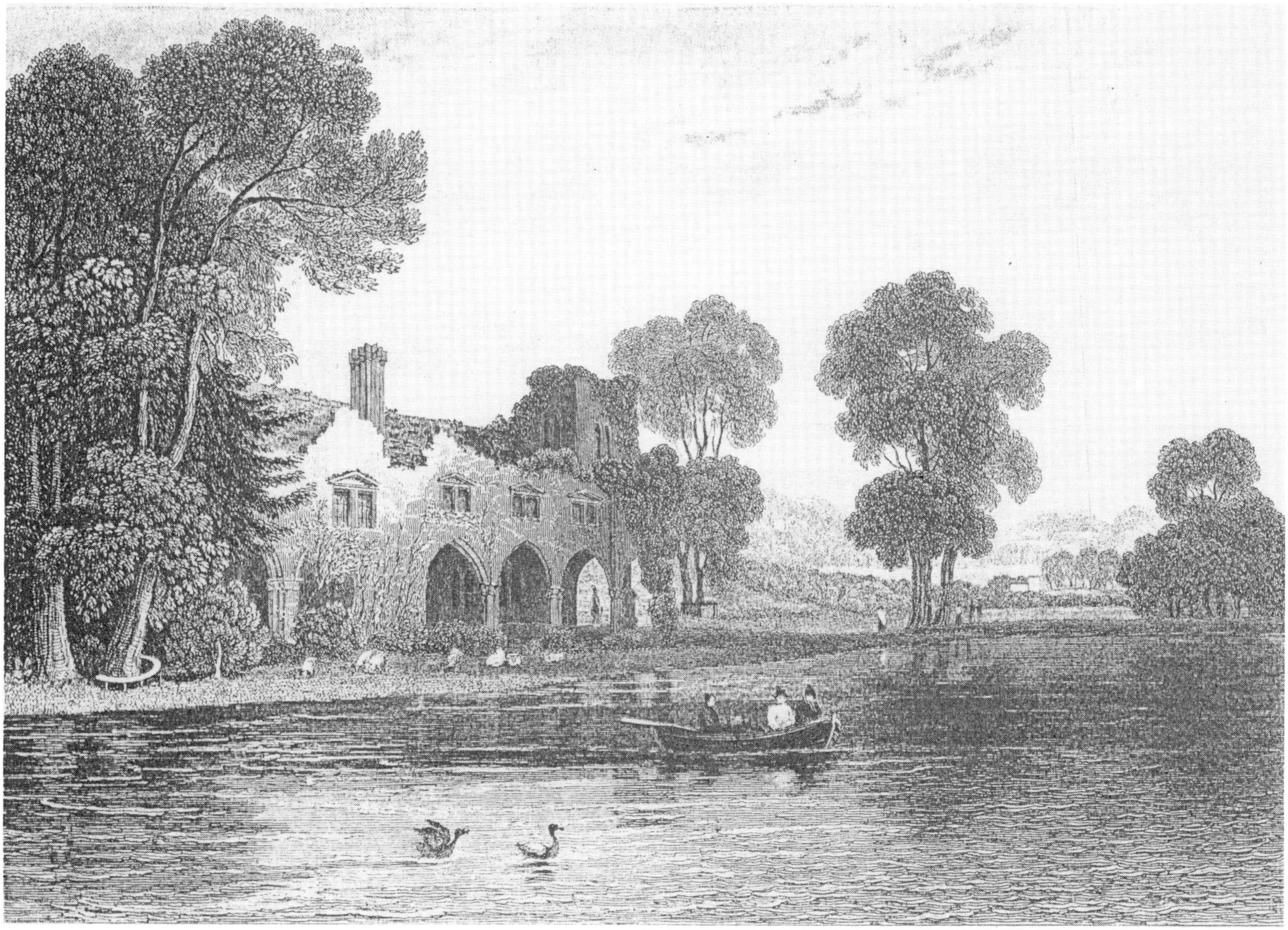

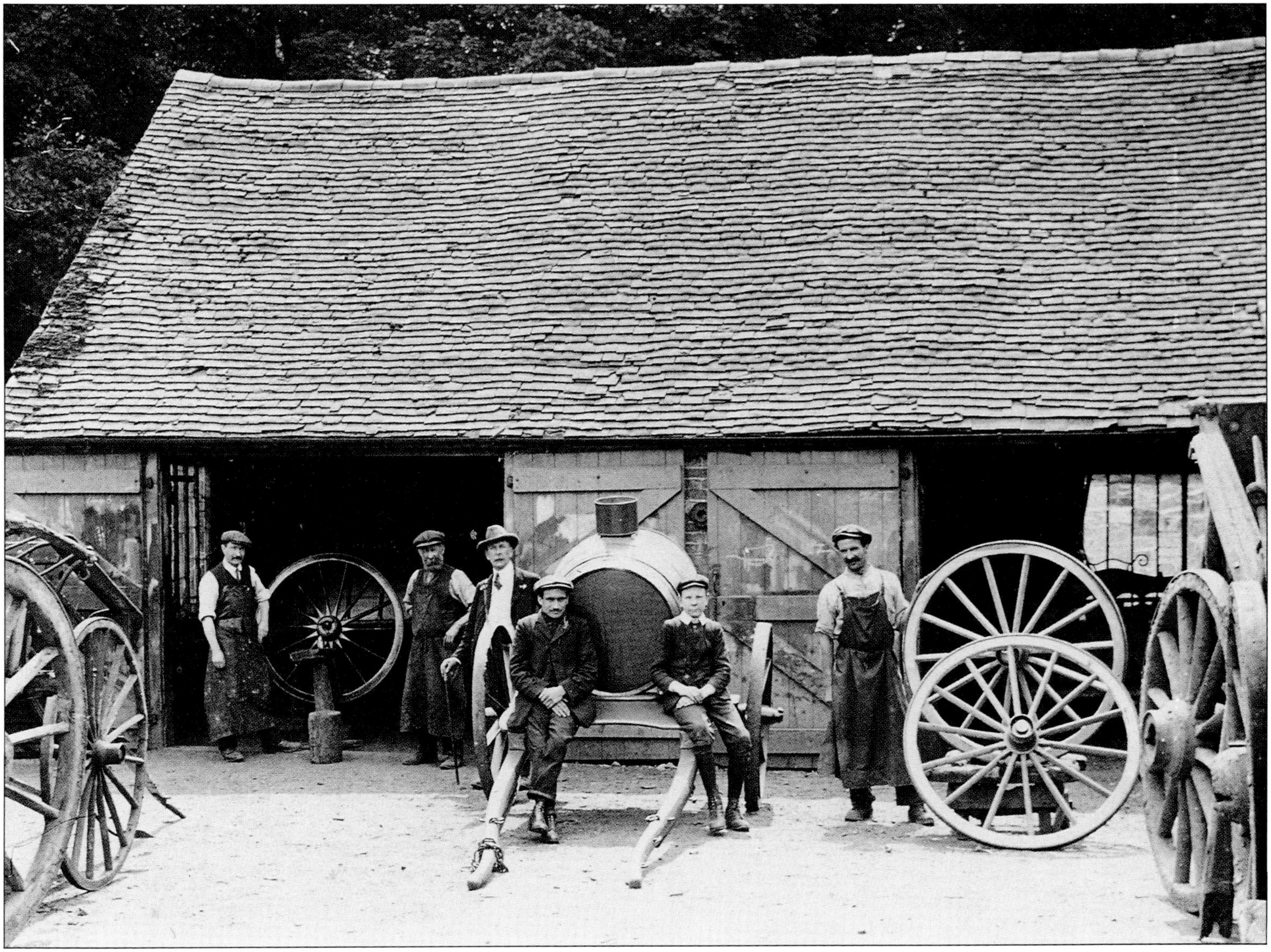

Wheelwright's shop, West Wycombe

The effect which the sight of such a visitor had upon them may be better conceived than expressed. Their attention had been so fixed upon what my master was saying, that they perceived not from whence he came; and his appearing so critically at the invocation, and in such a shape, made them conclude he was the Being invoked. Terrified out of their senses by this thought, they all roared out with one voice, 'The devil! the devil'! and starting from their seats, made directly towards the door tumbling over one another, and oversetting everything in their way.

A more worthy and lasting memorial to Sir Francis Dashwood is the unusual Church on West Wycombe hill which is referred to by the diarist Mr Thomas Phillibrown. He appears to have been a wine merchant, certainly living life to the full and the following extracts suggest that he encouraged others to do the same. Taken together, his diary entries convey a feeling of involvement surely as fresh as on the day they were first written. The 'golden ball' at West Wycombe was, in fact, still accessible until fairly recent times (D.E. remembers climbing in to the 'hollow globe' in 1953 and also that it felt quite 'choking').

Extracts from Thos. Phillibrown's Diary

Wednesday Sep 5th 1750

Messrs. John Hawkins, Wm. Sheppard and self set of for Wickham in Buckinghamshire about ¼ after one in ye afternoon on horseback . . . arrived at ye King Head at Beaconsfield about 11 (the following day) . . . Set out about one, stopped at Mother Redcap within a mile of Wickham and Hawkins treated each with a penny black pot of ale which pritty little tipple. Arrived at our customers Mr. Simkin's at ye Swan High Wickham about ½ past 2 . . . For supper boil'd fowl bacon and greens, 2 chickens roasted and a brace of partridges. After supper smok'd our pipes; about ½ past 10 Hawkins took a french leave vizt. (said nothing) and sneaked off to bed. Our company broke up at ½ past 11. Then Sheppard and I kiss'd our landlords daughter took our leave and went to bed. But first went, upbraided Hawkins for his dissertion.

Friday 7

Rose about 7 . . . Spoke to our Landlord to get some game to bring our friends in town. After breakfast walk'd into ye market place, it being market day. Came to our Inn where our landlord had comply'd with our request and had procur'd game for us. I bought a fine cock pheasant for which I gave 4s. for one partridge 1s.6d. Hawkins bought a brace of hare for 6 shillings and Sheppard 1 for 2s.6d.

Thursday 5th October 1752

In the afternoon about 4 o'clock by Mr. Simkin's persuasion, we rode to West Wickham (which is 2 miles distant on the road to Oxford) to take a view of Sir Francis Dashwood's seat, which is exceedingly fine and pleasantly situated . . . We rode up the hill on the right hand just without the town to the church which is very steep but yields a delightful prospect. With some difficulty and a little fear, we at last arrived at the Church which is situated on a very high chalk hill, the tower of which Church Sir Francis has (at his own expense) for the sake of a prospect to his House and Gardens, raised to twice the height it was before and on the top of the said tower is building a spire of timber, on the top of which is built of wood a very large hollow globe, the diameter of which is 8 feet and the outside of it is to be covered with gilt. We just went within the Church and up as high as the bell loft but had not courage to ascend higher. There are also to be, at Sir Francis's expense, a new flight of stairs, quite from the bottom of the church up to the new tower and from the gallery of the tower steps to ascend into the globe. Above the globe is to be a flag-staff which is to go through the centre of it.

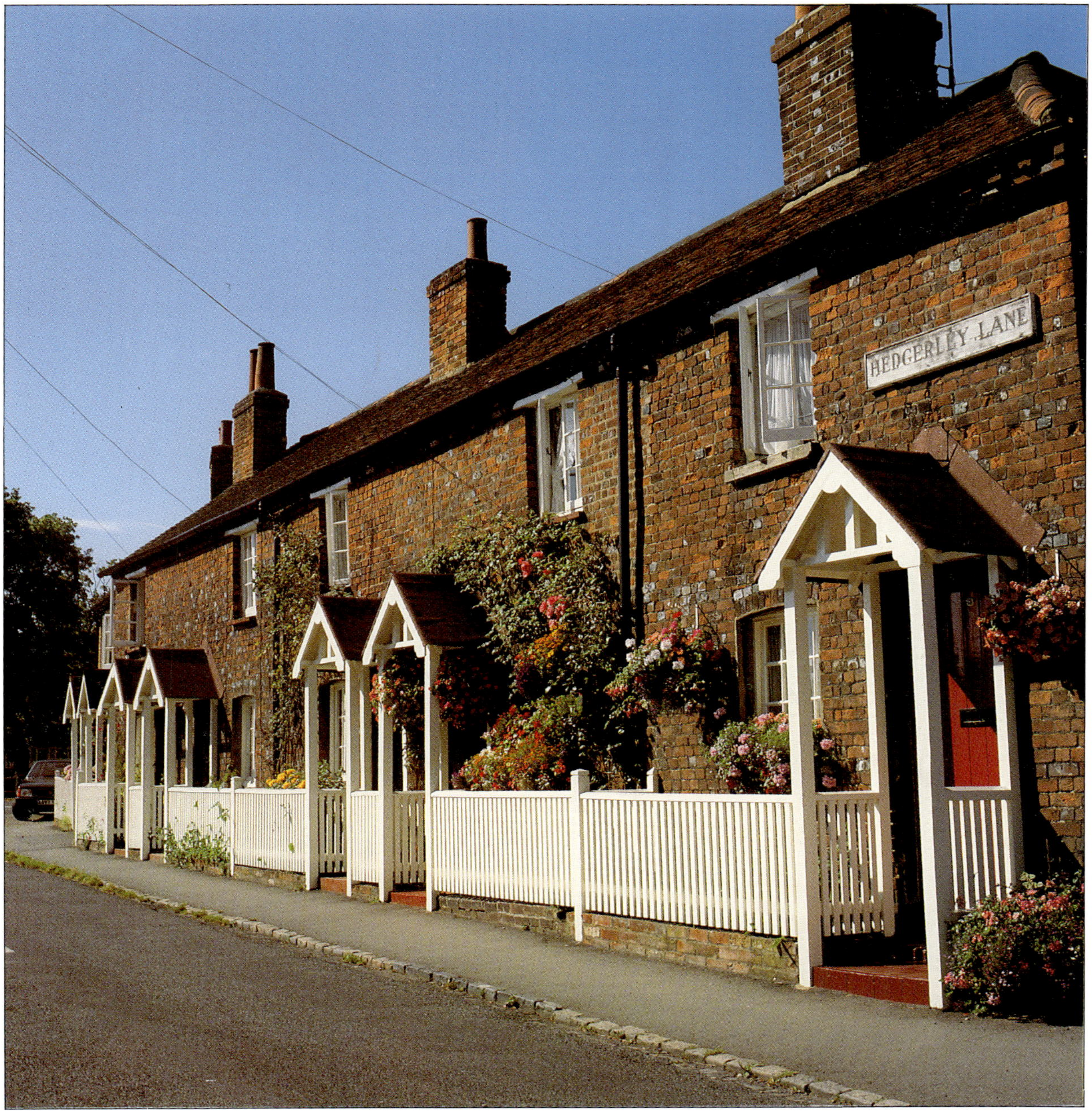

Beaconsfield

After entertaining ourselves with a delightful view of the country around Sir Francis Park, Gardens, Waters etc., from the church hill, we descended our lofty eminence from an easier descent than we ascended and by leading our horses down the precipice, arrived safe, just at the entrance of the town and remounting our steeds, returned back to High Wycombe very well pleased with our little excursion. Sir Francis is also making thro' his own ground, a good new broad road by the side of his park to High Wycombe and the old road which is a low, narrow, washy way, he intends to take in to his own Park. The Commissioners of the roads for this piece of publick service to allow £10. per annum for 3 years though 'tis said twill cost him £100 to finish it and was it not for the stupid obstinacy of an ill natured old woman, who would not part with a piece of her field on any terms (to complete so useful a work) Sir Francis would have widened and made good half the road from W. to High Wycombe.

Wednesday Oct 23rd 1754

. . . After dinner, Miss Simkins, my Bro and sister in ye chariot and Mr. Richardson and self of horseback, all went to see Sir Francis Dashwood's Gardens at West Wickham.

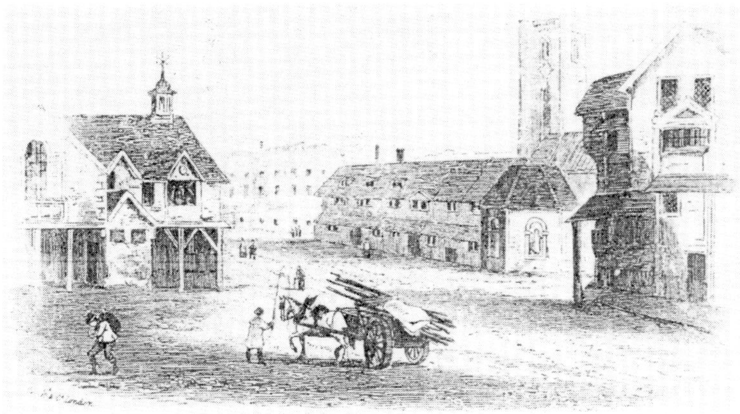

They are very pleasant and in which are green houses with exoticks and alcoves and temples decorated with statues, paintings etc. . . . In ye Grand Canal are various vessels, one of which is a Snow, Burthen about 60 Tun; it is completely rigg'd and carries several brass carriage guns which were taken out of a French Privateer and a sailor constantly is kept who lives aboard this snow to keep it in proper order; we all went on board it and there is a neat pretty cabin, forecastle or cork room and both under decks and outside is neatly painted and everything in missalure and quite pretty order and well worth seeing. There are also about three other vessels of various forms, a barge and boats which fleet afford an agreeable prospect.

In a previous entry for 1752 he describes the boats thus: 'There is also another smaller 2 mast vessel, a little in the venetian manner, also a 1 mast vessel like a sloop and also a barge.'

There are also swans on ye canal to add to ye beauty. We were told by ye sailor at one time a battery of guns in form of a fort was erected on ye side of ye canal in order to make a sham-fight between it and ye little fleet but in ye engagement a Capt. who commanded ye Snow comeing too near ye battery, received damage from ye wadding of a gun which occasion'd him to spit blood and so put an end to ye battle.

Thurs October 21st 1756

Rose before 7 Breakfasted on tea, toast and butter, set out at 10. Arrived at the Swan at High Wickham. Mr William Brickewell's (late Mr Bray Simkin's) at ½ past 11 Where my friend Zach Allnutt met us and drank with us and we invited him to supper. We walked before dinner by Lord Shelburn's (who is making great alterations and has cut out by his house a new road to Marlow and so up ye hills by ye beautiful beech wood by which Mr East ye late

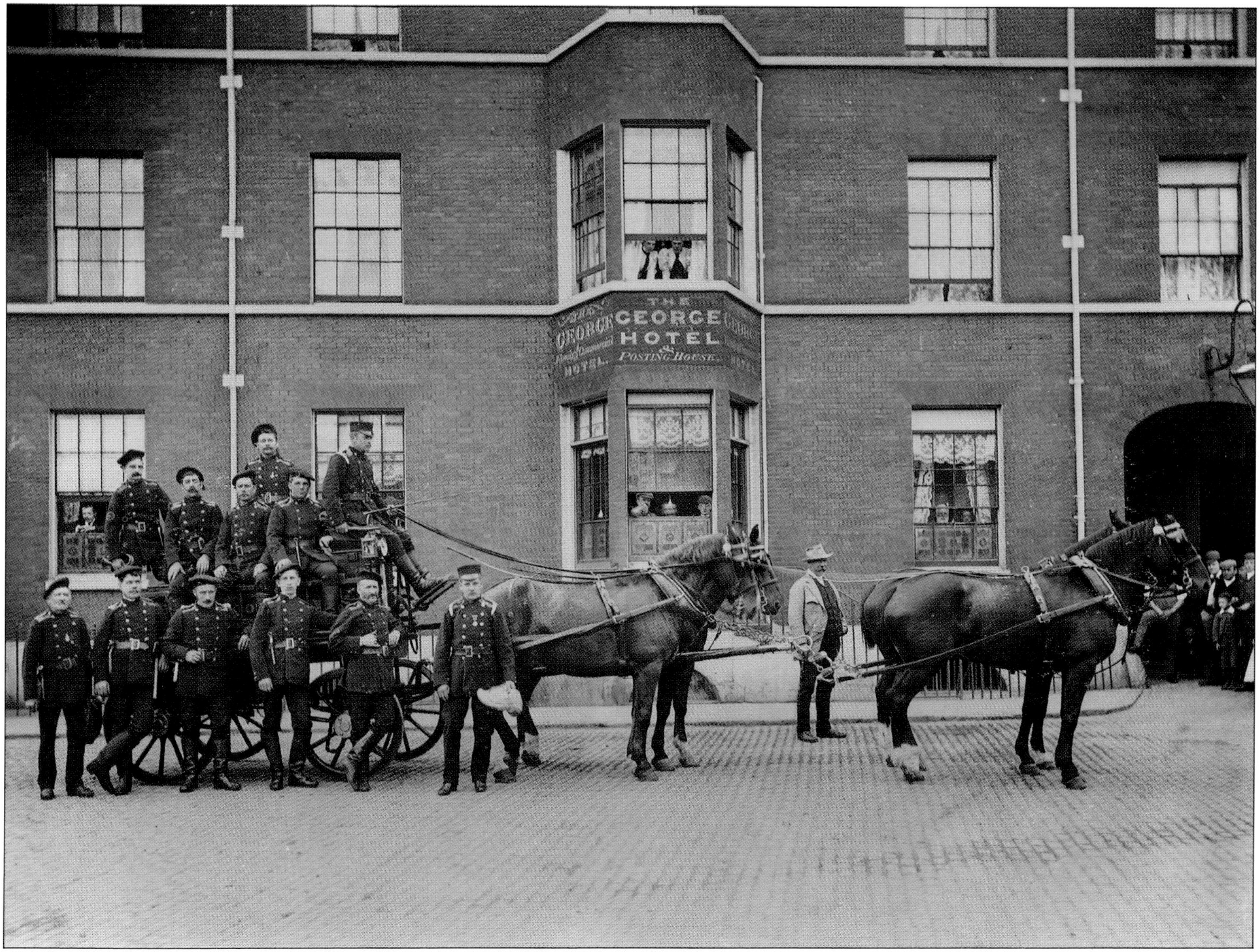

Aylesbury

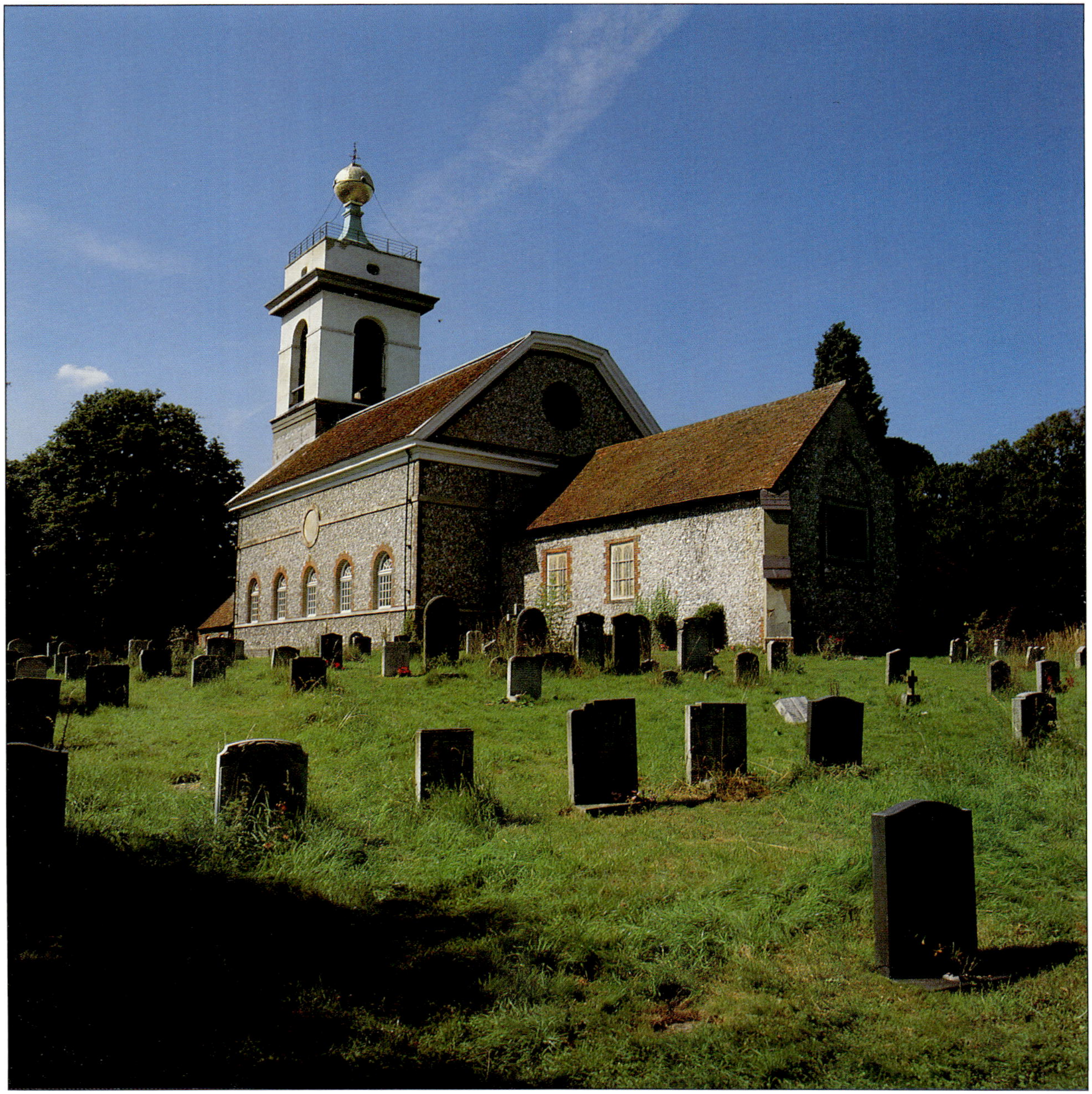

West Wycombe Church

Waggoner used to live. . . .) Afterwards returned to Mr. Brickwell's where our friends met with us and supped with us about 8 o'clock on. My friend and those invited by my landlord were in all 13. . . . After supper ye glass circulated cheerfully and Mr. Mayor toasted his Majesty and Royal Family which was pledged by ye whole company. After drinking, chatting and a song or two from Messrs. Pharsonage and Medwin (tho attended with frequent intervals of solemn silence, according to ye custom of Englishmen) about ½ past 10 Mr. Mayor and the rest of ye gents took their leave and went home except Messrs. Zach, Allnutt, Alder, Clarke ye drunken clergyman (who married Mr Rowswell's daughter; Rowswell keeps ye Red Lyon Inn at Wickham) Hill, the Surgeon, and Pharsonage the Attorney. They stayed to finish ye wine left on ye table and my Landlord Mr Brickwell came to help but he was dead drunk before dinner and was now scarce able to walk. As ye glass circulated, my Landlord and the parson grew so enfeebled that they could scarce fill their glasses. About ½ past 12 ye parson was forced to walk off and with great difficulty could get out of the door. About ¾ past 12 we all broke up. Zach and Allnutt and Pharsonage in good spirits. Hill with difficulty could walk in a strait line. Callamy and self in good sober order but my landlord Brickwell we left dead drunk in his chair.

Thursday 20th July 1758

We walked about and viewed the town. The present Lord Shelburn who is one of the members of Parliament for Wickham has at his own expense erected a new market house built of red brick with stone pillars ye bottom paved with stone. The Town Hall over it and the Gaol under ye Hall at one end of it. Lord Shelborn's Arms is very neatly cut in stone and put up in ye part of ye building as you come from London and on another part is ye Arms of the Corporation of Wickham, viz. A Swan neatly carved in stone. This building add greatly to ye beauty of ye town and is supposed will cost Lord Shelborn £2.000.

At 3 o'clock we set off for West Wickham 2 miles from High Wickham . . . We then walked up West Wickham hill to ye church in a most delightful prospect all over Sir Francis's gardens and ye country round about. We went up ye steeple into the belfry and quite up to ye new part of it built by Sir Francis on the front of which facing his house are cut in very large letters and blacked ye word.

MOMENTO

Mr Richardson went up ye ladder and out on ye leads of ye steeple, to view ye going up into ye great gilded ball. I afterwards took courage and went up quite round the leads tho with great fear and trembling for the great height makes it quite choking. We neither of us had courage to enter the ball which is considerably higher from the leads of the steeple; ye going up is on ye outside of a wooden spire with clamps of wood nailed like a ships side and ye ropes to take hold of it and a part of ye ball lifts up into which you can enter. We heard after that our coachman went into it. It is very large and is computed to hold 20 persons; there is a table in ye middle, seats around it and windows at top. Sir Francis with 12 or 13 of his friends has been up in ye ball at one time and drank punch there. There used to be a flag-staff above ye ball but it rotted so very fast that it is now taken down and workmen told us that Sir Francis proposes to have instead of it, on ye top of ye ball, the images of our saviour with the devil tempting him. After we had satisfied our curiosity and as we came down, we went into the bell loft and with my stick sounded the 6 bells.

We were all very agreeable and cheerful and several songs were sung after supper. Many stayed until the very last till we all broke up ¼ after 1 o'clock in ye morn. . . . All our friends who stay'd it out to ye last had their full charge but could walk off bonnily. Our ladies stayed up

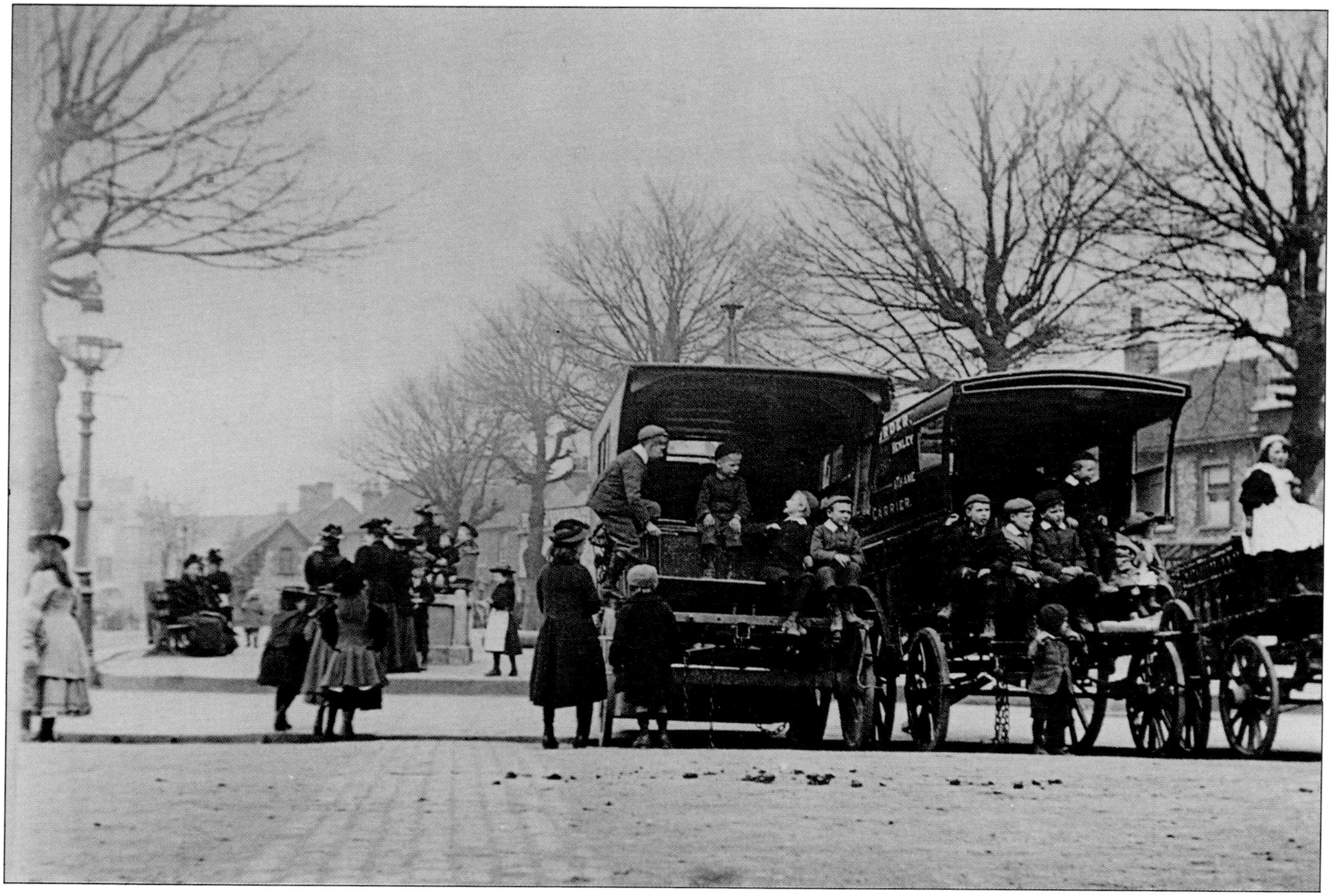

Jubilee Fountain, High Wycombe

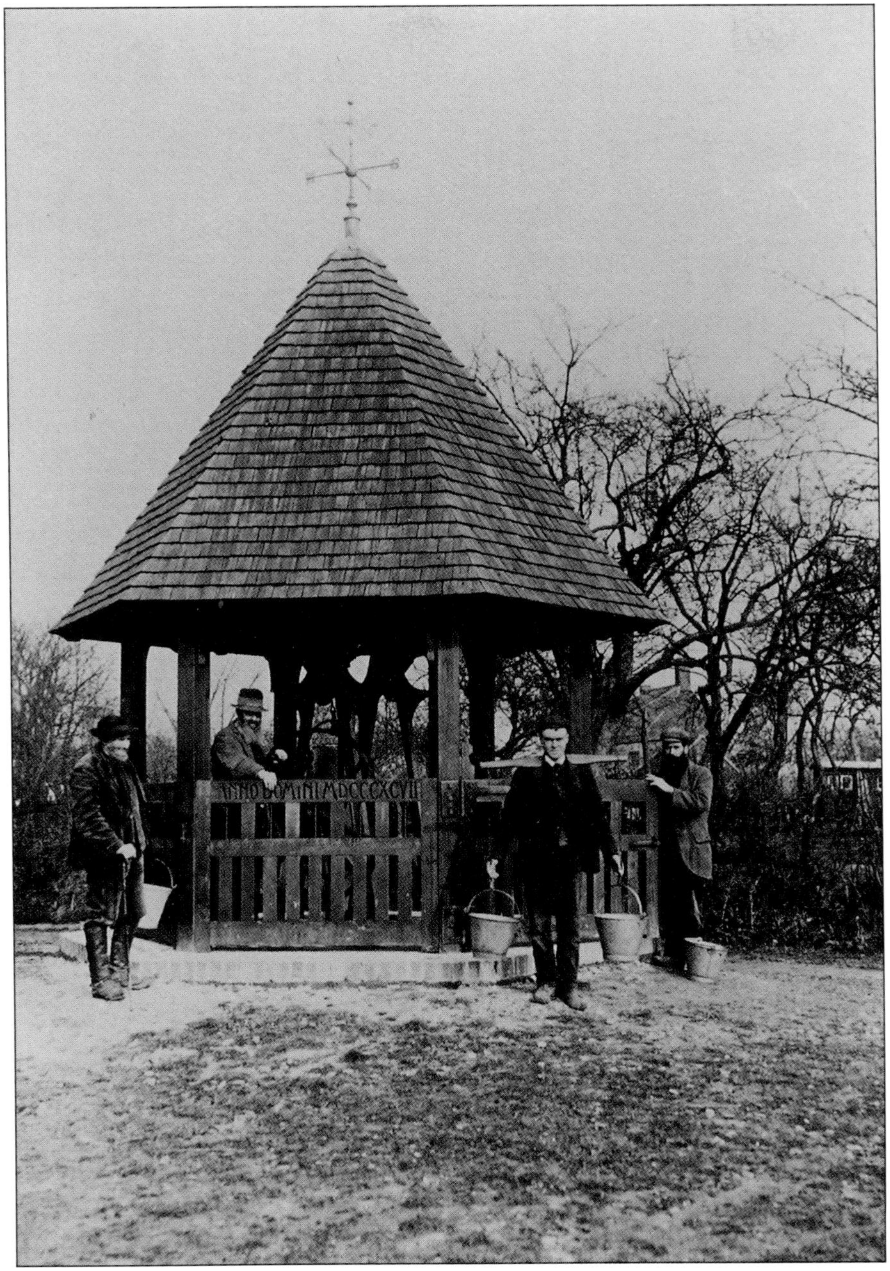

The Lee

till we had finished and frequently entertained themselves with coming on ye stairs and peeping through some light holes to see our droll figures and to hear our songs.

In THE PUBLIC AND DOMESTIC LIFE OF THE RIGHT HON. EDMUND BURKE by Peter Burke written in 1853, we are given an uncommon view of the private life of this statesman including his relationship with a part of the Chilterns and its inhabitants. A man of politics, at one point in his parliamentary career his seat in the Commons was representing Wendover, he was also a man of writing and literature, and developed long-standing relationships with Dr Johnson, Goldsmith and Garrick. It was at his house in Beaconsfield that he entertained such friends.

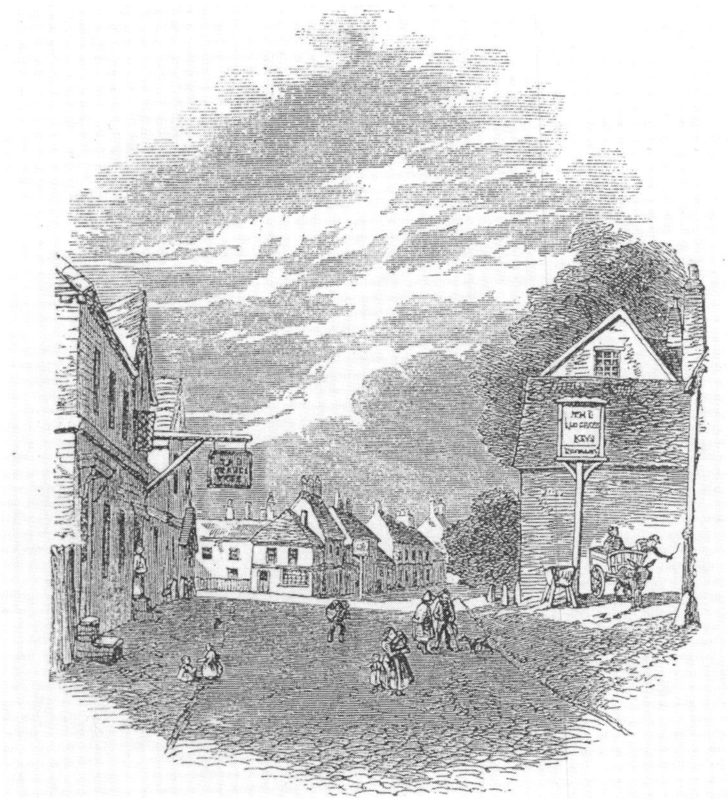

Edmund Burke always prefered a rural life, and dwelt in the country whenever he could. . . . in the year 1768, he purchased, for 23,0001., an estate in Buckinghamshire, called Gregories, or Butler's Court, situated about a mile from the market-town of Beaconsfield. His address from it, as he used to give it himself, was simply 'Beaconsfield,' or 'Beconsfeeld,' and consequently it became known and alluded to frequently by such designation only.

Lipscomb thus describes Gregories whilst in Burke's possession: 'The diversified combination of woods, hills, valleys, and beautiful enclosures by which the residence of Burke assumed a resemblance of Chiltern, Wotton, Cliefden; and the splendid colonnades which gave it, at a little distance, the dignity of a royal residence in miniature, by its similitude to Queen Charlotte's palace, called Buckingham-House, in St. James's Park, together with the magic name of Burke, rendered it an object of general curiousity. Once, however, in possession of his new estate, Burke applied his comprehensive mind so assiduously to the pursuits of agriculture, that he soon tripled the value of the land, and astonished his visitors and neighbours by his improvements. As a farmer he pursued the plan which had been found, by experience, to produce the best corn and cattle; and he was, in fact, without any unusual expense, one of the most successful farmers in the county. When in town he had his mutton, poultry, and all other meats, except beef, and also the various productions of the dairy and gardens, from his own estate, brought by his own horses and carts.

At Gregories, where the cheer was of course more in accordance with the dignity of the seat, he received his friends and admirers frequently and cordially. His house was the continual resort of rank, beauty, wit, and talent. In his domestic circle politics were readily laid aside. Various

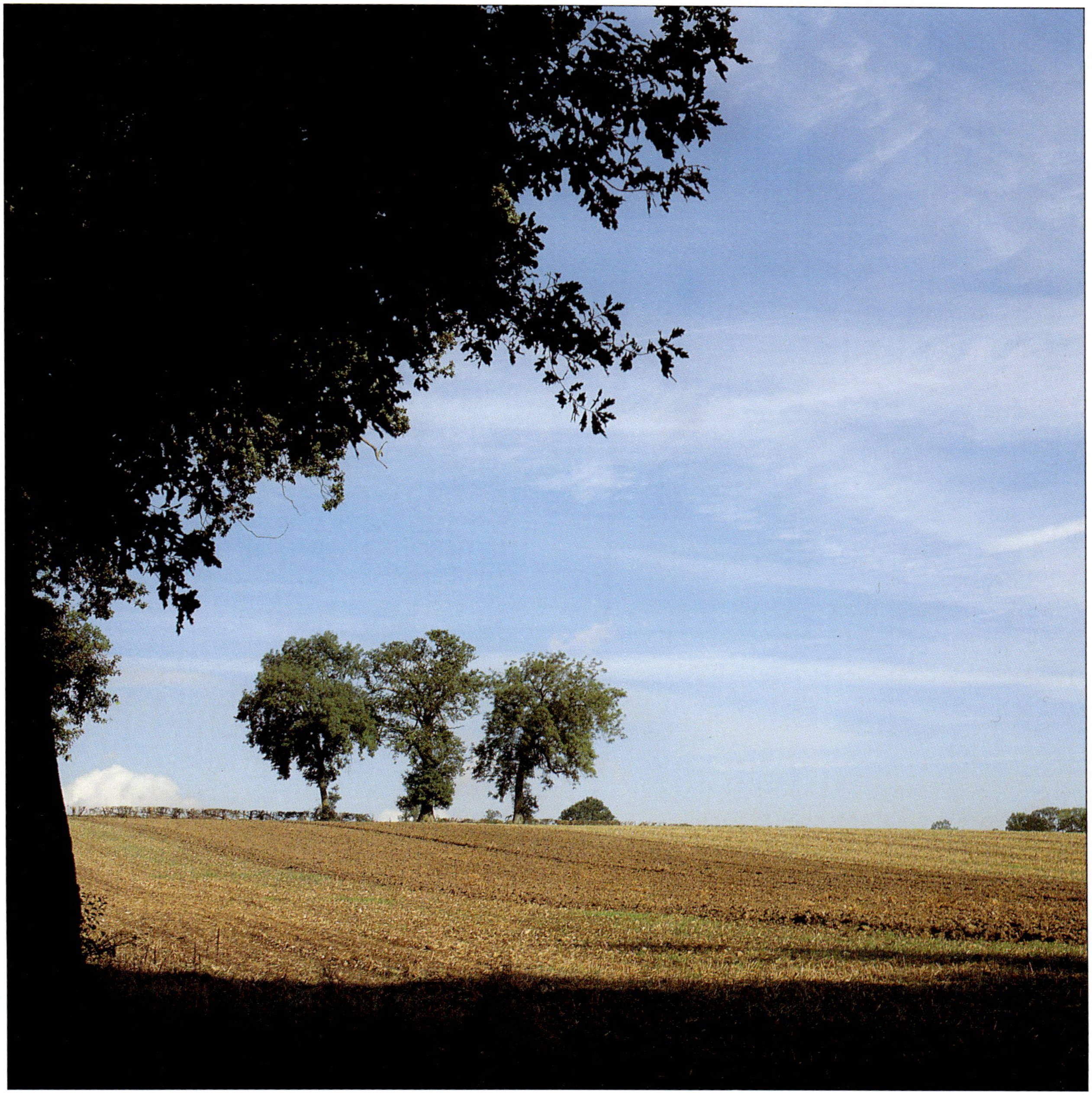

Penn

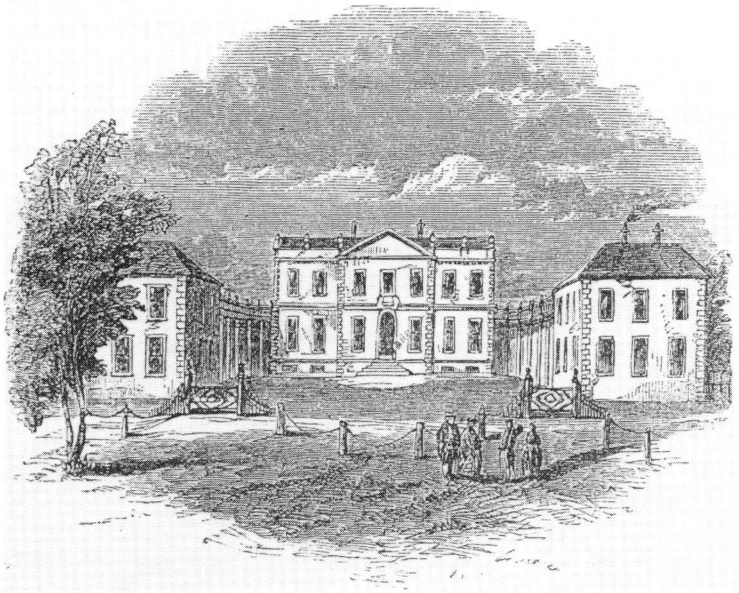

anecdotes represent the statesman entering with glee into the sports and pranks of the witty crowd around him; sharing earnestly in the games of schoolboys, and even listening to, or inventing with serious face, in the company of children, fairy adventures and infantine histories. He once observed to his friend Murphy, that 'Tom Thumb' and 'Jack the Giant Killer,' were both, 'from intrinsic merit, and from their popularity, fictions of no inferior stamp.' Of the interest he took in children of all classes, the following anecdote is related. Burke being one day with a friend at a country fair, observed a lot of boys in front of a show of attractive aspect, looking on with eager and longing countenances, but evidently with pockets too empty to enable them to penetrate into the interior. Burke forthwith went up to the showman, and agreed for the admission of the whole youthful crowd at his expense. On his friend asking him the reason of his strange proceeding, 'I could not,' he said 'miss the opportunity of making so many urchins happy.'

This attitude to children is seen in a more far-reaching way when we learn that Burke set up a special school for orphans of the French Revolution, having himself visited France in 1773 where he met a number of leading figures of the revolution. Robert Gibbs refers to this school in his BUCKINGHAMSHIRE MISCELLANY.

In the early part of 1796, Edmund Burke found active occupation in founding a school for the destitute children of emigrants who had perished by the guillotine or the sword of the French Revolution. With a view of being under Burke's immediate superintentence, the house of the late General Haviland, at Penn, was selected for the school, and through the representation of Burke, Mr. Pitt gave his assent to a grant of £600 per annum for its support. The school was opened in April, 1796, and Burke for the remainder of his life watched over the institution with the solicitude, not merely of a friend, but of a father; it was dissolved in 1820.

J. Prior in his LIFE OF BURKE (1824) leaves aside his principal character to introduce us to a particularly memorable elderly inhabitant of Penn:

Penn, to which Mr. Burke frequently resorted as the friend of General Haviland, and latterly as patron of the emigrant school, lies about three miles north-west of Beaconsfield. Many of the residents are distinguished for patriarchal longevity; not a few attaining a century of years. The family of Grove trace an uninterrupted descent from the Conquest as proprietors of the same estate. Mr. Edmund Grove died in June, 1823, at the advanced age of ninety-four; and being well-known in this part of the country as a fair representative of the ancient English yeoman, and was known to most of the surrounding nobility and gentry by the name Yeoman Grove – a name now disused for the appellation of Esquire, but formerly applied to those who farmed their own estate. Yeoman Grove was likewise known to George III, who permitted him an unusual freedom. Whenever they met in the street at Windsor, which was not infrequently on market-days, he would grasp the royal hand with fervour, and in a way peculiarly his own, inquire, 'How does your Majesty do? – How is the Queen? – How are all the children?' which commonly occasioned the Royal Personage a hearty good-humoured laugh.

In a different part of the Chilterns we make the acquaintance of another eighteenth-century diarist.

In 1526 Hardwick House was sold to Richard Lybbe of Tavistock and Shinfield, and the family remained in possession until 1909. Mrs Lybbe Powys married into the family and lived there from 1762–84 when, her family having grown up, she and her husband moved to Fawley Rectory where her brother-in-law was Rector. She was encouraged from an early age by her father to keep a diary, a practice she continued almost up until her death.

The following extracts provide a tantalizing glimpse of her social round and other vivid images including the severe winter of 1776:

Hardwick House October 24th 1762

We live at Hardwick (our father with us), in a large old house, about twelve rooms on a floor, with four staircases, the situation delightful, on the declivity of a hill, the most beautiful woods behind, and fine views of the Thames and rich meadows in front. Hardwick Woods you may perhaps have heard of, as parties come so frequently to walk in them, and request to drink tea in a cottage erected for that purpose in a delightful spot commanding a noble view of the Thames [the cottage was called 'Straw Hall'].

August 16th 1766

We all set out on an excursion for a day or two, and went first to Hedsor, Lord Boston's, near Clifden; but I think a still finer situation, a very indifferent very old house, (newly built 1788) but stands on such an eminence as commands a beautiful view of the Thames and fine country round that spot. We din'd at March's and in the evening went by water to drink tea at Monkey Island, belonging to the Duke of Marlborough. On this little island are two buildings, richly decorated on the inside. We went back to Maidenhead Bridge, and next morning went to Windsor. . . .

We lay again at Maidenhead Bridge, and the next morn went to see Lady Orkney's at Taplow, (Taplow Court) where is a terrace more, I fancy, adapted to the world landscape, as that of Windsor is to prospect; 'tis two miles and a half in length, a hanging wood below you; all the way the Thames runs along the bottom; the country all round highly picturesque; a Gothic root-house which hangs pendant over the river is exceedingly pretty; the building is like 'Straw Hall' in our woods, only the inside is Gothic paper resembling stucco; the upper part of the windows being painted glass gives a pleasing gloom.

May 12th 1767

Went to see the so-much talk'd of church built by Lord Le Despencer (Sir Francis Dashwood) near his own seat at West Wycombe, Bucks; I agree with Mr. Young that the difficulty of this ascent must be dreadful on the ancient and decrepid parishoners. The inside of the church is striking as a fine concert or ball room, 'tis indeed an Egyptian hall, and certainly gives one not the least idea of a place sacred to religious worship, having no pews or pulpit, but two sorts of ornamented writing-desks for the clergyman and clerk, and the font is shown as an elegant toy; the congregation sits each side on rows of forms, as at an assembly.

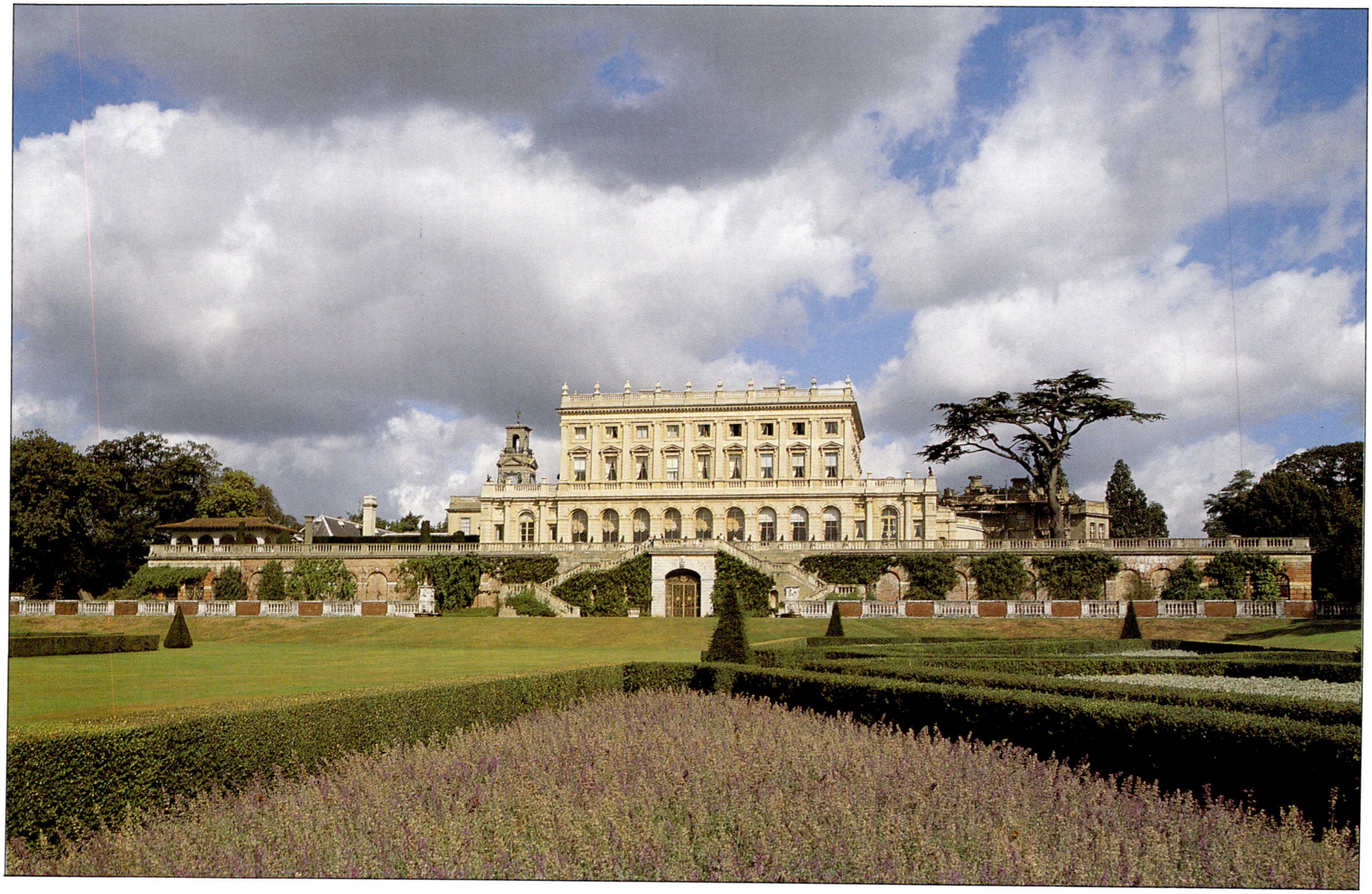

Cliveden

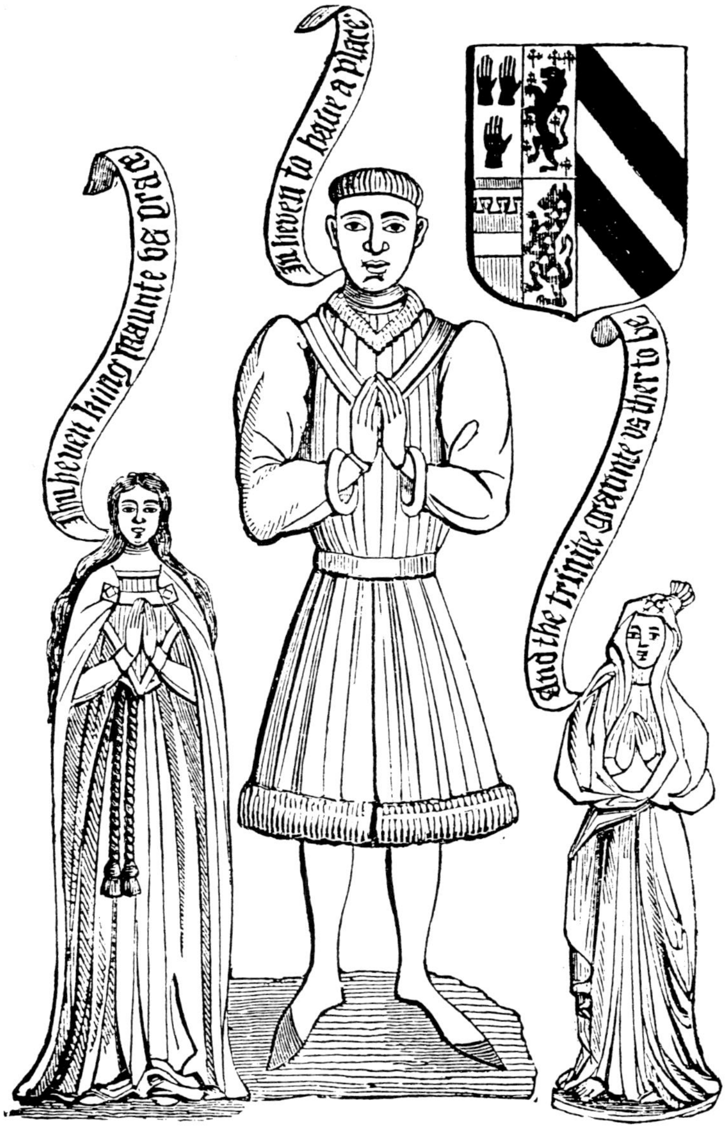

October 1771

Mrs Freeman's Fawley Court, Bucks, I've deferred mentioning, tho' so frequently there, till it was more finish'd. 'Tis in Buckinghamshire, built by this gentlemans father, but, though always an excellent house, had no ornaments till now, when Mr. Freeman has laid out £8000, I believe, in inside decorations, besides having the celebrated Mr. Brown to plan the grounds (Capability Brown). We spent a week there this year in the shooting season, and tho' one had seen it so frequently while the improvements were going on, one could hardly have imagin'd either house or its environs could have been so embelish'd by the artist's hand. . . . In this room (the saloon) are many fine pictures, a magnificent organ at the lower end, inlaid with many curious woods; a fine chimney-piece, two very beautiful marble tables, on each an elegant candlebranch of ormolu; the paper cost fifty guineas! . . . The best room is furnish'd with bed, &c., of the late Mrs. Freeman's work. One is seldom partial, I think, to ladies' work of this kind, as it generally carries the date of the age it was perform'd in, but this is peculiarly fine, differs from any one ever saw, and certainly does her honour. Her own picture is properly placed over the chimney of this room. The dressing-room to this is prettier than 'tis possible to imagine, the most curious India paper as birds, flowers, &c., put up as different pictures in frames as the same, with festoons, India baskets, figures, &c. . . .

1776

The most severe frost in my memory began January 7th and lasted till February 2nd. It began to snow about two in the morning as we were returning from a ball at Southcote, and kept snowing for twelve days, tho' none fell in quantities after the first three days, but the inconvenience from that on the ground was soon so very great, as strong

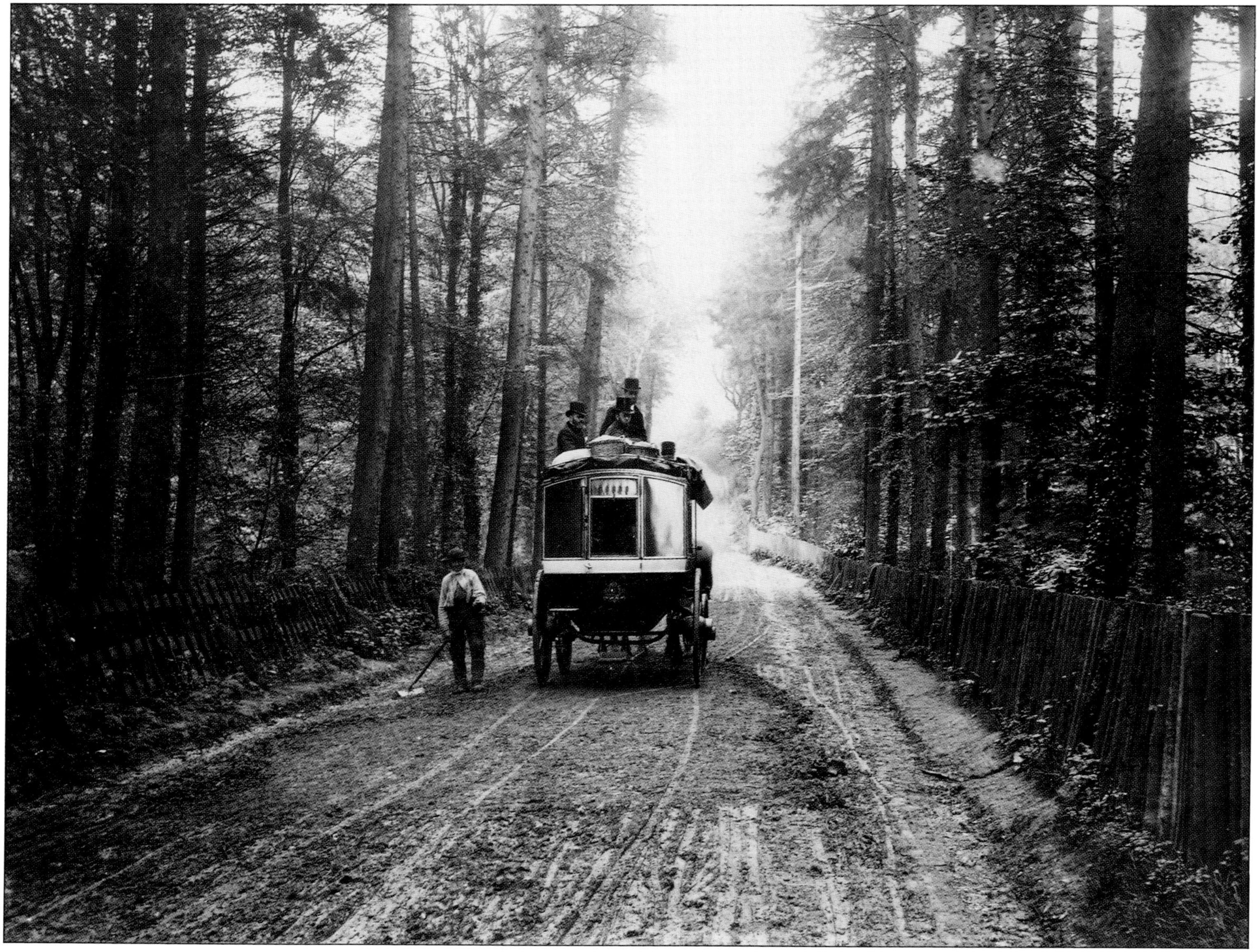

Chesham

north-east winds blew it up in many places twelve to thirteen feet deep, so that numbers of our cottagers on the common were oblig'd to dig their way out, and then hedges, gates, and stiles being invisible, and all hollow ways levell'd, it was with vast difficulty the poor men could get to the village to buy bread; water they had none, but melted snow for a long while, and wood could not be found – a more particular distress in Oxfordshire, as our poor have always plenty of firing for little trouble. As to our own family, we were fifteen days without the butcher from Reading being able to get to us, and then he came on foot, but luckily, we had sheep, hogs and poultry; our farmyard looked like a picture I've seen of all animals collected to enter the ark, as all our sheep, cows, horses etc, were obliged to be fodder'd there. We could have no news or letters from Henley or Reading for ten days, but then we began to be so impatient we got a man to venture on foot; no horse passed for a month or, cart for two. On the fifteenth day the butcher sent over two men with a little beef and veal, which then began to be scarce even there; not one team at Reading market the Saturday after it began – a thing never known. The two London waggons came in with sixteen and fourteen horses; but one horseman that day thro' the turnpike; all stages and machines stopped for ten or twelve days on the very best roads. It kept on freezing intensely after it had done snowing, the river being froze over from Whitchurch to Maple-Durham. Some of our people were silly enough to walk over it. Two hundred and seventeen men were employ'd on the Oxford turnpike between Nettlebed and Benson to cut a road for carriages, but then a chaise could not go with a pair of horses, and very dangerous, like driving on glass. . . . Our gamekeeper measured a piece of ice from a pond on the 29th; it was nine inches and a half thick. The beer and ale froze as they drew it, and the cream was forced to be put in the oven to thaw before they could churn it for butter, all my tender greenhouse plants died,

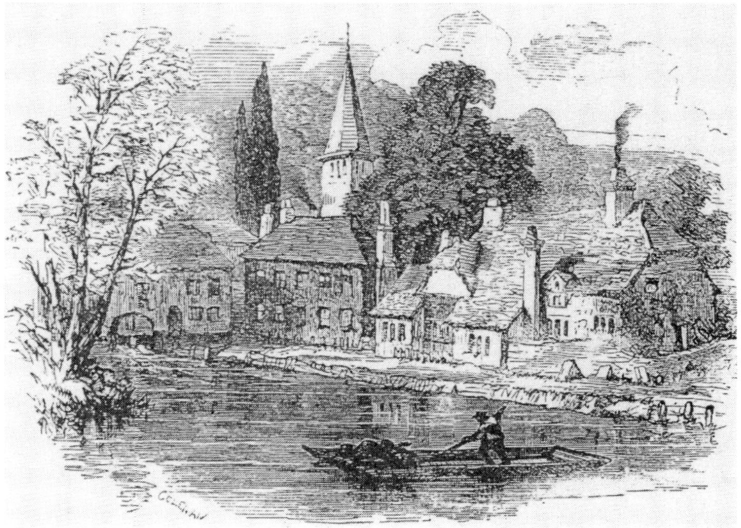

did not save one geranium, the oranges and myrtles not hurt, or any shrubs or flower-roots out of doors, the snow no doubt preserved them. Every one dreaded the so-much-wish'd-for-thaw; we by the river expected a deluge, but, thank God! never could such severe weather end more moderately. On the 2nd February began a most gentle thaw, and the immense quantities of snow melted away by gentle degrees to every one's astonishment. The road to Reading continued impassable till the 15th, after that the way was shovell'd, but when I went long after, it was in many parts a lane of snow above coach windows.

In 'A Village on the Thames' Mr Godlee writes for the January 1923 issue of the parish magazine: 'in forty years experience I have only once seen the river frozen over from side to side. That was in January 1893 when there were only a few open patches in Pangbourne reach, and above that it was completely frozen over as far as the islands, so that skating was in progress, with Ashley's men and a barrowful of life-buoys in attendance.'

June 1776

Tho' we never have any friends at Hardwick that we don't take them to see Caversham Lodge, (then the seat of 2nd Lord Cadogan) yet I've not here mentioned it, as I knew it was to undergo many alterations; those are nearly finished, and from always being a pleasing, 'tis now a very fine place, the situation beautiful, and these grounds laying out were the first performance of the since so celebrated Brown, who made a just tho' droll observation on the vast number of trees of an amazing growth all through the whole spot, 'that it was impossible to see the trees for the wood.' Indeed they stood so thick that this was literally true, they hiding each other. But by taking some down and leaving conspicuous the most noble, he has made it one of the finest parks imaginable, and at the time of the whitethorns being in blow, which at Caversham are by far the oldest and most beautiful I ever saw, 'tis hardly possible to describe the scene it offers. The terrace at Caversham (next to Lord Lincoln's), I've heard is the finest in England.

January 6th 1789

Tenants' annual feast at Fawley Court. We were there together with other principal tenants. The young people all as usual danced with the tenants six or eight dances; then we came up to cards and supper. The day always passes very agreeably, as it gives pleasure to see so many people all so happy. Many clever songs were sung by the gentlemen as well as farmers, and droll toasts given after dinner. Among the toasts were:

1 May the rich be charitable, and the poor happy.
2 Short shoes and long corns to all the enemies of Great Britain.
3 May all great men be honest, and all honest men great.
4 Peace and Plenty.

March 23rd. 1789

We all went to tea at Mr Cooper's at Henley (Phyllis Court), to see the illuminations at Henley town on the King's recovery [King George III first attack of insanity]. Every house was lighted up, and as we walked about for hours in different parties from the neighbourhood, the whole made a very fine sight. Fawley Court looked vastly well from the bridge. On the 25th my brother illuminated the parsonage, which look'd amazingly pretty from the bottom of the lawn, and at many distant spots, being a white house. We had the farmers, their wives, &c., to dinner. Had a large bonfire, and barrel of ale given to the village, and the day was pass'd quite to the satisfaction of all here on so truly joyful an occasion.

July 29th 1795

We had a water-party with the Freeman's of Fawley Court, who have a delightful boat, with awning, and every convenience of curtains, &c., to secure one from bad weather. We set off for Clifden Spring . . . It was too cold to dine as usual on the turf, so got out and walk'd while everything in the boat was got ready for dinner.

We had all a curiosity to see the ruins of the once magnificent Clifden House, so we set off, and mounted a very steep hill; the whole fabric, except one wing, a scene of ruin – the flight of stone steps all fallen in pieces; but what seemed the most unaccountable was, that the hall, which had fell in, and was a mass of stone pillars and bricks all in pieces, but two deal folding-doors not the least hurt, looking as if just fresh painted! They were the entrance into the inner hall; an archway over them had fallen in . . . The fire at Clifden was on May 20th. We din'd at Mrs Freeman's at Henley Park that night, and about 9.30 the servants came and told us Windsor Castle was on fire. On returning to Fawley Rectory, we saw the roof fall in – a tremendous sight; but on reaching the rectory, from my dressing-room window I saw it could not be Windsor Castle. The fire was caused by the carelessness of a servant turning down a bed. Very few articles of value were saved. The loss is estimated at £50,000.

Cliveden was restored in 1830 and after a second fire in 1849 rebuilt by the Duke of Sutherland to a design by Sir C. Barry.

Born in Great Marlow, the Revd Thomas Langley spent most of his working life in the Midlands. However, his native instinct led to his writing the prominent work the HISTORY OF THE HUNDRED OF DESBOROUGH AND THE DEANERY OF WYCOMBE which was published four years before his early death in 1801. A memorial to him can be seen in Marlow church, and here follows his description of this town in which he differs with Camden in his derivation of the name and says:

This learned antiquary has, I think erred in both derivation and illustration of the name . . . Marlow is Doomsday Merlaw, which appears to me to signify a mere or standing water; and this might be the situation of the place: for near the town are some peat moors; in which stags horns and other animal remains have been found, and these moors were probably standing water at that period.

There appears to have been a bridge over the Thames from very remote antiquity probably built by the Knights Templars of Bisham. Part of the bridge was pulled down by Major General Brown in 1642 when his army lay here, and in consequence parliament issued a warrant to levy a county rate for the repair of it. The old bridge becoming very ruinous and unsafe, application was made to the county in 1787 for rebuilding it; but the magistrates, not thinking the evidence of its being a county bridge conclusive (particularly as there was an estate of £20 per annum belonging to it, vested in bridgewardens appointed by the inhabitants) did not accede to this request. A subscription was therefore proposed by the Marquis of Buckingham, and £1800 was raised in 1789, when a handsome wooden bridge was built, which is very commodious, much improves the avenues of the town, and is a pleasing object to the surrounding county.

The church is a large ancient structure dedicated to All Saints. It consists of a body of two aisles covered with lead and a transept dividing it from the chancel. In the tower is a clock and six bells, and above a wooden spire built 1627. When the spire was new painted in 1790 a workman fell from the scaffold 70ft from the ground, escaped with a fracture and soon recovered from the confusion. It must be observed, that he fell first on the battlements of the tower and then on the roof of Mr Claytons family vault but still the escape was wonderful.

Remaining in Marlow we move into the nineteenth century. During his short and somewhat tempestuous life, the poet Shelley spent a brief interlude at Marlow around 1816. In a letter to Byron, Shelley appears to speak well of his contentment:

I have my books, and a garden with a lawn, enclosed by high hedges, and overshadowed with firs and cypresses, intermixed with apple trees now in bloom. We have a boat on the river in which, when the days are sunny and serene, such as we have had of late, we sail. May we hope that you will visit us?

Mary, his wife, re-emphasizes their pleasure in their surroundings:

The poem (The Revolt of Islam) was written in his boat as it floated under the beech-groves of Bisham, or during wanderings in the neighbouring country, which is distinguished by peculiar beauty. The chalk hills break into cliffs that overhang the Thames, or form valleys clothed with beech; the wilder portion of the country is rendered

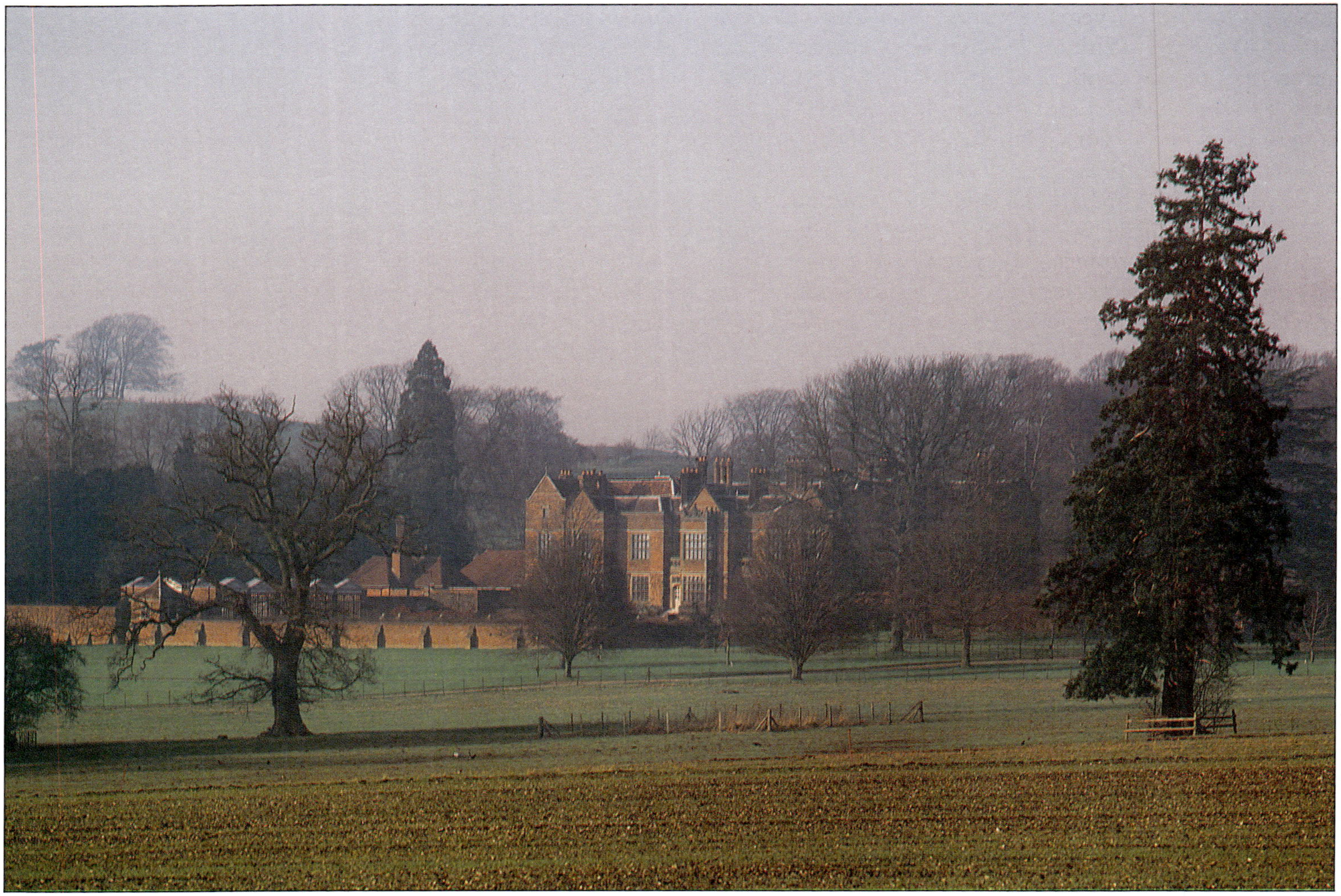

Chequers

beautiful by exuberant vegetation; and the cultivated part is particularly fertile. With all the wealth of nature which, either in the form of gentleman's parks, or soil dedicated to agriculture, flourishes around, Marlow was inhabited by a very poor population. The women were lacemakers and lost their health by sedentary labour, for which they were ill-paid. The Poor Laws ground to the dust not only the paupers, but those who were obliged to pay poor-rates. The changes produced by peace following a long war, and a bad harvest, brought with them the most heart-rending evils to the poor.

The latter remarks reflect a sincere awareness of those less fortunate in the community. In the same way, the pamphlets written at this time by Shelley under the pseudonym 'The Hermit of Marlow' portrayed a social conscience, and were frequently political in content.

In the early part of the nineteenth century improvements were being made to the arterial roads with the result that stage coach services to such places as Bath and Oxford speeded up. However, the benefits gained were soon overtaken by the provision of railway services and in 1838, when Brunel's line opened from London to Maidenhead (at this time more coaches passed through Maidenhead than any other town in England), passengers were making their journey partly by road and partly by rail.

Macadamizing was slower in reaching the lesser roads. A writer in the Cornhill Magazine *in 1861 makes the following observation about Ashridge:*

. . . There are men here yet living who remember that the only route hence to Dunstable was at your choice or chance, over the downs. Members of the then upper ten thousand, who ventured to and fro in their carriages to dinners, or on other pleasant occasions, sent men forward early in the day to smoothe down the ruts. The road was rendered discernible at night by the laying down of huge lumps of chalk, double lines of white buoys, through which the tipsy coachman steered his master and family, in comparitive safety, to the haven of their homes.

We find the Revd St John Priest in 1810 making the following observations:

The bye-roads of this county are extremely bad, some of them dangerous, and cautiously to be used; they have ruts so deep, that when the wheels of a chaise fall into them, it is with the greatest danger an attempt can be made to draw them out; nay, instances may be produced, where, if an attempt is made, the horse and chaise must inevitably fall into bogs; (in riding from Risborough to Bledlow, I turned my chaise out of the road, to avoid a waggon, and my horse fell into a bog up to his chest) and in the passages through lands under the open-field culture, not only are the roads bad, but the difficulty of discerning public roads from mere drift-ways, or from passages to lands of different proprietors, is so great that without a guide, some of them cannot be travelled by a stranger with safety. Witness the roads from . . . Tring to Dunstable, from Risborough to Thame . . . all the roads from Chesham; from Wendover to Chequers, and from thence to Missenden.

. . . But the principal causes to which the badness of roads are to be ascribed are two: first, the want of the residence of country gentlemen; and secondly, the number of dairy farms. No one requires proof, that the want of resident gentlemen in a county, can be assigned as a cause of the badness of the roads; because every one knows, that none but such can or will insist upon the execution of the laws respecting roads. Indeed, they alone feel chiefly the ill consequence of neglect in this respect in such a county as this; for as this county consists so much of dairy farms, farmers and the occupiers of land have but little traffic of corn with teams, compared with corn counties: they will, moreover, befriend each other, by omitting to complain of the badness of roads, some from one cause, and others from another; some in hopes that they themselves shall be exempted from the strict duty required of others; and others having no occasion themselves for more than a path for their horses to carry their butter periodically to the points agreed upon between them and their carriers. Thus the bye-roads are neglected and the great roads ill used.

Undeterred by the state of the roads William Cobbett travelled through many counties in England between the years 1821 and 1832 and his observations were published in his famous RURAL RIDES. We gather that his happiest moments were spent when riding through the countryside, taking note of the conditions of the country people, the crops being farmed and the continuously changing landscape.

His strong interest in America is apparent in his close comparison between that country and England. During the 1790s he spent much time in America which included having his own bookshop and publishing office in Philadelphia. Pennsylvania and the Chilterns are noticeably intertwined, the bond forged initially by William Penn, a link found here with William Cobbett, and later we have an enthusiastic American visitor in the Revd James Stone.

Set out at four this morning for Redbourn, and then turned off to the Westward to go to High Wycombe, through Hempstead and Chesham. The wheat is good all the way. The barley and oats good enough until I came to Hempstead. But the land along here is very fine: a red tenacious flinty loam upon a bed of chalk at a yard or two beneath, which, in my opinion, is the very best corn land we have in England. The fields here like those in the rich parts of Devonshire, will bear perpetual grass. Any of them will become upland meadows. The land is, in short, excellent, and is a real corn-country. The trees from Redburne to Hempstead are very fine; oaks, ashes, and beeches. Some of the finest of each sort, and the very finest ashes I ever saw in my life. They are in great numbers, and make the fields look more beautiful. No villanous things of the fir-tribe offend the eye here. The custom is in this part of Hertfordshire to leave a border round the ploughed part of the fields to bear grass, and to make hay from, so that, the grass being now made into hay, every corn field has a closely mowed grass walk about ten feet wide all round it, between the corn and the hedge. This is most beautiful! The hedges are now full of the shepherd's rose, honeysuckles, and all sorts of wild flowers; so that you are upon a grass walk, with this most beautiful of all flower gardens and shrubberies on your one hand, and with corn on the other. And thus you go from field to field (on foot or horseback), the sort of corn, the sort of underwood and timber, the shape and size of the fields, the height of the hedge-rows, the height of the trees, all continually varying. Talk of pleasure-grounds indeed! What, that man ever invented, under the name of pleasure-grounds, can equal these fields in Hertfordshire?

Hempstead is a very pretty town, with beautiful environs, and there is a canal that comes near it, and that goes to London. It lies at the foot of a hill. It is clean, substantially built, and very pretty place altogether. Between Hempstead and Chesham the land is not very good. I came into Buckinghamshire before I got into the latter place. Passed over two commons. But still, the land is not bad. It is drier; nearer the chalk, and not so red. . . .

Chesham is a nice little town, lying in a deep and narrow valley, with a stream of water running through it. All along the country that I have come, the labourers' dwellings are good. They are made of what they call brick-nog that is to say, a frame of wood, and a single brick thick, filling up the vacancies between the timber. They are generally covered with tile. Not pretty by any means; but they are good; and you see here, as in Kent, Sussex, Surrey and Hampshire, and indeed, in almost

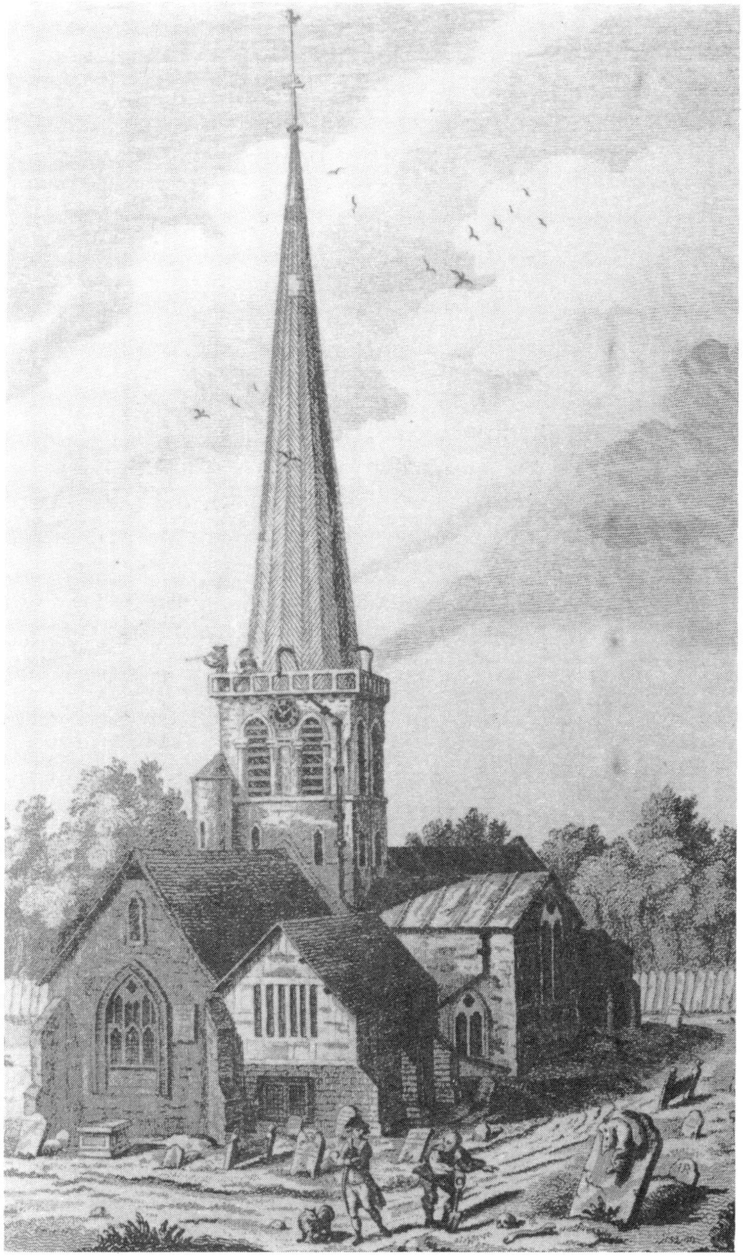

every part of England, that most interesting of all objects, that which is such an honour to England, and that which distinguishes it from all the rest of the world, namely, those neatly kept and productive little gardens round the labourers' houses, which are seldom unornamented with more or less of flowers. . . .

The Orchards all along this country are by no means bad. Not like those of Herefordshire and the north of Kent; but a great deal better than in many other parts of the kingdom. The cherry-trees are pretty abundant and particularly good . . . I saw the little boys, in many places, set to keep the birds off the cherries, which reminded me of the time when I followed the same occupation, and also of the toll that I used to take in payment. The children are all along here, I mean the little children, locked out of the doors, while the fathers and mothers are at work in the fields. I saw many little groups of this sort; and this is one advantage of having plenty of room on the outside of a house. I never saw the country children better clad, or look cleaner and fatter than they look here, and I have the very great pleasure to add, that I do not think I saw three acres of potatoes in this whole tract of fine country . . . In all the houses where I have been, they use the roasted rye instead of coffee and tea, and I saw one gentleman who had sown a piece of rye (a grain not uncommon in this part of the country) for the express purpose. It cost about three farthings a pound, roasted and ground into powder. – The pay of the labourers varies from eight to twelve shillings a-week. Grass mowers two shillings a-day, two quarts of what they call strong beer, and as much small beer as they can drink.

After quitting Chesham, I passed through a wood, resembling, as nearly as possible, the woods in the more cultivated parts of Long Island, with these exceptions, that there the woods consist of great variety of trees, and of more beautiful foliage. Here there are only two sorts of trees – beech and oak: but the wood at the bottom was

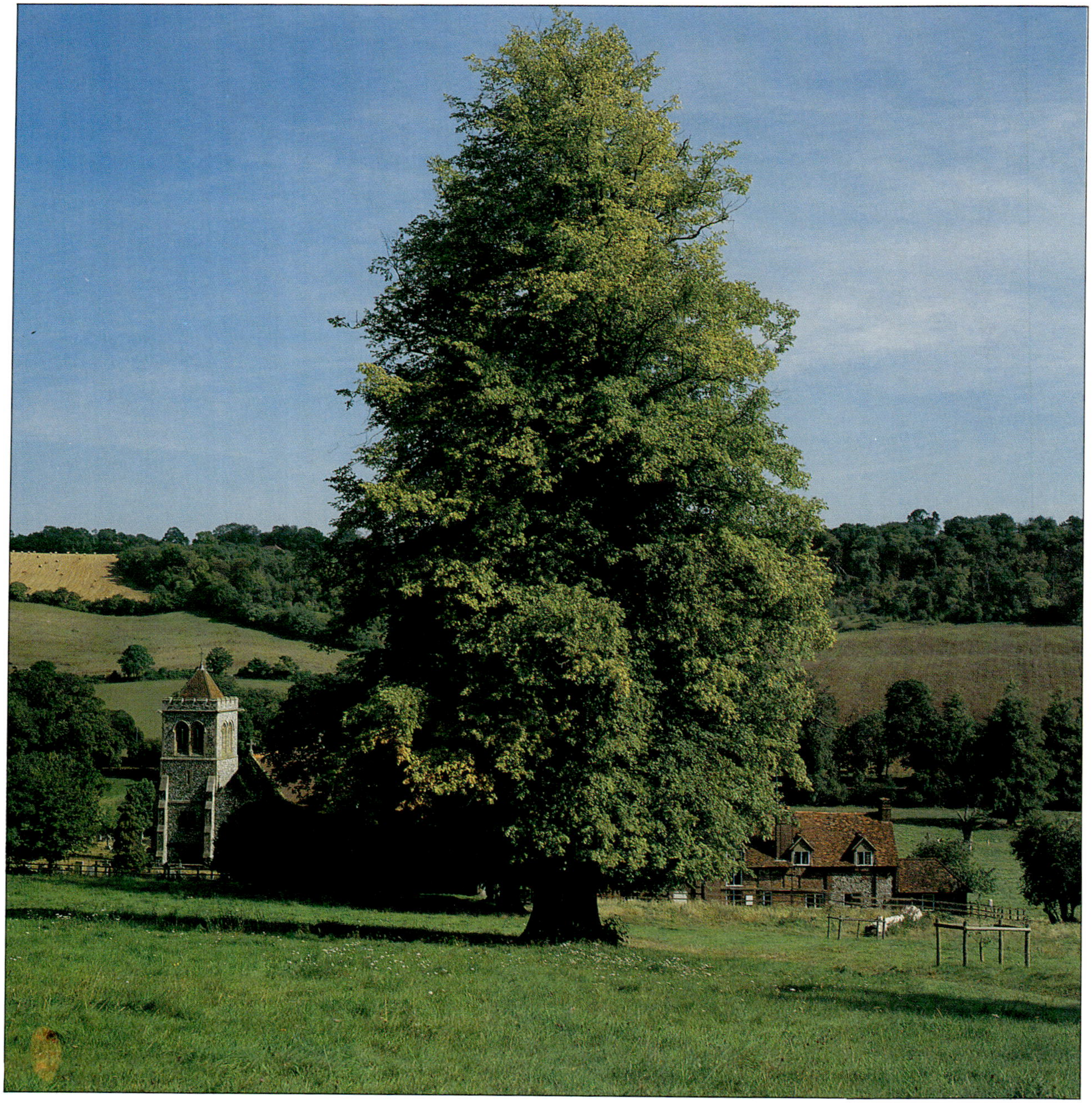

Hughenden Church

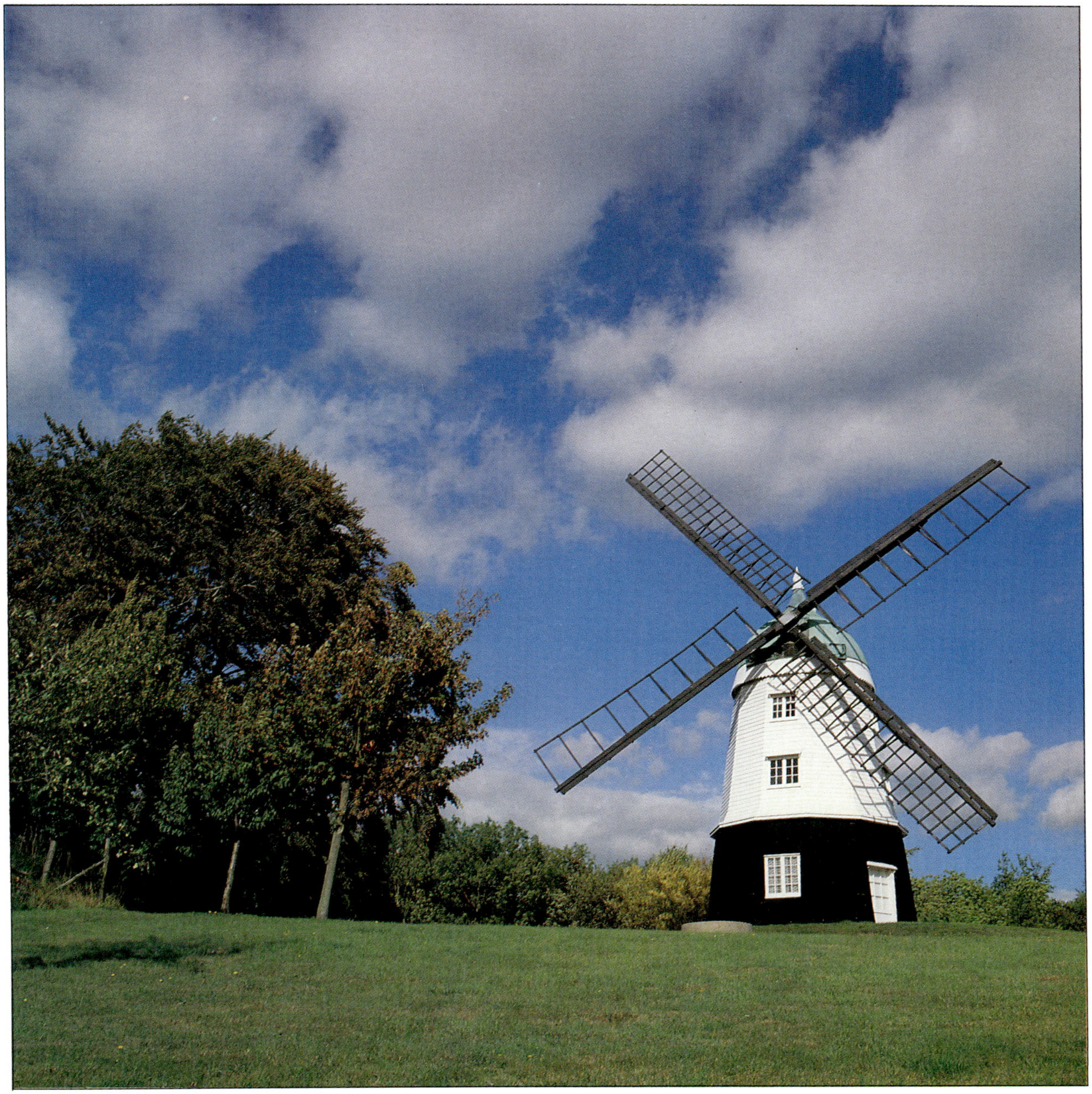

Turville

precisely like an American wood: none of that stuff which we generally call underwood: the trees standing very thick in some places: the shade so complete as never to permit herbage below: no bushes of any sort; and nothing to impeded your steps but little spindling trees here and there grown up from the seed. The oaks seem here to vie with the beeches in size, as well as in loftiness and straightness. I saw several oaks which I think were more than eighty feet high . . . This is by far the finest plank oak that I ever saw in England. The road through the wood is winding and brings you out at the corner of a field, lying sloping to the south, three sides of it bordered by wood and the field planted as an orchard. This is precisely what you see in so many thousand of places in America. I had passed through Hempstead a little while before, which certainly gave its name to the Township in which I lived in Long Island, and which I used to write Hampstead, contrary to the orthography of the place, never having heard of such a place as Hempstead in England. Passing through Hempstead I gave my mind a toss back to Long Island, and this beautiful wood and orchard really made me almost conceit, that I was there, and gave rise to a thousand interesting and pleasant reflections.

On quitting the wood I crossed the great road from London to Wendover, went across the park of Mr. Drake, and up a steep hill towards the great road leading to Wycombe. Mr. Drake's is a very beautiful place, and has a great deal of very fine timber upon it. I think I counted pretty nearly 200 oak trees, worth, on an average, five pounds a-piece, growing within twenty yards of the road that I was going along. . . . When I got to High Wycombe, I found everything a week earlier than in the rich part of Hertfordshire. High Wycombe, as if the name was ironical, lies along the bottom of a narrow and deep valley, the hills on each side being very steep indeed. The valley runs somewhere about from east to west, and the wheat on the hills facing the south will, if this weather continue, be fit to reap in ten days. I saw one field of oats that a bold farmer would cut next Monday. Wycombe is a very fine and very clean market town; the people all look extremely well; the girls somewhat larger featured and larger boned than those in Sussex, and not so fresh coloured and bright-eyed. More like the girls of America, and that is saying quite as much as any reasonable woman can expect or wish for. The Hills on the south side of Wycombe form a park and estate now the property of Smith, who was a banker or stocking-maker at Nottingham, who was made a Lord in the time of Pitt, and who purchased this estate of the late Marquis of Lansdowne, one of whose titles is Baron Wycombe. Wycombe is one of those famous things called Boroughs, and 34 votes in this Borough send Sir John Dashwood and Sir Thomas Baring to the 'collective wisdom'.

So famous was Aylesbury for its duck breeding that a particular breed of duck was named after the town. J.F. Fowler, a writer on country life and owner of Prebendal Farm near Aylesbury, provides us with a good description: 'The pure Aylesbury breed, long bodied, white plumage, without spot, with pale flesh-coloured bill and bright orange-coloured legs and feet, is prized everywhere for its great size, delicacy, and merchantable quality.' However, duck breeding could not necessarily provide a steady and secure income. Much depended on the demands of the market, and the 'duckers' ability to keep his flock free from disease. The Revd St John Priest in his GENERAL VIEW OF THE AGRICULTURE OF BUCKINGHAMSHIRE, *written in 1810, gives some interesting insight into duck breeding at that time.*

Ducks form a material article at market from Aylesbury and places adjacent: they are white, and as it seems of an earlier breed: they are bred and brought up by poor people, and sent to London by the weekly carriers. One poor man whom I visited, had before his door a small pit

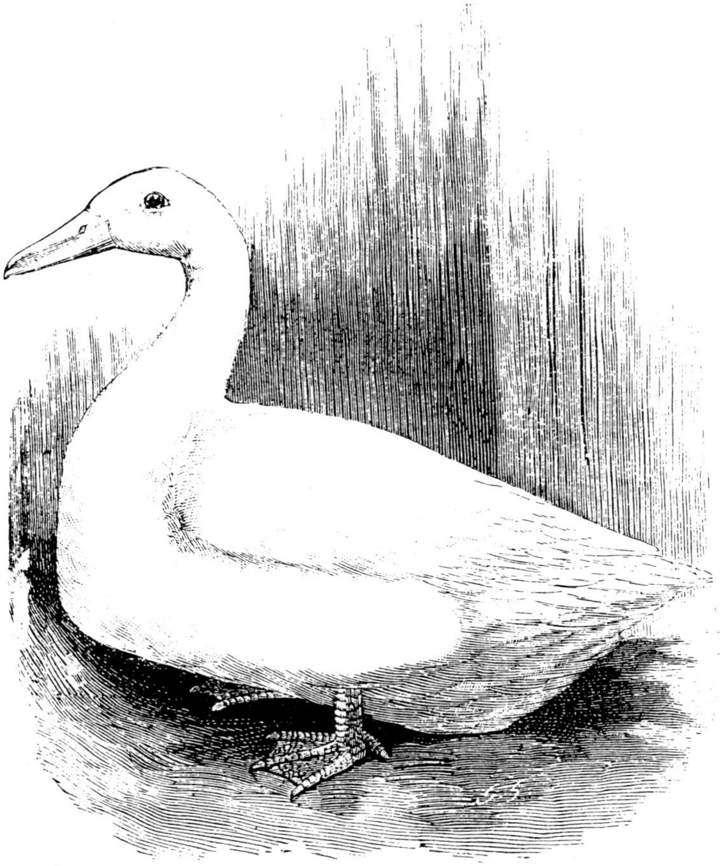

of water, about three yards long and one yard broad: at two corners of this pit are places of shelter for the ducks, thatched with straw: at night the ducks are taken into a house. (These pits make an unsightly appearance, and are rather dangerous, certainly incommodius, to travellers, by the side of the streets, and accordingly have been ordered to be removed.) In one room belonging to this man (the only room he had to live in), were ducks of three growths, on the 14th of January, 1808, fattening for London market: at one corner about seventeen or eighteen four weeks old; at another corner a brood about a fortnight old; and at a third corner a brood a week old. In the bedroom were hens brooding ducks' eggs in boxes, to be bought off at different periods: ducks six weeks old at that time for 12s. a couple. Besides the above, there are other persons who breed many more ducks than the person now mentioned, and as far as it was possible to discover, I understood this person sends 400 ducks in a year to London. Allowing then forty persons to send only as many, at an average of 5s. per duck, the return of ducks from Aylesbury alone will amount to 4000l per annum. This return has been magnified into 20,000l. per annum: but upon such conjecture the whole neighbourhood must be taken into consideration, and I have not sufficient data to ascertain the truth of it.

This unsalubrious habit of duck rearing in the breeders' own houses was to lead to human tragedy as we learn from Captain W.H. Smyth, writing in 1851, who makes a comparison between the breeders in the village of Hartwell and those in Aylesbury: 'they manage without being so intrepidly reckless as their friends of Aylesbury, into whose dirty duck-rearing bedrooms the grim blue-visaged Cholera found a suitable welcome, when he first visited England at the close of 1831.'

From Aylesbury we move to another important duck breeding area – Aston Clinton. In vol. 1 of the RECORDS OF BUCKS we find a piece of country history, investing the Chiltern slopes with shades of Arcadia, and also drawing our attention to the tradition of cutting motifs in the chalk hills. The contributor records a visit made to this site in 1847.

There is a spot on the Chiltern hills, in the parish of Aston Clinton, called the Shepherd's Grave. It is a lofty eminence commanding a wide and picturesque view of the surrounding country. Tradition states that a shepherd named Faithful, delighted with the panorama, used to make this spot his common resting place, while attending his master's flock. Becoming at length so attached to it, he exacted a promise from his fellow shepherds that at his death they would bury him here. This promise they fulfilled, and cut in the turf the following epitaph:

> Faithful lived and Faithful died,
> Faithful shepherd on the hill side;
> The field so wide, the hill so round,
> In the day of judgement he'll be found.

The rustics of the neighbourhood used carefully to keep the letters clear; but, having for some time ceased to do so, the word 'Faithful' alone was legible when I saw it. The spot, however, was still held in reverence, and my guide approached it with unmistakeable awe, and narrated the story with grave solemnity. This was about 1847; and I am afraid the ground has since been ploughed over.

It would be fair to claim that two of the most productive maufacturing industries associated with the Chilterns – as with the neighbouring regions – were lace-making and straw-plaiting for the hat trade. These industries were cottage based rather than factory based, with the workers usually receiving raw materials and returning finished articles to a lace or straw dealer. Lace-making was freely found throughout Buckinghamshire; while straw-plaiting mainly took place in the north-east of the Chilterns, an area which included parts of Buckinghamshire and Hertfordshire.

From their origins in the seventeenth century these industries became an essential part of the livelihood of many farm labourers' families, with wives and daughters anxious to supplement the all-too-meagre wage of the bread-winner.

We find reference to lace-making provided by many authors, referring to towns and villages throughout the Chiltern region. In THE COMMISSION ON THE EMPLOYMENT OF CHILDREN, YOUNG PERSONS AND WOMEN IN AGRICULTURE 1867–8, *we are given a visual description of the lace-making and straw-plaiting schools which even very young children were forced to attend to learn a skill to support the family income.*

In the lace district a farm labourer treats it as a matter of course that his daughters will be sent to a lace school at 4 or 5 years of age, and that from the time of their leaving the school to the time that they leave his house for good, it is his wife's business to see that they stick to their lace pillow, and work at least as many hours as he does himself. Lace making, from the fact that it entails sitting in a stooping position with the hands out in front of the body, and must generally be performed in the cottage room, causes fully as much physical injury to the frame of the worker as straw plaiting, though there are not such loud complaints of its effects on the morals. Lace schools, in their arrangements, and the extent to which they injure children by close confinement in badly ventilated rooms and interfere with their education, so much resemble plait schools that the description of the latter, which will be presently given, may be held to apply equally to them.

The earnings of girls engaged in lace making are very difficult to get at, but according to the evidence of the lacemakers themselves and those who knew them best, the earnings . . . when the trade was very much depressed, as it has been for some time, were about as follows: – Working 11 or 12 hours a day girls of from 10 to 12 years of age could earn about 1s per week, and girls of from 16 years and upwards from 2s.6d. to 3s. per week.

As farm labourers in the lace district send their daughters to lace school, so farm labourers in the plait district send their children, both male and female, to plait schools, where for a payment of 2d. to 3d. per week, a master or mistress (generally a mistress) teaches them to plait, and sees that they execute the task set them by their parents, the plait so made being the property of the parents, who buy the straw and sell the plait when made.

A return of the number of children attending such

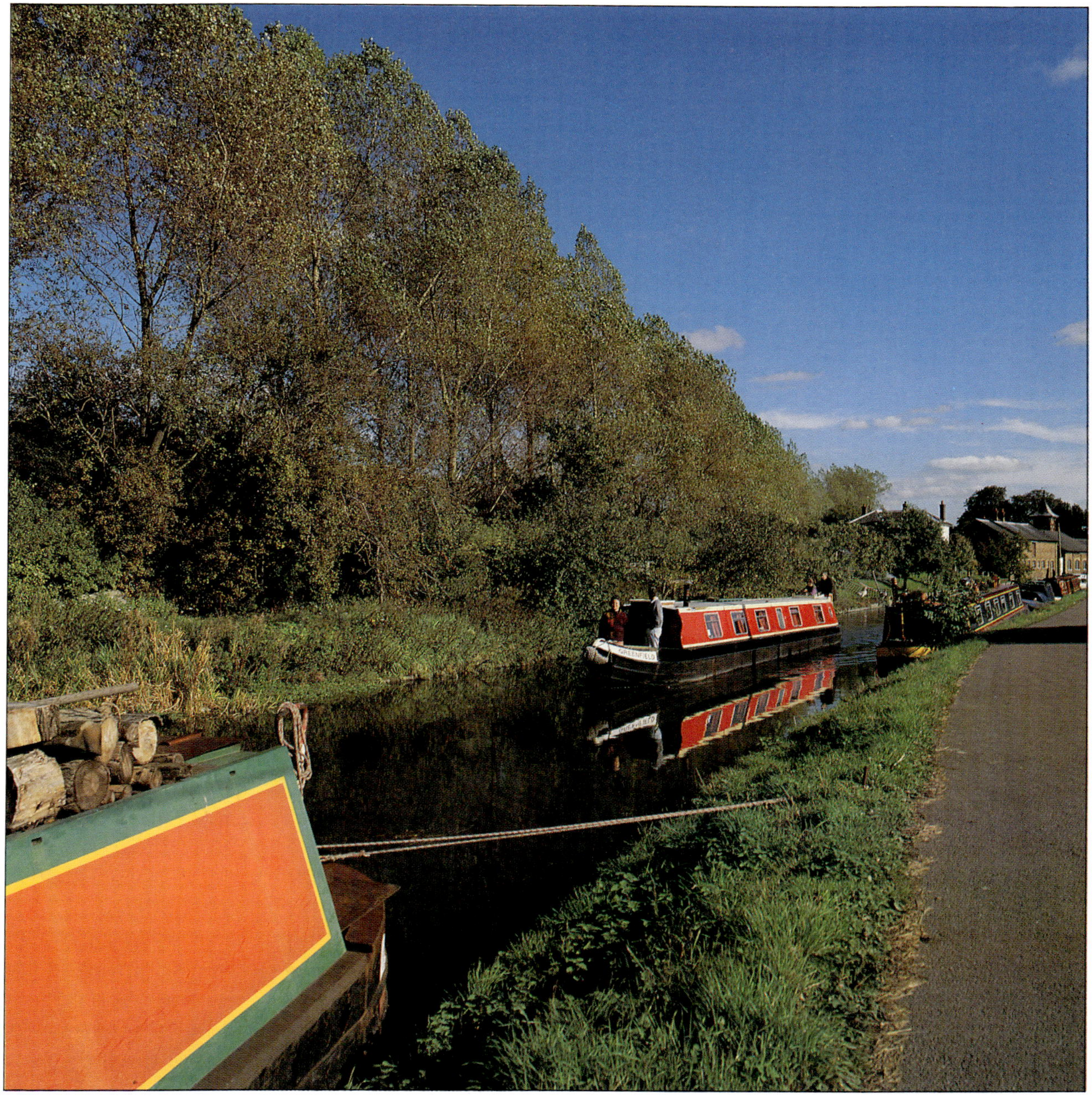

Bulbourne

schools in the centre and south-eastern divisions of Bucks was kindly given to by the chief constable, from which it appears, that there were 1,457 children, of whom 658 were under 8 years of age, in attendance at 102 plait schools in those districts, and there can be no doubt that if the straw plaiting trade had not been in an unusually depressed state at the time the return was made, a very larger number of children, especially of the younger ones, would have been found in attendance. I visited several schools at the time the return was being collected, and in three of these where I asked the question the teachers confessed to having from 30 to 40 per cent. more children when 'plait was good.' From these returns it will be seen that the hours of work most common in schools at the time the returns were made were six or seven hours, which, however, are lengthened to nine or ten when 'plait is good,' or the extra three or four hours considered necessary to make out a fair day's plaiting are worked out at home. Some of the schools I visited, even with the reduced number of learners, were very close and offensive, and the accounts I received of their state in times when plait 'went well' were enough to justify the very strong feeling existing in the plait district that some legislative interference is necessary, if only to protect the children from the physical injury sustained by working in close heated rooms. Warmth appears to be necessary to insure sufficient suppleness of the fingers, that in cold weather every breath of air is carefully excluded from the little cottage kitchen where 30 or 40 children are packed together as closely as they can sit.

It is particularly noticeable in the report above that the health of these children suffered at school and even into adult life due to their occupation. Captain W.H. Smyth when talking of Hartwell in his AEDES HARTWELLIANAE (1851) brings to the forefront this problem and others which were to prove even more crucial – 'the only manufacture it possessed was that of lace-making with bobbins, an injurious employment for women, and wretchedly ill paid, which has happily been reduced almost to zero by the frame workers of Nottingham and other factory places.' By the 1840s machine-made lace was proving a competitor to this 'cottage industry'.

In the following short report written in 1862, Thomas Gilbert, a lace dealer from High Wycombe, explains his working practices. One wonders if his occupation and that of his 'workpeople' would have had a greater chance of suvival if the manufacturers had not taken the hand-made lace of the East Midlands, including Buckinghamshire, as the model for many of their machine-made products.

I am a pillow lace manufacturer employing lacemakers over the greater part of southern Buckinghamshire and the adjoining strip of Oxfordshire and in these districts there is no other lace manufacturer of importance. The greater part of the whole pillow lace trade is in the hands of three or four manufacturers. I employ 3,000 persons. They are not absolutely employed by me as workpeople; but I sell them the materials, patterns and silk or thread and there is a mutual understanding, though no legal obligation, that I should take all the lace for which I have sold patterns whether there be a demand for it or not and that the lace-makers should bring it to me and not to any other buyer. From some I buy in their own villages, travelling round for the purpose . . . In some places I do not deal directly with the lacemakers themselves, but through the agency of small buyers to whom I supply the materials and patterns and who in turn deal with the lacemakers in the same way as myself.

In the same way that hand-made lace was under threat, the straw-plait industry was feeling the pressure of foreign imports. Large quantities of straw hats were imported from Leghorn in Italy in the eighteenth century; in the nineteenth century imports from China and Japan were to cause the complete demise of the industry.

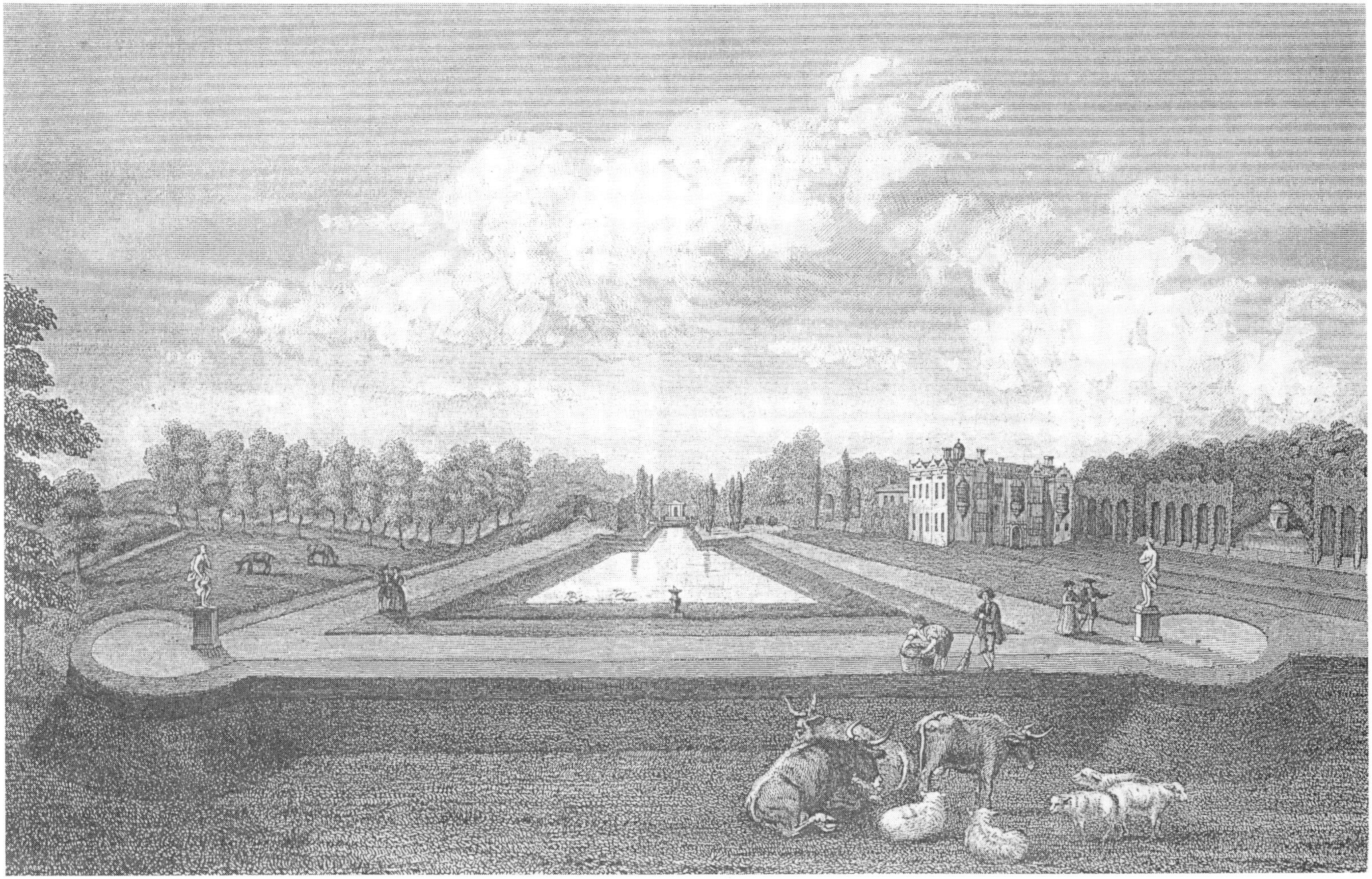

As these industries became depressed so the wages of the workers suffered. Comments made in 1867 by Mrs Crutchley of Chesham, and Mrs Rush of Hitcham near Maidenhead, portray only too clearly their shortage of money and the misery of their living conditions:

My husband has 12s. a week, and in hay time about 15s. My eldest child is a girl 11 years old, she plaits and earns 1s., as I hinder her a good deal. My second girl, 8 years old, earns 1s. I ain't against education, but with all they can earn, it isnt' over good living.

Mrs Crutchley (husband a farm labourer) from Chenies

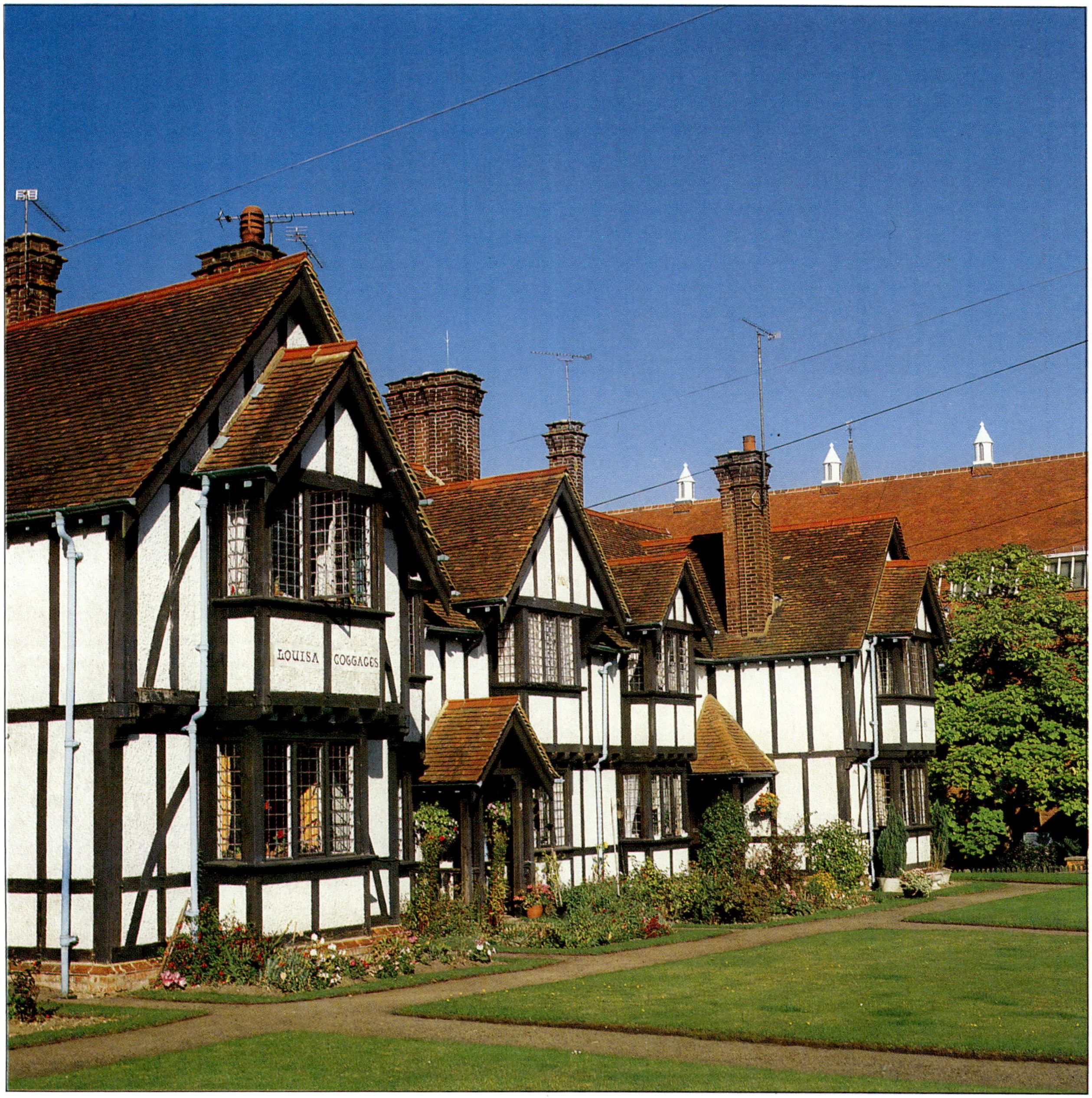

Tring

We pay 2s. and have about 10 to 15 poles. My husband is a farmer; is a labourer: he is truck-filling today; he earns a day-work 2s.9d. to 3s., but I can't rightly tell, not if you give me a guinea. I have seven children, and my father sleeps here. Three go to school, and we pay for them. I'm obliged to work to keep them at school. The eldest at school is 9, I think, but I'm no scholar: my husband puts them in the book.

Mrs Rush, living in one of six one-bedroomed and very poor cottages at Hitcham New-town.

John Werge Howey Esq., landowner and occupier of Coleshill near Amersham, in the same year as the above remarks, confirms in detail the state of some cottages in the Chilterns and the poverty of those living in them.

Cottages have two rooms, one on the ground, one above, as a rule 12 ft. by 12 ft., height, 9 ft. Ventilation, door, chimney, or a broken pane of glass. No drainage, except to the road. The number of the family not taken into consideration. Water bad, and scarce in dry seasons; this hamlet is better supplied than generally the parish. A small out-house, a small pot garden; when obtainable, a piece of potatoe ground. Owners, some out of business, some in trade. Rent, 1s. to 2s. per week. Cottages, as a rule, miserably poor in furniture, the bedding of the scantiest and most wretched description. After a meal, nothing left in the cottage, no bacon, no cheese, no lard, perhaps a piece of bread left for a young child. Beer shops are the curse of the hamlet.

As a northern man, I cannot help contrasting the difference between a hind's house in the north, and a labourer's cottage in the county of Bucks. In the first you see useful substantial furniture, crockery ware, good beds and bedding. Overhead side of bacon, cheese, bread; in the dairy, butter, milk, etc. The people go to work with a heart and good will. Now in Bucks, look into a cottage. You will see a want of furniture, scanty bedding, perhaps the remains of a quartern loaf, and a mug smelling of beer. The family not having a good meal smelling of victuals once in twelve months, do their work (except piece-work), accordingly without a will. As a rule, they are honest and well conducted, but their enemies are want of economy, ignorance, and the beershop.

It is hardly surprising that the solace of beer was sought to drown a world of sorrows. In 1868 Mr W. Brown, land agent of Tring, offers strong condemnation on the evils of this liquid:

My experience since that time (last year) confirms my opinion that the greatest drawback to the improvement of the agricultural labourer is the confounded beershop and the temptation to men to drink more than is necessary for their good. The beershops are the curse of the country. It is seldom that an honest, temperate, and industrious man allows his family to be brought up improperly, and so long as such temptations are held out for drunkenness, I see but little chance of improvement.

Mr. W. Brown, land agent of Tring 1868

Although the preceding cottage-based industries were eclipsed by competition from outside the area, chair-making in contrast went on from strength to strength. The following extract from Knights BRITISH ALMANACK of 1861 was written when factory production of chairs in High Wycombe had become firmly established. The first factories were attributed to Thomas Widgington and Samuel Treacher, and started in the late eighteenth century, but for many years the wood turner or 'bodger' was still making legs and stretchers in the woods supplying the factories, and women did the caning or rushing of chair seats in their homes.

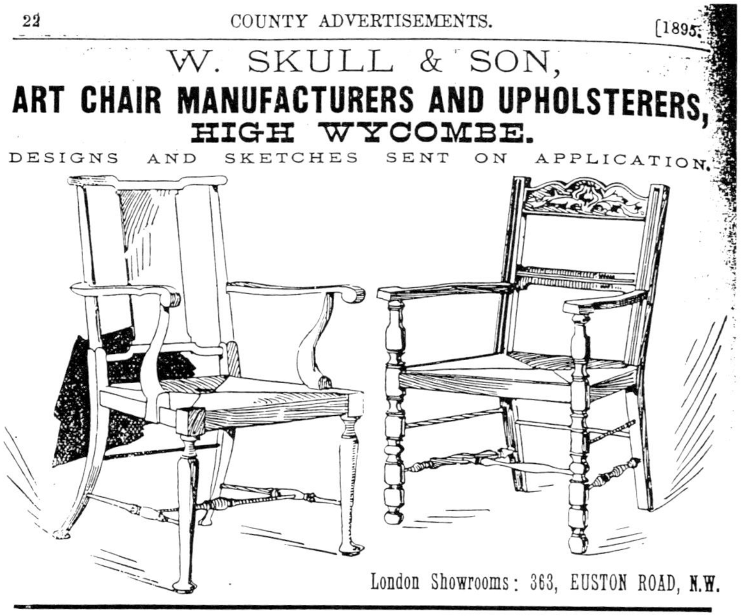

(D.E. remembers being told by women sewing machinists in the furniture factory about the stench of the rushes kept by their mother's back doors.)

In a happy hour the people dwelling amidst the beech woods of the Chilterns took to chairmaking, and so vigorously pursued the occupation that the Buckinghamshire weed is becoming scarce, as the oak was becoming scarce in the 16th century. It is remarkable how suddenly manufacturers are localized under favourable circumstances. Chairs were, no doubt, always made in these districts. The Windsor chair has a fame of some antiquity; but the Wycombe chair-making trade was scarcely known as something remarkable twenty or thirty years ago. The demand for the chairs has grown with the enormous increase of general population; the facilities of communication with the metropolis; the rapidly extending demand of our colonies. 'When I began the trade,' said a

JAMES COX,
MANUFACTURER OF ALL KINDS OF
CANE AND FANCY CHAIRS,
IN BIRCH, CHERRY, SYCAMORE, MAHOGANY, AND WALNUT WOODS;
ALSO OF WINDSOR AND RUSH CHAIRS,
AND EVERY VARIETY OF
ROCKING, FOLDING, SMOKING, & EASY CHAIRS, &c., &c.
SHIPPING ORDERS EXECUTED WITH DISPATCH.
OXFORD ROAD, HIGH WYCOMBE, BUCKS.

large manufacturer to me, 'I loaded a cart and travelled to Luton. All there was prosperous. There was a scramble for my chairs; and when I came home I laid my receipts on my table, and said to my wife, "You never saw such money before."' This manufacturer now sends his chairs to London, Liverpool, and Manchester; to Australia, New Zealand, and Constantinople. He made 8,000 chairs for the Crystal Palace; and, being a person of true English humour, rejoices to tell how he took his family to a Crystal Palace musical festival, and asked the attendents where they got so many chairs of the same pattern, which seemed to him one of the greatest wonders of the place. Another manufacturer provided 2,500 chairs, of unusual strength, for the evening services at St. Paul's; and he is providing similar chairs for the services of Ely, Exeter, and other cathedrals. . . . We need not then be surprised that Wycombe boasts of making a chair a minute all the year round – chairs that would not be unsightly in the handsomest sitting room, and which can be sold at 5s. each. More costly chairs are here produced, as well as the commonest rush-bottom chair of the old cottage pattern. But the light caned chair, stained to imitate rosewood, or of the bright natural colour of birch, and highly polished, finds a demand throughout the kingdom – a demand which might appear fabulous to those who have not reflected upon the extent to which a thriving industrious people create a national wealth which gives an impulse to

B. NORTH & SONS,
WEST WYCOMBE, BUCKS.
London Showrooms: 90 & 92, CITY ROAD, E.C.

Wholesale Chair Manufacturers.
CANE, WOOD AND RUSH FURNITURE.
FRAMES AND UPHOLSTERED GOODS.
FANCY ARTISTIC CABINET FURNITURE.

every occupation, and fills every dwelling with comforts and elegances of which our forefathers never dreamt.

In the same year J.J. Sheahan wrote of West Wycombe:

The trade here is almost exclusively chair-making. One manufacturer alone (Mr Benjamin North) employs about 100 workmen. Mr North has registered the pattern of the chairs called the 'Wellington,' the 'Raglan,' and the 'Napoleon.' Here too was made the first 'American Rocking Chair,' and also the 'Smoking Chair.' In fact about 400 different patterns of chairs are manufactured in this one establishment alone.

Cornmilling, already mentioned in an earlier century as a major source of Wycombe's wealth, was the trade entered by Robert Stone, the son of a chairmaster. In 1867 he was bound apprentice to Mr Pearce of Temple Mill in High Wycombe. Reading the entries in his diaries one is amazed that he found enough spare time to keep them. Far from being inhibited by his work, which sometimes went on into the night, he seemed to be involved in every aspect of community life. His propensity for physical activity led him to ride one of the first bicycles to take to the streets of Wycombe. The type mentioned would have been that which preceded the penny farthing and on the cobbled streets must surely have lived up to it's name of boneshaker.

The intitials R.C. which appear frequently in his diaries are those of his youthful love – Rachael Cooper – who later became his wife.

February 1869

28 Sunday My Seventeenth Birthday!!! Windy all day. Went for a walk over Amersham Hill before Church in the morning and for a walk to the Marsh in the afternoon. Church again in the evening and after which I spoke to R.C. Grandfather and Grandmother Atkins came to our house to tea to celebrate my birthday. G. Mother gave me a pocketbook and Aunt Iris a box of fishing tackle. Walk in the evening.

March

26 Good Friday Holiday Made arrangements in the morning for a holiday on the water at Fred. Stone, Charles Barton and W. Tyzack. We started at 12.45 in a hired 'trap' for Marlow Road where we hired a boat at the 'Watermans' Arms' and rowed towards Gt. Marlow intending to take tea there, but when within about half a mile from the town we were interrupted by a gang of about fifteen young men commonly styled 'Marlow Donkeys', and driven back by large stones thrown at us, one coming into the Boat, we then proceeded down the street to Cookham, thinking to have our tea there, but could not be accomodated, and we were obliged to return to the 'Watermans' Arms' where we partook of an excellent Tea, consisting of Fifteen eggs, etc., and after having various amusements we rode home to Wycombe, and finished a fine holiday. Spoke to R.C. after my return at 9 o'clock, and afterwards went to M.S. for my Likeness, but did not get it – Fine all day.

May

14 Friday Grand Review of the Bucks Militia attended by the Slough Lancers in Wycombe Park – together with

the Presentation of New Colours to the Regiment by the Duchess of Buckingham. I went & saw them for about two hours. Work from 7 to 8.15. Went for a walk down street with F. Stone, Grand Ball at the 'Lion' Hotel. The Velocipede from Devonshire came by train to be inspected, and if not like to be returned. Fine.

15 Saturday Work from 8.15 to 8.30. Fred fetched the Velocipede from the Railway station and took it to Mr Hooper's, London Road. And after work we went and rode on it. It has good wheels and cranks but very bad action, and requires a deal of uncomfortable labour to keep up to any speed.

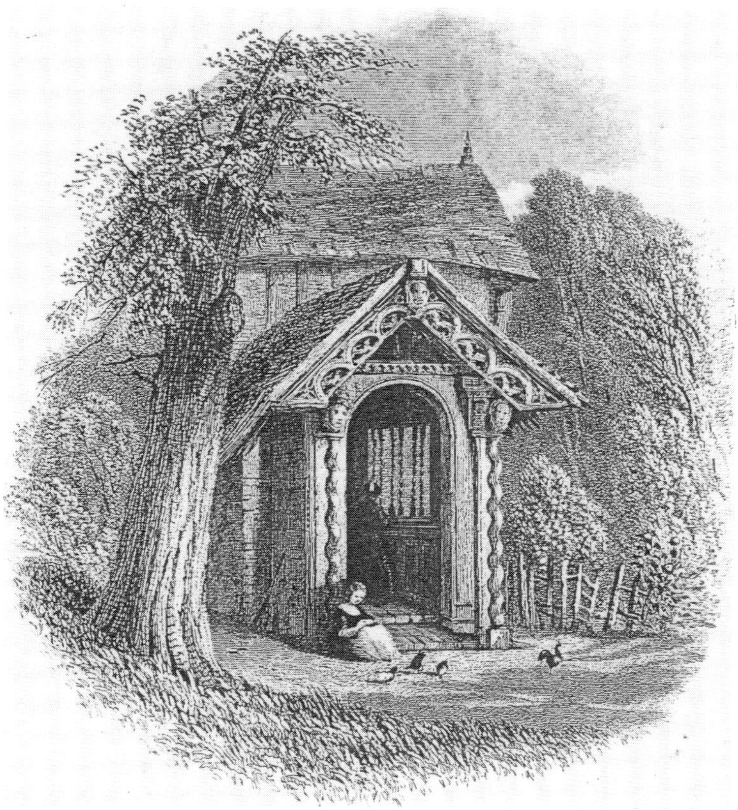

June

7 Monday Work from 7 to 8. Went with H. Hills, J. Cage etc. and had a splendid bathe in the Dyke, first time this year. Very Warm. Father, Mother, Aunt Fred and six of the little ones went to Dropmore Gardens and then to Burnham Beeches with the Wesleyan Choir. Went to have my tooth extracted but must go again.

July

12 Monday Holiday. Cricket Match at Bisham Abbey between eleven of Father's workmen, and Eleven of those employed by G.H. Vansittart Esq. The men started from Wycombe with most of their wives and children in six vans, numbering about 100, at 8.15 a.m. On arriving at Bisham they began cricket, and played one innings each after which we all did justice to the dinner provided by Host Hockley of the 'Bull'. Dinner over, we again began our sports, I went boating, some went swinging, dancing, and racing, other paid a visit to the abbey. Tea at 5. after which I went in a canoe, & had a bathe in the Thames, swimming across it. All sorts of games continued till past 8. when supper was called, then a few suitable speeches, and afterwards preparation for the return home which we finally reached without any accident at 11.30 p.m. after having enjoyed a pleasant day by the Thames.

20 Tuesday Work from 8.30 to 3.45. Went home and changed my clothes, and then went to the Park to the 'Band of Hope' Fete. There was a steam circus, and a number of velocipes and bicycles for public amusement. Fred and I had a ride on a bicycle but found it very difficult, after which I had a game with R.C. and a few others. There was a little dancing but people all complained of 'no amusements'. There was also a cricket match in Wycombe Park, between the Drapers' and Grocers' assistants in the town – Shops being closed. The former won.

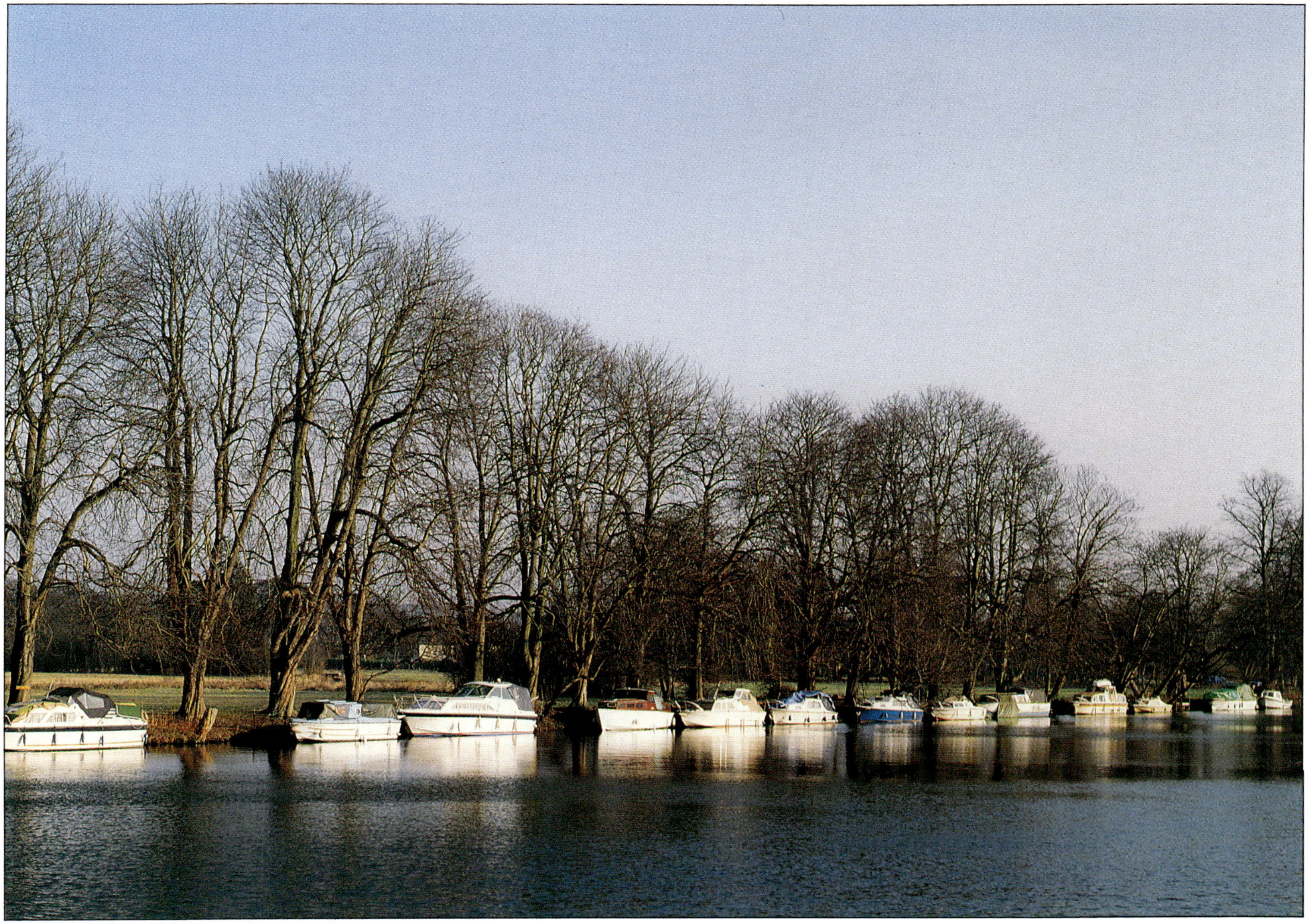

Pangbourne

August

18 Wednesday Work from 6.30 to 9 a.m. Changed my clothes and started with the Church Choir from Mr. Poulter's to Velvet Lawn at 10.30. On arriving there cricket & croquet were commenced after which dinner was disposed of by the hungry appetites. A glass of wine, with 'Church & Queen', after which all sorts of games were resumed. After tea I went for a walk to a small water mill at Ellesboro' and was shown all over it by the proprietor. About 8 o'clock we started for our jolly ride home, which after singing, hollaing and all sorts of games we finally reached at 9.30 – after having spent a fine holiday amidst the pleasant scenery at Velvet Lawn.
21 Saturday . . . Several velocipes are now parading the street 'on hire', and bicycles are coming more into use. Three or four persons own such things in the town. Fred and I are anxious to have one.

April 1870

11 Monday Breakfast at 7.30. Went which Fred and the other second class shots, in the Park, and shot for the badge of a rifle and stars. These recruits passed the first class – myself 32 points . . . Work from 9.45 to 6.30. Went home and put on my Rifle Corps Uniform and then went to drill at the Abbey. The new Colonel (Chester) was present. Told that we are not allowed to go to the Brighton Review next Monday because of Small Pox at Wycombe. After a short drill we had a march out with the band to the Marsh and stayed about ten minutes and then returned to Wycombe.
20 Wednesday Work from 8.30 to 9. Went home and had my supper. About half past three an alarm of fire was raised and both engines started to 'Pegs Mills' at Marlow Road, which was on fire. I went with two others on my bicycle and stayed till about half past five, then rode home and went flour carting at the mill. The mill was half burnt by fire.

May

6 Friday Work from 8.30 to 8.30. About which time an alarm of 'Fire' was raised, it proved to be the workshop and show room of Mr. Loosely, Upholder, Oxford Street on fire. In a short time four engines were at work on the flames, which at one time seemed to threaten the houses adjoining but through the abundant supply of water it was got under control in about two hours, having destroyed property to the value of near £650 (Estimated) in furniture, timber, and other stock. I went home at 10.30. No Choir Practice in consequence of the fire.

July

27 Work from 8.30 to 4.30. Grand Rural Fete in Wycombe Abbey Park. Shops closed at 12 o'clock. Went to the Park after tea, and saw some dancing etc, heard the Life Guard's Band till the evening. Saw the games 'grab', 'drop-glove', etc, etc, with M.E.W., Mary Dean and Miss Cooper, had a ride on the horses and amused ourselves till 9 – At 9.15 the Fireworks were let off on the opposite side of the Dyke, they looked splendid. M.E.W. and I walked about and enjoyed ourselves from 7 to 11, dancing, japanese jugglers, singing etc was carried on during the day. Fine.

February 1871

7 Tuesday Last day at Mr. Reuben Pearce's Temple Mill, High Wycombe, Bucks. Work from 8.30 to 12.45. Worked the water down at night. Mr. Pearce gave me my Apprenticeship Indentures dated four years from March 14th 1867 . . . Bought a ledger and day book ready for Pangbourne Mill. Uncle Alfred Atkins lent me a box to pack my goods in. Bought some rat traps. Chas. Moxham expected to go with me to Pangbourne tomorrow to help dress the stones. Rained nearly all day.
15 Wednesday Worked from 7 to 3.30. Changed my

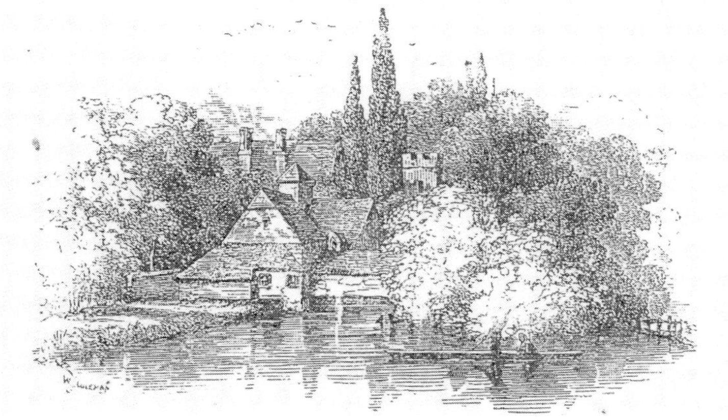

clothes and walked along the Thames bank to Mapledurham, saw Mr. W. Wooster and went to his house to tea. Then went to his mill, and looked over it – Afterwards went back to his house and had a chat and a pipe. Supper at 9 – then walked back by the Whitchurch Road at 11 o'clock.

27 Monday . . . dressed a pair of wheat stones and furrowed one till 9 o'clock. Caught a slight cold, had some onion gruel and went to bed. Received a very nice book by post from R—— C—— Wycombe about the 'Christian Year' as a Birthday Present – tomorrow being my nineteenth birthday – Read some of it at night. It has a bookmark in it worked with blue letters LOVE. . . .

28 Tuesday My nineteenth birthday – Work from 7.30 to 3. Went with George Hillesden and Harry to Mapledurham to see Mr. Wooster about foreign wheat. Had tea and walked home by 8 O'clock. Wrote a letter to Ernest, Fred, and one to R.C. at night, afterwards played a few tunes on my violin. Received a letter from R.C. in the morning. Damp and dull weather. Caught cold. Millwrights worked all through night last night. Condition of Peace between France and Germany nearly settled.

Mr J.F. Fowler, who has already introduced us to the Aylesbury breed of duck, writing in his ECHOES OF OLD COUNTRY LIFE recollects an unusual equestrian event which took place in his town. Until 1784 horse races took place annually at Haydens Hill and, in spite of later attempts to revive them, they failed through lack of support. In Mr Fowler's time Aylesbury steeple chase meetings and fox hunting were both keeping the horse riding tradition alive.

In the year 1851, at one of the early meetings of the Aylesbury Aristocratic Steeplechases, and during the stewards dinner at the White Hart in the grand old Rochester Room, the following event occurred.

The conversation turned to the fact that the Marquis of Waterford had once taken a noted hunter up the stairs and led him round the dining-table in this very room, whilst the noble Master of the Buckhounds, the Earl of Erroll, and his guests fed the horse on biscuits and apples – the Marquis afterwards leading him down stairs again into the entrance hall. One of the young Oxford gentlemen, well known for his splendid riding in the steeplechases which were then being held, turned to old Charlie Symonds and said, 'I believe, Charlie, the little grey would come up these or any other stairs.' It was asked if the trial might be made, and, on consent being obtained, down went two or three choice spirits into the stable-yard, and, to the astonishment of the party (nearly fifty people being present), a lumbering noise was heard on the stairs, and presently in walked the gallant grey. After leading him round the table and resting him before a large fire which blazed in the fine old grate before which many a time and oft poor Nellie Gwynne had warmed her dainty feet, the horse, led by a halter, was induced to jump over the backs of a couple of chairs. Then, J. Leech Manning, a sporting farmer of the neighbourhood, said he would undertake to ride him over the dinner-table (it should be mentioned that the dinner was still in progress, the third course was being

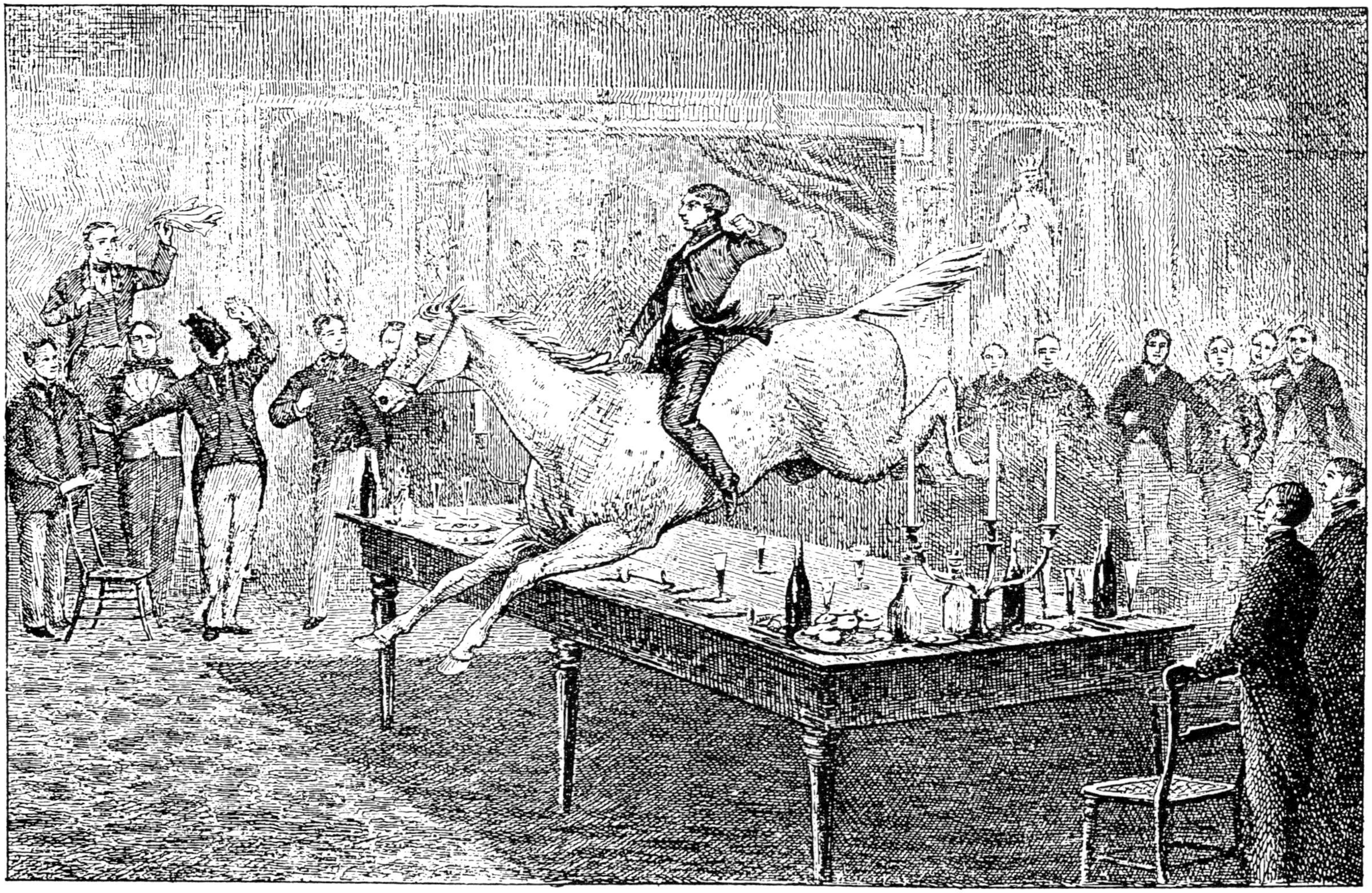

consumed, the decanters of wine going their round, the candelabra was alight, and the various wax lights as well were sparkling on the board). No sooner said than Manning jumped on to the barebacked horse, and taking the halter in his hand, he rode him up into the corner of the room, which was about forty feet long by twenty two feet wide, the table in the meantime having been slightly slued round: Manning struck the horse with his heel, and with a slap on his neck with his right hand he sent him flying over the table, covered as it was with all the usual appurtenances to a repast: he cleared it well, then to the surprise of all, he turned the horse in splendid style and jumped him back again.

The gentleman who first suggested the attempt, now a noted parish priest in an extreme northern county, then essayed the same feat. The horse answered to his cry of 'Come up,' and just cleared the table, but caught one of his heels on its edge, and pulling the cloth over smashed a few plates and glasses, which fell with a loud clatter, whereupon the rider struck the gallant steed with his open hand, and again he cleared the whole in much better style than before. Of course, immediately a dozen others, emulous of fame, wished to essay the same feat, but I thought there had been enough done to try the temper of the noble little horse, and a veto was put on any more displays of circus riding. Then the difficulty arose – How are we to get the horse to descend the stairs? From the Rochester Room to the top of the staircase there was a long gallery with a floor of polished oak, and this gallery had to be traversed before the descent commenced; a narrow carpet ran the entire length, and along this the horse went quietly enough, but on coming to the top of the stairs he stoutly refused to make the descent. Nothing we could do would induce him to put his foot downwards on to the first step, and although all the time he was as quiet as a lamb, no one could suggest a means of overcoming his scruples at taking so unusual a course. In this dilemma a learned Q.C. who was staying in the house, who had started as a candidate to represent the ancient borough of Aylesbury in Parliament, and, with him, his elder brother, a worthy baronet and M.P. for a county borough, hearing the noise on the stairs came from their sitting room, and at once suggested an easy solution of the difficulty, viz. to tie a wet towel over the horse's head, blindfold him, take him to the end of the long corridor, and then to lead him steadily along without stopping a moment, but to keep him going without any hesitation. This advice was no sooner given than it was put into practice, and the horse coming along freely enough, he began to go down the stairs, but getting frightened he stumbled and fell on his knees, but did not cease to scramble on. The two men who held him tightly by the head evidently reassured the well trained dining-room performer, and in the end he landed safely in the entrance hall, merely breaking three or four of the carved oak balusters.

Mr Fowler brings a farmer's ribald sense of humour to bear when relating his stories of Disraeli; someone of whom he was, in fact, a great admirer.

In addition to Lord Beaconsfield's desire to be an authority on agricultural matters, he was anxious to also pose as a farmer – in full costume. At one of the annual general meetings of the Royal and Cenral Bucks Association, at Aylesbury, those attending the show-yard were startled by the appearance of their beloved M.P. entering in full panoply of agricultural mail, or, as he thought, in full farming costume. He had discarded the traditional top-boots, but appeared in a brown velveteen shooting-coat, with flapping waistcoat, and over his black trousers he had drawn a pair of long dark-brown leather gaiters, with wooden buttons covered with leather up the side, reaching from his dandy Wellington boots to his hips, and fastened there with leathern straps to his brace-buttons; his head was covered with a black 'billycock' hat, and a blue bird's-eye silk handkerchief was tied loosely round his neck, and he carried a big stick with a spud at the end; in fact he looked like a well-dressed gamekeeper. Everyone was screaming with laughter, but he thought he was paying us agricultural folk a compliment by wearing what he considered to be the typical dress of the British farmer – he must have been surprised to find many of the real article dressed in the modern style, and several with coats by well known Mr Poole, of Savile Row. These little idiosyncrasies of his rather showed in reality how much he wished to identify himself with his own country people.

Lord Beaconsfield – whilst Mr Disraeli, as M.P. for

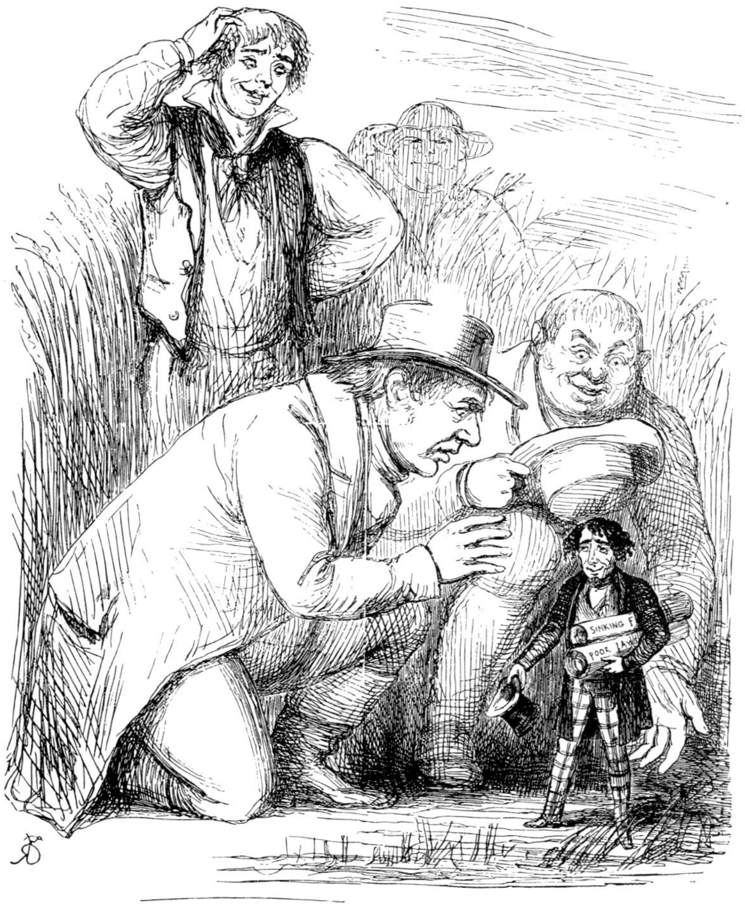

Bucks – was always particularly anxious to pose as the British farmer, and phrases in many of his speeches have become household words. In one of his after-dinner speeches, at which I was present, he had a chance to show off his agricultural knowledge, and in speaking of the advantages of farmers breeding their own stock, he told them, as a great piece of original discovery in sheep breeding, 'that they should cross their Downs with Cotswolds.' As this had been the practice for many years with nearly three-fourths of his hearers, there was not much valuable information in the advice; but our facetious contemporary, Mr Punch, seized upon the phrase, and recommended him to cross his party with a dash of his bitterest opponents.

On another occasion at Hughenden I noticed how luxuriantly the trees grew, especially the cedars and the pines, and instanced a young cedar of Lebanon which had grown to a large size. He told me he had brought it himself with a few others from the valley of Lebanon when some years ago he travelled in Palestine, and that he had given one to Lady Grenville at Dropmore, a place about six miles distant, and that there was great rivalry between them as to which grew the best, her ladyship annually coming over to see his tree and compare notes, whilst he returned the visit. 'I was always pleased,' he said, 'to find mine was by far the finest specimen, notwithstanding old Frost, her gardener, took especial care of hers.'

I remember once when visiting at Hughenden, that Mr Disraeli put on his billy-cock hat, and with his legs enclosed in leather gaiters and a spud in his hand, he suggested taking a walk through that portion of the beech-woods surrounding the north-west of the Manor House, which he called the 'German forest'. We were talking on many subjects, and as we passed an opening in the woods, he said, 'Come here, and sit ye down', and he led the way to a rough seat made of some split larch firpoles, and completely out of sight of the 'madding crowd'. He remarked, 'This is a favourite resort of mine. You can see no trace of human being. I only have the beech-woods, primroses, and wild flowers about me, and more than all, it shuts out any view of Wycombe' – and he smiled complacently, and talked of farming, and the future prospects of that business.

The reference to primroses is not without significance. These were Disraeli's favourite flowers and ever since Queen Victoria

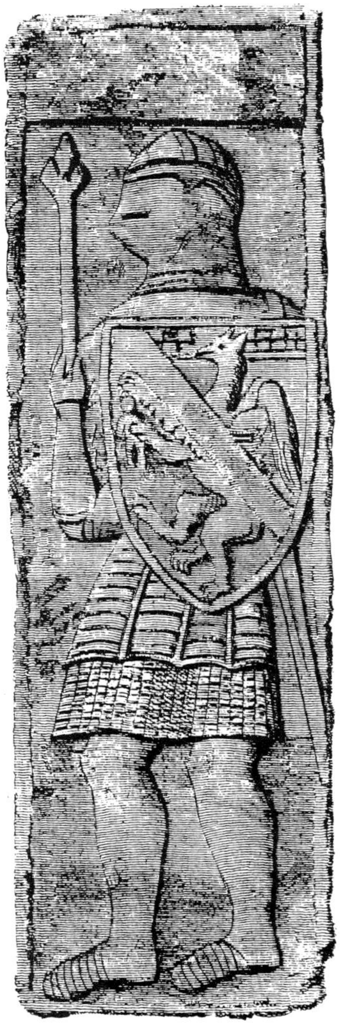

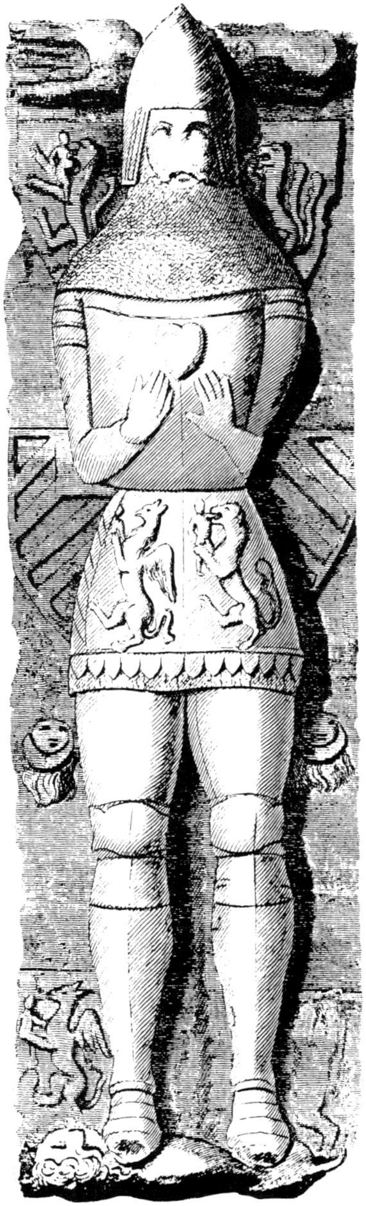

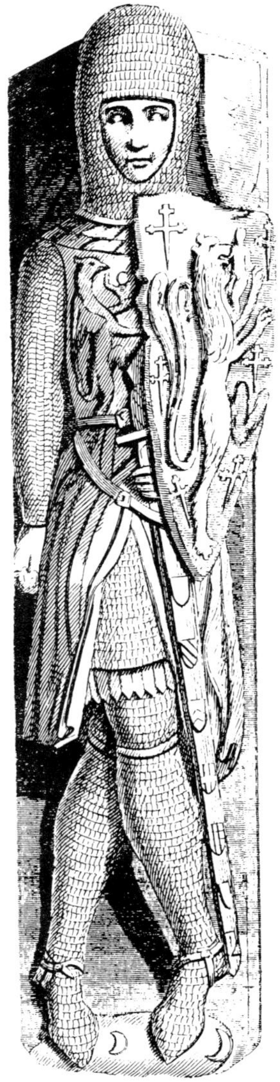

brought these to his grave there has been an annual Primrose Sunday at Hughenden Church.

The Earl of Beaconsfield was on good terms with his tenants and labourers and visited them in their cottages. He called them, according to Fowler, 'a stalwart race, shrewd, and open to reason'. In 1860 he wrote:

I find great amusement in talking to people at work in the woods and grounds at Hughenden. Their conversation is racy, and the repose of their natural manners agreeable. . . . I don't know any men, who are so completely masters of their business, and of the secluded, but delicious world in which they live. A forest is like the ocean, monotonous only to the ignorant.

Disraeli clearly loved Hughenden; he further writes, one October:

The limes all golden, the beeches ruddy brown, while the oaks and elms and pines are still dark and green, and contrast well with the brighter tints. But not a leaf has fallen; they want the first whisper of the frost, and then they will go out like the lamps when the dawn breaks on a long festival.

The strong literary undercurrent is unmistakable in these brief extracts and that is to be expected. Disraeli wrote many books, some of them like CONINGSBY, SYBIL *and* TANCRED *becoming justly renown. Of his library he writes:*

I have a passion for books and trees. I like to look at them. When I come down to Hughenden I pass the first week in sauntering about my park and examining all the trees, and then I saunter in the library and survey the books. My collection is limited to Theology, the Classica and History. Anything miscellaneous in it is the remains of the Bradenham Collection, but the great bulk of the *Belles lettres* I parted with after my father's death.

Leaving Disraeli, who was an established figure in the Victorian literary world, we find ourselves in the company of Mr J. Leadbetter, a writer with a rather different accent. Let us enter into the spirit of his writing and allow ourselves to be immersed with him in his subject. His A PILGRIMAGE TO THE SHRINES OF BUCKINGHAMSHIRE *was written in 1860 and encourages us to let our imaginations wander through a time now even further in the past.*

First he considers Cliveden:

Come with me, then, and enter this little boat. Resign yourself to my guidance, and I assure you that our voyage shall be fair, and that no cloudy sky shall intervene with its blighting shower, to mar our joyous holiday. We slowly pull down the river, fanned by the cool breeze, wafted over the smiling meadows that border with their 'draperie of green' the silver waters. Soon we pass Cookham Church, half embowered among the trees, and half shrouded with ivy, whose verdant garniture clothes the time-worn walls, and towers above its battlements. We pass a loch, and then bursts upon our view the scene, in all its fair splendour of woodland and rural beauty. Oh! traveller, who with weary feet marcheth along the borders of the Rhine to behold its ancient beauties, you should be with us today, on your own English Rhine, and I would show you a scene that equals any of its boasted beauty. Before us lie the 'wood-crowned heights,' with the sun-beams playing in light and shadow over their verdant surface, now lighting up the pale green of the fragrant beech, and resting on the dark branches of the sombre pines which stand amidst their fairer brethren like an ancient time-worn castle frowning over a pleasant landscape. . . . Soon we come to a little lodge near the river, and turning our boat, enter a small cove, and, on leaving it, find ourselves in the far-famed pleasure-grounds of Cliefden. . . . We . . . advance along a pathway, until we reach the mansion. It is a large building of Italian architecture, and surrounded with terraces, commanding

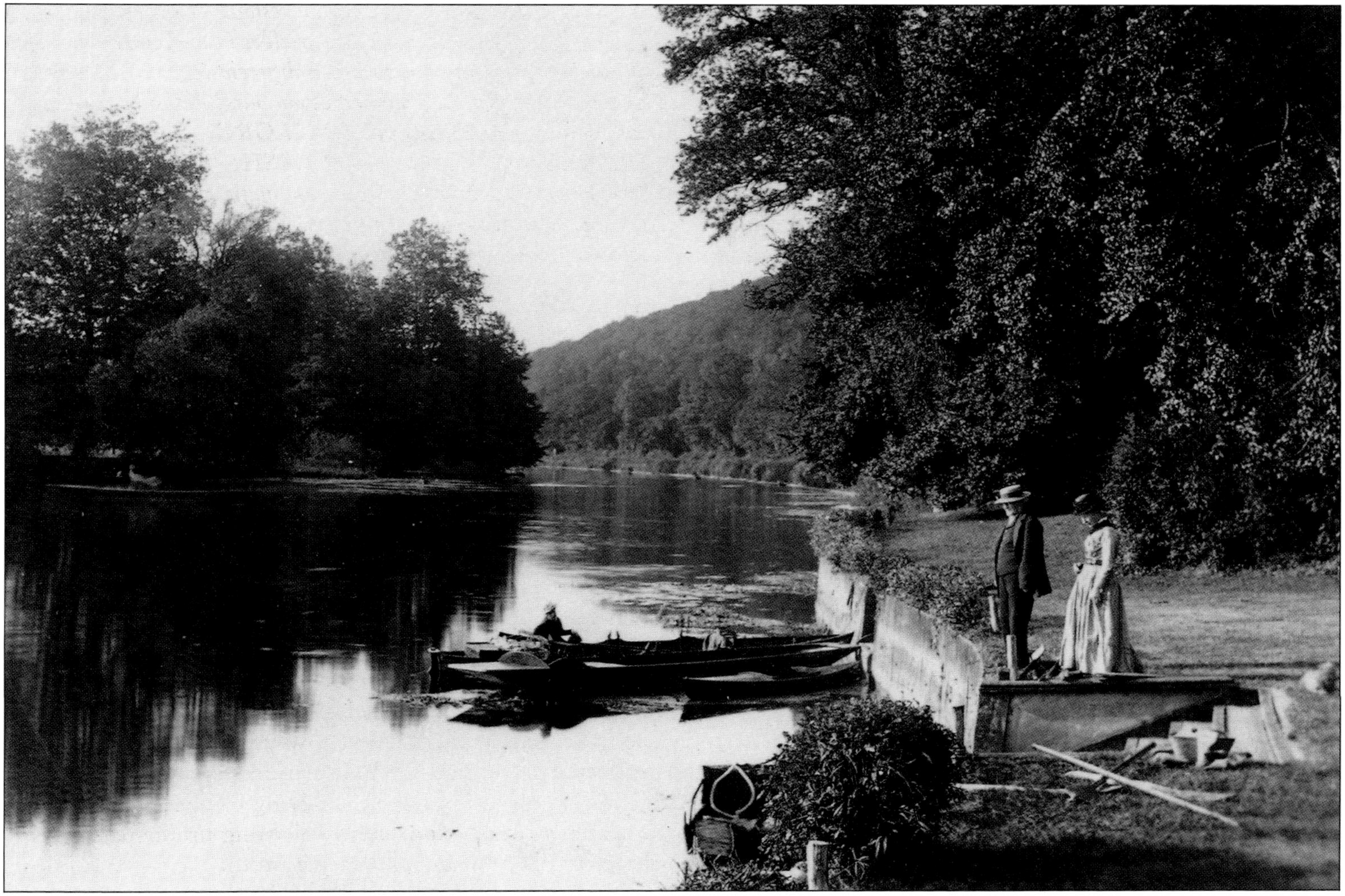

Cliveden

from their balustraded heights beautiful views of the surrounding country. At a small gateway we ring a bell, and a guide comes whose duty it is to accompany visitors over the pleasure-grounds and ornamental gardens. At the foot of the terrace we pause to gaze at the glorious scene before us. . . . We wander on, pausing to catch, between the trees, glimpses of the surrounding country in all its extent of woodland and plain, the lucid Thames winding, like a silver thread, through the landscape, flashing and sparkling in the sun's rays. Soon we come to where, formed by the gardener's skill, is a 'true lover's knot,' filled with forget-me-nots.

It is amidst this charming scene, and on the site of the present house, in 1740, that Thomson, assisted by Mallet, wrote the 'Masque,' for which 'Rule Britannia' was written, and the first sounds of 'Britons never never will be slaves,' echoed through the lofty rooms, and resounded upon the listening ears of a numerous suite attendant upon the Prince and Princess of Wales, who were staying at Cliefden.

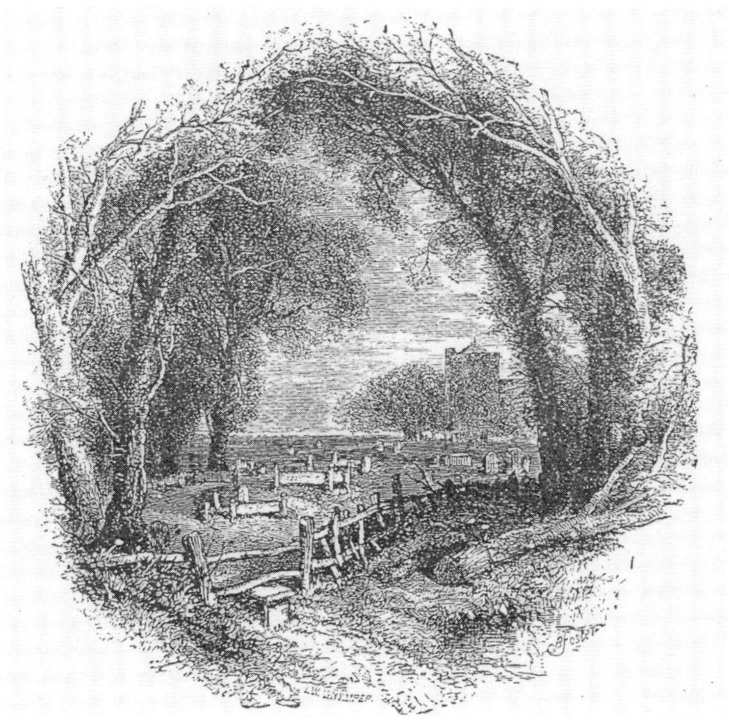

And so Leadbetter whisks us from Cliveden to Burnham Beeches which he endows with even more romanticism.

We have reached the object of our search, and are at 'Burnham Beeches.' What a wild and picturesque spot it seems, as it lays before us in all its rugged verdant beauty . . . We advance down one of the forest paths, that winds along beneath the shade of these venerable trees, pausing to gaze at their huge and half ruined forms, which are formed in all fantastic shapes, as though Puck and his legion of mischievous elves had played their sport with them but yester-even. Time worn as they are – tarnished as is their rustic beauty by the summer's sun, and the winter's storms that have passed over them – yet they are not dead, still do they struggle in the hard grasp of old Father Time, and from their hoary heads there sprouts forth a gay coronal of leaves that blooms like the bay wreath on the venerable head of a poet, and dower them still with the charms of youthful beauty.

Burnham Beeches obviously inspired Leadbetter but we are left in no doubt by his letter, a hundred years earlier, to H. Walpole that the poet Thomas Gray was also very strongly influenced by this same atmospheric environment. It has been suggested that the 'nodding beech' of his Elegy *was to be found on the southern fringe of this woodland. His memorial and tomb can be seen in Stoke Poges' churchyard.*

My comfort amid all this is, that I have at the distance of half-a-mile, through a green lane, a forest – the vulgar call

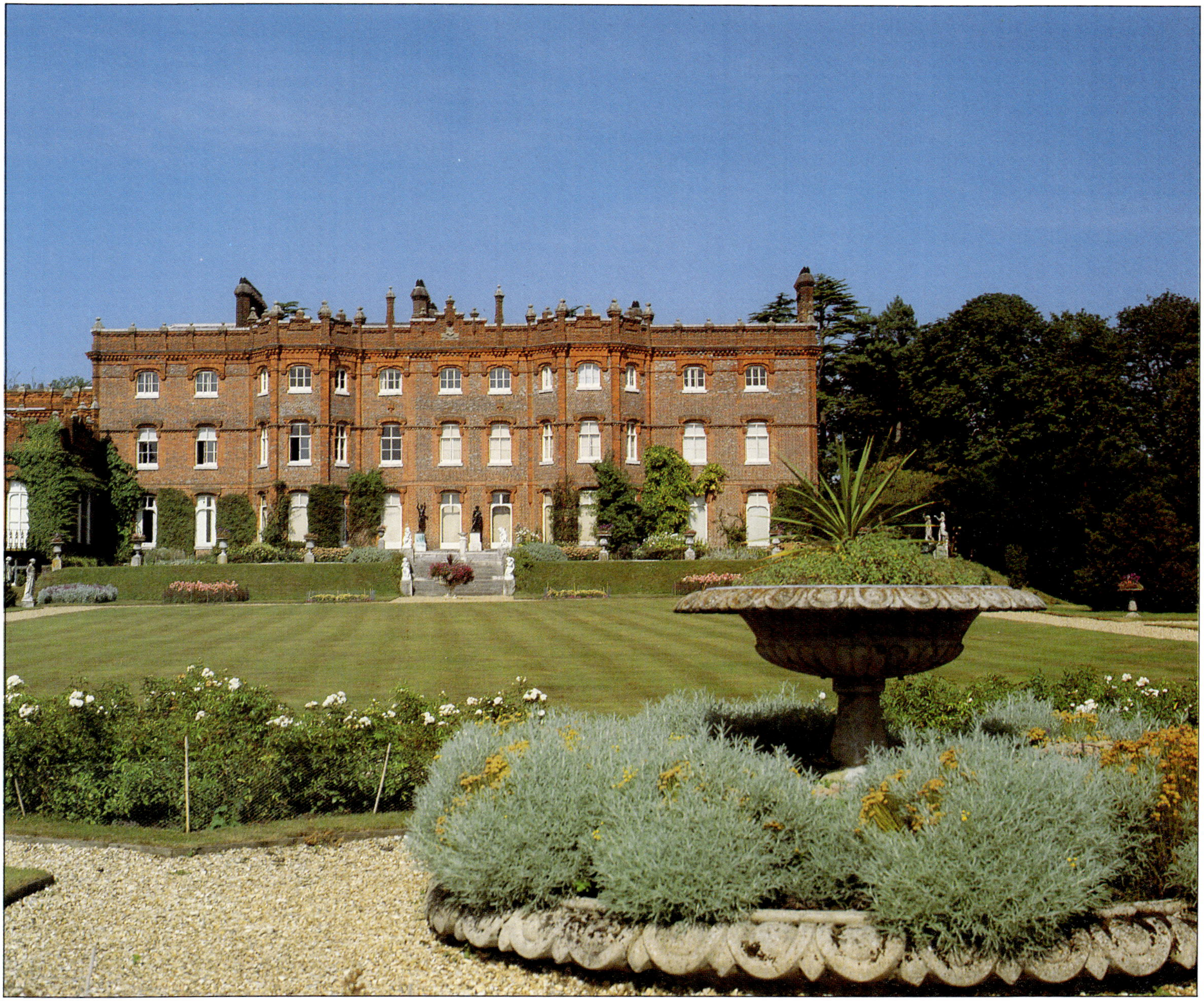

Hughenden Manor

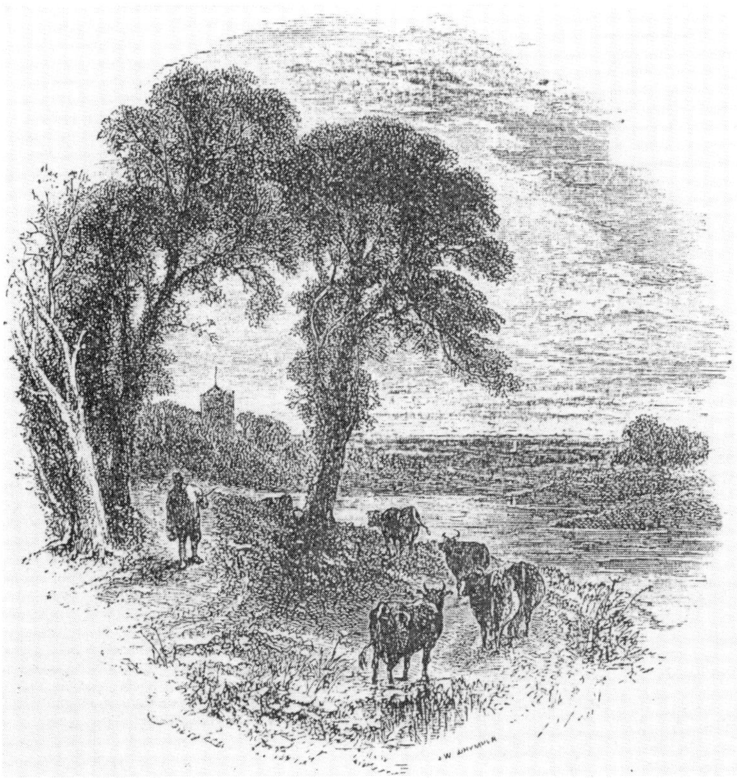

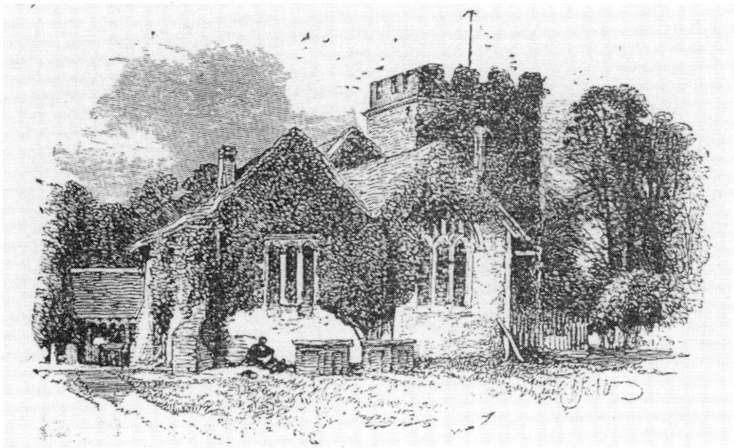

it a common – all my own, at least as good as so, for I spy no human being in it but myself. It is a little chaos of mountains and precipices, mountains it is true, that do not ascend much above the clouds, nor are the declivities quite as amazing as Dover cliffs; but just such hills as people who love their necks as well as I do, may venture to climb, and crags that give the eye as much pleasure as if they were more dangerous. Both hill and vale are covered with most venerable beeches, and other very reverend vegetables, that like most ancient people, are always dreaming out their old stories to the winds –

> And as they bow, their hoary lips relate,
> In murmering sounds, the dark decrees of fate;
> While visions, as poetic eyes avow,
> Cling to each leaf, and swarm on every bough.

Along the Chiltern heights it was not unknown in former times for beer to be cheaper than water during times of drought. Stoke Row, like many other places in the region suffered from water shortages, but in 1864 through the beneficence of the Maharajah of Benares and his friendship with Mr E.A. Reade of Ipsden a well was sunk. The system of lifting the water was designed jointly by Mr Reade and Mr Richard Wilder (Wilder, in fact, made many less exotic well-heads, some of which can still be seen) and entailed the use of two nine-gallon buckets to raise the water from a depth of 368 feet.

In 1872 the recovery of the Prince of Wales from typhoid fever was to be the cause of a further act of generosity by the Maharajah. The Berks and Oxon Advertiser *of 1872 records the day of celebration. One of the highlights of this was a spectacular fireworks display:*

Then after an interval followed the illuminations, which had been entrusted to Messrs. C.T. Brock and Co. the well known pyrotechnisists of the Crystal Palace, and it is only due to them and their assistants to sum up the whole matter in one word – perfection. The displays were made

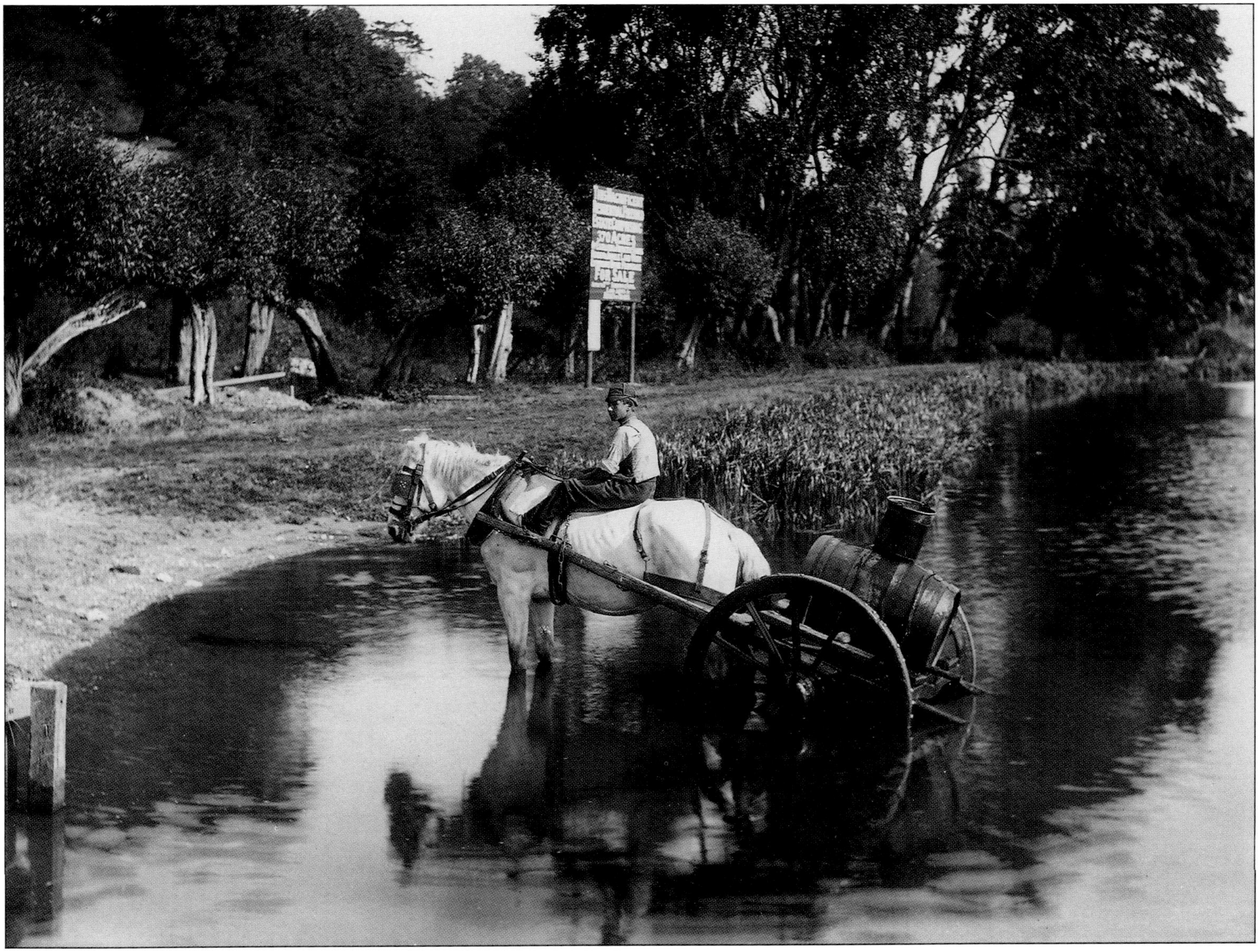

Watercart at Shiplake

in the well ground and orchard, the spectators having a full view along the line of the public road, several waggons also having been provided by the farmers of the neighbourhood for the accommodation of the children and visitors. . . . At the signal given, 17 aerial maroons were fired with the precision of artillery practice, as the Maharajah's salute. Then followed rockets, saucissons, tourbillions, sheels, a nameless and profuse variety of other descriptions, and the ascent of a balloon, which gently soared away, bursting after a time into magnesium stars and coloured fires. These displays were interspersed with special devices. Of these a fiery fountain, mock suns in various parts of the enclosure, and parachute rockets were only a foretaste of more splendid exhibitions. One of these was the Maharajah's name ISHREE, which suddenly burst forth in dazzling brightness on a raised frame in front of the well, followed by a cascade of fire, which spread fan like across the width of the well enclosure, casting out jets of many colours, so as to elicit not only admiration but the astonishment of the spectators. Next followed the illumination of the well structure by coloured fires, more impressive from the stilness and the duration of the display than any other. The grand device of the Prince of Wales' feathers and motto on a framework 20 feet square was of course reserved for the last. It was most magnificent, surrounded by wheels and cascades of fire, and was followed as the illumination declined by the startling effect of a single flight of 100 rockets. . . . All combined to make this a happy day for Stoke Row. The weather was fine, the night was still, the wind in just the right direction to keep the smoke from the spectators. The Nettlebed band was in great force, the crowd was enormous, but orderly, and the Chiltern Hills never resounded with louder and more loyal cheers for the Queen, the Prince and Princess of Wales, the good Maharajah of Benares, and his heir apparent, or the young Rajah, as the rustics shouted, from inability to give out his proper name.

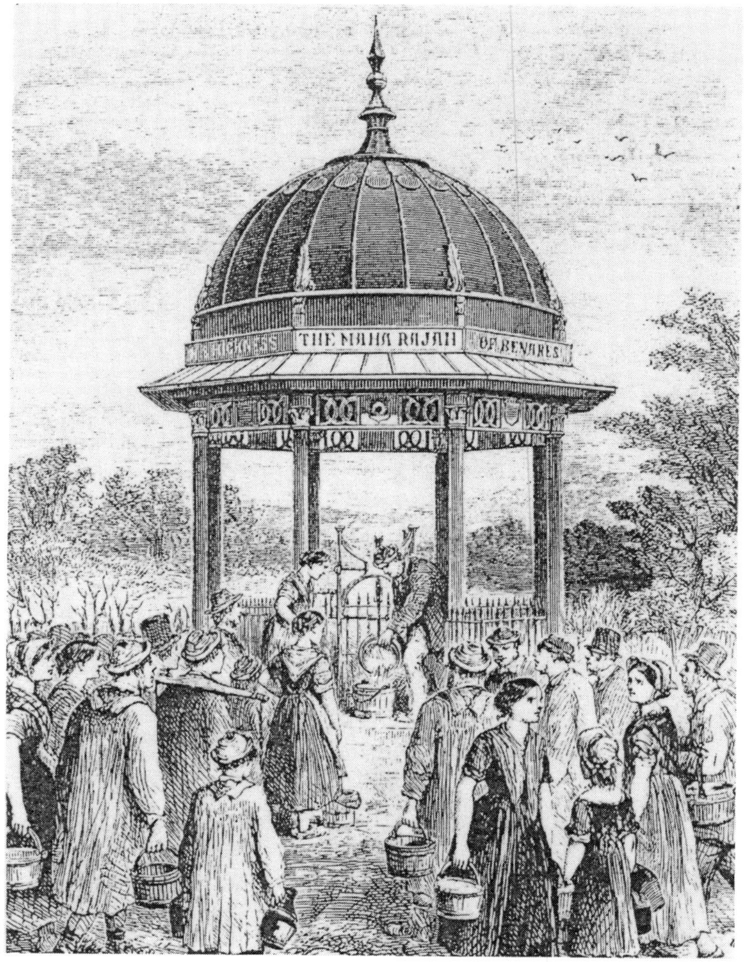

Another gentleman from overseas who established a connection with the Chiltern area came from America. The Revd James Stone, a Philadelphian, following a visit to this country, put pen to paper on his return home to write THE HEART OF MERRIE ENGLAND, which was published in 1887. 'Where is the Heart of this Merrie England? There are twenty border counties and twenty inland counties, and in none of them is old

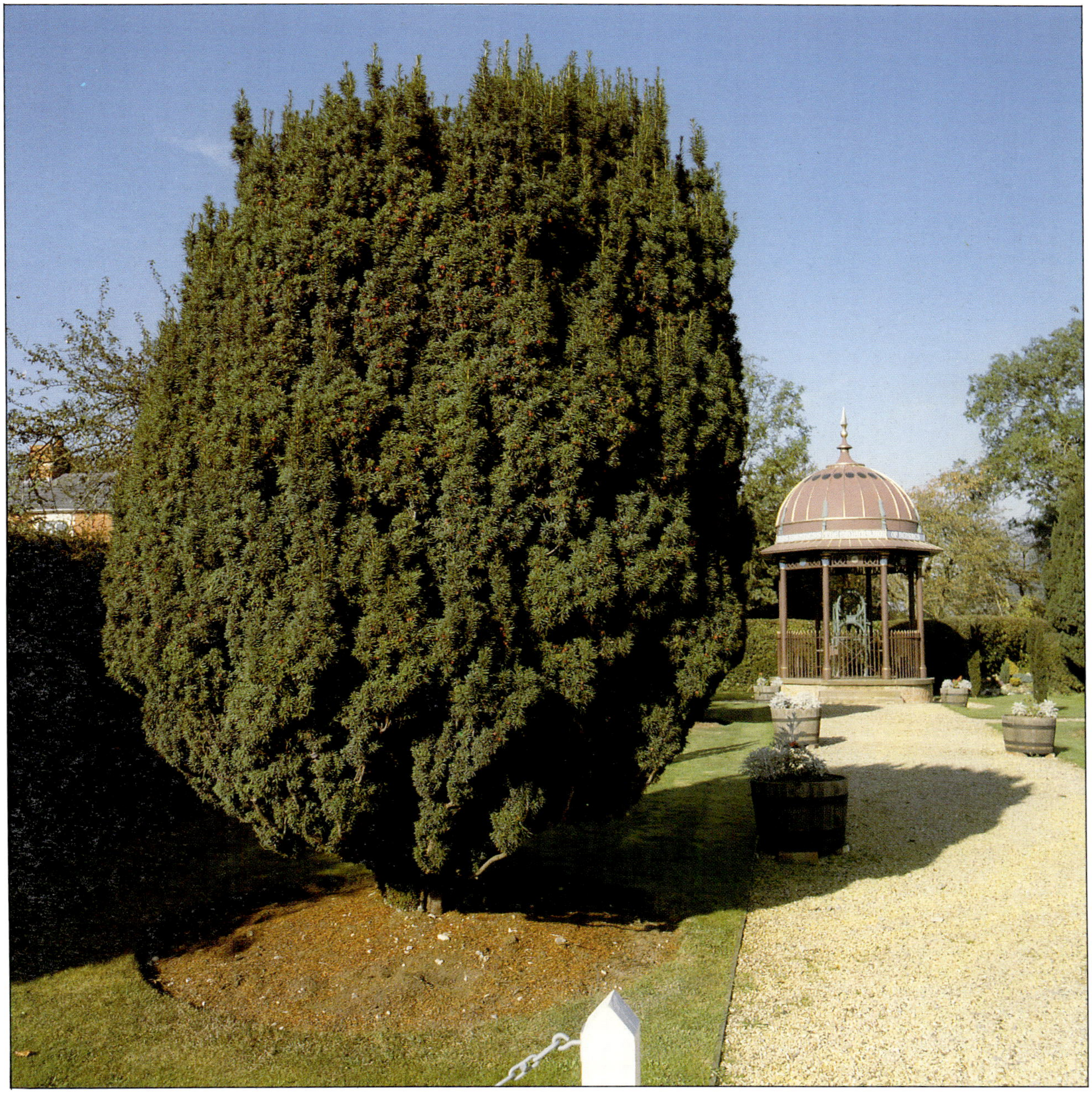

Stoke Row

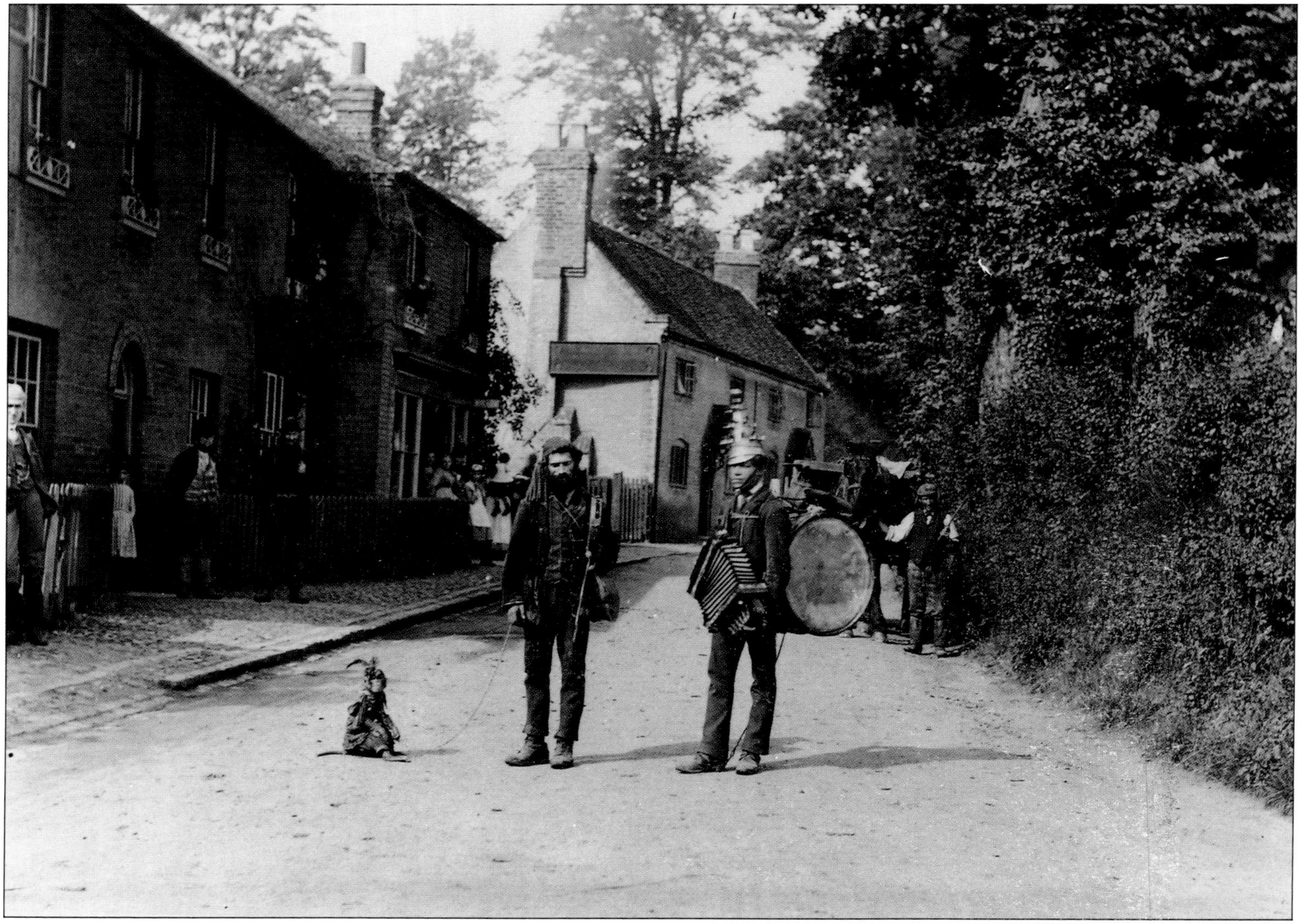

Taplow Street musicians

Merry England better seen than in the fair counties of Warwick, Worcester and Oxford.'

His fascination for the English character is immediately established in his preface with the comment: 'In no part of the book is a character given that is not sketched from life – sometimes so faintly disguised that not a few into whose hands this volume may come will easily recognize the author's model and purpose.'

Our intrepid American visitor walks from Thame to Watlington and there records for us a slice of old England.

As the twilight darkens, the moon floods the country with her silvery beams. Beyond this long wall is the road leading to Pyrton, a small village with an Elizabethan mansion where Hampden's father-in-law lived. Another field and a close, and Watlington begins . . . There is a house – we passed it when we entered the town – which was many years since occupied by a wheelwright. A jovial happy go lucky sort of fellow was he, a workman of the first rank, well to do, employing several men and apprentices and holding some respect and position in the neighbourhood. He made most of the wagons and carts used hereabouts, and once a year, after a season of good work, he gave supper to his friends and workmen, his best customers also being invited. Instead of the smoking hoop of the wheel, the boys saw the vaporous offrisings of the big boiler into which every Monday throughout the year was put the washed linen of the household, but which contained hams, legs of mutton and rounds of beef, carrots, potatoes, and cabbage. . . . His hospitality was boundless, nor did he reach the acme of his joy till he knew that every one around his board was stuffed to the full, and that even the rubicand and ale-soaked farmers were so far gone as to need somebody to see them safely home. For one or two of his neighbours a wheelbarrow stood in the yard, and about midnight the good natured apprentices would bowl them off to their domiciles with right hearty glee. . . . Later on everybody went to bed – that is to say, everybody except the apprentices, whose couch in the attic being occupied by visitors from over Chinnor way obliged them to sleep on the floor with the dogs before the kitchen fire.

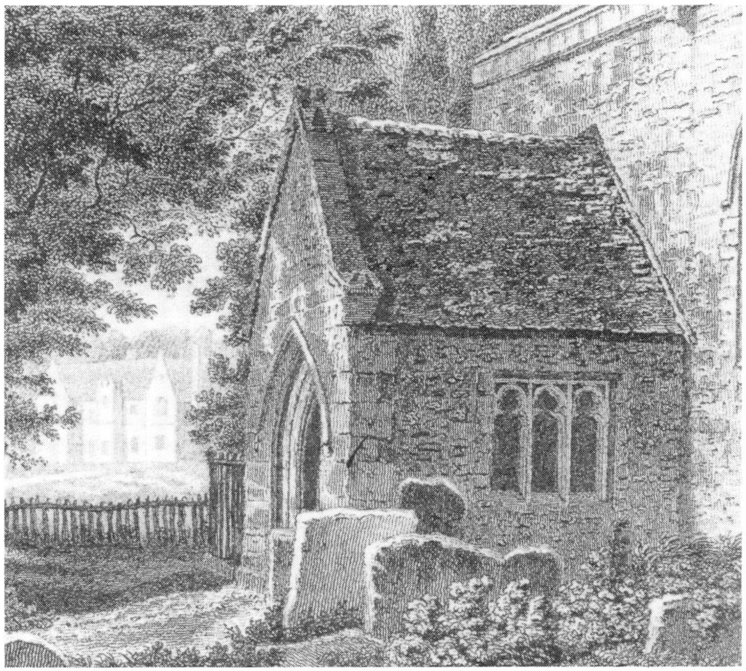

But we must away to other parts of this interesting town. Once in a while a Punch-and-Judy show comes and exhibits near the town hall. There is then much excitement – even greater than that caused by the monthly visit of the 'scissor grinder.' The latter fairly rivals the travelling tinker, who does a fair trade for two reasons – first, because of his handiness at mending old pots and kettles; and secondly, being a gypsy, he is suspected of a capability of stealing fowl by way of revenge for not having work given him. If he cannot have bread honestly – Well, that is what some think. The children are half afraid of him because gypsies have been known to steal boys and girls

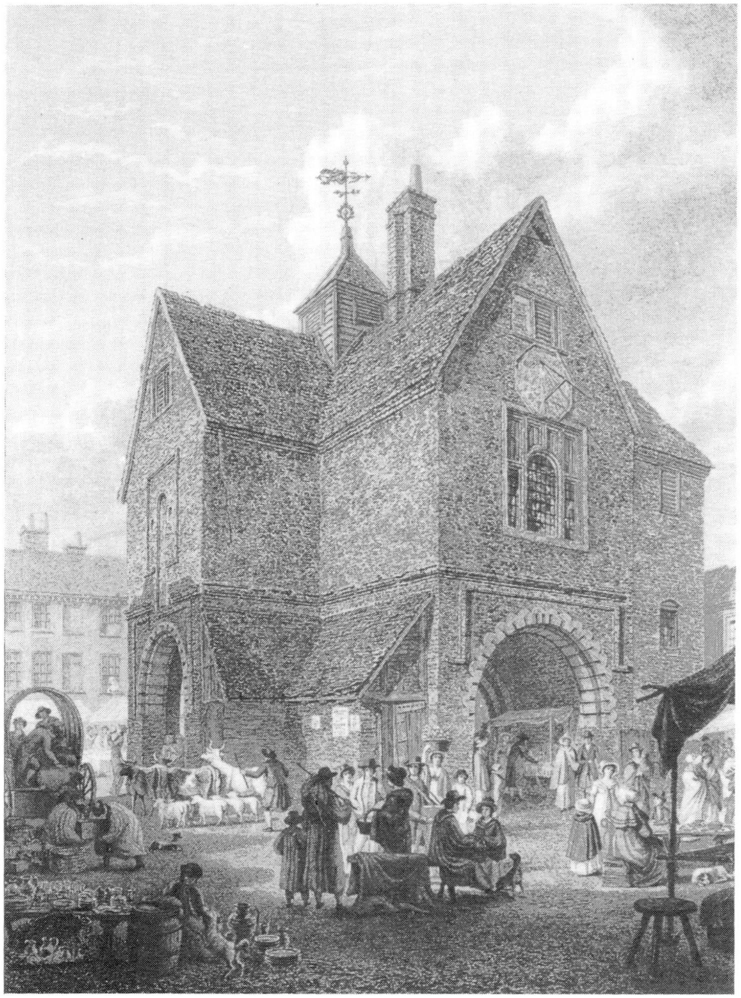

and make acrobats, and sometimes aristocrats, out of them. As to the grinder of scissors, he is commonly supposed to live somewhere in the neighbourhood, though where nobody knows. He is even suspected of being an itinerant preacher, but the weight of opinion is rather in favour of regarding him as a pretty straightforward sort of man. He is quiet, low in his charges, sober and respectful. For a penny he will sharpen all the cutlery of a small establishment. He also mends umbrellas and sells paper windmills. When he comes wheeling his little machine down the street, boys run after him with their pocket knives and women with their scissors, and as the sparks fly from the tiny grindstone everybody looks on with profound interest. But he shines only in the absence of the sun. The luminary of luminaries is the puppet show man. Here in this open space in front of the White Hart – one of the best inns, by the way, in the country – he goes through the tragedy of Punchinello. Between the acts he performs on a primitive musical instrument consisting of a row of small pipes fastened in the front of his coat. This 'wind organ,' being level with his mouth so that he can use it at his convenience, and if need be beat a drum at the same time, produced music similar to that which is obtained by blowing over the open end of a key. Occasionally he uses a jewsharp; sometimes, a cornet; less frequently a violin. If he has any artistic vanity, it is helped by the lusty cheers of the crowd; his pocket is filled with their pence. Only let Punch kill the devil, and every man in the company will give the 'price of a pint.'

From the market-hall southward is a street called Couching and this ends in the road leading from Henley, the oldest place in the county, to Oxford, the most celebrated. A pleasant road it is too, running in one direction over the hills to Nettlebed, on which a windmill spreads its sails to the breezes and thick furze bushes dot the unenclosed common. . . . There lie the hills – graceful lines against the horizon, the green of the fields and the woods making more intense the white of the chalk pits and roads. At the foot of the Mark are the wheat and barley fields . . . A pleasant sight it is to see the harvest moon shining on the standing shocks of corn; pleasanter to see the poor and needy leasing after the reapers. How strange appears the one tree in the middle of yonder field, thick with leaves and casting a deep shadow in which the sheep rest during

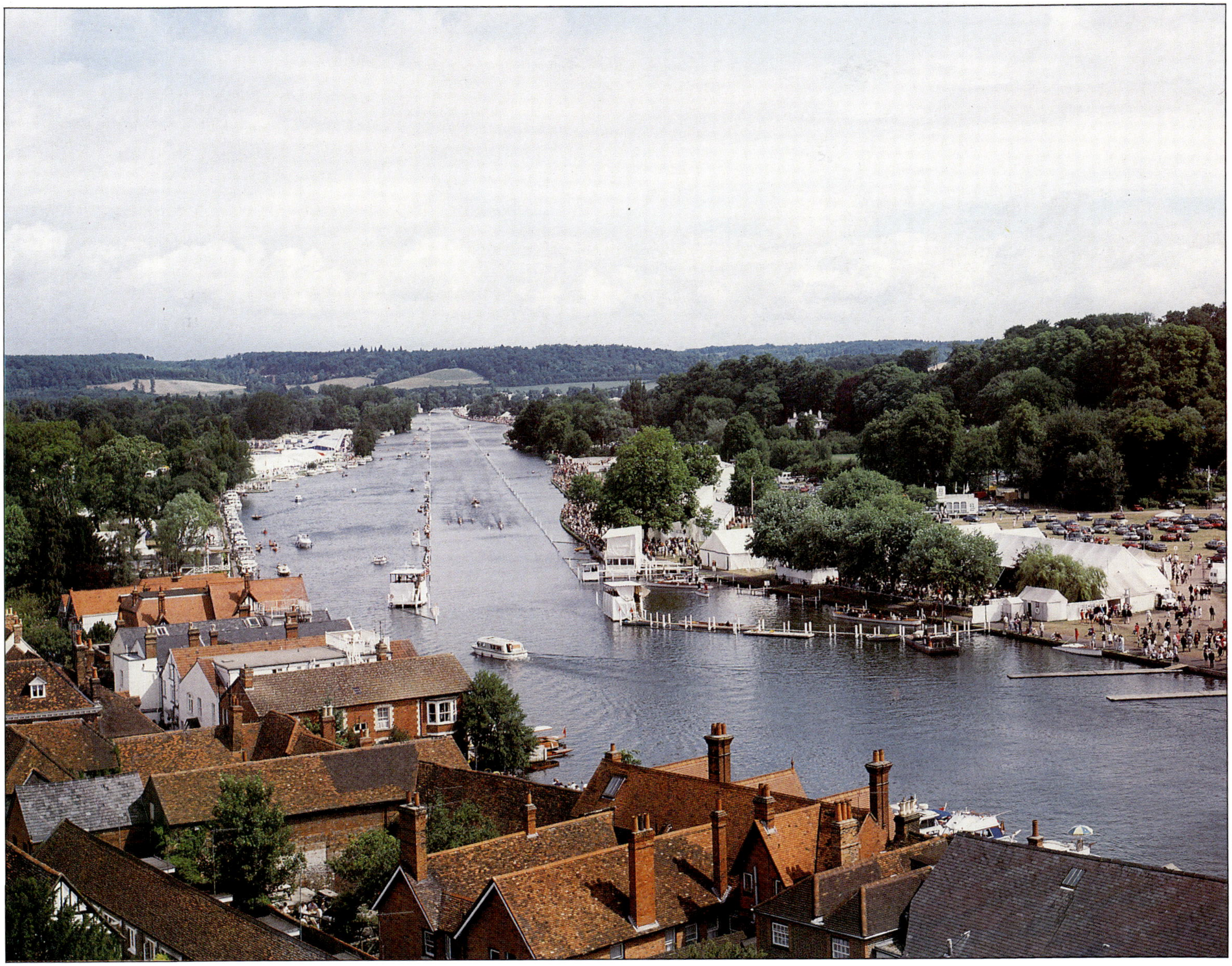

Henley Regatta

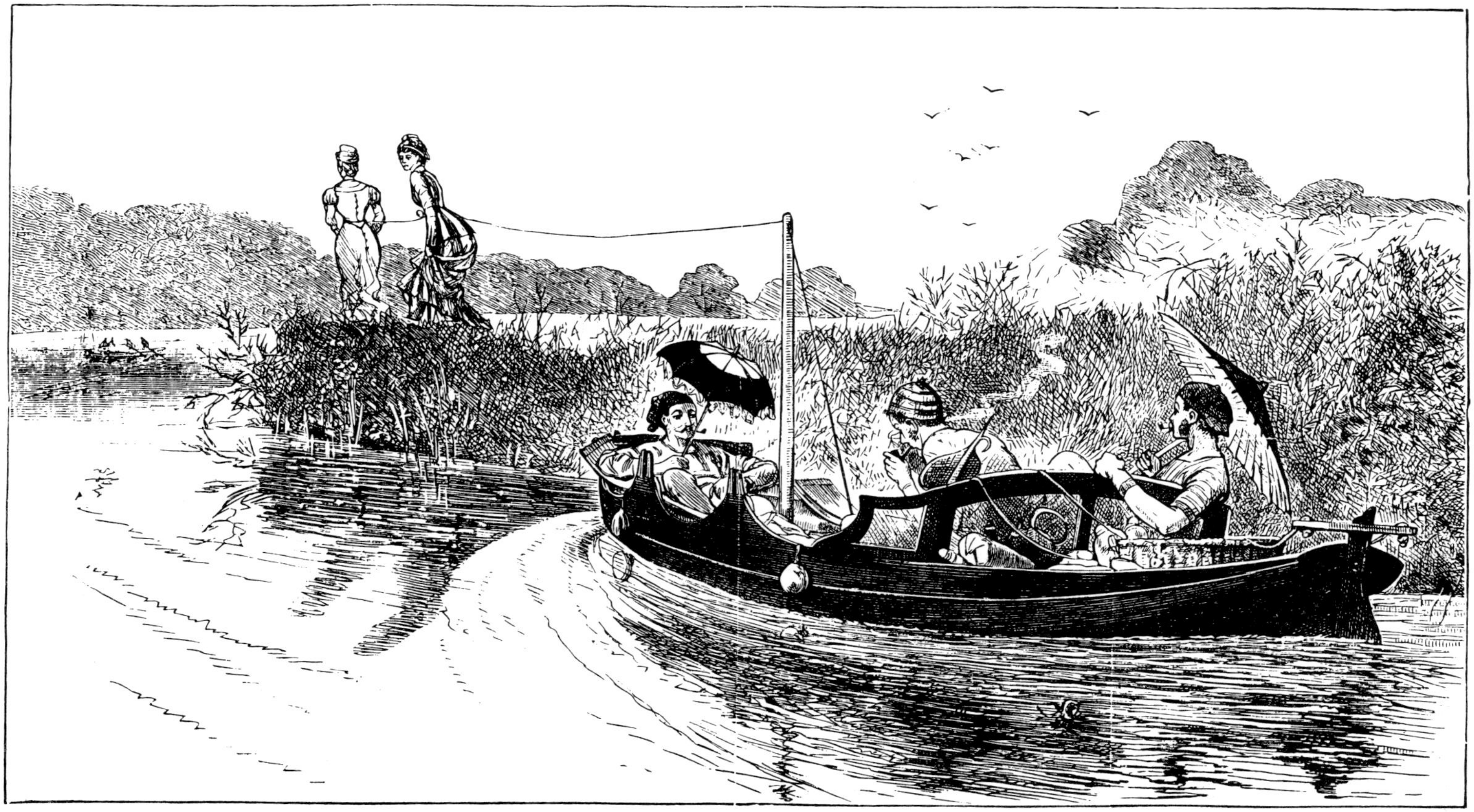

the noontide heat, but seemingly lost in its solitude! . . . Crooked streets old houses, shops with tiny windows and with bow windows, residences hid away behind high walls and seen only through great iron gates, walls built of flint with brick facings and broken glass bottles along the top, cobblestones and pebbles under foot, antique taverns, a gentle, drowsy, restful, self satisfied life – that is Watlington.

To encompass the River Thames in our travels about the Chilterns and not to mention Jerome K. Jerome would be a serious omission. For the famous river journey made by his THREE MEN IN A BOAT surely must be one of the most memorable and humorous ever described. Here we find the intrepid oarsmen in and around Marlow:

Marlow is one of the pleasantest river centres I know of. It is a bustling, lively little town; not very picturesque on the whole, it is true, but there are many quaint knooks and corners to be found in it, nevertheless – standing arches in the shattered bridge of Time, over which our fancy travels back to the days when Marlow Manor owned Saxon Algar

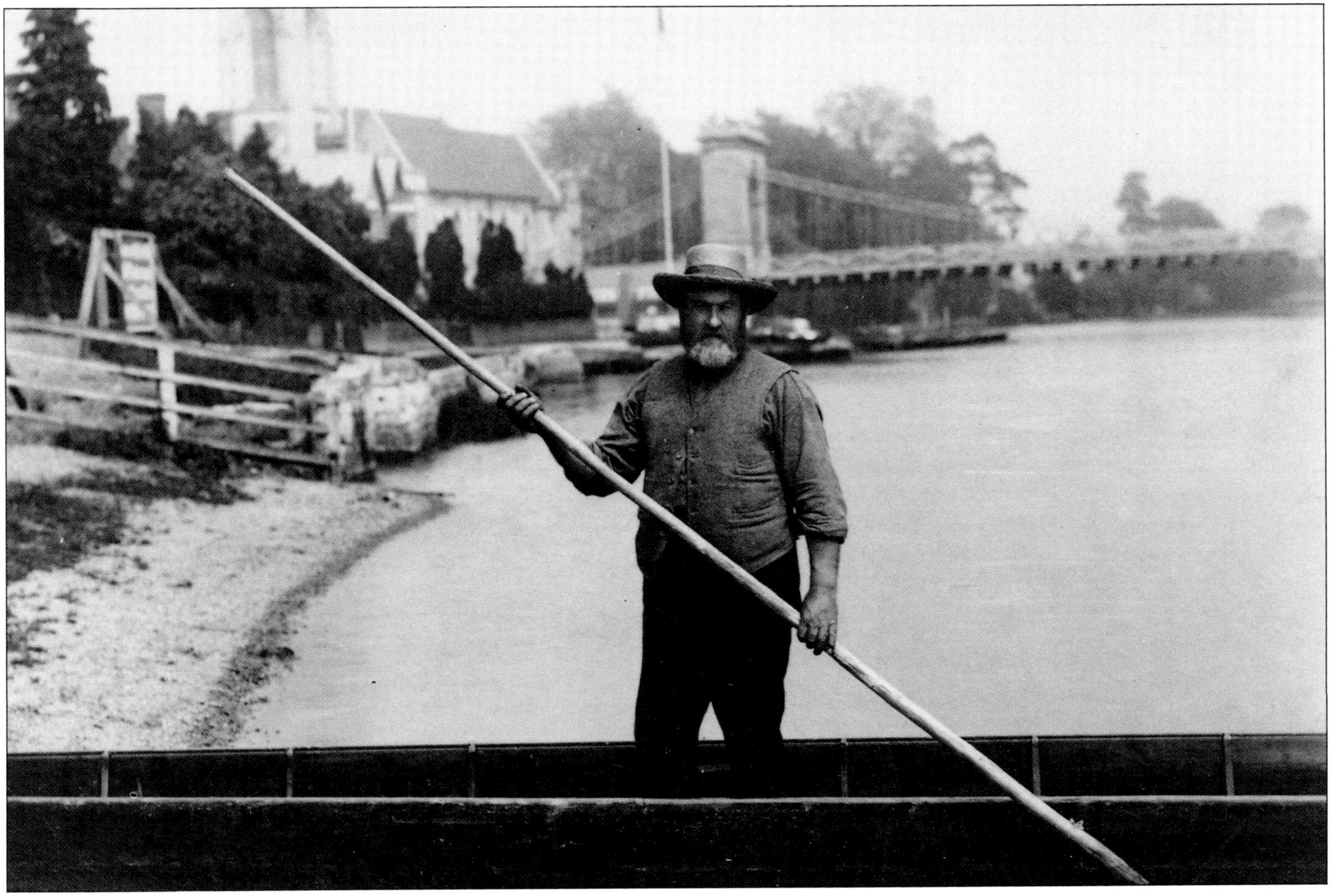

Marlow

for its lord, ere conquering William seized it to give to Queen Matilda . . .

We got up tolerably early on the Monday morning at Marlow . . . did our marketing after breakfast, and re-victualled the boat for three days. . . .

Our departure from Marlow I regard as one of our greatest successes. It was dignified and impressive, without being ostentatious. We had insisted at all the shops we had been to that the things should be sent with us then and there. None of your 'Yes, sir, I will send them off at once; the boy will be down there before you are, sir!' and then fooling about on the landing-stage, and going back to the shop twice to have a row about them, for us.

We went to a good many shops adopting this principle at each one; and the consequence was that, by the time we had finished, we had a fine collection of boys with baskets following us around as heart could desire; and our final march down the middle of the High Street, to the river, must have been as imposing a spectacle as Marlow had seen for many a long day.

The order of procession was as follows:

Monmorency, carrying a stick.
Two disreputable-looking curs, friends of Montmorency's.
George, carrying coats and rugs, and smoking
a short pipe.
Harris, trying to walk with easy grace, while carrying a
bulged-out Gladstone bag in one hand and a bottle of
lime-juice in the other.
Greengrocer's boy and baker's boy, with baskets.
Boots from the hotel, carrying hamper.
Confectioner's boy, with basket.
Grocer's boy, with basket.
Long-haired dog.
Cheesemonger's boy, with basket.
Odd man, carrying a bag.
Bosom companion of odd man, with his hands in
his pockets
smoking a short clay.
Fruiterer's boy, with basket.
Myself, carrying three hats and a pair of boots, and trying to
look as if I didn't know it.
Six small boys, and four stray dogs.

When we got down to the landing-stage, the boatman said: 'Let me see, sir; was yours a steam-launch or a house-boat?'

On our informing him it was a double-sculling skiff, he seemed surprized . . . There is lovely country round about it (Marlow), too, if, after boating you are fond of a walk, while the river itself is at its best here. Down to Cookham, past the Quarry Woods and the meadows, is a lovely reach. Dear old Quarry Woods! With your narrow, climbing paths, and winding glades, how scented to this hour you seem with memories of sunny summer days! How haunted are your shadowy vistas with the ghosts of laughing faces! How from your whispering leaves there softly fall the voices of long ago!

Quarry Woods, recently devastated by severe gales and no longer retaining the wild beauty found a hundred years ago, is reputed to have been 'Wild Woods' in Kenneth Grahame's WIND IN THE WILLOWS.

The wintry view of the landscape given by Mole is bleak, and yet his words capture the intensity of feeling generated by the Chiltern countryside at this season.

. . . the Mole had a good deal of spare time on his hands, and so one afternoon, when the Rat in his arm-chair before the blaze was alternately dozing and trying over rhymes that wouldn't fit, he formed the resolution to go out by himself and explore the Wild Wood and perhaps strike up an acquaintance with Mr. Badger.

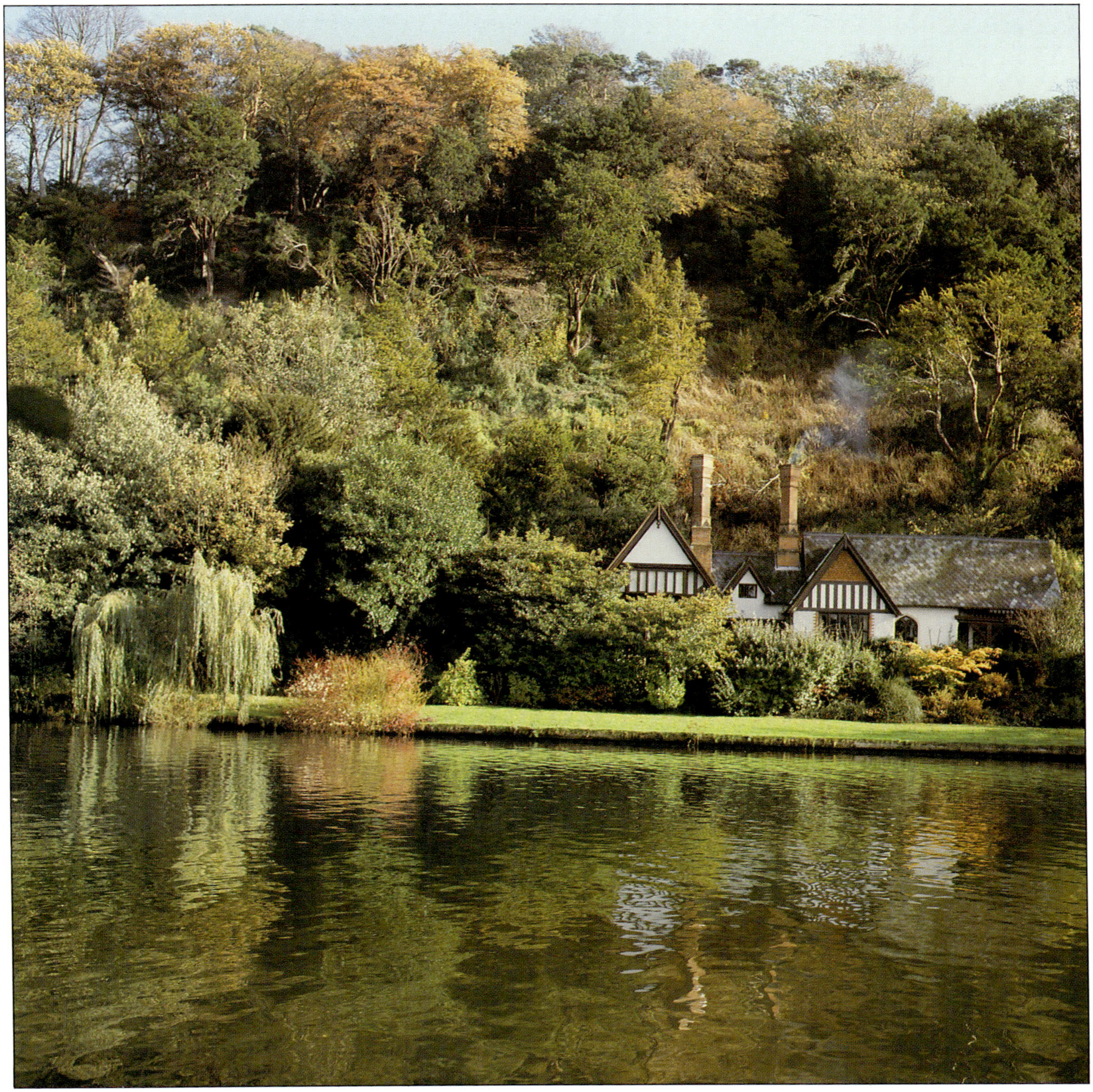

Cliveden Reach

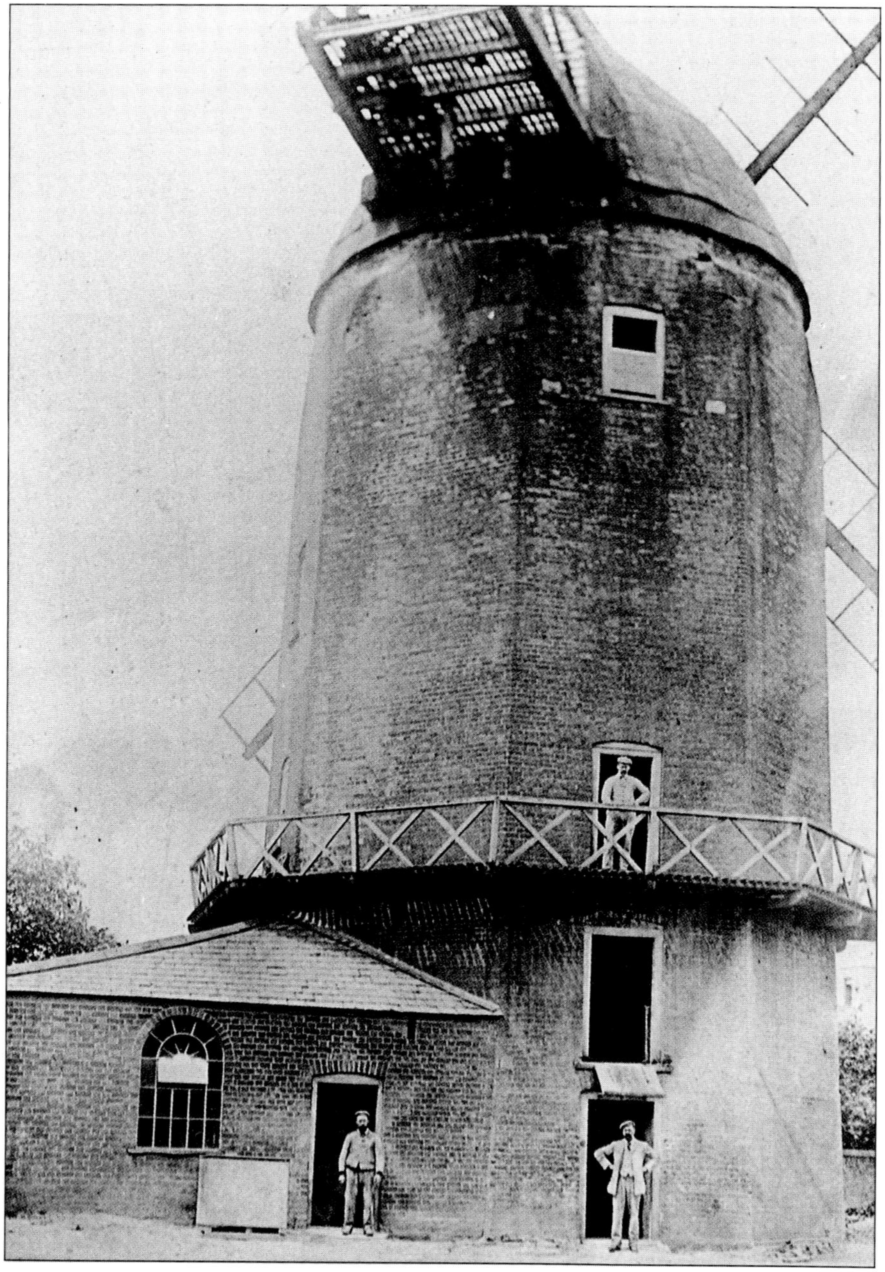

Wendover

It was a cold still afternoon with a hard steely sky overhead when he slipped out of the warm parlour into the open air. The country lay bare and entirely leafless around him, and he thought that he had never seen so far and so intimately into the insides of things as on that winter day when Nature was deep in her annual slumber and seemed to have kicked the clothes off. Copses, dells, quarries and all hidden places, which had been mysterious minds for exploration in leafy summer, now exposed themselves and their secrets pathetically, and seemed to ask him to overlook their shabby poverty for a while, till they could riot in rich masquerade as before, and trick and entice him with the old deceptions. It was pitiful in a way, and yet cheering – even exhilarating. He was glad that he liked the country undecorated, hard, and stripped of its finery. He had got down to the bare bones of it, and they were fine and strong and simple. He did not want the warm clover and the play of seedling grasses; the screens of quickset, the billowy drapery of beech and elm seemed best away; and with great cheerfulness of spirit he pushed on towards the Wild Wood, which lay before him low and threatening, like a black reef in some southern sea.

There was nothing to alarm him at first entry. Twigs crackled under his feet, logs tripped him, funguses on stumps resembled caricatures and startled him for the moment by their likeness to something familiar and far away; but that was all fun, and exciting. It led him on, and he penetrated to where the light was less, and trees crouched nearer and nearer, and holes made ugly mouths at him on either side.

Everything was still now. The dusk advanced on him steadily, rapidly gathering in behind and before; and the light seemed to be draining away like flood-water.

John Davidson in 1894 produced his book THE RANDOM ITINERARY, which largely centres on the Chilterns and lives up to its title. In his own words:

There is little hope for anyone who does a thing right the first time; the chances are that he will never be able to do the thing better than right. This applies to visiting the Chiltern Hills as well as any other branch of art. The artist has often more interest in the rough sketch . . . than in the finished picture, which is a fulfilment without further promise; and the itinerant thinks that his mistaken wanderings over the Chilterns were more to his mind than a well-ordered journey would have been.

Firstly he takes us on a voyage of discovery which begins in Wendover and ends in Princes Risborough:

Shortly after noon he arrived at Wendover, and picked up the way where he had left it. But first he sauntered about Wendover, an ancient sunny village on a hill slope. Every third house seemed to be an inn. The Rising Sun, with tiled panels of the four seasons on one of its gables, the Rose and Crown, The Pack Horse, The Nag's Head, were all equally inviting; but, for a change, he lunched in the Coffee-House, an antique, high-shouldered, steep-roofed building beside the church. . . . In Wendover a mill stood up forlorn, its arms shivering idly in the wind: it seemed to look out across the fields tinged green with the coming harvest – not so forlornly either; hopefully, rather, if with a little anxiety: there will be work for the wind and it yet.

Past Ellesborough Church, standing on a hill, a footpath led through Chequers. The Chilterns are famous for their beeches; none are finer than those that grow in this estate. High up on knolls they stand, letting the light hide among their fluted stems. In glades, boxwood, with its dark-green glossy leaf, muffles their smooth trunks. In a bay that runs deep into the hill they throng together on either side, masses and clouds of foliage – a green sea cleft asunder by some enchanter's rod. . . .

Through fields, populous with ant hills, the itinerant

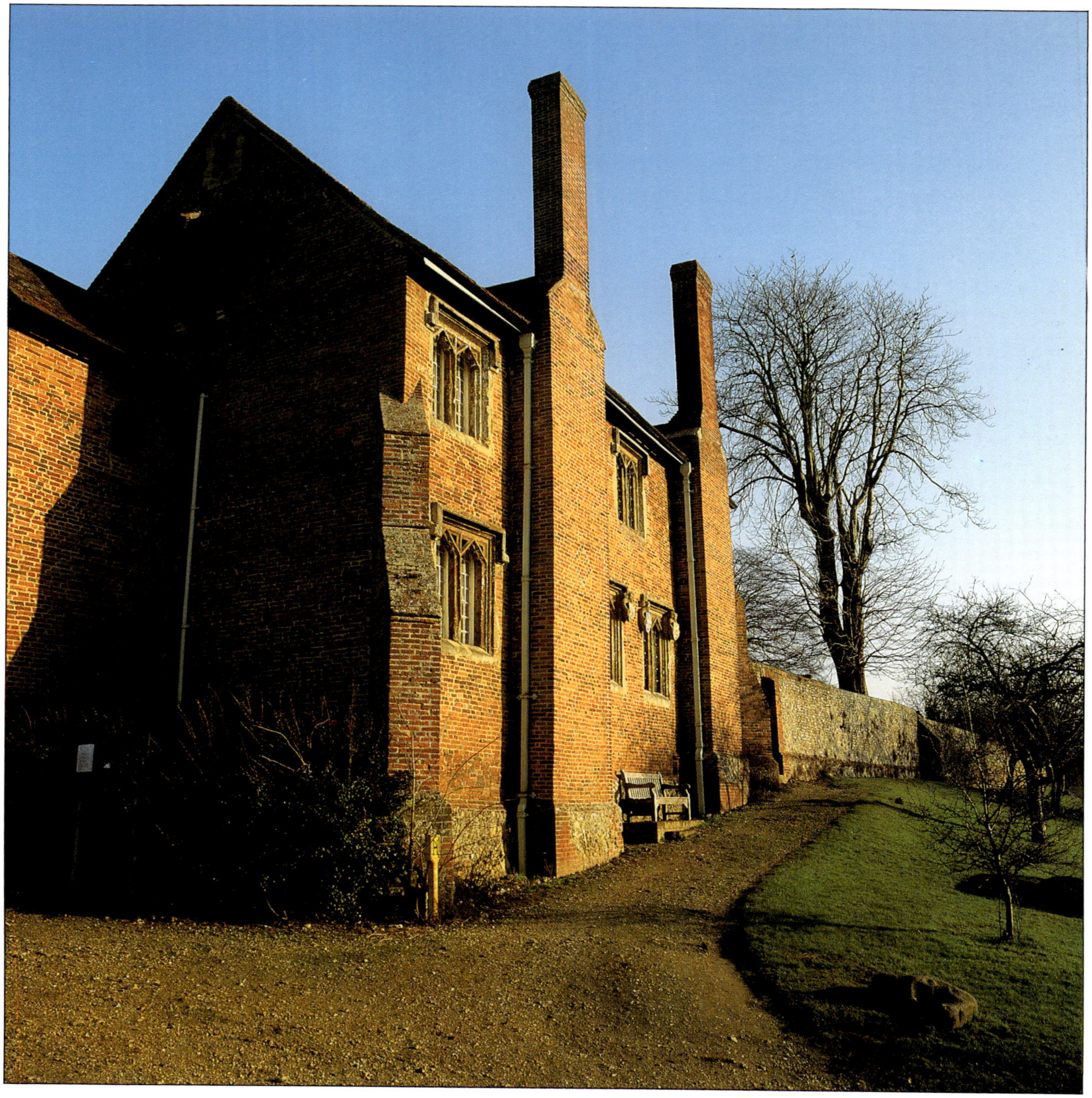

Ewelme

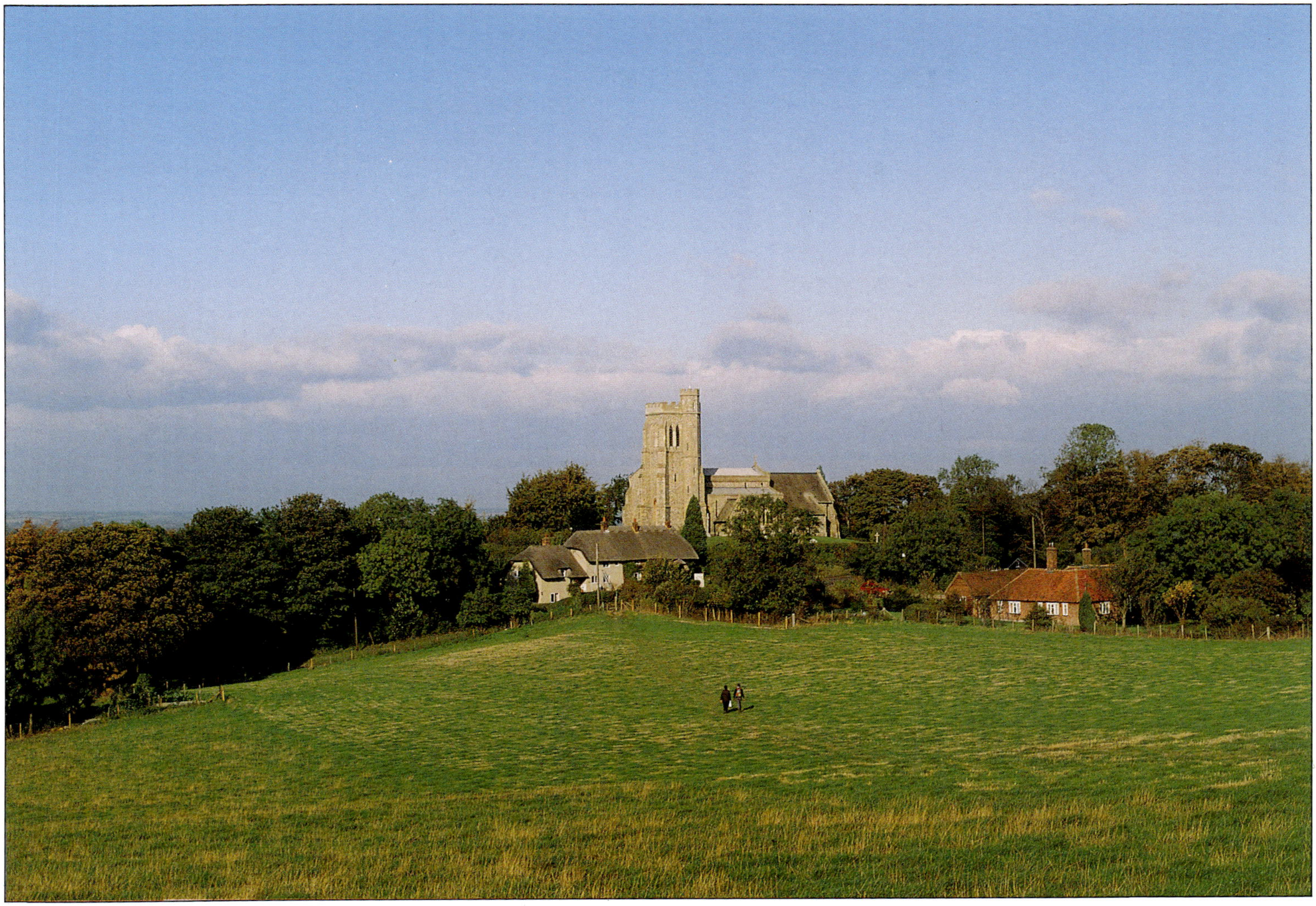

Ellesborough

came to the highway, to Little and Great Kimble, reposeful upland hamlets. At Great Kimble he enjoyed for the first time in his life a wash at a pump. It is impossible, in words, to convey an impression of the delights, after a long walk, of being pumped to and on, of yellow soap, and a huckaback towel. . . .

Between Great Kimble and Monk's Risborough, under the eave of a hill, is the village of Whiteleaf. Old thatched houses among trees, sitting above the world, overlooking the highway from a distance, steeped in memories, good friends with Time; a place to live in: exquisite, under the eave of the hill; a place to die in.

Prince's Risborough is called after the Black Prince, who built a castle there, hoping to retire from the world. The name of the place and two Black Prince inns are the only memorial of him left. Larger and more modernised than Wendover, Prince's Risborough is a pleasant market town. Prosperous old vines grow against gables in the open street. It is a well-sheltered place, with a thriving look about it.

Our second foray into the Chilterns with Davidson is to Amersham, and after an informative and amusing interlude here we find ourselves heading for Chesham.

The footpath lead down into Amersham past a walled churchyard with sombre yews, and cypresses more sombre still. It was after twelve, but there were few people in the street. Broad and clean, the main thoroughfare came short of being picturesque through want of height in the buildings. No two houses seemed of the same pattern. Shops, inns, residences, were of all ages, from the wood and plaster and projecting front of the Tudors to the red brick and immortal stone-facings of the Guelphs. With many differences in height and shape, conformity in one matter marked most of the buildings, even the newest and shoddiest. The windows had more breadth than length, and were set low in the wall, and those of the upper storey were crowded up under the eaves. This old fashion is not perhaps in itself highly aesthetic, but by contrast with the monotonous regularity of most modern glazing it is quiet beautiful. Thatch, slate, red tile, the last predominating, were no small part of the effect of variety which the town presented. Amersham is compact and airy though lying in a valley; a very pleasant, old-fashioned little town, quite unchanged as yet by the railway. It was worth seeing; above all, it was worth while to come suddenly on it out of the beech-wood. The itinerant came into and walked through it, before he quite realized that there was a town there.

One of the great delights of an itinerant is the half-hour in the inn when it is time to eat and drink. It may be that for a whole day the only opportunity of converse he has is with the innkeeper or the taproom-maid, and if he be a practised itinerant, he selects his inn carefully, supposing he has a choice; stalks it so to speak, and enters it with some excitement and expectation. The choicest inn in Amersham had indeed an enticing, antique air, and the sign was of the quaintest; so was the old innkeeper, a surly, indignant looking person. The itinerant asked him whose whisky he kept.

Innkeeper. My own.
Itinerant. Oh yes, of course! But whose?
Innkeeper. My own.
Itinerant. Are you a distiller then?
Innkeeper. No; but you asked me whose whisky I kept, and I said my own. It belongs to me.

The innkeeper began to look very savage; this was evidently a standard joke of his, and it seemd as if it weren't going to come off this time. A judicious laugh, however, set matters right; and the innkeeper without much change in his surly and indignant expression, developed a communicative and reminiscential mood; he

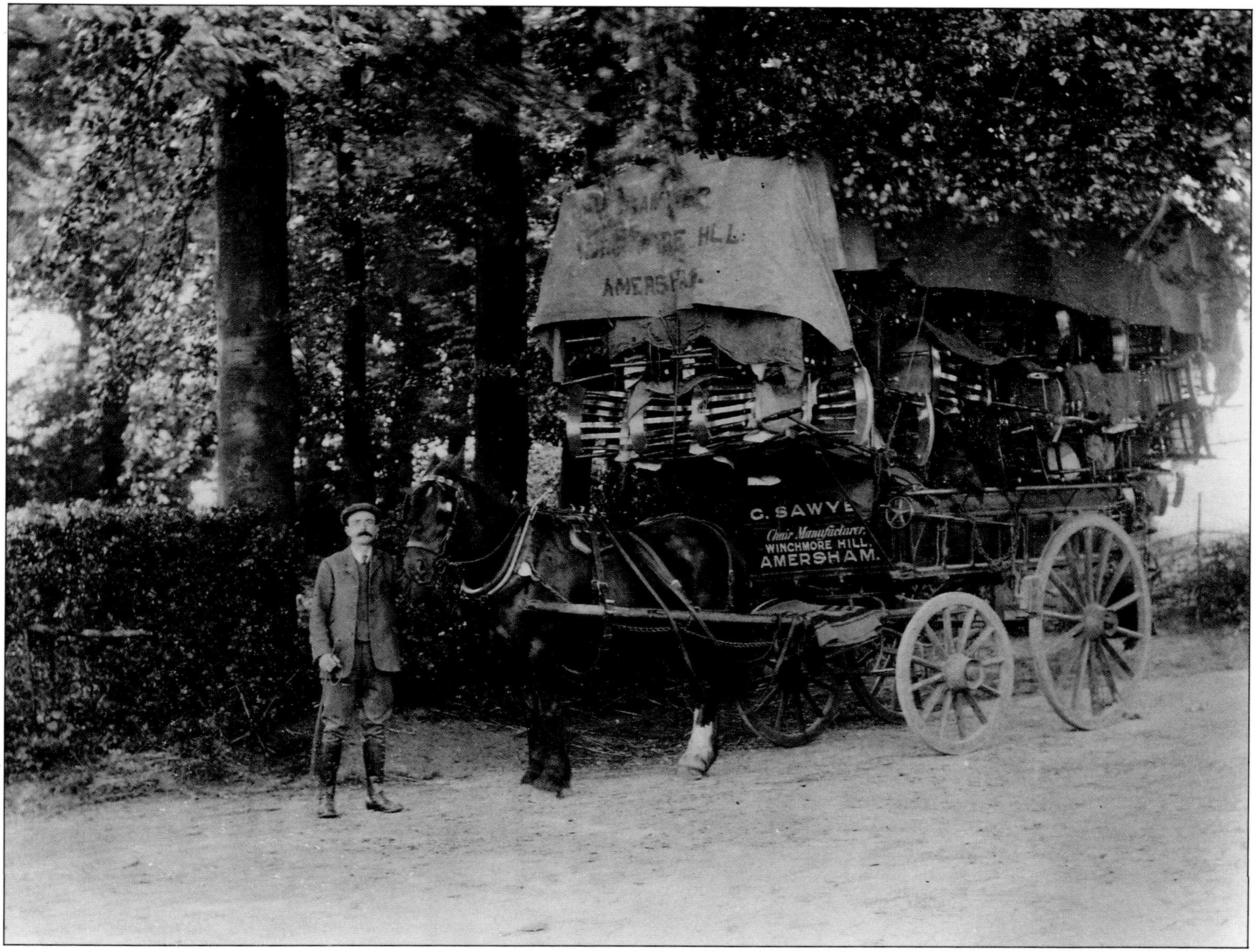

Amersham

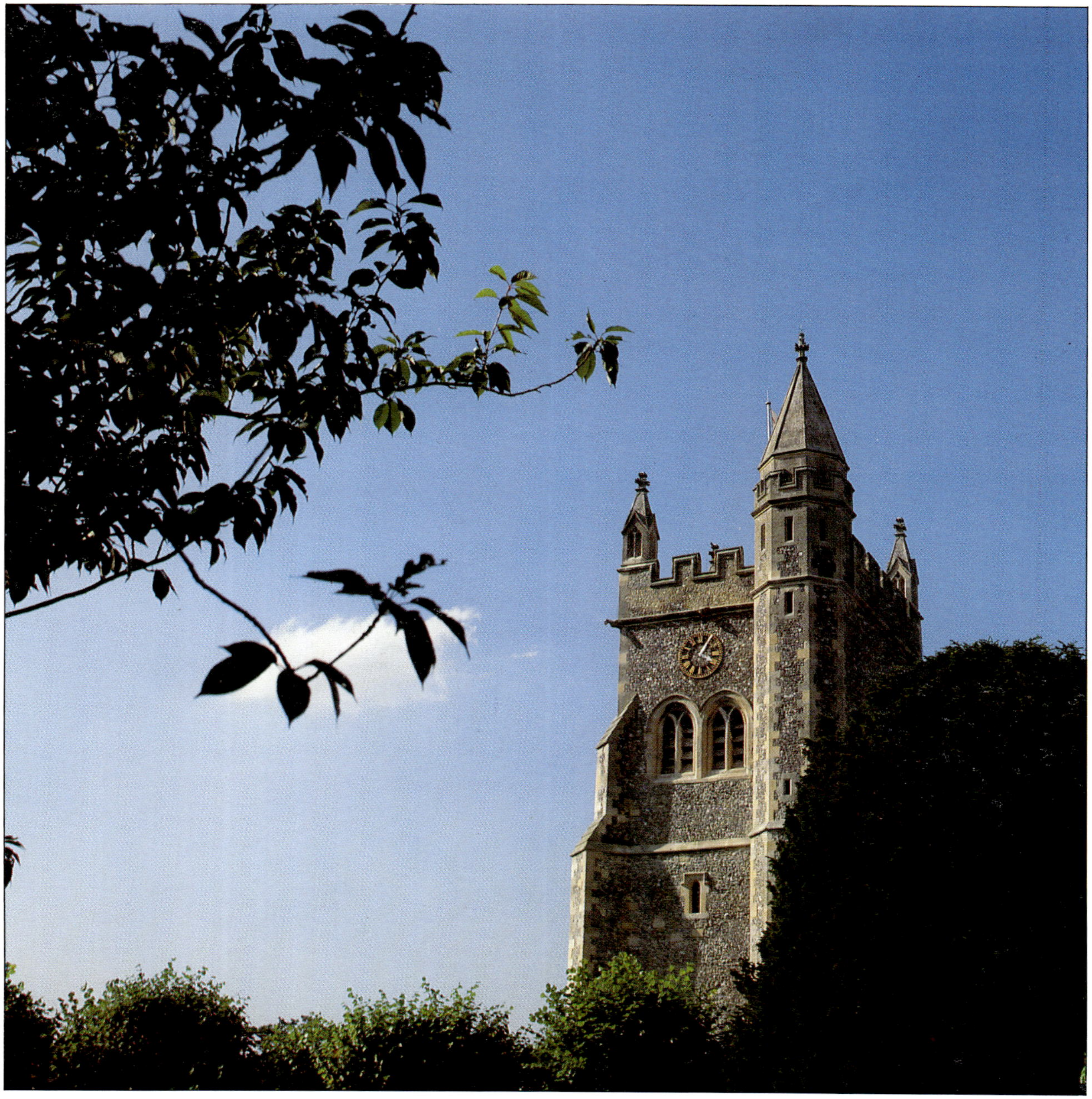

Amersham

had a very odd appearance talking pleasantly, with his fixed look of exasperation. Asked if he had been in Amersham all his days, he replied, No, he had lived in London for a dozen years, but had been born and brought up in Amersham.

Itinerant. And has Amersham changed much in your day?

Innkeeper. Not much; the streets grow a little longer by a house or two every half-dozen years, that's all. I remember, although I was only a boy at the time, when the Reform Bill of '32 was passed. People used to say that Amersham would turn into a great place; they seemed to think that the Reform Bill was a promise to pay, and they would all get money and be butchers and innkeepers and manufacturers; and Amersham would grow bigger than Aylesbury. Long after the bill was passed they came and stood about the Market hall in the evening, waiting, you would have said, for the money to fall from the skies.

Itinerant. Was that the Market Hall I passed a little way down the street – a curious-looking building, standing on cloisters, like a house on a bridge?

Innkeeper. Yes; that's the Market Hall. I remember seeing an election before the Reform Bill, when the town returned two members. After it was over the members stood up on stones in front of the hall, like duxes in a school, and recited little speeches, and then drove about the town in carriages with four horses apiece. After that came the funniest thing; it was a custom here, and I saw it myself, for my father kept this inn before me. Into all the inns the women came, high and low, rich and poor, married and single; and the two members went about from inn to inn and kissed 'em every one.

Itinerant. The election, I suppose, wouldn't have been valid unless they had done so.

Innkeeper. Perhaps not. Anyway I saw the members do it in the public room of this inn. Very solemn and regular they were about it – a piece of business. And as soon as they had gone over them all, the young fellows in the town came after them, and there was such a kissing match as you never heard. I was only a boy then, and before I was old enough it was changed times.

Itinerant. Old enough?

'To take my share of the kissing,' replied the innkeeper, looking more irate than ever.

After some desultory remarks, the itinerant expressed a wish to walk about a little, and asked the innkeeper to recommend a road. 'Go to Chesham,' said the innkeeper. 'Is it a pleasant road?' 'A good road.' 'And what is there at Chesham?' 'Woodware. They make chairs, and bats, and tennis-racquets and toy spades; brushes too, and boots; and there's a cress ditch.'

Having never seen a cress ditch, the itinerant felt that Chesham was the place to go to. . . .

Half-way between Amersham and Chesham, there lies a furze common. It was all in bloom, and the sober hue of the skies gave the gold of the whins a deeper tone. A shepherd's boy tended some goats and sheep that fed among the bushes; from more than one neighbouring smithy the anvils rang; and the cuckoos sounded in the beechwood. Here were some delightful acres of old

GEORGE PEARCE,
ENGLISH AND FOREIGN TIMBER MERCHANT,
TURNER AND MANUFACTURER OF
Corn & Malt Shovels, Spades, Hoops, Yokes, Scoops, Butchers' Trays, Bowls
AND ALL KINDS OF
ASH AND SIEVE HOOPS. LAWN TENNIS STICKS.
Saw Mills, Townfield Yard, Red Lion Street,
CHESHAM, BUCKS.
PRICE LIST FREE ON APPLICATION. (5) Also Buyer of all kinds of English Timber.

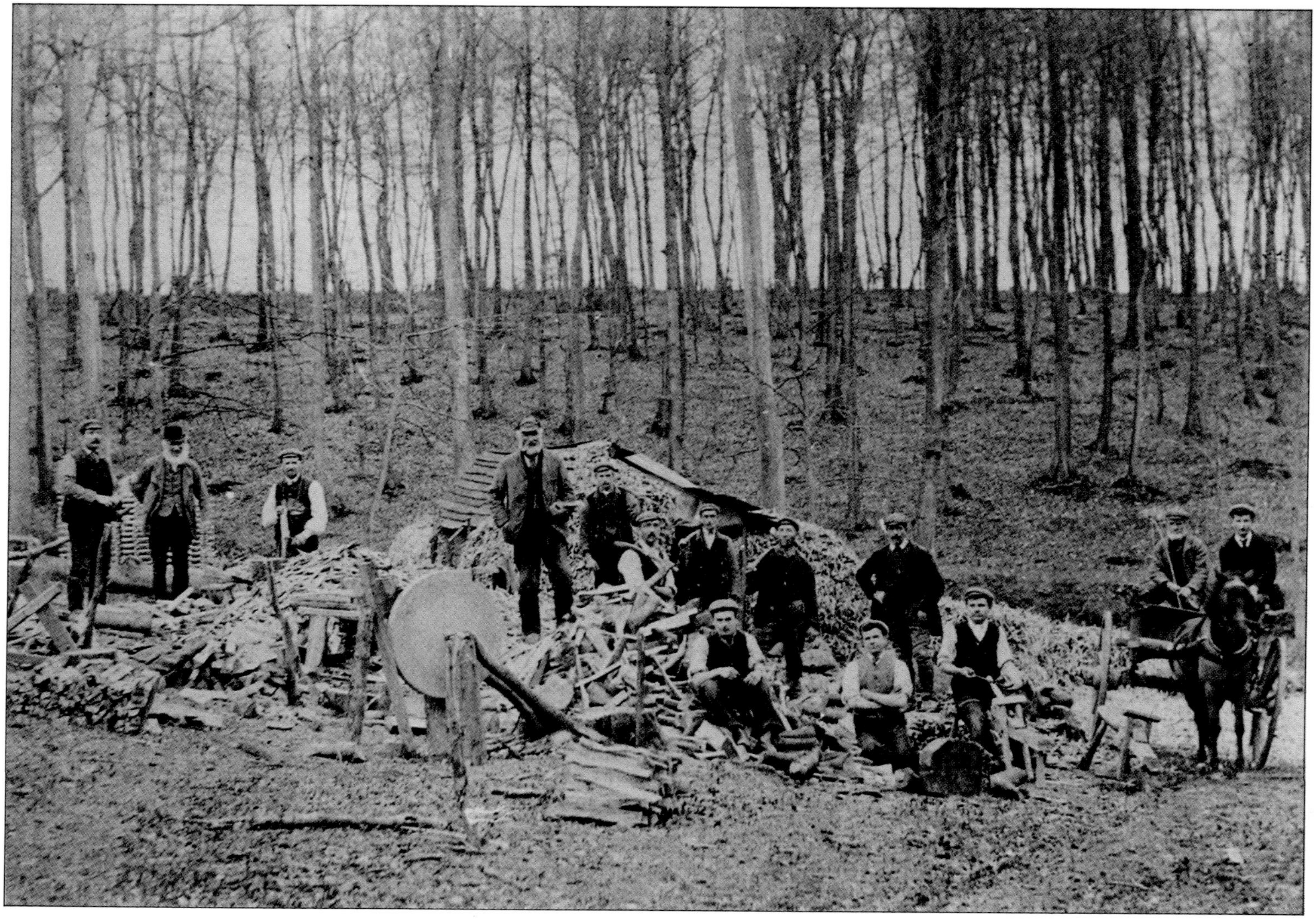

Bodger encampment

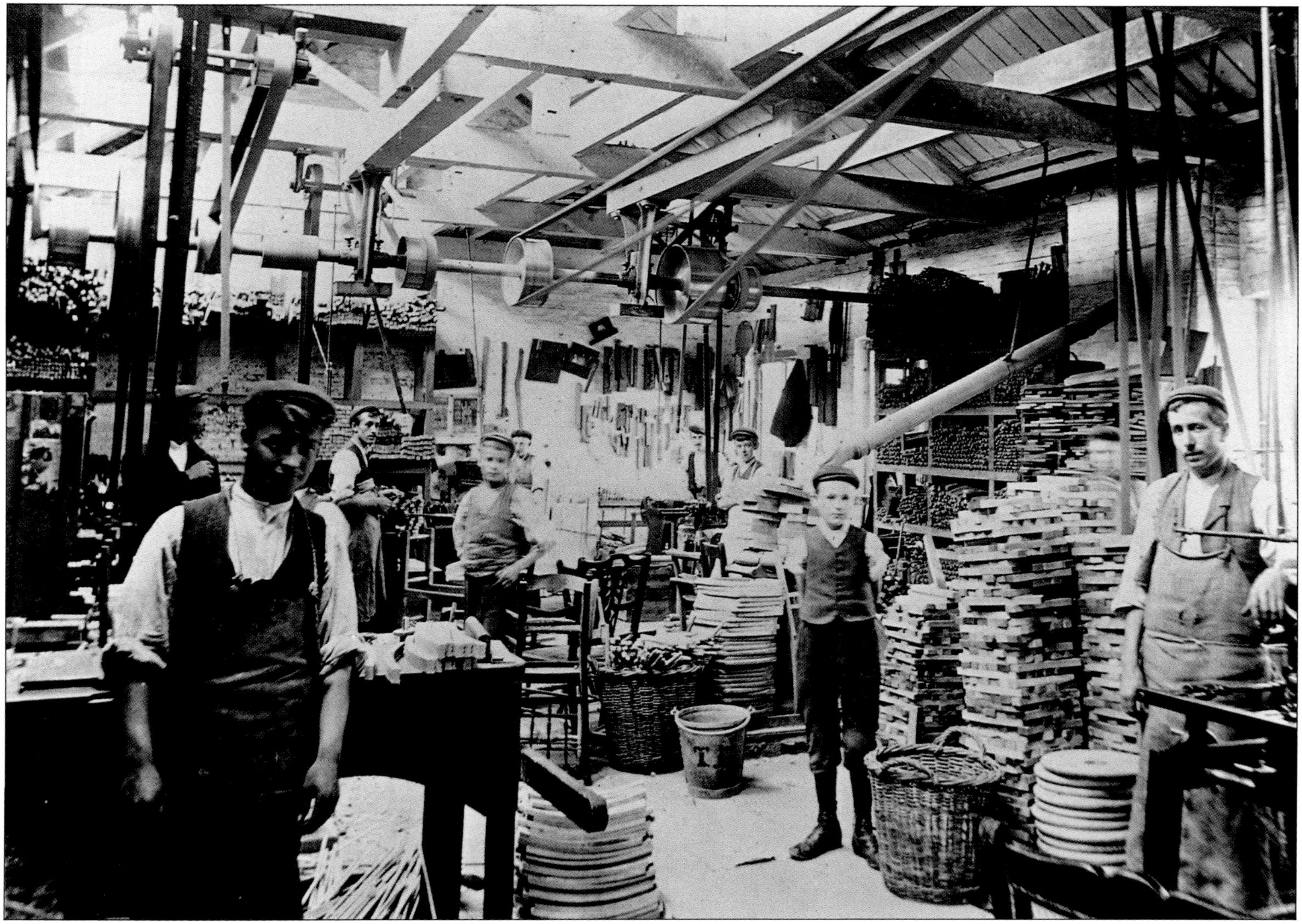

Glenister's chair factory, High Wycombe

England, a little island between two railways only a mile off on either hand.

It was to see a cress ditch that the itinerant went to Chesham; but he found the town more interesting and picturesque than Amersham. The High Street contained higher buildings than the main thoroughfare of the latter town, with as much variety in style. It was not nearly so wide either; and narrowness in a street has great aesthetic value when the buildings are not imposing. As for the cress ditch, he had some difficutly in finding it. Those people he asked were profuse in their directions, and seemed quite proud of their ditch. He began to look upon cresses as the staple of Chesham, and was somewhat dismayed when told that he had just walked past the ditch without observing it. Retracing his steps, he found, instead of the great moat he had expected, a small stream of water on one side of the road, containing forty-four baskets face downwards and tightly packed for Covent Garden; and on the other a small artificial marsh where the plant grew, occupying a portion of ground that could have been easily covered by a good-sized carpet. Doubtless it was a capital cress ditch, but the itinerant did not share the enthusiasm of the Cheshamites. He preferred their fine old church from whose tower curfew rings every night.

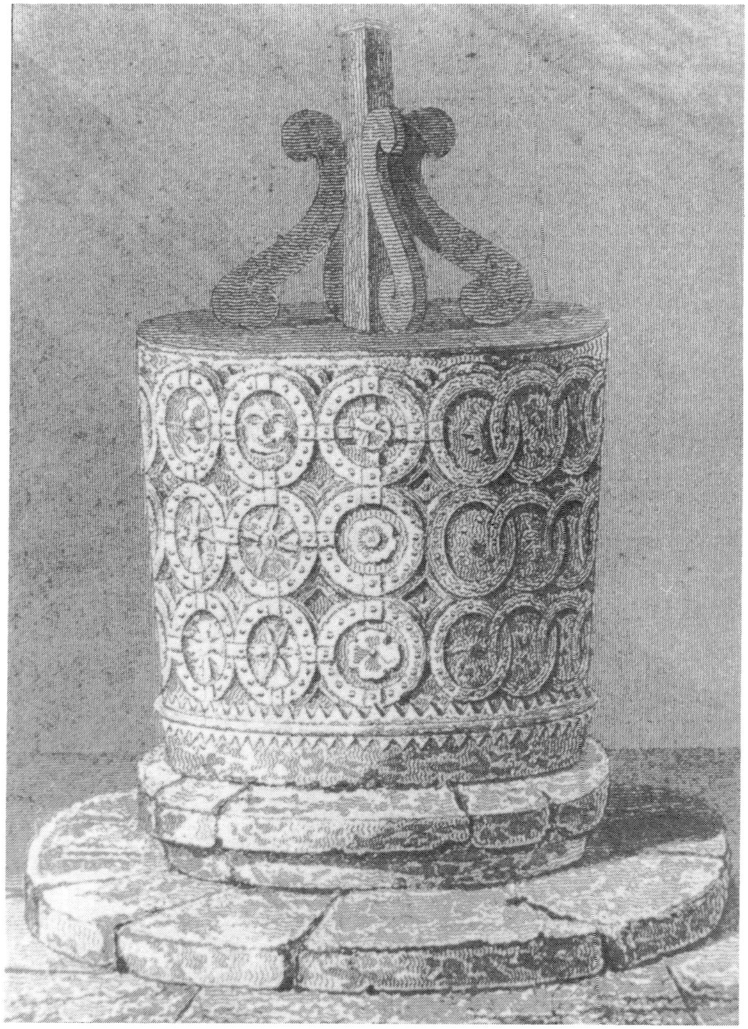

Henry Kingston writing in his HISTORY OF HIGH WYCOMBE in 1848, gives a more graphic account of the watercress industry in the Wycombe area. The same crop was also grown further afield in the Chilterns, notably at Ewelme but also at Lewknor and Bledlow.

Every visitor to Wycombe will naturally be attracted with a comparatively modern source of employment amongst a great number of industrious families – the cultivation of water cresses. The many shallow currents which flow along the valleys of Hughenden, West Wycombe, and continuing their course towards Wycombe Marsh, Loudwater and Wooburn are admirably adapted for the growth of this new universal addition to the breakfast table. Hereabouts the industrious cresser may be seen stalking heedlessly in his jack boots, knee deep in water, and thus adorned in person, with the addition of his striped jersey, he vigorously pursues his allotted task, and immersing his bare and sinewy arms in the gurgling brook, dextrously plucks his emerald crop. Thus secured – on the bankside may be observed an adjunct to these labours, in the shape of a somewhat primitive vehicle, half truck half donkey cart, to which the patient animal becomes speedily attached, and the proprietor thereof hastily proceeds home, while yet early, with his packed baskets, awaiting a speedy transit to the metropolis. Scores of hampers are sent to London, during the season, from hence, and generally realize high prices; sufficiently remunerative to induce the cultivator to bestow the most unlimited pains in rearing plants for an early market.

John Davidson, like many before and since, enjoyed walking through the Chiltern region. Joining this illustrious band who recorded their experiences is the eminent Hertfordshire historian Mr Herbert W. Tomkins. Writing in 1902, he was clearly a man obsessed with sauntering down country lanes, and through his words gives us a clear picture of the Chilterns before it was overrun with angry cars and angry motorists. He leaves us with a feeling that the industrial revolution has made itself felt and that the clamour for urbanization is growing louder.

After passing the signpost on the Berkhampstead road, a long descent, shaded by many trees on the southern side, leads me once again to the towing path of the Grand Junction Canal. Here, however, the scene is not like that of the usual canal side, but far more picturesque. I have passed through a little gateway near the bridge, and scrambled down a most precipitous path to the water side, where –

By the margin, willow-veil'd,
Slide the heavy barges trail'd,
By slow horses;

A steep hill, well shaded by larch and beech, leads me towards the village of Wiggington near Tring. Turning to the left presently instead of keeping straight on into the town, I find myself clambering up a perfect precipice . . . I would not have remained at the bottom among meaner minds for a king's ransom; for here, on a spur of the Chiltern Hills, the villagers of Wiggington can look upon one of the finest prospects in the county. To the north east are the green heights of Ashridge, crowned by the Aldbury monument; southward, in the foreground, lies Champneys, an ideal homestead, with Tring Common and the varied greenery of Buckinghamshire in the farther distance. I can see too, a train winding into the Northchurch tunnel; beyond is Berkhampstead, wreathed round

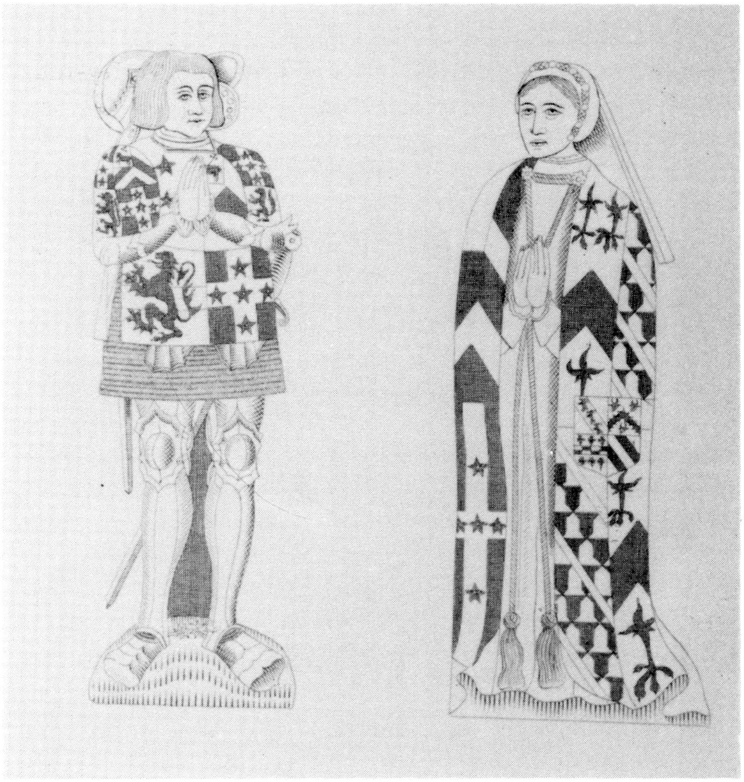

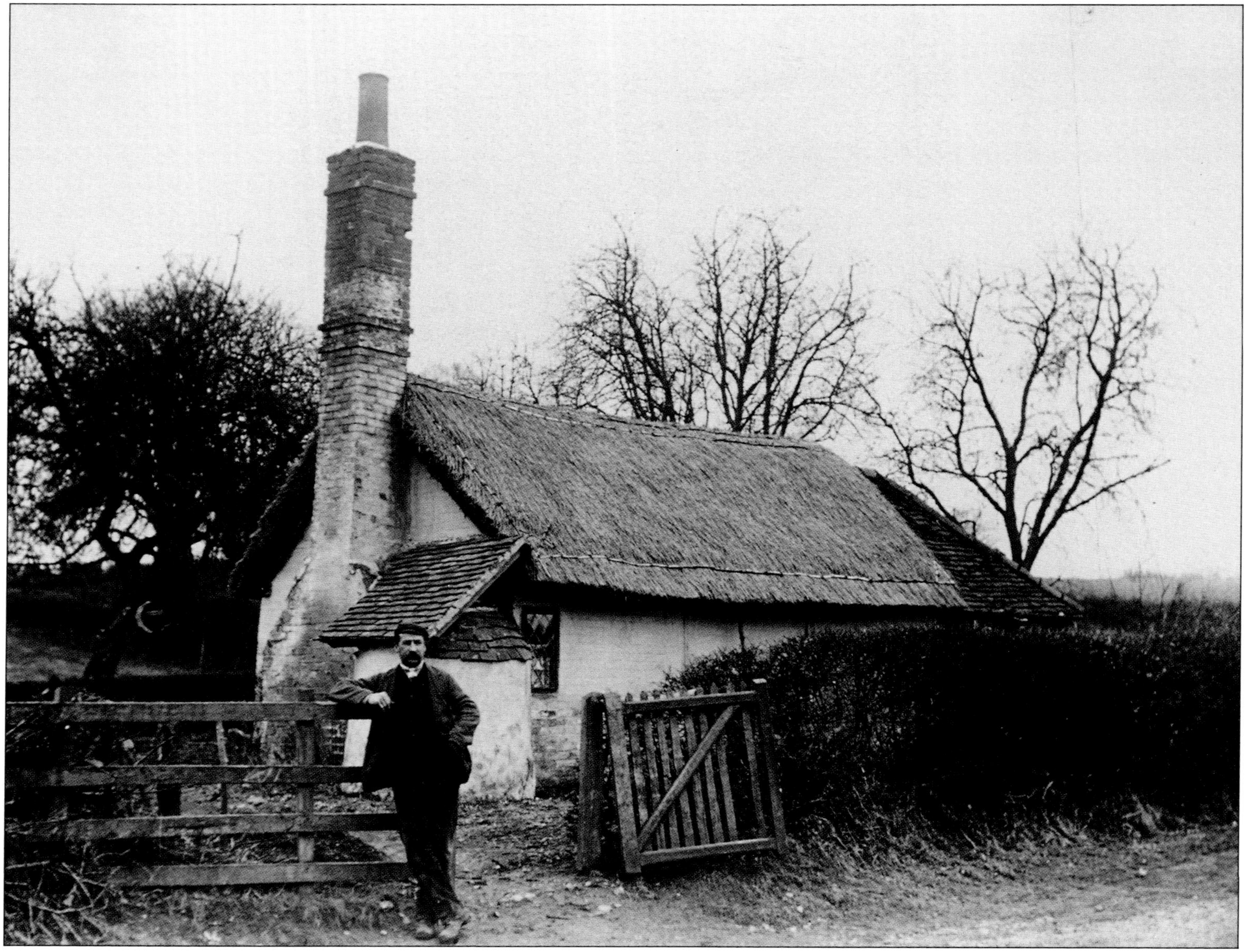

Coleshill

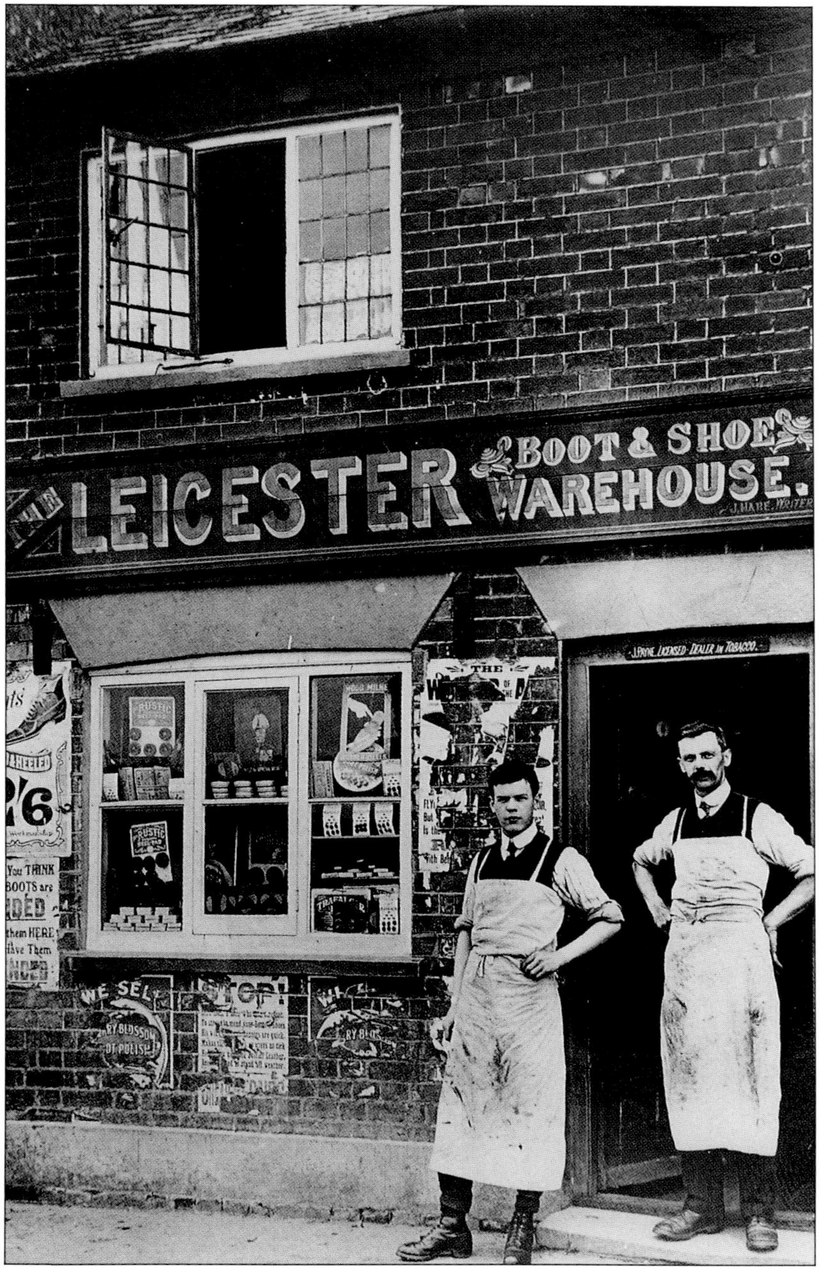
LEICESTER
BOOT & SHOE
WAREHOUSE.
J. PAYNE. LICENSED DEALER IN TOBACCO.

Tring

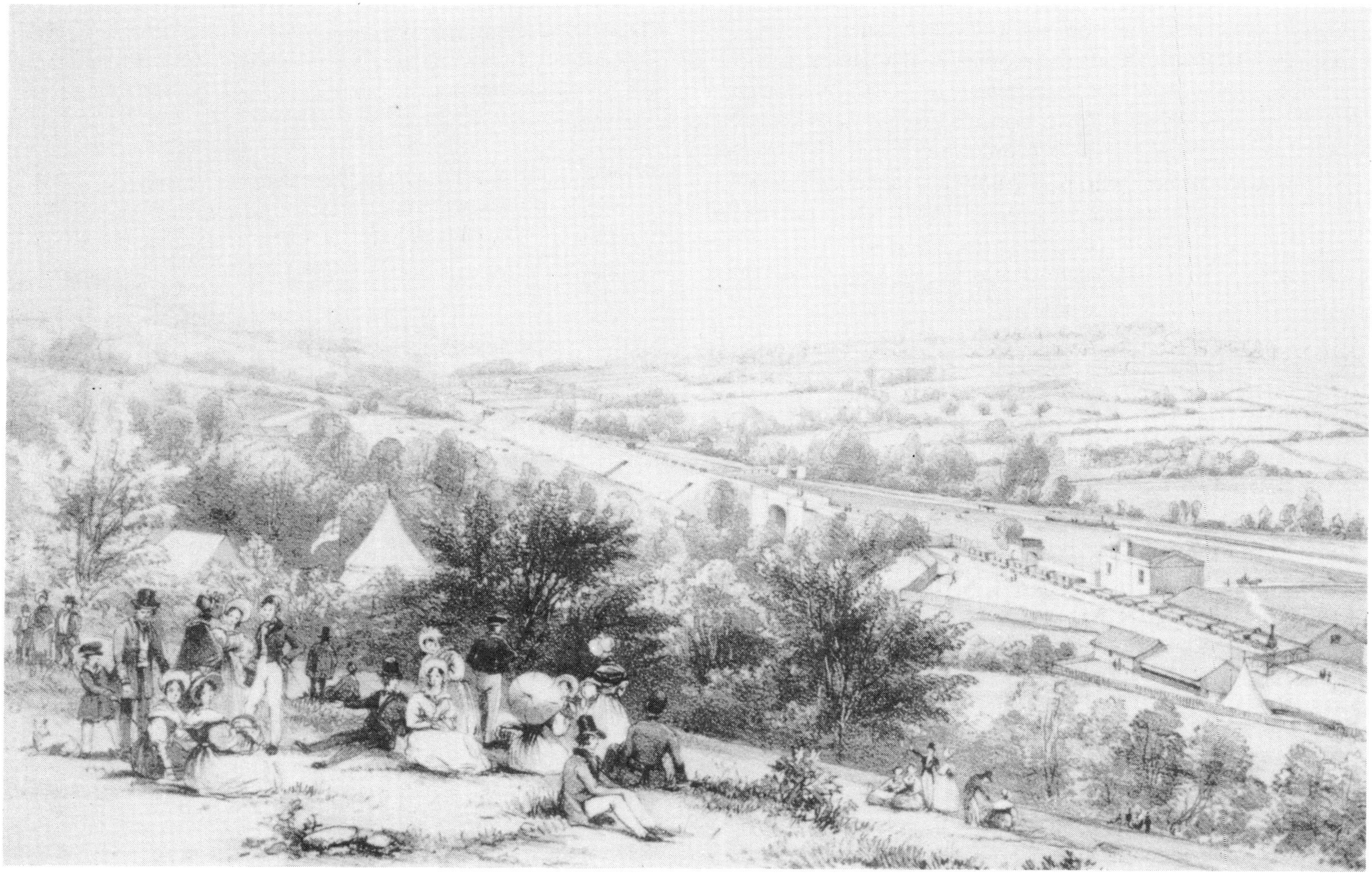

with light grey smoke from its many chimneys; beyond that again stands a conspicuous clump of pines on the hill top near Boxmoor.

That Tring is an 'ancient town of England' is, I believe, indisputable; but this morning I have been wondering how it has contrived so effectually to conceal its antiquity . . . A bird's eye view of the disposition of the streets of Tring would readily convince you that the town grew up in the 'golden days, long, long ago', for it is dotted and dispersed irregularly around four main, twisted streets; but few of the houses are of great age . . . I have been peeping up courtyards and under arches, and trespassing in Willow Court and Tabernacle Yard and Denmark Place, where clusters of tiny cottages are hidden away under the very shadow of inns and in the rear of shops; where groups of children are playing at fivestones or squabbling about nothing, and women are at the wash-tub with their sleeves rolled up, or gossiping from door to door with their arms a-kimbo. . . . Had I visited Tring some years ago I might have sought out one who new many a snatch and legend of the district. This was old Betty, a well known person in this far west corner of Hertfordshire, who went 'a-fagging' every wheat harvest, and was over one hundred years old when she last gleaned in the fields near here. Farmer and labourer alike knew old Betty; she was fond of her snuff, and, when asked how she did, invariably answered that she was well enough but her box was empty. There was a touch of Meg Merrilies in her, too; for she would rail on occasion against those who endeavoured to enclose public land, plough public footpaths, prosecute the poacher, or infringe the gleaner's immemorial rights. I am told that she died in her hundred and tenth year, and she was hale and reasonable almost to the last. . . . Our Saxon forefathers chose wisely when they made their homes, as they so often did, in the little leafy valleys of old England. How picturesque those 'denes' invariably are! Gaddesden, Nettleden, Flaunden, Harpenden, [plus many others in the Chilterns] are all in the valley, as their names denote. You come upon these homesteads unawares as, emerging from the tangled lanes, or from some footpath through the cornfields, a sudden turn shows you the village almost at your feet. They are small and scattered, these valley villages, for the sons of Hodge love not the tasks to which Hodge was bred, and have gone away from home to fill the towns.

Writing at the end of the last century, Mr Fowler says:

The smock coated farmer has almost ceased to exist, but still some survive and hold small occupations of from fifty to a hundred acres, leading an industrious, hard-faring life, living offtimes more frugally than their labourers, and going on, as the saying is on the Chiltern Hills, 'From cherry time to cherry time,' and getting 'no forrarder.'

The oral historian Mr H. Harman, when recording dialects in various parts of the Chilterns, was simultaneously setting down for posterity the last vestiges of long-established traditions. Here he is talking about Askett in 1923:

Churry Pies and Su-ut Pudduns

B. Aint it clooas! It a bin like this all the arternoon. I had mi jackut off neeurly all day, and I a ony jest put it an to come in heeur. I rickun we shull git a storm afu-ur the night's out, and I shoont be surprised if we git it very soon. My gals a bin a-blackburrying all the arternoon and a come home wi a good lot. They filled biggish baskut full and so I suppoase we shull be havin blackburry pies and blackburry pudduns fur the nex few days. But I doant like em! I wunt taiast em. They can have em! I shan't. Lots a people a bin out a-gethering em this arternoon. They come out heeur from Aiuhlsburry and git no eend an em, ispecially tuther side a Meadull. They clambur up the hedges and clah em neeurly all off, so when they be gone thaiur aint many left fur anybody else. Gi me straaburries or churries – they be my favourite fruit; a the two I like straaburries.

A. I doo-ant; gi me a churry – them big black uns; the real ole Bucks black churry. I think they call em 'Croons.' They can't be bait.

B. I know em, the big black and the little black. I like the big black fur ettin and the little black fur pies. Thaiur's no churry as can come up to em. Thaiur's nothing I like in this world like a real ole Bucks churry pie as be well pinched. I used t' have em ivvery yeeur when I was young – my mother allus used to maiak em ivvery summur, but I dooant git em now. Tis like ivverything else, all the ole custums gooin out a deeat. I ull tell ye what it is! Women can't pinch em now-a-deeas, tis too much trouble; and if they could they woont. I sin em many a time maiad jest like half a moon gooin to the baiakhus an a tin, as many as ten at a time. They looked bootiful – ivvery one pinched up as reglur as clockwurk. And waunt they good when they were done!

A. Ah! that's it; ivvery ole Bucks woman in this part a the country could pinch em once an a time, but they can't do it now.

B. Then thaiur was the ole churry puddun as we allus had wi broad beeans and biled baiacon. You know it!

A. Yis I know it, but I ant sin one for a good time now. You meean a su-ut puddun wi cherries mixed up in it. That's a reeal ole Bucks summur dish, but people dooant have it now.

B. No, because nine parts out a ten a the women can't maiak a su-ut puddun now-a-deeas as it should be maiad. Thaiur's one thing they can't do – they can't get the right linge when they be mixin up. You want a nice bit a su-ut well chopped up and no gret hunches left in it, then mix it wi the flour, and put in a bit a salt. Then a you got to put the water to it and stir it up well till yet git the right linge, nuther too wet nur too dry, and this is what they can't do. Now it has to be tied up in the cloth as tight as it can be tied, and when it comes out a the pot it rolls out jest like a futball. You can then put yur knife an it and it almosts falls a-two. That's when they be good and wuth ettin, and what can be bettur fur anybody when ye a got a nice drap a greeavy from a bit a baif or a rearin baiaked ovur a sahcer of inen and saiage? Tis the finist thing fur anybody, ispecially childern, fur they dooant want much mait ar-ur they had a good bellyful a that. I tell ye a slice or two aich day puts a colour in the chaiks, and if ivvery gall had em ivvery day, half the chimist shops in the country ood soon be shet up.

One would not expect the author of such novels as KING SOLOMONS MINES and SHE to be an authority on farming. In fact, H. Rider Haggard was himself a Norfolk farmer who recorded the events on his farm in a diary for 1898 called 'A Farmer's Year.' He also wrote RURAL ENGLAND (1906) from which the following extract is taken:

Mr Aubrey J. Spencer, of Wheatfield, Tetsworth, in the southern division of the county, where he owns an estate of 800 acres, has kindly furnished me with a report on the labour conditions in that district . . . He said that the land in his neighbourhood was pretty good, although on the Chiltern Hills things were in a very bad way. They had been hard hit by the depression, but were to some extent kept afloat through the help of the London milk trade. . . . Rents in Oxfordshire had, he estimated, fallen about 30 per cent. on good land, and much more on the light land of the Chiltern Hills, which hardly seemed worth cultivating. Landlords were constantly poor, and were also called upon to spend their income on repairs and improvements to an extent that was unknown in the old days. Mr Spencer thought that labourers were in any case likely to drift away to towns in order to better themselves, but he was of opinion that the loss would be diminished by the provision of good cottages and a liberal supply of allotments and small-holdings. Many of their young men had gone soldiering, and some of them had come back from the ranks to work on the land. Two young fellows who had served their time returned to the village to milk cows and do other agricultural work, but, rather to their disgust, were called up with the Reserve and sent to South Africa.

Many men went to the Boer War from this region with the Imperial Yeomanry and many never returned. On the hill above Wendover, visible for miles around, stands a monument to them. The list of men though poignant is short in retrospect. By the end of the Great War such monuments

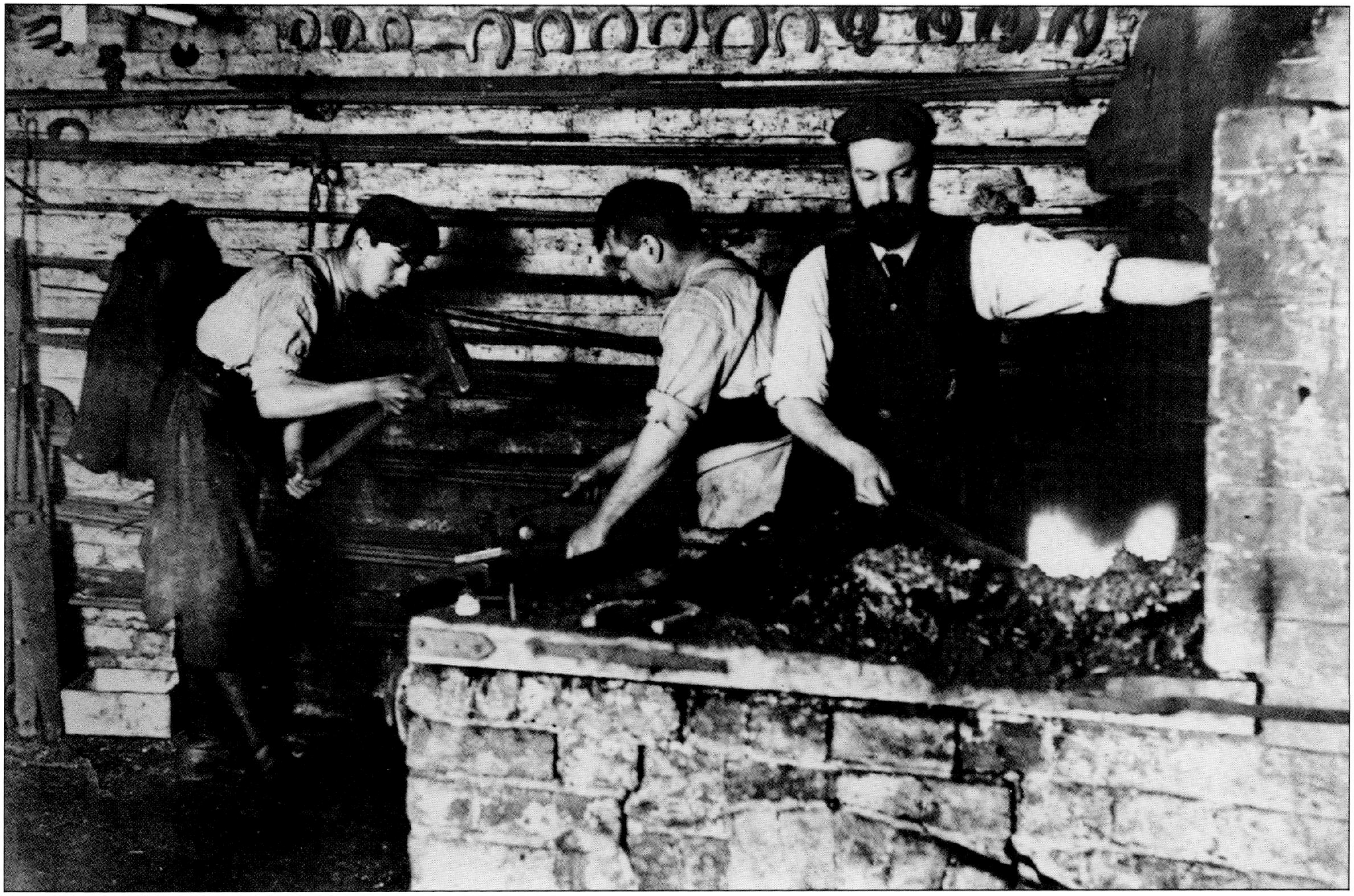

Frieth smithy

had sprung up all over the country marking not only the passing of many lives but the end of an era.

A writer of novels as well as several books about the region surrounding his beloved 'Pilgrim Cottage' near Henley, Cecil Roberts conveys with real insight life in the country between the wars. Our final extract chosen from GONE RAMBLING (1935) reflects in microcosm the effect of the 1914–18 war on family life and also on the rural scene generally.

22 June

I found the blacksmith's cottage anything but tranquil as I entered. It seemed crammed with relations and friends, all smiling, all talking, and trying to make themselves useful. The sitting-room, which I knew in winter's cosy lamp-light, with a kettle singing on the hob, as well as in summer's open windowed sweetness, was now completely transformed. A long table filled the room, with rows of chair on either side. There was a gathering of tea-pots on the hob – many a neighbour must have helped out with a tea-pot on this occasion. The centre of the table was dominated by two enormous iced cakes, one the present of a married daughter, the other of a local resident, and all down the table were dishes of jam and great plates of bread and butter, and teacups, saucers, knives, forks, spoons, pots of flowers, and gay festoons of paper bunting.

It was a real farmhouse tea, with everyone talking, and the old dames passing the tea-cups, and much coming and going with full plates and empty plates and jugs of hot water. What a scene of good cheer, like a chapter out of Dickens, with daughters and their husbands, and grand-children, and neighbours, old, middle-aged and young. And there at each end of the table sat the hero and heroine of this bright occasion, and for a moment, as I looked at Mrs. Harman, with her rosy cheeks and bright blue eyes, with such happiness and vitality sparkling in them, I caught a glimpse of another festive table set fifty years ago, with its bride brought to this village by the stalwart young blacksmith.

The blacksmith just now would have passed for a bishop, so neat was he in his black suit, so benign with his patriarchal domed head and white beard. He recorded this celebration of his golden wedding with the utmost serenity. At eighty four there is nothing much to get excited about. Time has become a pageant in which one has ceased to enact a part. As I looked at him now, I saw a figure of a dead era. The forges are passing from the village greens of England. If they do not fall into decay, then they are converted into petrol stations. When he was young and strong the blacksmith rose with the dawn to shoe the squire's horse – there were eighty of them on the estate. Now there are not half-a-dozen. Today another blacksmith pays a visit to the smithy once a month, and an odd horse is produced for shoeing. The squire's estate has shrunk too, and his woods have been felled. The village through which he motors is now no longer his, and on the edge of his most sacred coverts there are weekenders who have Elizabethened the farm-labourers' cottages with old oak, inglenooks, settles, tankards, grandfather clocks, and sundials.

Mr. Harman, sitting serene at the head of his table, must regard us all as transitory visitors. How long his forbears have lived here it is impossible to say. There are records in the Fawley Church Register of his progenitors through nearly four hundred years . . . As I sat at my host's board, among his married daughters, grandsons, and granddaughters, there was one seat vacant. The long line of Harmans is broken for ever. When the blacksmith is gathered to his fathers in Fawley Churchyard, his male line, preserved down the ages will be ended. The only son, a boy of twenty, lies in French soil, killed in the last week of the Great War. . . . I had taken Mr. Harman aside and had gently probed his memory. You must decant an octogenarian's memory much as you do old wine. Gently done, it will come sweet and clear; clumsily done, its bouquet will be shattered by sediment. Cautiously I lead him back down the years.

'When did you first start work, Mr. Harman?' I asked.

'When I was little more than fourteen I was apprenticed to a blacksmith.'

'Here at Fawley?'

'Oh, no, sir, that was at Turville Heath. The old smithy's a private house now. When I'd been there about three years the blacksmith died, and I carried on by myself.'

'But most of your life was passed here, at Fawley. You were born here?' I asked.

The old blacksmith drew at his pipe, and taking it out of his mouth, looked at me with a roguish twinkle in his eye.

'I've lived here in this very house for the last fifty years, but I wasn't born in Fawley, sir, I was born at Lower Assenden.'

'What! in my village!' I exclaimed.

'In your cottage, sir!' he said with a chuckle.

Now I have talked with the old blacksmith through many an evening as he sat by the fire nursing their enormous cat, but never before had I heard of this. He enjoyed the surprise he had given me.

'I was born in part of your house, sir,' he explained, 'for it was then two cottages – but which of 'em it was, I can't say. You see, I left when I was a month old.'

This, I felt, was one more strand in our friendship. By a strange fate I own the cottage in which he was born and the cottage in which he has passed his life. I also own the smithy in which he has done his life's work. The word 'own' sounds disagreeable in my ears. That smithy, I feel, belongs for all time to Mr. Harman. From early dawn to eve he has sweated by the furnace, his blows have rung out on the anvil, his strong hands and knees have gripped the fetlocks of cart-horse and hunter . . . Mrs. Harman was the last to bid me goodnight. It is her custom to accompany her guests to the little iron gate that separates her garden from the village green. Here she will stand, white haired and smiling, until the visitor has gone beyond sight. But this evening she went along the road with me a little, to take the usual evening constitutional. 'It's the Fawley air, sir,' when I alluded to her alertness. 'Do you know, when I came here a bride, they didn't think I was going to live, my lungs were so weak! . . .'

And how little we have seen! We had intended to go rambling afar, and we have stepped but a short distance from 'Pilgrim Cottage'. Over those hills and beyond those woods lie villages whose beauty and wealth of legend we have not tapped – a vintage of the years that may yet prove the best at our feast.

But we must end. The lights are lit in Henley town. The log burns brightly in the grate, the tea-table is set, and the slippers are warming by the fire. This evening we will take our ease, and perhaps, God willing, go –

To-morrow to fresh woods and pastures new.

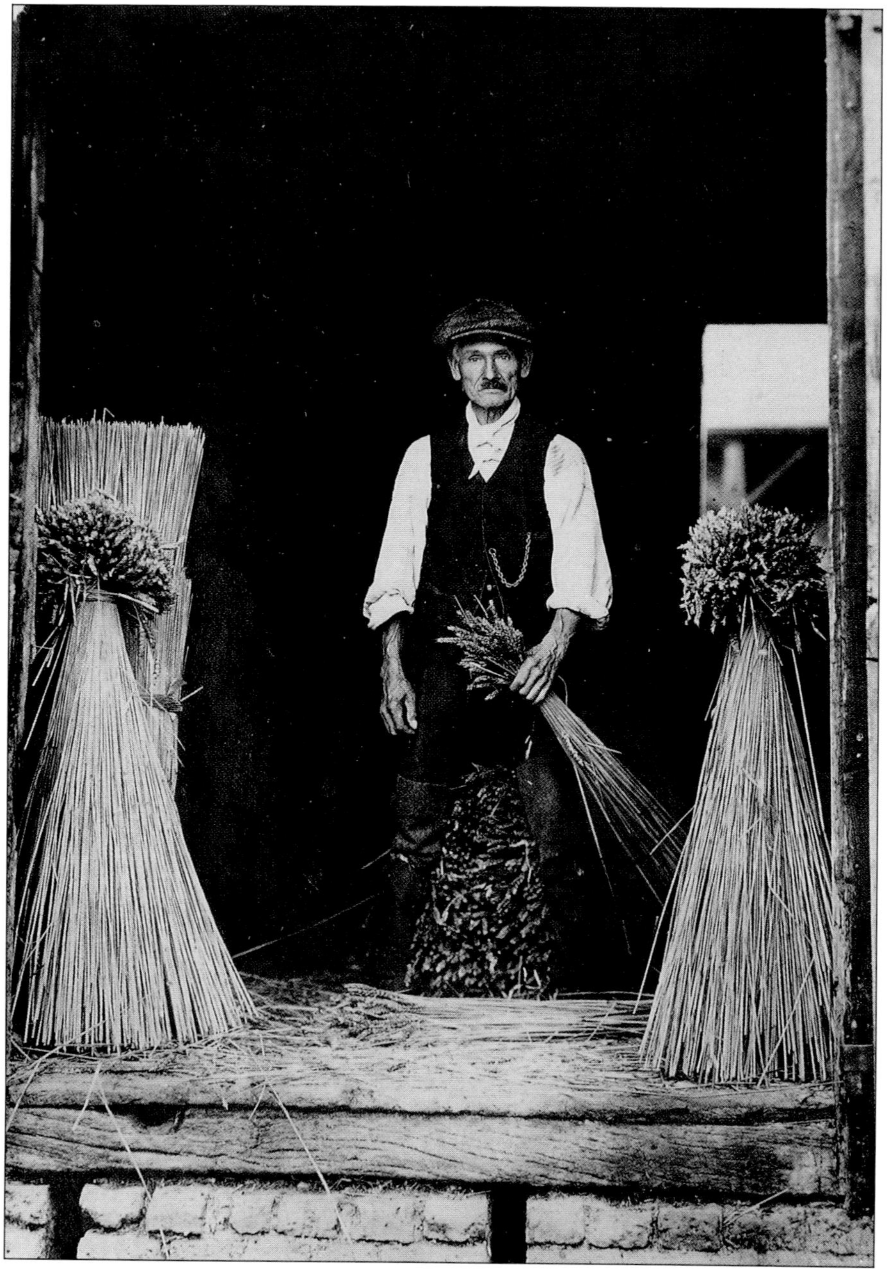

Pitstone

Acknowledgements

We wish to thank Gillian Arney, Pitstone Historical Society; Philip Crouch, Wycombe Chair Museum; Percy Stone; and the staff of the following institutions: Aylesbury Local Studies Library, Buckinghamshire County Museum, Centre for Oxfordshire Studies, Hertfordshire Local Studies Library and Reading Central Library.

The credits and information on all of the illustrations used in the book are given in page ascending order. The following key of initials refers to sources which appear frequently in the list of illustrations: B.A.S. Berkshire Archaeological Society; B.C.M. Buckinghamshire County Museum; C.O.S. Centre for Oxfordshire Studies; P.F. Paul Felix; P.H.S. Pitstone Historical Society; R.M. Reading Museum; W.C.M. Wycombe Chair Museum. The sepia-produced photographs fall within the period 1880 to 1920.

Page **2** Donkey boy in Burnham Beeches; **3** Straw plaiting at the cottage door, P.H.S.; **6** Spring head at Peppard, R.M.; **7** The Hampdens, B.C.M.; **8** Effigy in Ivinghoe Church; **9** Coombe Hill, P.F.; **11** Whiteleaf Cross, B.C.M.; **12** Bradenham, P.F.; **14** Ewelme; **15** Wallingford; **16** Radnage, P.F.; **17** Fingest, P.F.; **19** Henley, B.A.S.; **20** Great Missenden, P.F.; **21** Stoner Park, P.F.; **22** Berkhamstead Castle; **23** Prospect of Berghamsted 1724; **24** Saunderton, P.F.; **25** Watlington, P.F.; **26** Chenies almshouses; **28** Cymbeline's Mount, P.F.; **32** Princes Risborough, P.F.; **33** Thame, P.F.; **34** Ashridge House; **35** Shirburne Castle; **36** Marlow, P.F.; **37** Masks of Thames and Isis on Henley Bridge; **40** Milton's cottage at Chalfont St Giles, P.F.; **41** Poynatts Wood, near Skirmett, P.F.; **44** Nettlebed, P.F.; **45** Caversham Bridge; **46** Sonning, B.A.S.; **47** Bisham, B.A.S.; **49** Wooburn Green, P.F.; **51** Stokenchurch; **53** Jordans, P.F.; **54** Chinnor, B.C.M.; **55** The Ford, Hardwick; **57** Great Hampden, P.F.; **58** Hampden House and Church; **60** Aylesbury, P.F.; **61** Turville Church; **62** Maidenhead, B.A.S.; **63** Waller brass in Beaconsfield Church; **64** Penn Street, P.F.; **66** Plucking ducks at Chinnor, B.C.M.; **67** Thame, C.O.S.; **68** Mapledurham Mill, P.F.; **70** Sheep shearing, P.H.S.; **73** Latimer house; **74** Hurley, B.A.S.; **75** Bray, B.A.S.; **76** Milton's well, Chalfont St Giles; **77** Milton's cottage, Chalfont St Giles; **79** Monks Risborough, B.C.M.; **81** John Bigg the Dinton Hermit; Dinton Church door; **82** Hurdlemaker at Little Gaddesden, P.H.S.; **83** Timber hauling, P.H.S.; **85** Shiplake Church; **86** Packing pheasant eggs at Cholesbury/St Leonards, B.C.M.; **87** Plough in use with Mr Ellis at Little Gaddesden; **88** Bridgewater Monument, Ashridge Park; **90** Chimney corner in Bucks.; **91** Cherry pickers, B.C.M.; **93** Charcoal burning near Tring, P.F.; **95** Pitstone, P.H.S.; **96** Medmenham Abbey, B.A.S.; **98** Medmenham Abbey; **99** Wheelwrights shop, West Wycombe, W.C.M.; **101** Beaconsfield, P.F.; **102** High Wycombe 1752; **103** Aylesbury, B.C.M.; **104** West Wycombe Church, P.F.; **106** Jubilee Fountain, High Wycombe, B.C.M.; **107** The Lee, B.C.M.; **108** Beaconsfield; **109** Penn, P.F.; **110** Edmund Burke's house, Beaconsfield; **112** Cliveden, P.F.; **113** Brass in Taplow Church; **114** Chesham, B.C.M.; **115** Whitchurch; **118** Chequers, P.F.; **121** St Mary's Church, Hemel Hempstead; **122** Hughenden Church, P.F.; **123** Turville, P.F.; **125** Aylesbury duck; **127** Bulbourne, P.F.; **129** Hartwell House; **130** Tring, P.F.; **132** County directory advertisement 1895; **133** County directory advertisement 1895; **134** Dropmore Lodge; **135** Pangbourne, P.F.; **137** Mapledurham Mill; **138** 'The Jump over the Dinner Table'; **140** Punch cartoon of Benjamin Disraeli 1850; **141** Effigies from Hughenden

Church; **143** Cliveden, C.O.S.; **144** Gray's *Elegy* 'Beneath those rugged elms'; **145** Hughenden Manor, P.F.; **146** Gray's *Elegy* 'Parting Day'; Stoke Poges Church; **147** Watercart at Shiplake, B.A.S.; **148** Maharajah's Well, Stoke Row; **149** Stoke Row, P.F.; **150** Taplow street musicians, C.O.S.; **151** Pyrton Church porch; **152** Watlington market; **153** Henley Regatta, P.F.; **154** Illustration from 'the Graphic' 1878; **155** Marlow, C.O.S.; **157** Cliveden Reach, P.F.; **158** Wendover, B.C.M.; **160** Ewelme, P.F.; **161** Ellesborough, P.F.; **163** Amersham, B.C.M.; **164** Amersham, P.F.; **165** County directory advertisement 1895; **166** Bodger encampment, W.C.M.; **167** Glennister's chair factory, High Wycombe, W.C.M.; **168** Lewknor Church font; **169** Brasses in Aldbury Church; **170** Coleshill, B.C.M.; **171** Tring, P.H.S.; **172** Railway at Boxmoor; **175** Frieth smithy; **178** Pitstone, P.H.S.

Bibliography

Bell, Vicars; *To Meet Mr Ellis, Little Gaddesden in the Eighteenth Century*, 1956.
Berkshire & Oxon Advertiser, 1872.
Burke, Peter; *The Public and Domestic Life of the Right Hon. Edmund Burke*, 1853.
Camden, William; *Brittania*, 1586.
Church, Samuel Harden; *Oliver Cromwell*, 1894.
Clarenden, Edward; *History of the Rebellion 1702–4.*
Cobbett, William; *Rural Rides*, 1853.
Davidson, John; *A Random Itinerary*, 1894.
Defoe, Daniel; *A Tour Through the Whole Island of Great Britain 1724–6*, 1753.
The Dictionary of National Biography.
Drayton, Michael; *Polyolbion*, 1622.
Ellis, William; *Chiltern and Vale Farming*, 1733.
First Report of the Commissioners on the Employment of Children, 1862 (Parliamentary Paper).
Fowler, J.F.; *Echoes of Old Country Life*, 1862.
Foxe, John; *Acts and Monuments*, 1563.
Fuller, Thomas; *The History of the Worthies of England*, 1662.
Gibbs, Robert; *History of Aylesbury*, 1885.
——; *The Buckinghamshire Miscellany*, 1891.
——; *Worthies of Buckinghamshire*, 1888.
Goodlee, Sir Rickman; *A Village on the Thames, Whitchurch Today and Yesterday*, 1926.
Grahame, Kenneth; *The Wind in the Willows*, 1908.
Haggard, H. Rider; *Rural England*, 1906.
Harman, H.; *Bucks Dialect*, 1929.
Jerome, K. Jerome; *Three Men in a Boat*, 1899.
Johnstone, Charles; *Chrysal, or the Adventures of a Guinea*, 1760–5.
Kingston, Henry; *History of High Wycombe*, 1848.
Langley, Revd Thomas; *History of the Hundred of Desborough and the Deanery of Wycombe*, 1797.
Leadbetter, J.; *A Pilgrimage to the Shrines of Buckinghamshire*, 1860.
Leland, John; *The Itinerary of John Leland 1535–1543.* Edited by Lucy Toulmin Smith, 1907–10.
Lipscombe, George; *History and Antiquities of the County of Buckinghamshire*, 1847.
Lybbe Powys, Mrs Philip; *Passages from the Diaries of Mrs Philip Lybbe Powys of Hardwick House, Oxon, AD 1756–1808.* Edited by Emily Climenson, 1899.
Milton, Deborah; *Deborah's Diary Fragments 1665–80.*
Oxfordshire Record Society; *Journal of Sir Samuel Luke*, 1950.
Phillibrown, T.; *Diary* (typed extracts re High Wycombe 1750–8), High Wycombe Central Library.
Plot, Robert; *The Natural History of Oxfordshire*, 1676.
Priest, the Revd St John; *General View of the Agriculture of Buckinghamshire*, 1810.
Prior, J.; *Life of Burke*, 1824.
Records of Bucks.
Roberts, Cecil; *Gone Rambling*, 1935.
——; *Gone Afield*, 1936.
Royal Commission on the Employment of Children, Young Persons and Women in Agriculture, 1867–8 (Parliamentary Paper).
Sheahan, James Joseph; *History and Topography of Buckinghamshire*, 1861.
Smyth, W.H.; *Aedes Hartwellianae*, 1851.
Stone, Revd James; *The Heart of Merrie England*, 1887.
Stone, Robert; *Private Family Diaries.*
Tomkins, H.; *Highways and Byways in Hertfordshire*, 1902.
Verney, Margaret; *Bucks Biographies*, 1912.

Index

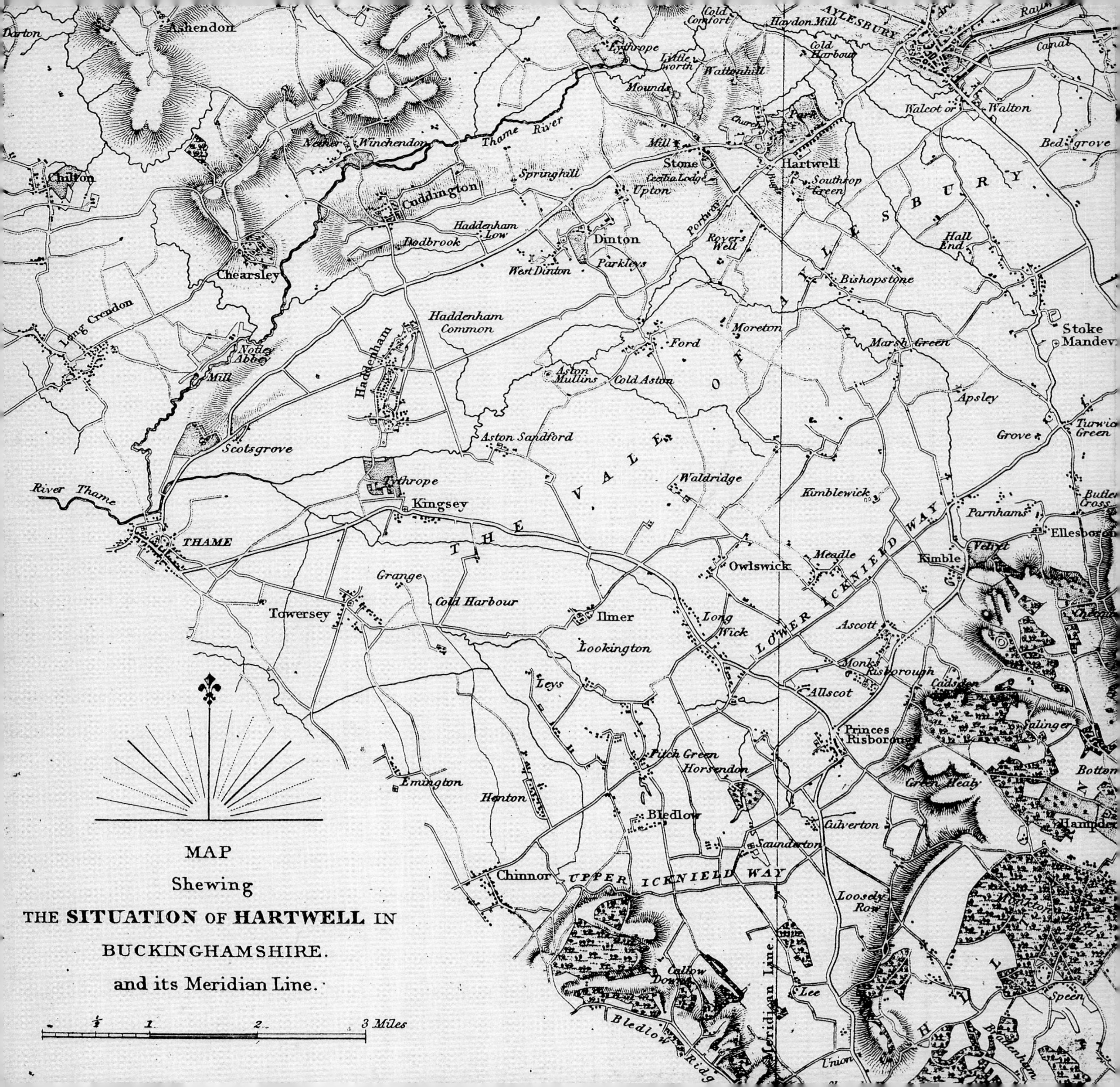

MAP
Shewing
THE **SITUATION** OF **HARTWELL** IN
BUCKINGHAMSHIRE.
and its Meridian Line.